Westering Women
and the Frontier Experience
1800–1915

W. H. D. Koerner, *Before the Railroad Came*. The character and self-confidence of Westering women is captured in this painting. (Courtesy Ruth Koerner Oliver.)

Westering Women and the Frontier Experience 1800–1915

Sandra L. Myres
University of Texas at Arlington

HISTORIES OF THE AMERICAN FRONTIER

Ray Allen Billington, General Editor
Howard R. Lamar, Coeditor
Martin Ridge, Coeditor
David J. Weber, Coeditor

University of New Mexico Press
Albuquerque

Library of Congress Cataloging in Publication Data

Myres, Sandra L.
  Westering women and the frontier experience, 1800–1915.

  (Histories of the American frontier)
  Includes bibliographical references and index.
  1. Women—West (U.S.)—History—19th century.
2. Frontier and pioneer life—West (U.S.) I. Title.
II. Series.
HQ1410.M96   305.4'2'0978   82-6956
ISBN 0–8263–0625–X   AACR2
ISBN 0–8263–0626–8 (pbk.)

© 1982 by the University of New Mexico Press.
All rights reserved.
Manufactured in the United States of America.
Library of Congress Catalog Card Number: 82–6956
International Standard Book Number:
0–8263–0625–X (cloth)
0–8263–0626-8 (paper)
First edition
Design by Emmy Ezzell

For John Hudson
and
In Loving Memory of Ruth Younkin

Contents

Illustrations

Maps

Foreword

On March 3, 1981, Ray Allen Billington, distinguished historian of the American West and founder of the *Histories of the American Frontier Series*, died at his home in San Marino, California, at the age of seventy-seven. Although Professor Billington was long identified as a defender of Frederick Jackson Turner's famous hypothesis that the frontier experience played a major role in shaping American institutions and the American character, he was truly a historian of the entire sweep of this nation's past. That range is suggested by his early volume on *The Protestant Crusade, 1800–1860: A Study in the Origins of American Nativism* (1938), his magisterial textbook, *Westward Expansion* (1949), his delightful narrative, *The Far Western Frontier, 1830–1860* (1953), and his prize-winning biography, *Frederick Jackson Turner: Historian, Scholar, Teacher* (1973). His twenty-fifth book, *Land of Savagery/Land of Promise: The European Image of the American Frontier* (1980), promises to be one of the most significant scholarly histories to appear in a generation.

Ray Billington's range and distinction are also attested to by the fact that during the years when the Turner thesis was under heavy critical attack, he successfully launched the *Histories of the American Frontier Series* in 1961 and was elected President of the Organization of American Historians (1962–63). The immense respect his colleagues in Western history had for him prompted the founding of the Western History Association in 1962 and his election as that organization's first president. The reasons were not difficult to find, for during Professor Billington's lifetime he trained many hundreds of scholars in American history and American Studies here and abroad. Whether they encountered him during his career as a member of the faculty at Northwestern University (1944–63) or in his role as Senior Research Associate at the Huntington Library (1963–81), all would acknowledge his mentorship as the most productive and dynamic scholar of frontier and Western history in this century.

When Professor Billington invited me to join him as coeditor of the *Series* in 1973, I discovered that he had in mind the completion of an initial set of volumes devoted to the regional and topical histories of the frontier experience and the launching of an additional series that would embrace the Indian-White Frontier, the Mexican Borderlands, the Pacific Basin Frontier, the Lumber Frontier, the Urban Frontier, and volumes on the Frontier Family and Women in the West. Alastair Hennessey's *The Frontier in Latin American History* (1978) and David J. Weber's *The Mexican Frontier, 1821–1846: The American Southwest Under Mexico* (1982) are the first volumes to appear in the new series.

Now, once again, the value and promise of the new series has been demonstrated with the appearance of Sandra L. Myres's impressive study, *Westering Women and the Frontier Experience, 1800–1915.* Not only is it important as the first volume in the *Series* to be devoted to the history of women, it is equally important that a scholar of Professor Myres's excellence and experience should have undertaken this difficult task. Since 1961 she has written or edited six books and many articles dealing with the history of the American West, among them her recent *Ho for California! Women's Overland Diaries from the Huntington Library* (1980). As a teacher of both Latin American and Western American history at the University of Texas, Arlington, she brings to this volume a valuable comparative perspective.

Since the history of women on the frontier has been studied by relatively few scholars, Professor Myres has had to craft the narrative out of materials found in more than four hundred collections about Western women. Only a few days before his death, Professor Billington commented that "The evidence of Sandra Myres's vast scholarship so well displayed in the voluminous notes, are bound to impress any reader . . . they provide one of the most remarkable bibliographies to materials in this new field, both published and unpublished, that I have ever seen."

By making extensive use of their own words, Myres has given frontier women a voice they never had before, whether the statements were matter of fact, poignant, eloquent, or all three, as captured in the diary of a woman who wrote: "go put on a clean dress, smooth hair with side combs, brew a cup of tea, set and rest and rock a spell and count blessings." Professor Myres has also recorded the statements and acts of Mexican and French pioneer women along with those of Anglo-American women. And, where possible, she has included the reminiscences of black and Indian women.

Professor Myres succeeds in placing the experiences of pioneer women in context; that is to say, she has included them in the main narrative of Western history rather than isolating them. Thus her account is both new and complementary. Finally, she has provided an imaginative format by reviewing common myths about frontier women before presenting the more realistic account based on her findings. Without saying that all of the old stereotypes were wrong, she goes far to replace them with more factual accounts and with far more complex explanations. Whether the subject is popular images of "Westering" women themselves, or women's responses to the Western environment, or to Indians, homemaking or their actual role in the suffrage movement, the result is a strikingly original and highly readable and informative history that will be used by scholars and lay readers alike.

The publication of *Westering Women and the Frontier Experience* also marks the occasion to announce the formation of a new editorial board for the *Histories of the American Frontier Series* to carry on the work that Ray Billington had begun. The University of New Mexico Press and I are pleased to announce that Dr. Martin Ridge, Senior Research Associate at the Huntington Library, and Dr. David J. Weber, Professor of History at Southern Methodist University, will join with me as editors of an ongoing *Series* dedicated to the memory of its distinguished founder—Ray Allen Billington.

Howard R. Lamar
Yale University
Spring 1982

Preface

> Up to our own day American history has been in a large degree the history of the colonization of the Great West. The existence of an area of free land, its continuous recession, and the advance of American settlement westward, explain American development.

Thus began Frederick Jackson Turner's famous essay on the significance of the frontier in American history. Nearly one hundred years later, Americans still find the frontier experience exciting and significant, and they are still discovering aspects of the frontier experience that were not explored by Turner or his successors. In recent years, Western historians have turned their attention to new fields such as music, art, folklore, the role of various minorities in the development of the West, and most recently, the study of women on the frontier.

Unfortunately, many of the first studies of women were not based on sound research or careful interpretation. The "discovery" of minorities, including women, spawned a number of scissors-and-paste books for classroom use or utilized government documents, newspapers, and other contemporary accounts written by men rather than examining what women themselves had to say about their frontier experiences. Other studies subjected westering women to a microscopic analysis outside the context of the total frontier experience. By isolating women from the social and cultural milieu in which they lived, such studies distorted the role of women on the frontier and often replaced old myths and stereotypes with new ones. Women were an important part of the American frontier experience, but they must be viewed within the context of that experience, not isolated in pristine splendor or tacked on at the end of a chapter on the winning of the West.

The study that follows is an attempt to view women within such a context. It is intended not as women's history but as frontier history. It is an account of women's participation in a unique human experience—the settlement and development of the North American continent—based on what women wrote about their experiences. Although the text includes the Spanish, French, and English colonial frontiers and the trans-Appalachian region, the emphasis is on the nineteenth-century trans-Mississippi West. I have included something of Indian, Hispanic, and Negro women's perceptions of the frontier experience as well as those of white women of predominantly English ancestry. I have examined, in some detail, women's preconceptions about the frontier, and I have tried to suggest how those ideas were changed and modified by life on the frontier. I have also attempted to suggest something of the similarities in and differences between men's and women's preconceptions of and reactions to the frontier.

Several topics are not included. I have not discussed immigrant women. Their experiences were colored not only by the frontier but by the adjustment to the new society and culture, and often language, with which they had to contend; demographic data are not included either. We have always assumed that there were comparatively few women on the frontier, but some recent studies suggest that such a generalization is inaccurate. Women were "scarce" in some frontier areas, but in others they were equal, or superior, in numbers to men. A number of regional and local studies need to be done before we can reassess the demographic distribution of women in the West. I have not attempted to compare Western women's lives to those of Eastern or Southern women during the same time period. Such a study should be done, but it is outside the framework of the present volume.

Note on Sources

This study is based on the many diaries, journals, letters, and reminiscences written by frontierswomen. Some have been published, and a few, such as Sarah Royce's *A Frontier Lady* and Susan McGoffin's *Down the Santa Fe Trail,* are considered minor classics. Most of the material, however, comes from little-known manuscript sources in various libraries, state historical societies, and archives. Until recently, it was assumed that there were few primary materials documenting the experiences of nineteenth-century women. Such is not the case. Although much of this material has been ignored or overlooked and is frequently uncatalogued or not clearly identified, there is a treasure trove of material written by women. Most university libraries, every state historical society, and many local institutions have such materials. In the course of the research, I have examined over four hundred such collections as well as a number of diaries and reminiscences published in various state historical journals. These are identified in the notes. In most cases the footnotes not only identify specific quotes but include "see also" entries which indicate the rich source material available on topics related to women's lives on the frontier. In no case are these exhaustive. They are simply suggestive of the wide range of source material.

A few of the women cited in this study (such as Elizabeth Custer, Susan Wallace, and Mary Austin Holley) are fairly well known. But most were ordinary women who lived very ordinary lives. Their only claim to fame was that they left, either as conscious chroniclers of their age or as a means to satisfy their own emotional and psychological needs, a written record of their lives. The fact that they did, and could, write does make them special, of course. Obviously, most were educated, middle-class women, but they were also fairly typical of westering Americans in the nineteenth century. The westward movement was primarily a middle-class activity; few of the very poor or the very rich undertook the move to the frontier.

Moreover, it should be noted that although a few of the women cited had an excellent education or were endowed with some modest literary talent, most were only marginally familiar with the niceties of spelling, punctuation, proper grammar, and style, and many wrote laboriously, carefully recording their thoughts and experiences in phonetically sounded-out words without any attempt at punctuation or capitalization.

In addition to the sources on women of primarily English, middle-class background, the notes also suggest sources for the history of Indian, Mexican, and black women. The best sources on Mexican women are oral histories, especially those in the Bancroft Library, and in the voluminous provincial archives in California, New Mexico, and Texas. Helpful on the subject of Indian women are the many anthropological and ethnological reports dealing with Indian societies and the oral histories prepared under the auspices of the Doris Duke Foundation. Also helpful for Oklahoma are the many interviews with Indian women in the 120 volumes of the Indian-Pioneer Papers gathered by the Federal Writers' Project. Although these interviews are uneven and some seem to reflect the words and views of the interviewer or transcriber rather than the women themselves, they nonetheless provide information about a number of women whose stories would otherwise have been completely lost. Source material on black women in the West is more difficult to locate, but the Indian-Pioneer Papers and other oral history projects do provide a key to this material, and new sources on the history of black women continue to come to light.

Of course, primary source materials must be used with some care. Reminiscences are particularly unreliable, either because the writer forgot the details of the initial experience or because she, or he, chose to delete, add to, or embellish certain events. Pioneer reminiscences were a recognized literary form with an established format and content, and writers, both men and women, often added events which they had not experienced but included because they were expected parts of the typical pioneer story. Thus, one or two Indians intent on stealing livestock became a "horde of screaming savages," a snow storm became a "raging blizzard," a few grasshoppers became "a plague of locusts." Reminiscences were frequently nostalgic, as well, full of comments about the "good old days," when life was simpler but somehow more satisfying.[1]

Diaries posit their own particular problems. There are four generally recognized types of diaries: the travel diary, the public journal, the journal of conscience, and the diary which serves as a record of the day's events.[2] Some, principally travel and public journals, were written to be read by others; others were intended only for the eyes of the writer, and the content and tone of the diary were often determined by the expected audience.[3] For example, there is a very different point of view and different kinds of information in Mary Maverick's memoirs, written for her children and grandchildren, and in her tiny pocket diary in which she recorded her most intimate thoughts and fears. Letters also must be used with some care. Here, too, the expected audience must be kept in mind. A woman writing to elderly parents or friends in the East may deliberately downplay her fears in regard to Indians or other dangers while she may elaborate events in writing to a young friend.

In preparing this study, I have not attempted the type of elaborate content analysis employed by John M. Faragher in *Women and Men on the Overland Trails* (New Haven, 1979);[4] however, I have attempted to keep in mind the intended audience and the particular circumstances under which the material was written. For example, most travel diaries were intended for at least a limited outside audience, either friends or family members back home or for future generations. Most men and women who traveled the overland trails had a clear sense that they were participating in an historic event. They believed that they had stepped, however briefly, onto the public stage of great events, and their diaries and journals reflect this participation. Most diaries from the settlement period are daybooks or journals of events, usually intended for private use. Women's diaries of this type often include elements of the journals of conscience as well. Girls in the nineteenth century were encouraged to keep spiritual diaries and to look to their religious development so that they might be better wives and mothers and direct the family's religious life. Thus their diaries were often more introspective than those of men and included minute examination of their inner lives.

In working with these materials I have tried to keep in mind not only the intended audience and the circumstances in which the writers found themselves but the constraints of language with which most were forced to deal. Many of the women had a limited vocabulary and thus used a simple word or phrase to express a wide range of emotions. "Felt a little sad" might mean anything from a brief twinge of homesickness to an almost overwhelming melancholia. "A pleasant view" might describe a quiet river valley, a spectacular sunset, or a broad vista of snowcapped mountains. Even the most literate of the writers had some difficulty in expressing themselves. As one authority pointed out in a little-known but provocative article, the frontier experience "brought a cultural background of wide reading in English literature into conflict with the physical background of the new country," and pioneers were forced to express new and unfamiliar experiences within a narrow framework of conventional beliefs and language which were often inadequate to their purposes.[5] I have tried to give readers a feel for the language and the mind set of the times and the women who lived in those times by using their terms such as "forting up," "laide over," and "make-do." In addition, the original spelling and punctuation of the writers has been retained in the quotes, and I have made only limited use of the intrusive *sic*.

There is no comprehensive bibliography on Western women. The best available guides to the secondary literature are Sheryll and Gene Patterson-Black, *Western Women* (Crawford, Ne., 1978) and the extensive bibliographic notes in Joan M. Jensen and Darlis A. Miller, "The Gentle Tamers Revisited: New Approaches to the History of Women in the American West," *Pacific Historical Review*, 49 (May 1980), pp. 173–213. Also helpful, although not confined to Western women, is Cynthia E. Harrison, ed., *Women in American History: A Bibliography* (Santa Barbara, 1979) which provides a guide to recent periodical literature. Of some assistance for minority women are Rayna Green, "Native American Women," *Signs*, 6 (Winter 1980) pp. 248–67; Robert Cabello-Arandona, et al., *The Chicana: A Comprehensive Study* (Los Angeles, 1975), and Lenwood G. Davis, *The Black Women in American Society: A Selected Annotated Bibliography* (Boston, 1975). Several state historical societies have published preliminary or partial guides to their collections relating to women. For Texas, Ruthe Winegarten, ed., *Texas Women's History Project Bibliography* (Austin, 1980) lists both primary and secondary sources. Helpful on a regional level is Lynn Donovan, "Women's History: A Listing of West Coast Archival and Manuscript Sources," *California Historical Quarterly*, 55 (Spring and Summer 1976), pp. 74–83, 170–185. The best guide to the primary materials is the extensive survey undertaken at the University of Minnesota under National Endowment for the Humanities auspices and published in Andrea Hinding and Clarke Chamber, *Women's History Sources*, 2 vols. (New York, 1979). As a result of the Minnesota project, a number of libraries and archives identified, for the first time, material by women which was previously catalogued under the name of the family, husband, or father. Most institutions with extensive materials related to women are recataloguing or otherwise identifying women's sources as such and making this material more easily accessible.

Acknowledgments

This study was first conceived in discussions with Ray Allen Billington during the summer of 1977 when I was a reader at the Huntington Library in San Marino, California. During the course of many talks about the role of women in the American West, Ray asked if I would be interested in preparing a book on the subject for the Histories of the American Frontier Series which he and Howard Lamar edited. Needless to say, I was delighted, and over the course of the next three years, Ray helped me outline the topics for inclusion and gave me continued encouragement and support. Both he and Howard Lamar were patient and understanding; and their continuing assistance and many helpful comments made my task a pleasant one. I am especially grateful to Howard Lamar for seeing this book through the final stages of writing, editing, and production. It was an honor and privilege to work closely with Ray Billington during the many months I spent in San Marino preparing the manuscript, and I learned a great deal from him about the historian's craft. Ray was not only an internationally recognized scholar and a fine writer, he was also a warm and witty colleague, an exacting critic, and a superb teacher. He never failed to balance a well deserved criticism with encouragement, and he never failed to praise where he felt praise was due. I am especially pleased that he was able to read, and comment on, all but the last chapter of the manuscript before his unexpected and untimely death in March 1981.

The research and writing were accomplished with the aid of a generous research grant from the National Endowment for the Humanities supplemented by grants from the Huntington Library and the University of Texas at Arlington Organized Research Fund. Like all historians, I am deeply indebted to those unsung heroines and heros of the profession, the librarians and archivists who make our work possible. Without a word of complaint they filled my often vague requests, suggested additional sources of information, and shared their knowledge of and expertise in their collections with me. For the many services and favors they rendered, a heartfelt "Thank You." I am especially grateful to the scholars and staff of the Huntington Library who provided generous quarters and a delightful atmosphere in which to complete my writing. My thanks also to the many colleagues who offered constructive criticism and research assistance, especially Glenda Riley, Rodman Paul, Martin Ridge, Terry McDonald, and others acknowledged in the footnotes. My special thanks to two extraordinary people—John Hudson, Librarian at the University of Texas at Arlington, and Ruth Younkin, friend and confidant, without whose continuing support and encouragement this book would never have been completed and to whom this volume is gratefully dedicated.

Sandra L. Myres
The University of Texas at Arlington
December 1981

1

The Madonna of the Prairies and Calamity Jane

Images of Westering Women[1]

Perhaps no image in American history and literature is more deeply embedded in the American mind than that of the frightened, tearful woman wrenched from home and hearth and dragged off into the terrible West where she is condemned to a life of lonely terror among savage beasts and rapine Indians. Overworked and overbirthed, she lived through a long succession of dreary days of toil and loneliness until, at last, driven to or past the edge of sanity, she resigned herself to a hard life and early death. This tragic figure appeared so often in American literature that she assumed almost legendary status. From Hawthorne to Hemingway, American literature is replete with examples. Typical of this stereotype was Hamlin Garland's description of his mother:

> Her life had been always on the border—she knew nothing of civilization's splendor of song and story. All her toilsome, monotonous days rushed through my mind with a roar, like a file of gray birds in the night—how little—how tragically small her joys, and how black her sorrows, her toil, her tedium.[2]

Another part of this portrait was the isolation of the woman cut off from her own kind, from the network of womankind and sisterhood. The space, the wind, the emptiness of the prairies and plains drove her to melancholia and eventually to suicide or, at best, to an insane asylum. Such women appeared in the novels of O. E. Rölvaag and Dorothy Scarborough, and their story was retold in the pictures and newspaper accounts of insanity, suicide, and violent death in the recently published *Wisconsin Death Trip.*[3] The image was that of a refined lady of a sensitive and emotional nature who, unable to adjust to the frontier way of life, was "dashed and buffeted by the winds of western life till her frail body broke."[4]

Unfortunately, these literary stereotypes have found their way into

1

historical portraits of frontier women. "It is a well-known fact," one author wrote in 1940, "that women, as a rule find it harder to leave friends, relatives, and associations than do men."[5] Women, especially Western women, according to another male "authority," were conservative, home-loving creatures, "hating with a passion those three concomitants of the Western frontier—poverty, physical hardship, and danger."[6] It was women, charged another historian, who were responsible for the retreat from the frontier.

> These solitary women, longing to catch a glimpse of one of their own sex, swept their eyes over the boundless prairie and thought of the old home in the East. They stared and stared across space with nothing to halt their gaze over the monotonous expanse. . . . Hollow-eyed, tired, and discouraged . . . Some begged their husbands to hitch up the team, turn the wagon tongue eastward, and leave the accursed plains. . . .[7]

Recently feminist historians have embellished this image with psychoanalytical overtones. Women's lives in the American West, one wrote, were dominated by the "patriarchy of masculine power and prerogatives." Women, he declared, "always controlled . . . always confined," resigned themselves to "a mild kind of rural American purdah."[8] Yet another feminist historian, in a gloomy analysis of women's diaries, concluded that women were generally reluctant to go West, that their life there, whether on an isolated farm or in a frontier community, was one of unending toil and unnatural labor, that suicides and insanity were common, and that their trail journals, "with their relentless record-keeping of the graves passed, were ultimately indictments of men."[9]

Concomitant with the image of the weary and forlorn frontier wife, a sort of helpless heroine, is the stereotype of the westering woman as sturdy helpmate and civilizer of the frontier. She, too, was reluctant to go West, but once the decision was made, she trod westward with grim-faced determination, clad in gingham or linsey-woolsey, her face wreathed in a sunbonnet, baby at breast, rifle at the ready, bravely awaited unknown dangers, and dedicated herself to removing wilderness from both man and land and restoring civilization as rapidly as possible. She was a woman of some culture and refinement, "domestic, submissive but sturdy, moral," the guardian of all that was fine and decent.[10] She was a hardy heroine, an example for others of her sex, and her story was familiar to nineteenth-century readers. An 1850 description of Catherine Sevier was typical of this genre:

tall in stature, erect in person, stately in walk with small piercing blue eyes, raven locks, a Roman nose, and firmness unmistakable in her mouth and every feature. . . . It could be said of her without any question that she "reverenced her husband" and she instilled the same Scriptural sentiment in the minds of his children. . . . She relieved him of his cares at home, and applauded his devotion to the service of the people.[11]

The sturdy helpmate could fight Indians, kill the bear in the barn, make two pots of lye soap, and do a week's wash before dinnertime and still have the cabin neat, the children clean, and a good meal on the table when her husband came in from the fields—all without a word of complaint or even a hint of an ache or a pain. She was the Madonna of the Prairies, the Brave Pioneer Mother, the Gentle Tamer so familiar in Western literature. We encountered her in James Fenimore Cooper's Esther and Emerson Hough's Molly Wingate, and we find her still in historian Richard Bartlett's 1974 portrait of the pioneer woman:

The new country woman held her head high, and her bright eyes searched the horizon for what lay ahead. She shared with her husband a faith in their future. . . . She was a builder, along with her husband; she knew her value.[12]

If this image seems more positive than that of the drudge, it still had its negative aspects. The Gentle Tamer was still fearful, if somewhat self-sufficient, and she had to be protected from danger. Such women feared and hated wilderness and thus, by extension, they feared and hated Indians and other wild creatures. It was these women who, in their fear, insisted on killing or at least removing the "savage" with whom the lone white male once had a positive relationship. This popular image, according to one historian, "led recent writers to identify the 'invasion of feminine sentiment' into the wilderness as the major cause of historic racism in America."[13] This same writer went on to explore, in depth, the literary and historical images which led to this conclusion, and pointed out that modern literary critics would go so far as to have us believe that it was the entrance of women into the wilderness that destroyed "the Second Paradise" and brought about the destruction of both the woods and the Indians.[14] The arrival of the gentle tamers in the wilderness also curtailed male freedom and forced unwanted control upon men's self-imposed rejection of civilized values. The frontier was a fine, free, male place until the petticoat pioneers arrived bringing law and order, cleanliness, and religion. Once women arrived, there was no more "zestful combat" with frontier dangers, "and to destroy these traditional testers of human endurance was to destroy something male in the race."[15] A psychohistorian went one step further and named the pioneer mother the historical prototype of that twentiety-century horror, "Mom."[16]

There was yet a third image of the Western woman prevalent in American literature, that of the bad woman. Sometimes she was the backwoods belle, "hefty, grotesque, and mean with a pistol."[17] Like the Prairie Rose described by nineteenth-century army officer and explorer Randolph Marcy, she was occasionally shocking in her speech and manners and "just as wild, untamed, and free from tyrannical conventionalities of society as the mustangs that roamed over the adjacent prairies."[18] Or she was the soiled dove or female bandit, the Calamity Jane who drank, smoked, and cursed and was handy with a poker deck, a six-gun, and a horse. She was the antithesis of the civilizer-helpmate; she was more masculine than feminine in her behavior, but she always had a heart of pure gold. In a less malevolent image she was the backwoodswoman of Eastern writers—unlettered, crude of manner, superstitious. She displayed many strange habits of speech and dress, and although she was often kind and considerate, the image she projected was still primarily negative.[19] There were, and are, other images of the frontier woman, of course, but they were generally derived from these three basic stereotypes.

It is also interesting to note that, despite cultural differences, other frontierswomen—Mexican, French, and Indian—shared the basic stereotypical fate of their Anglo sisters. Writers and historians tended to place Spanish frontierswomen in either the gentle tamer or soiled dove categories. There was the strong, saintly señora presiding over her family, peons, and Indians with a kind but firm hand. Her portrait was heavily influenced by the cult of the Virgin which permeated Spanish views of women whether on the frontier or in more settled society. She was sometimes garbed as a nun; she was usually of noble blood, well educated, genteel—a version of the frontier lady of later myth. She was best known to American readers as Señora Moreno in Helen Hunt Jackson's *Ramona* or as Ana Robledo in Angelico Chavez's *Lady from Toledo*, but she appeared in Spanish literature as well.[20] A related image was the of La Conquistadora, a blend of helpmate and backwoods belle. She was strong, self-sufficient, able to withstand great hardship and fight side by side with her husband. She was reminiscent of the female warriors of Visigothic Spain, the heroines of medieval pastoral romances, and the famous Virgin of New Mexico, Nuestra Señora del Rosario (who was familiarly titled La Conquistadora). She appeared in literature and history as the merry widow of the Anza expedition or Doña Eufemia de Penalosa in New Mexico who rallied the women to defend the rooftops against Indian attack until the men returned.[21] In the nineteenth century, westering men added a third stereotype, that of the seductive señorita. With black eyes flashing, cigarillo held delicately in her lips, provocative shoulders bared, she charmed men with her skills in love, cooking, and often, like the notorious La Tules of New Mexico (Gertrudis María Barcelo), gambling as well. But, like the soiled doves, she had a good heart and a gentle spirit.[22]

Similar images could be found on the French frontiers. There was the saintly nun who braved terrible dangers to bring Christianity and civilization to remote Indian villages and the legendary Madeleine de Vercheres who fought the Indians and saved the fort. There were the unrefined but sturdy women who accompanied the French *coureurs de bois,* helped them in their work, and often saved them from the Indians. And there were the convict-belles of colonial Louisiana who shared the toil and hardships of a remote frontier.[23]

Black women were an almost invisible part of the mythology of westering women. There were black women on all of the American frontiers, and on the Spanish and French frontiers as well, but even modern writers on the black experience have generally overlooked them as a part of the frontier experience. They have remained an unrecognized part of the Western American past. When they were portrayed in the literature, the images were Southern, not Western. Usually they were seen as the devoted slave bravely sharing the hardships and dangers with a beloved mistress or as the faithful old family retainer so dear to the heart of white Americans in the post-Civil War period. Occasionally a "beautiful mulatto" or a striking "lady of color" joined the soiled doves, but most westering black women, when they were included, were pictured as passive, not active, participants in the Great Adventure of the West.[24]

Indian women, of course, were rarely seen as frontierswomen. In European literature they were usually portrayed as a part of the wilderness that must be conquered and civilized. Indian women, like Indian men, might be either "noble savages" or "thieving, murdering redskins." Occasionally the Indian woman was described as a princess, a Pocahontas figure, who rescued the brave white man from his cruel captors. Sometimes she was a sex object, the sensual Indian maiden of "Hiawatha" and the *Leatherstocking Tales* or the mountain man's "squaw" described in overland diaries and journals. More commonly, Indian women were portrayed as badly abused, abject drudges, victims of cruel and barbarous Indian society, forced to perform the most difficult and menial tasks while her stronger "brave" lolled before the fire or went hunting with his friends.[25]

Views of frontierswomen, then, were numerous and often contradictory. Whatever the frontier, women were there, but they were described by

generally negative, semiromanticized stereotypes which obscured their
real lives and character. Most of these stereotypes derived not from the
reality of women's lives but from nineteenth-century ideas of what women
should be. In the first decades of American settlement, as on the later
Western frontiers, all members of society worked together to clear land
and build homes. Most family needs were supplied through a system of
home production which involved the entire family, a system in which
women's economic role was a recognized and valued one. But as frontier
conditions gave way to more stable, structured communities and men
moved into the marketplace, producing goods and services for monetary
gain, women's work ceased to be seen as productive or necessary for family
survival. Women, and women's work, were relegated to a secondary, subordinate position within the society they had helped to establish. Banned
from the marketplace and displaced from their earlier economic roles
within the family, women sought a new meaning for their lives, and this
was provided by the idealization of women as the moral guardians of
home and family life. Women were assigned a new role confined within
the carefully defined sphere of woman's place. Women were expected to
remain domestic and demure, withhold themselves from competition with
men, and shield home and family from the rapidly changing and often
frightening values of an increasingly materialistic society. By the nineteenth century, this portrait of woman's place was enshrined within the
cult of true womanhood.[26]

Purveyed to the public by various ladies magazines such as *Godey's
Lady's Book,* and reinforced by essays, novels, school texts, and sermons,
the cult of true womanhood demanded that women be pious, pure, submissive, and domestic.[27] Women, the publicists of this doctrine suggested,
were important, not as workers, but as the repository of true virtue and as
the moral guardians of the family and, by extension, the Republic. Women
were physically weaker and probably mentally inferior to men, the proponents argued, but they were morally superior. Women were thus not
inferior to men but equal and possibly even superior within their separate sphere. Pushed onto a pedestal from which she was expected to "up-
hold the pillars of the temple with her frail white hand,"[28] the idealized
nineteenth-century woman was expected to be modest, submissive, educated in the genteel and domestic arts, supportive of her husband's efforts, uncomplaining, a perfect wife and mother, and an example to all.
But this example was to be private, never public. Women should be neither seen nor heard outside the sacred confines of the family circle. "A
woman is essentially a being of retirement and seclusion," one writer ed-
itorialized, "and her nature becomes deteriorated by any employment

which brings her before the public."[29] Woman's mission was "in the inculcation of high and pure morals" and it was "within the circle of her own family and dependents" that she performed "her sacred duty" and fulfilled "her destiny."[30]

Such an idealized role provided a rationalization for the subordination of women, but it did not conform to the reality of most women's lives. Many women simply could not afford the luxury of the pedestal. Only middle-class and upper-class families could allow their women to retire into domesticity—usually assisted by one or more servants—and the steady round of visiting, shopping, sewing, and adding loving touches to their homes described and recommended in the magazines, on the lecture circuit, and in the Bibles of new domestic life written by Catherine Beecher and Lydia Maria Child.[31] On most farms and in city working-class families, women's roles were far different. Farm women continued to work in the fields and pasture and exchanged their domestic produce for essential goods. Working-class women and girls labored in mills and factories or took domestic positions outside their homes in order to help support their families. Nonetheless, the ideal of true womanhood and its corollary cult of domesticity remained the goal, the normative behavior toward which women should strive.

Western migration and frontier conditions seriously threatened to undermine this carefully constructed separation of the sexes. Far from the familiar, stable communities of the East, out on the edges of civilization, families again had to become self-sufficient, and women had to assume new roles, undertake new tasks outside the proscribed sphere of woman's place. Their new duties provided women opportunities to regain their former economic importance and to gain some legal and political power, but in the process it was feared that they might lose their claim to moral superiority. Some writers argued that frontier conditions allowed women to expand their role as guardians of social and cultural values and morals. By helping to reestablish traditional society in the West, women, within their accepted sphere, might become not simply the guardians but the creators of civilized values and help direct these new societies into proper channels of "moral rectitude and social refinement."[32] But other writers argued that the frontier was too "savage," "barbarous," and "violent" for women to overcome. They would be victimized by rapine savages and white men turned "cruel and savage" by years beyond the restraining influences of civilized society. Working alongside men in "inappropriate" tasks, they would lost their femininity, even their looks. "Their skin," one writer warned, "becomes shriveled, their complexions like coal, their features coarse and homely, and they fall into a premature decrepitude, more hideous than that of old age." Even more disastrous, they would be forced from woman's sphere and "lose their value in the eyes of society."[33]

Whether seen as valued civilizers or victims, Western women were conceded to be different. Some writers attempted to adapt the Eastern ideal of frontier women and pictured them as courageous, benevolent heroines or portrayed them in the tradition of Catherine Sevier as helpful helpmates and sturdy pioneer mothers. In a similar vein, other writers argued that Western women, although "not so refined, so deeply schooled in that which is delicate and beautiful" still had "those qualities which were the developments of their nature's purity, uninfluenced by the fashion and artifice of society." Western women were somewhat more masculine than their Eastern sisters, such writers concluded, but only "if you term that masculine, which prompted them to defend, aye die, for their husbands, their children."[34] More frequently Western women were caricatured as "coarse," "crude," "unlettered," drudges who were both "slovenly" and "unfeminine."[35]

Such stereotypes were reinforced by a twentieth-century interpretation of frontiering as primarily a male enterprise in which women played a largely invisible and subordinate role. Frederick Jackson Turner's frontiers were devoid of women. His pioneers were explorers, fur trappers, miners, ranchers, farmers, all of them male. Succeeding generations of historians continued to interpret the westering movement in masculine terms.[36] Women, after all, as a modern day historian has reminded us, "did not lead expeditions, command troops, build railroads, drive cattle, ride Pony Express, find gold, amass great wealth, get elected to high public office, rob stages or, lead lynch mobs,"[37] and such activities were what built the West. If, occasionally, a woman did such things, she was not a woman "in the true sense of the word" but an exception, an aberration, a masculine rather than a feminine participant.

Aside from the literary images presented by Cooper, Irving, and Kirkland and the penny dreadfuls and dime novels (many of them written by women) which portrayed such interesting female characters as Hurricane Nell, the Trapper's Bride, and Zilla Fitz-James, the Bandit Queen,[38] a few nineteenth-century histories also dealt with Western women. They displayed a strong pioneer mother bias which pictured pioneer women as perfect ladies who were nonetheless capable of defending home and family and holding the fort until their husbands returned and who also brought enlightenment and civilization to the benighted red folks and other denizens of the "dark and bloody" frontier.[39] Most twentieth-century writers, following in the Turnerian tradition, ignored women as a part of the westward movement or, if they did include a token woman or two, they were usually Princess Sacajawea, brave pioneer mother Narcissa Whitman, or one of the bad girls, most often Belle Starr or Calamity Jane. A recent (1974) survey of standard textbooks used in college and university courses in Western history concluded that these texts all "come close to ignoring women entirely."[40] As recently as 1979, a major study of the overland trail contained only a few brief passages related to women's participation in the Western migration.[41]

During the 1940s and 1950s, a few serious studies of westering women were published, but most were written primarily from government documents, newspaper articles, and men's accounts or used only a few carefully selected women's journals and reminiscences. For example, Georgia Willis Read's "Women and Children on the Oregon-California Trail" (1944), was based on government documents and the observations of J. Goldsborough Bruff.[42] Nancy Ross, *Westward the Women* (1944), and Helena Huntington, "Pioneers in Petticoats" (1959), did use women's accounts, but their sample was very limited, and their interpretations, although more realistic than the nineteenth-century versions, were within the brave pioneer mother tradition. In a similar vein, historian and novelist Dee Brown portrayed Western women as civilizers and culture-bearers, an attitude reflected in his title—*The Gentle Tamers* (1958).[43] William Sprague's *Women and the West: A Short Social History*, published in 1940, utilized a number of women's source materials, but unfortunately it incorporated the prevailing stereotypes of women and was limited in its objectivity. For example, Sprague contended that women suffered more than men from the fevers and ague prevalent in many frontier areas, that they endured greater hardships than men, and that their real difficulties came when they were deprived of "shipping facilities, material luxury, and attention by men."[44] A similar interpretation of frontier women as overworked and discouraged drudges was presented in Everett Dick's 1937 *The Sod-House Frontier.*[45]

In recent years, the interest in women's history has led to the publication of a number of new studies of frontier women. Several books and articles dealing with women's role on the overland trails and on the frontier have appeared[46] within the past decade, and several journals devoted entire issues to Western women's history.[47] Unfortunately, some of these authors, in an attempt to demolish the old myths about westering women, succeeded only in creating new ones.[48] Several authors, writing from a militant, feminist perspective, pictured Western women as exploited, downtrodden drudges deprived of the liberating virtues of the West. These authors contended that women on the frontiers were forced into unfamiliar roles, and that although women in the Western settlements continued to try to reinstate a culture of domesticity, their work as virtual hired hands prevented them from either returning to older, more familiar roles in the social structure or creating new roles. "They refused to appropriate their new work to their own ends and advantage," the authors of one such article concluded, and thus "in the deepest sense of themselves they remained estranged from their function as able bodies."[49] A similar interpretation in an 1977 article stressed the conflict between women's sense of woman's proper sphere and the new roles and conditions imposed by the frontier, and concluded that the frontier worked against women rather than offering new opportunities as it did for men. Writing from a somewhat different perspective, another historian also questioned the application of Turner's thesis to women's frontier experiences. Women, he decided, were physically, as well as socially and emotionally, unable to take advantage of the opportunities offered by the frontier. Even if one accepted Turner's "own assumption that economic opportunity is what matters and that the frontier was significant as the context within which economic opportunity occurred," he argued, ". . . for American women . . . opportunity began pretty much where the frontier left off."[50]

In 1979 two important books on Western women appeared which have aroused a good deal of comment and controversy. John M. Faragher's *Women and Men on the Overland Trail* and Julie Roy Jeffrey's *Frontier Women: The Trans-Mississippi West 1840-1880* took very different approaches and provided very different pictures of Western women.[51] It should be pointed out, however, that the title of Faragher's book is misleading. Although the book focuses on the overland immigrants, it is primarily a study of Midwestern farm families at a particular time. Since there were few diaries and reminiscences of Midwestern farm life, Faragher used the diaries which those folk who moved West wrote about the trail and from these later writings attempted to reconstruct family life before emigration. He also utilized a number of demographic techniques and an elaborate content analysis of diaries, memoirs, and even folksongs and folklore of the period as a basis for examining the role of men and women and their own perceptions of those roles. Writing from a Marxist orientation, Faragher defined all relationships in terms of the class, race, and sexual struggle, and within this struggle Faragher saw women as exploited, subordinate, and powerless. He viewed immigrant women as passive participants who only reluctantly went West "because of the terms of obedience which marriage had imposed. . . ." The West, he concluded, did not provide new opportunities or more equal status for women. Rather, "the frontier extended the impact that agricultural settings have historically had on relations between the sexes" and westering women, like their Midwestern sisters, remained "confined to the domestic space, left without social power, were dependent for status upon their relations with their husbands."[52]

Jeffrey's study was based on a broader geographical area, and, using more traditional methodology, she reached very different conclusions. Although Jeffrey also failed to find a new egalitarianism for women in the West, she portrayed frontier women as spirited, if selfless, participants who were able to take advantage of some of the opportunities offered in the new country. She also pointed out that although Western women remained conservative and "few responded [to the frontier] by casting off convention," they played an active role in frontier life. "None thought to reject the civilizing mission they assumed they had consciously performed," she concluded, and they wrote of their contributions with pride and appreciation of their value. "Had they not known it before these women realized now how strong and successful they had been in meeting the challenges of frontier life. . . . They had been not weak but strong; they had been not passive but active. They had triumphed over frontier conditions heroically."[53]

Jeffrey's work and several other recent studies have done much to counterbalance the old nineteenth-century myths and the more recent feminist stereotypes of frontier women.[54] These studies stress the fact that westering women came from different backgrounds, had different experiences, and responded to frontier conditions in different ways. "If there is a truth about frontierswomen," one author contended, "it is that they were not any one thing."[55] The drudge and the brave pioneer mother were stereotypes but not myths. That both existed is evident from the literature. So did the soiled doves and the bad girls, but they were the exception. Their stories stood out because they differed from the lives of most pioneer women. If we are to understand the variety of women's frontier experiences and finally put the Madonna of the Prairies and the Calamity Jane images to rest, there are a number of questions which need further examination. What preconceptions did women have about the frontier? How did they view the physical wilderness? What preconceptions did they have about Indians, Mexican-Americans, and other groups they would encounter in the West? How, if at all, were these ideas changed by life on the frontier? What adaptations in social, economic, cultural, and intellectual life were necessary or came about as a result of the frontier experience? Did women's ideas about their role in the family and the community change as a result of the westering experience? Did women take on new roles in the West, and did these new roles change both individual and national perceptions of woman's place? In what ways did women's reactions and adaptations to the frontier differ from those of men? In the following pages some of the answers to these questions are suggested in the words written by women about their frontier experiences.

2

The Pleasing Awfulness[1]

Women's Views of Wilderness

Perhaps no concept, no theme in American history has had a greater impact on the popular imagination than the idea of the West, the frontier.[2] Long before Frederick Jackson Turner penned his famous essay on the significance of the frontier in American history, Americans had been intrigued, almost mesmerized, by the land out there beyond the settlements. Once Anglo-Americans had braved the perilous oceans to reach the New World, they seemed drawn, almost impelled, to continue their probings of the unknown, or at least the little-known, land beyond. Between 1607 when the first colonists landed in Virginia and 1763 when the British government attempted to limit, or at least confine, settlement to the area east of the Appalachians, Anglo hunters, traders, land speculators, and settlers had roamed far into the backcountry seeking new opportunities and new areas for expansion and settlement. By the end of the American Revolution these same restless people were ready to push well beyond the old British-French-Indian frontier line into the lands between the Appalachians and the Mississippi River. By the close of the War of 1812 they had occupied these lands, established homes and farms and towns, and were ready, with an ever restless spirit, to move into the newly acquired lands of the Louisiana Purchase. By the end of the Civil War they had pushed to the Pacific and were already probing beyond the continental limits westward to Hawaii and northward into Alaska.

To the south and west was another expanding European frontier, older in date of settlement, but different in character from that of the Anglos. In the sixteenth century, Spanish conquistadors, searching for new deposits of gold and silver and new Indian peoples to subdue, convert, and exploit, moved out of the Valley of Mexico into the desert lands to the north. Using a unique combination of military, religious, and civilian institutions, they established a far-flung frontier line which stretched, at one time, from San Augustine in the Floridas, west to Altár on the Gulf of Sonora, and north along the Pacific coast to San Francisco Bay. Although seen by the Spanish authorities as principally a defensive bulwark against European and Indian aggression, the Spanish borderlands frontier attracted a hardy breed of settlers, mostly *mestizos*, who saw opportunities for economic and political advancement not available to them in the established society of New Spain. The Spanish frontier was more rigidly controlled by officers of church and state than was the Anglo frontier, but the vigor of its institutions and the skill of Spanish frontiersfolk can best be seen in the strong imprint that they left on the land and the people and in their success in maintaining their far-flung boundaries for over two hundred years.[3]

To the north was yet another European frontier. Dominated by the commercial interests of the fur trade, French Canada differed markedly from both English and Spanish America. Rather than promoting an expanding area of settlement, French policy encouraged concentration of the European population along a stretch of the St. Lawrence River from Quebec to Montreal. From this metropolis, the French dominated the hinterland and controlled the fur trade but made little attempt to populate the backcountry. French rule ended in 1763, and both Canada proper and much of the interior Mississippi Valley came under the influence of English institutions and settlement patterns.[4]

The seemingly inexorable progress of the European nations in exploring and settling the North American continent is a well-known part of our historic tradition in the United States. But at the same time that Americans looked forward with eager anticipation to westward expansion, there was an ambivalence in attitudes toward what has become known, in modern usage, as the frontier experience. The first settlers, and their pioneering descendants, were both attracted to and repelled by the wilderness land beyond the setting sun. From the first tenuous probings out from the settlements along the Atlantic shore and from the Valley of Mexico, Americans saw what they regarded as the vast "unsettled"[5] interior of the continent both as the land of promise and as the dark beyond. In a later age, Frederick Jackson Turner referred to the frontier as the "meeting point between savagery and civilization,"[6] and it was in terms of savagery and civilization that Americans viewed the essential paradox of the frontier.

Particularly for Anglo-Americans, the West was the land of opportunity, the place of beginning again, but the West was also an unsettled area fraught with danger, a place

> Where none inhabited
> But hellish fiends, and brutish men
> That devils worshiped[7]

The West might be the land of opportunity, but it could also be a Howling Wilderness; and wilderness implied untamed elements, unknown dangers, a territory haunted by savage men and ravenous beasts. When settlers came into a newly opened frontier area, they had to meet the wilderness on its own terms; they were told they "must accept the conditions which it furnishes, or perish."[8] Progress and economic betterment required sacrifice, and that sacrifice meant people "had to forsake all the niceties of society and return to primitive conditions."[9] Wilderness bred savagery in man and beast alike. Not only the Indian but the white person could be influenced by this hostile environment. Life in the West, warned popular geographer Jedidiah Morse, produced a "strange sort of lawless profligacy, the impressions of which are indelible. The manners of the Indian natives are respectable compared with this European medley."[10]

Despite these dangers, the vacant lands to the west still offered the opportunities for material progress which were becoming a national creed. The Western area might be wilderness now, but potentially it was the Garden of the World.[11] Wilderness was a temporary condition, "thro' which we are passing to the Promised land," wrote one New England colonist, and his words were repeated by succeeding generations of pioneers.[12] Wilderness could be conquered and civilization reestablished. "Thus is the period already arrived, when this state so lately a wilderness, blossoms like the rose," wrote geographer Herman Mann in 1818, sentiments echoed by historian W. H. Venable over half a century later: "Wilds where but a few years since, the note of the owl and the howl of the wolf were heard, have given way to cultivated fields."[13] Like the Israelites of old led by God to the land of promise, New Englanders believed their wilderness colony was a refuge, "a place of Safetie" which might be transformed into a "fruitfull place . . . where trees flourish faire, and prosper well. . . ."[14] In a like manner, early nineteenth-century Western boosters, both male and female, were positive their land and their society were favored above all others. The West, boasted popular writer Eliza Farnham, was to be "preferred over all other portions of the earth. Its magnitude, its fertility, the kindliness of its climate, and the variety and excellence of its productions are unrivaled in our country, if not on the globe."[15] Describing the future prospects of the trans-Appalachian country, Ohio Senator Ben Ruggles rhapsodized, "This surely is the greatest region of the country on 'that little speck called Earth.' "[16] This garden land, as anyone could see, was destined to be "the power center of America, as America will be of the whole world," proclaimed a proud Westerner in 1838,[17] and decades later Americans still repeated and believed in the ultimate destiny of the Western lands.

Despite the differences in their motivations, organization, and expectations, the French and Spanish also saw both the wilderness and garden aspects of the American continent. French priests and *coureurs de bois* knew well the dangers and perils of wilderness travel and trade, but they also saw the potential for harvesting both souls and furs and living off the "bounteous" products of the country. Although they sometimes commented on the "scorching sun," the "dark thick woods," the "violent and furious" rivers, and the "dry and barren" stretches of countryside, their histories and descriptions of the new land were replete with references to "pleasant meadows," "a fruitful champayne country," "fertile soil," trees which "droop under the weight and multitude of their fruit," and all manner of game and other wildlife.[18] Spanish conquistadors hoped to find another El Dorado, but Spanish colonizers, although disappointed by the lack of rich mineral resources, were more interested in exploiting the extensive pasturelands and gaining the highly prized status of *hidalgo*. Explorer Juan Bautista de Anza grew almost lyrical in his description of the opportunities of California. "I have seen no other region," he recorded, "so advantageous as this for the raising of all kinds of stock and the production of the principal grasses. . . ."[19] The Spaniards also saw the new land in Biblical terms. Captain Gaspar Pérez de Villagrá piously pointed out in his great epic poem on the conquest of New Mexico that the province lay in the same latitude as "Jerusalem the Holy," and he later described one exploring expedition's stopping place along the Rio Grande as the "Elysian fields of happiness" where they had arrived after "traversing vast and solitary plains where the foot of Christian never trod before."[20] Here were opportunities for both the colonizer and the church—stockland for the settler and converts for the priests.

This paradoxical view of the West as both wilderness and paradise continued throughout the nineteenth century. As Anglo-Americans crossed the Mississippi River and gained new frontier territory at the expense of the French and Spanish, the same dilemma over the nature of the land and its opportunities which had concerned earlier pioneers remained. There were rich valleys and prairies in the trans-Mississippi West; inviting new areas called pioneers westward, but there was also a Great American Desert, a wilderness as frightening as anything encountered before. Somewhere between the ninety-eighth meridian and the Rockies (the geographers differed in its exact location), was a wilderness country unfit for human habitation, "a barren, trackless waste" inhabited only by "the mustang, the buffalo, the antelope and their migratory Lord, the Prairie Indians," a place to hurry across on the way to California or Oregon.[21] The new Western frontier, like the old, both beckoned and repelled. Where there was opportunity, there was also danger; where there were potential gardens, there were also barren wastes.

Whether Americans viewed the West as Howling Wilderness or Promised Land, they did not go into the frontier areas unprepared. In addition to tools, seeds, clothing, and household items they also packed a good deal of at least theoretical knowledge about the region to which they were immigrating. During the sixteenth and seventeenth centuries official government reports of expeditions and letters and journals of the priests who accompanied them were available to Spanish and French frontier settlers although many of their ideas about the *tierra afuera* probably came from the speculations of friends and word-of-mouth reports. Throughout the eighteenth and nineteenth centuries books of geography and description, travel accounts, and reports of expeditions were popular reading material. In the closing years of the eighteenth century, a number of Western travelers published accounts and descriptions of the trans-Appalachian region, and these books were generally available and eagerly read both in North America and Europe.[22] These, along with gazetteers and guidebooks, such as Cramer's *Navigator* and Cummings's *Western Pilot*,[23] and newspaper and magazine articles were avidly read by prospective immigrants, both female and male. Thus, American women approached the Western land with a number of preconceptions about the new regions.

Considering the comments by some historians, sociologists, and political scientists concerning the differences in men's and women's attitudes about westering, the similarity in their perceptions about the West is, at first glance, surprising. This is especially true in regard to the physical wilderness. Yet, on careful consideration, the similarities are not difficult to explain. Most of the widely read publicists for the West were men, and it was from their writings that women gained most of their preconceptions and ideas about the West. Generally the accounts which shaped women's ideas of the West were positive and optimistic; they stressed the productivity of the soil, the luxuriant forests, and rich mineral resources of the Western lands. Indians, wild animals (other than those useful as game or for fur), and other dangers were rarely mentioned, or at least not emphasized, except as curiosities. Popular and widely read authors extolled the beauties of the Ohio River Valley, Kentucky, and the Illinois country. Kentucky, Western publicist John Filson assured his readers in 1784, "is more temperate and healthy than the other settled parts of America." The soil was fertile, he continued, and "exceeding luxurious in all its productions. The western waters produce plenty of fish and fowl . . . and serpents are not numerous." Even the Indians were "not so ignorant as some suppose them, but are a very understanding people . . . of a very gentle and amiable disposition to those they think their friends. . . ."[24] Tennessee was no less desirable. "The soil is not only fertile," one author informed his public, "but easily cultivated. Six hogheads of tobacco . . . does not require more labour than three hogheads in the Atlantic states."[25] To the south, East and West Florida had a perfect climate according to explorer Bernard Romans and were capable of producing "all the products of the torrid zone as well as of the temperate."[26] Obviously the region needed only more settlers and a vigorous outside trade to make it truly an Earthly Paradise.

The lands to the north of the Ohio River also offered rich and fertile soils and a salubrious climate. According to one guidebook author, "the valleys of Ohio and Illinois comprise, perhaps, the finest region in the world. If soil, climate, vegetable and mineral production are added to its commercial advantages, this opinion can not be considered extravagant. . . ."[27] "No part of the federal territory," geographer Jedidiah Morse reported, "unites so many advantages in point of health, fertility, variety of products, and foreign intercourse."[28] Yet another Western booster confidently predicted that soon the new states which would be carved from the territory would become "very bright stars in the galaxy of the republic."[29] Immigration into the country along the "beautiful Ohio" and the other water courses was a pleasurable experience. As the traveler's boat floated along, he could enjoy

beautiful spring mornings, when the verdant forest, the mild and delicious temperature of the air, the delightful azure of the sky of this country, the fine bottom lands on the one hand, and the romantic bluff on the other, the broad and smooth stream, rolling calmly down the forest, and floating the boat gently forward.[30]

Even an overland journey was not "so uncomfortable a business as it may generally appear to be," one writer assured the prospective settler, and "as for the dreadful stories told of wild beasts, believe me they are vain."[31]

Not all the writers were so ebullient in their assessment of the Western prospects. The West was "no poetical 'Arcadia,' " one author cautioned, and anyone planning a move to the West "should examine and re-examine every statement; exercising the most deliberate caution."[32] The way west was not nearly so easy as pictured but was beset by a number of difficulties, including treacherous roads, raging streams, and violent storms. Other Western experts cautioned that the broad prairie regions yielded little timber for buildings, fuel, and fences, and one went so far as to opine that these lands could not be "inhabited by whites."[33] The numerous popular accounts of the Indian wars, such as Matthew Bunn's narrative, reminded the prospective settler that the Indians were not as amiable and friendly as one might have been led to believe.[34] Such cautious notes did little to deter immigration, however. Americans continued to take a utopian view of the West as a land flowing with milk and honey, a new Canaan, a second Garden of Eden. These, and similar opinions, were frequently reflected in women's as well as men's accounts of the West.

Books of travel and emigrant's guides were not the only source of information for prospective Westerners, of course. Newspapers and magazines carried numerous articles about the Western territories. Geographies, school texts, and other books of instruction, familiar to most parents and children, echoed the spirit of optimism in relation to the Western lands. "If we glance an eye over this immense region," declared one textbook writer,

> if we regard the fertility of the soil, the variety of productions, and if we combine those advantages offered by nature, with the moral energy of the free and active people who are spreading their increasing millions over its surface—what a brilliant prospect opens upon us through the darkness of future time.[35]

With such descriptions to influence their opinions, Americans expected much from the new country beyond the Appalachians; most of them were not disappointed. Even women, who were supposed to be reluctant pioneers, reflected the country's optimism, and joined their voices in the national hymns of praise to the prospects of the new country. Writing from Ludlow's Station on the Ohio frontier in 1802, Charlotte Ludlow referred to the Mad River area as the garden spot of Ohio, and went on to describe its "beautiful extended plains," "lofty forests," and "clearest streams."[36] Other women, writing to family and friends in the East, gave similar descriptions of the delights of the Western country.

Caroline Kirkland, whose popular *A New Home* (1839) and *Forest Tales* (1842) were widely read in the East, poked fun at some of the more exaggerated male views of Western potential. She described the West as seen through the magic glasses of a political friend. Through these glasses, she wrote, "Snake Hill, an elevation which had always before appeared to me covered with stunted oak bushes" was crowned instead with "luxurious sugar maples and lofty elms, with fantastic arbors." Of the wild oak grove, she continued, there was nothing left save some "delicately fancied garden chairs."[37] Despite her gentle jibes at the overly enthusiastic reports of some Western propagandists, Kirkland agreed that great progress had been made in clearing the land "so lately the home of the deer, the bear, and the wild wolf, now fast becoming one wide expanse of industry and abundance."[38]

Other women, too, saw the great potential of the Western lands, and their reports differed little from those of male writers. "The most buoyant and playful imagination must be outstripped by the prosperity which will, at some future day, smile on this favored portion of the earth," wrote an enthralled Catherine Stewart; she confidently predicted a day when the West would realize "the wealth that is slumbering in the fertile soil and science shall have reared her temples in these western groves."[39] Many women writers, like their male counterparts, compared the Western lands to the "promised land beyond the Jordan," and saw the West as the recipient of special Heavenly blessings. "No spot on earth," boasted Caroline Kirkland, could rival the West in natural beauty and productivity. The region boasted the "richest meadowland, shut in by gently swelling hills . . . lakes in unparalleled variety . . . studded with islands and tenanted by multitudes of wild fowl. . . ."[40] In a somewhat more realistic vein, Eliza Steele pointed out that a great deal of labor would be necessary to make the land productive, but the effort "would well repay the agricultists labors," and the great rivers and rapid streams would "place a great amount of manufacturing power at the disposal of the settlers."[41] Kirkland, Stewart, and Steele, like Eliza Farnham, were well-known nineteenth-century publicists—professional writers who prepared their comments for an eager public audience. But the same enthusiasm for the Western country was reflected in the diaries and letters of ordinary women, some of whom had undoubtedly read their books and had been influenced by them.

Many Western settlers were promoters, eager to attract new settlers to help civilize the country and buy up surplus land, and women were as enthusiastic in their boosterism as their menfolk. As one woman promoter reminded her readers, the country where once "there was little to be seen or heard but the red man of the forest . . . and the yell of the prowling wolf," soon would become an area of "productive farms, with splendid mansions, inhabited by intelligent and enterprising farmers" where here and there one could find "beautiful villages which will vie with any."[42] Although men and women often approached the remote areas with a combination of hope and fear, their fears quickly gave way to the ideas of progress and national pride which dominated nineteenth-century American life. Wilderness vanished as rapid expansion and rural and urban growth helped fulfill the prophecies of exuberant nineteenth-century pundits who proudly proclaimed that the West offered "the golden opportunity to spread America's economic, political, and social systems into an environment which will nurture this already established ideal society."[43]

If the nineteenth century was the Age of Progress, it was also part of the Age of Romanticism, and Americans subscribed to the concepts of sublimity and deism which provided the climate for a "cult of wilderness." Romanticism, as one historian noted, implied "an enthusiasm for the strange, remote, solitary and mysterious," and for the romantic, wilderness evoked feelings of "awe and delight rather than of dread and loathing."[44] This was an age which enjoyed "pleasing awfulness," and the West offered abundant opportunities to view and experience such scenes. By the early nineteenth century, the romantic viewpoint was clearly apparent in books of Western travel and description, even in those intended primarily for instruction and advice. In guidebooks such as *The Navigator,* the "romantic appearance" of the countryside, the "monstrous growths" and "towering heights" which reportedly filled the beholder with astonishment, found their way into the detailed instructions on the locations of rapids and the best passageways along the rivers.[45] Even geographers had their romantic side. Along the Great Lakes, Timothy Flint noted, "the precipitous crags" and "black masses of primitive granite" filled the observer with "ideas of loneliness, grandeur, and desolation."[46] Cramer and Flint were not alone in their romantic musings on the wilderness. Almost every book of geography and travel, including advice to immigrants, written in the late eighteenth and early nineteenth centuries, combined practicality with the concept of sublimity.

Women who traveled into the trans-Appalachian region also linked the progressive pioneer spirit with Romantic enthusiasm for nature. Julia Kinzie recalled her early longing for "the region of romance" and "spelled out the long word 'Michi-i-li-mach-i-nac,'" that distant land with its vast lakes, its boundless prairies, and its mighty forest had possessed a wonderful charm for my imagination."[47] Eliza Steele rhapsodized over her first sight of an Illinois prairie. "A world of grass and flowers stretched around me, rising and falling in gentle undulations as if an enchanter had struck the ocean swell."[48] Even the usually practical Catherine Stewart succumbed to the romantic spirit of the age as she described the "lofty magnificence, or reposes on the magic rillings of nature."[49] Perhaps women's enthusiasm for the romantic appeal of wilderness is best illustrated by Mary Dewees' description of her journey to Kentucky:

> arrived at the top of the cloud capt Allagany [sic]. It was really awfully pleasing to behold the clouds arising between the mountains at a distance. . . . I think [in] this and many more of the scenes we have passed through we have seen nature displayed in her greatest undress; at other times we have seen her dressed beautifully beyond expression.[50]

There was a darker side to all this wilderness of beauty, of course. Muddy roads, bogs, and swamps; pine barrens and sterile stretches of land; mosquitoes, wolves, panthers, and rattlesnakes; and "lurking savages" infested the land and made it less an earthly paradise for the potential pioneer. Dewees' romantic musings were immediately followed by the comment that the road was "excessive bad." But even discomforts and dangers moved women writers to romantic description:

> The vast plain over which we were moving, seen through the dusk of a cloudy night, seemed a fitting place for dark deeds—a fine Hounslow heath, or Indian lurking place. . . . Suddenly a low plaintive wail sounded over the waste.[51]

Such descriptions added yet another element to women's sense of exultation and awe.

Many of the women and men who wrote so exuberantly about the West were tourists rather than settlers. Those who had to deal with the day-to-day aggravations of living beyond the edge of civilization were more realistic in their assessment of the wonders of wilderness. Caroline Kirkland, who admitted that her ideas of the West had been shaped by "Hoffman's tour or Captain Hall's 'graphic' delineations," was appalled by her first encounter with the Michigan wilderness. Her reading, "touched by the flowing pencil of fancy, gave me but incorrect notions of a real journey through Michigan." Immigrants also complained about the lack of suitable accommodations for travelers. In most wilderness taverns, reported Mary Dewees, one was lucky "to escape being fleased [sic] alive."[52] Primitive roads, dark, tangled woods, and their first glimpse of Western home life did little to inspire the immigrants' first impressions of the country.

Once they arrived at their destination most were not attracted by the open prairies in the new country. Earlier experience on American frontiers had seemingly taught pioneers that fertility of soil could be judged by the forest growth and that open fields indicated barren lands. Anglo-Americans generally were a forest people who distrusted open places, and early Western settlers preferred land with wood and water. Thus Kentucky pioneers named their smiling meadows The Barrens and cleared farms in the depths of the forest. To the north, settlers skipped over the rich prairie lands of Illinois and Indiana to take up their claims on inferior wooded hills. Forests provided building materials for fencing and for building a cabin, fuel for the fire, game for the table, and mast for farm animals. More important, the forest offered physical and psychological shelter from the fury of prairie fires and the terror of blinding winter blizzards. The prairies were unfamiliar and open, the forest familiar and sheltering, and "only gradually did American settlers overcome their natural repugnance to a shelterless, timberless farm home."[53] This aversion to open land was a frequent theme in writing of both men and women. Although most settlers found the prairies beautiful, they preferred to make their homes in the more familiar woods.

Immigrants also believed the prevailing theory that it was the open prairie lands which gave rise to the fevers and agues which plagued the region. Almost everyone was affected when they first arrived, and although some became rapidly acclimated, others continued to suffer from the aftereffects for some time. These malarial fevers often turned the skin "yellow as an orange," sapped the victims' strength, and left them with low vitality for many months.[54] Living conditions, at least during the early years of settlement, were crude and put additional strains on tired and worried women. It was difficult to appreciate the beauties of nature when all one's time and energy were absorbed in devising ways to "secure a comfortable living in that new and rough country."[55]

Women were especially concerned by the darker side of human nature which they found among their fellow pioneers. They were disturbed by the rough talk and hard liquor, the lack of attention to religious duties, and the lack of "timely beauties of cultivated life" which did "not spring up in wilderness nor in prairies nor in log cabins."[56] Almost every woman who wrote about the trans-Appalachian country had something to say about the seamier side of the Western character. Catherine Stewart's comments were fairly typical. "The brightest picture must have its dark shades," she wrote:

> Vice and degradation are diffused through every society; and it is well that a man should be armed at all points to turn aside the arts of the wily and selfish, who always contribute to the heterogeneous mass of a new community.

"It is too true," she continued

> that moral obligation in many cases, sits too lightly; the natural consequence of infidelity, which ever prevails where the light of the Gospel is withheld, or but partially administered. The desecration of the Sabbath occurs in many places.[57]

Romantics might stress the close association between religion and nature, but many women wondered if God truly inhabited the wilderness. Even if God had not forsaken the wilderness, it was clear that many wilderness dwellers had forsaken, or at least conveniently forgotten, God. Women were more inclined to point out the godlessness of the Western country and to dwell on its effects on society, but men also were disturbed by these "dark shades."[58]

Despite the defects in Western prospects and character, pioneers remained optimistic about the future. After a long recitation of their many difficulties in establishing a home in Illinois, Rebecca Burlend confidently wrote that their "circumstances kept improving" and that "the soil and mineral productions of America" provided everything necessary to "make a community great, independent, and happy." In a similar vein, Mary Dewees told her sister in a letter from Kentucky, "I can assure you I have enjoyed more happiness the few days I have been here than these four or five years past . . . and am in full expectation of seeing better days."[59] Like their menfolk, women were confident that wilderness could be conquered and rampant nature tamed. After all, God had given men "dominion over the fish of the sea, and over the fowl of the air, and over every living thing that moveth upon the earth." Good Christian men and women, working together, could overcome the excesses and evils of wilderness and hasten the day when peace, prosperity, and godliness would dominate the land.

Americans had no sooner begun to settle and civilize the trans-Appalachian country than another garden beyond the Mississippi beckoned. In 1803 the United States purchased the Louisiana Territory, and the area was quickly hailed as the new Promised Land. Despite the reports by Stephen Long and Zebulon Pike which gave rise to the Great American Desert theory, there were obviously well-watered and well-timbered lands and fertile prairies lying along the western banks of the Mississippi River. By the 1830s much of the land east of the Mississippi had been settled, farms and villages dotted the landscape, and already a restless race looked for new land, new resources. The vast expanses of the trans-Mississippi West stretched invitingly toward the Pacific, and frontier families, who a decade earlier had hurried into Kentucky, Tennessee, and the Ohio country or into the new cotton lands of Mississippi and Alabama, quickly decided that the new territory offered more land, more opportunity, more promise than the old. There was a New Canaan, richer, more fertile, than the old. Once again the wagons rolled westward into Missouri, Iowa, and the Minnesota country while to the southwest the Mexican government opened Texas land to Anglo settlers.

Pioneers wrote glowing reports of the new country and urged friends and relatives to join them. By the 1840s the myth that the open prairies were inhospitable, unhealthy, and could not produce crops had been dispelled. "We had heard so much of the beautiful prairies of Iowa," wrote a young Pennsylvania girl. "We could see for miles and all my longings for the vast open spaces were satisfied." Men and women were enthralled by the new country. The woods and prairies along the Western watercourses teemed with deer, wild turkey, prairie chickens, and quail. Indians were more a nuisance than a menace. The soil was rich and fertile, one woman reported, and even uncultivated lands were "covered with wild rye, higher than the tallest man's head, and so thick that you could not see a man, on horse-back, at five paces distant." Undoubtedly this, announced another, was the "most magnificent dwelling place prepared by God for the abode of man."[60]

Then came a new cry. "West to Oregon!" "Ho for California!" It was two thousand miles across the plains and mountains to the final golden green Paradise on the Pacific, but Americans were ready to go. Some cautioned patience. The way was too hard; land in California and Oregon was no better than that in "the States." It would be better to fill in the existing areas and proceed carefully into the new areas. The West should be approached, counseled one newspaper, "striking at him with one hand while the other holds fast to the world behind, and he loses all his terrors, and meets the stranger with a smiling welcome."[61] Many women, reluctant once again to pull up stakes and move to yet another farther frontier supported such opinions. "I used to have the same contempt for Clark & Lewis' explorations as I have since had for Franklin L. Kane," wrote a disgusted Harriet Williams. "I felt that the same energy, time & money spent in some other way would be such a benefit to mankind, and who would go to Oregon as long as there was land to live on anywhere else."[62]

But many Americans did not share these sentiments. By the 1840s first single men and then families headed for the Willamette Valley, and within a few years the first cries of "Gold!" from the California slopes sent first the gold-seekers and then the land-seekers on the perilous journey across the continent. It was on this journey that men and women encountered even greater wonders of nature than they had seen before—spectacular mountain scenery, gorgeous desert sunsets, violent yet thrilling storms, strange new plants and animals. It was this epic journey which produced hundreds, perhaps thousands, of diaries, journals, reminiscences, and letters with rich descriptions of the many sights along the trail and the adventures the pioneers experienced both on the trail and in their new homes.

The nineteenth century was an age when both men and women were encouraged to keep journals and diaries, and overland travelers were especially anxious to record their experiences, either for their own pleasure or to inform friends and family back home about the journey. Others saw the trip as a "Great Adventure" and wanted to preserve, and possibly publish, an account of their participation. Many who did not keep a daily record of their crossing later wrote reminiscences for their children and grandchildren in order to recall and relate the story of their own part in the opening of the West. Women's diaries and reminiscences constituted an important portion of this trail literature. One survey of the travel accounts on just one overland route along the South Platte revealed that over 10 percent were written by women,[63] and women's journals contained some of the most detailed accounts of the trip and vivid descriptions of the countryside.

As before, in the move into the trans-Appalachian West, potential immigrants armed themselves with as many facts as possible about the trip and the new land. Men and women considering the journey eagerly read geographies and school texts, travel accounts and emigrant guides, newspapers and magazines for information about the new country and the best routes for crossing the continent. These reports helped to shape their preconceptions and expectations. "I have been reading the various guides of the route to California," wrote Lodisa Frizzell, and "they have not improved my ideas of the pleasure of the trip, no very flattering account I assure." But she remained optimistic and hoped "we may find it better not worse." But other women approached the journey with eagerness and a sense of anticipation. "Ho—for California—at last we are on the way," extolled an excited Helen Carpenter, "and with good luck may some day reach the 'promised land.' "[64] Such seemingly conflicting comments were shaped by the conditions women left behind, their motives for undertaking the journey, and by various descriptions of the new country which they read.

It is not surprising that westering women were often ambivalent about the undertaking. As they poured over geographies, travel accounts, guidebooks, and other descriptions of the Western country, they were presented with a number of contradictory opinions. The writers of these accounts were by no means unanimous in their assessment of the nature of the Western areas. Although most were enthusiastic in their praise of the far Western lands, they offered conflicting impressions of the territory between the settlements and the coast. The area was still a wilderness, geographer William Woodbridge told his readers; the country consisted "chiefly of immense plains . . . inhabited only by Indians, and a few soldiers." The entire region 300 miles east of the Rocky Mountains, another writer warned, was only "a burnt and arid desert, whose solemn silence is seldom broken by the tread of any other animals than the wolf or the starved and thirsty horse which bears the traveller across its wastes." Other accounts, however, made the way seem more pleasant. Geographer

S. A. Mitchell wrote that although much of the northern plains area "may be likened to the great steppes of Central Asia," there were, even "in the most sterile parts a thin sward of grass and herbage," and the entire area teemed with "droves of buffalo, elk, and deer." Even the Great American Desert did not offer as formidable a barrier as might be supposed, one newspaper informed its readers, for there were "deep ravines in which the brooks and rivers meander, skirted by a few stunted trees. . . ."[65]

Even more contradictory than the descriptions of the country were the warnings about the dangers and hardships of the journey, especially for women and children. Beginning with the first large-scale Oregon migrations in the early 1840s, newspapers throughout the country offered conflicting advice and opinions. Some declared the trip an exciting adventure while others pronounced it palpable homicide. The more optimistic editors assured potential immigrants that although there were certain dangers and hardships, the trip was really quite pleasant. "The way is now completely smooth and easy," the New York *Morning News* informed its readers, and yet another paper declared the trip "merry as a marriage bell" and recommended it for honeymooners.[66] On the opposite side, the naysayers, led by Horace Greeley's influential New York *Tribune*, warned that the trip had an "aspect of insanity" and grimly predicted that not "nine-tenths of the immigrants will ever reach the Columbia alive." Other anti-immigration papers echoed these warnings and gave particular attention to the perils of trying to take women and children across the country. Even Western papers such as the St. Louis *Daily Missouri Republican* argued that although the trip might be undertaken by young, single men, in their view it was an "absurdity" and an "injustice" to subject "their wives and children to all degrees of suffering."[67] Such dire predictions did little to deter women from undertaking the trip, but they undoubtedly added to their apprehensions.

The discovery of gold in California increased the newspaper coverage of the overland trails, and it also intensified the debate over the feasibility of the trip and the possible dangers and hardships which might be encountered. Some papers continued to insist that to take women and children was "folly in the extreme" while others assured their readers that the trip was a perfect "pleasure excursion," and women and children could make the trip with "ease and facility."[68] Moreover, newspapers in the later forties and early fifties began to provide practical and useful information about the trip—what to take, how to pack, the advantages and disadvantages of the various routes. They also supplied information on points of interest, forts and trading posts, and the unusual plants and animals which the immigrants might see. Perhaps even more than the books of travel and instruction which were more likely to be read by well-educated, upper middle-class folk, the newspapers supplied much of the information available to common men and women who were contemplating the westward journey and helped to color their opinions.

Guidebooks, too, were a frequent source of information for all classes. Although the guidebooks all stressed the fact that the journey to the coast could be made, and described the means and routes for doing so, they were not unanimous in their assessment of the difficulties of the journey. Some warned of the hardships and dangers of the trip and of the "expansive desolation along the road," while others assured their readers that one might make the trip "without suffering any of that extraordinary toil, unheard-of hardship or eminent danger, which his own fruitful imagination, or the kind regard of his numerous friends, may have devised."[69] Most guidebook writers tried to prepare their readers for the extraordinary scenes which they would experience and included detailed descriptions of the plants, animals, climate, and topography, often in lyrical terms. For example, one guidebook described the plains as a "vast, beautiful, and perfect picture, which nature herself had drawn, and the hand of man never violated. . . . All was natural, beautiful, unbroken." Even the shorter, more terse guidebooks entries provided short descriptions of the curiosities such as Chimney Rock, Scott's Bluff, Devil's Gate, and the Sink of the Humboldt which undoubtedly influenced later immigrants' descriptions. One guidebook writer described the bluffs along the Platte as "resembling ancient fortifications, castles, etc. in ruins." Independence Rock, another told his travelers, "is well worthy of attention," while yet another directed his readers to take time to visit the celebrated Soda and Steamboat Springs.[70]

Travel narratives, newspaper accounts, guidebooks, and word-of-mouth descriptions did much to help prepare immigrants for both the difficulty and the romance of the overland journey. Thus, women ventured into the new West with a number of preconceptions—and misconceptions—based largely on what they had read or heard. But what did women actually say about the trip? How did westering women view the plains, the deserts, the mountains? How did they describe the strange new animals and plants they saw? Were women repelled by the new wilderness landscape, or did they find beauty in even the most unlikely places?

Some women's diaries were almost as sterile as was, presumably, the land over which they were traveling—a dreary recital of weather, distance, and the availability of wood, water, and grass:

No change in looks of land. Considerable wild sage. Passed 15 graves. No wood nearer than three miles. Very cold and cloudy. Traveled 20 miles.[71]

Such entries were not uncommon. The trip across the plains by either the northern route along the Platte or the southern road from Santa Fe or Texas and out the Gila took from four to six months of slow travel (ten to twenty miles a day by wagon, less than thirty minutes on today's highways). Much of the way the scenery was flat and dreary, and the overwhelming sentiment expressed by most travelers was boredom. Even the most vivacious diarist included many entries such as "another day of bad roads," "warm and dusty still," "nothing of note occurred today," but most women's diaries and reminiscences of the Western journey also provided long narrative passages, rich in descriptive detail.

The physical features of the land attracted much of the attention of the diarists. Women, as well as men, could tell fertile soil and something of the potential of the land, and women's evaluations of the land they were crossing were often perceptive and well informed. "This country looks rather poor," wrote Caroline Richardson as she traveled through part of Iowa; "only once and while [sic] a place that looks like living." "Poor soil . . . but some good springs," opined Maria Shrode of one spot, while Nellie Slater revealed some knowledge of the earlier attitude towards the open prairie lands when she wrote, "We have been traveling over beautiful prairie but there is no timber therefore it is thinly settled."[72] Certainly the women saw the possibilities for future development. "Never have I seen so varied a country, so suitable for cultivation," Tamsen Donner wrote of Nebraska. Near Grand Island, Kate Dunlap reported a new town which was "in the heart of a fine farming country" and "bids fair some day to be a flourishing town."[73]

Not only did women see the potential for future development in the new country, they rarely alluded to the Great American Desert metaphor. A recent survey of 150 women's travel accounts revealed that only a few of them used this phrase in describing the region east of the Rockies, although they occasionally applied the term to the Great Basin area west of Salt Lake City.[74] Perhaps because they traveled through the region during the temperate and generally pleasant months of May and June, overlanders were less inclined than the geographers to view the plains as barren desert. It is clear, however, that women were aware of the desert concept. Jennie Wriston wrote that her family had looked in geographies for "The Great American Desert!" that the books described as " 'an arrid waste, inhabited by savages, wild beasts, and serpents, and on which no rain ever fell in a reasonable natural manner. . . .' "[75] Other women's comments also made it clear that they were familiar with the desert concept, but they nonetheless described the plains in generally positive terms.

Some women saw the plains scenery as barren and desolate, or as "offering no variation whatsoever,"[76] but others were pleasantly surprised.

"The hills look like orchards, and there are a great many hills on the South Fork of the Platte," wrote Agnes Stewart; "I did not expect so much variety on the road to Oregon." "I could not help but wonder at the beauty . . . surrounding us on all sides," rhapsodized Lavinia Porter.

> Above us was the bright dome of a heaven so free from all earthly smoke and vapor, so clear and transparent, that the stars seemed closer and shone with an exceeding brilliancy. The air was filled with a balmy sweetness, and yet so limpid and clear that even in the starlight we could catch glimpses of the shimmering trees in the distant river.[77]

Women frequently compared the plains to the sea. Julia Lovejoy described the Kansas prairies as "undulating like the waves of the sea," while according to Lodisa Frizzell, the plains "were not so level as I had supposed, quite undulating like the waves of the sea when subsiding from a storm." Dayelle Kittredge also likened their journey across the plains to a storm at sea. "Nothing," she wrote, "could more strikingly resemble the tumultuous breakers of the sea."

> The emerald waters brake around us in heavy irregular billows, high and proud, their sides creased with deep indentations like the rushing of a mighty current through the whirling floods of the deep. . . . Sometimes a house appeared in sight like a ship lying calmly in the restless billows, or a lovely group of trees loomed up like an island in the midst of the sea. Charmed I watched the impetuous waves lashing headlong into the broughs between while we rose grandly on the swells.

Although few employed such elaborate language, about half of the women's books surveyed applied the land/sea analogy to the plains country.[78]

The Western mountains elicited even more comment than the plains landscape. Some women saw the mountains only as a barrier and obstacle and described them as "nothing but huge boulders" with bad weather and worse roads.[79] Others reveled in the spectacular mountain scenery and described the "wonderful grandeur" and "magnificent scenery." Nothing, wrote Susan Wallace, could compare with the "surpassing loveliness" of the mountains of New Mexico, while Eveline Alexander painted a delightful word-picture of her first journey through the Raton Pass:

> when we reached the summit of the mountain . . . we had a view of the surrounding country which was only limited by our powers of

vision. At our right the bleak rocky summit of Fisher's Peak reared itself above our heads, and at the left the Spanish Peaks towered above the clouds. . . . At our feet lay many a rocky cañon and lovely valley, enameled with gay flowers, through which we could trace our winding path for many miles.

Anna Gordon found the Rockies "divinely beautiful" while Mary Bailey suggested that "it is not worthwhile for anyone to go to Switzerland to see mountains" for "some of the finest views of mountain scenery that was ever seen by mortals" was available in the American Rockies. Elizabeth Cumming was almost overwhelmed by the mountains of Utah. "Never have I imagined any thing like what I have seen," she wrote. "Do not think me affected when I say my heart *ached*. It was *physical* pain produced in me by what I saw. . . . The most unearthly, weird, wild scenes crowd on my memory."[80]

What was described as the "many curiosities" and "wild and romantic scenery" along both northern and southern overland routes also attracted women writers, and they taxed their imaginations to find suitable words to describe such scenic wonders as Chimney Rock and Scott's Bluff along the Platte, Devil's Gate in Wyoming, New Mexico's Raton Pass, and the Painted Desert and vast saguaro cactus gardens of Arizona. Perhaps because such spectacular sights offered a break in the generally tiring and monotonous landscape, they were favorite topics for the diary and letter writers, but it is difficult to find a single diary that does not include at least one description of a particularly pleasing or impressive scene. Such areas also offered opportunities for women to expound on the beauties of nature and on the relationship of man and God as revealed in nature. On the northern routes women wrote of "the wild prairies covered with luxuriant grasses and wild flowers," "the beautiful landscapes on the Plains," "the turbid Platte . . . within its crumbling banks," "the desolate, wild [and] grand arrangement" of the rocks and the "immense mountains covered with evergreens."[81] In the Southwestern desert areas they described the "remarkable mirages," the "mysterious mounds formed by drifting sand," "the welcome springs," the "beautiful cañons . . . and huge granite mountains and great looming peaks."[82] They were interested in seeing everything the journey had to offer and sometimes took side trips to visit the Soda Springs or to inscribe their names on Independence Rock or to admire the view from a high vantage point. For, as Harriet Ward observed at Devil's Gate, "No one will regret spending half an hour in admiring its grandeur, even enroute for California."[83]

Influenced by the romanticism of the age, nineteenth-century pioneer women exalted nature and pondered the religious significance of the natural wonders they encountered. Viewing enormous piles of volcanic rocks along the upper Platte, Lodisa Frizzell concluded:

> what has caused the earth to be to its center shook? Sin! the very rocks seem to reverberate. Sin has caused them to be upheaved that they may be eternal monuments of the curse & fall of man; viewing these symbols of divine wrath, I felt humbled; I took a small stone & wrote upon a flat rock beside me, Remember me in mercy O lord. I shall never forget this wild scene, & my thoughts & reflections there.

Mary Blake reflected a similar sense of the relationship between God and nature when she wrote of the Rocky Mountains, "O' heavenly heights, fair Mountains of the Snow! will we ever again look upon anything so wonderful until we cross the border-land to the Blessed Country. . . ." Even women not moved to religious contemplation were inspired to flights of romantic fancy. In a dramatic mood, Ellen Biddle described the "most remarkable mirages" of the Southwest, "great cities and castles, and churches with domes; it was almost impossible to believe they were not real." Annie Tallent let her imagination "run riot" as she drove through South Dakota's Black Hills:

> In passing through some of the deepest, darkest canyons of the Hills . . . I could not help glancing furtively from side to side of the ravines to see whether there were any gnomes or hobgoblins peering out at us from between the crevices of the great rocks, where these irrational creatures are supposed to hold high carnival. . . .[84]

Not only the grand and the awe-inspiring but the ordinary and mundane found their way into women's musings. Seemingly no natural phenomenon or objects were too small or insignificant to escape the travelers' chronicles. "There were so many beautiful stones along the road," Helen Carpenter recalled,

> that we did a great deal of walking just for the pleasure of picking them up to admire for a little while. All the colors of the rainbow were represented. There was cornelian, amber, emerald, topaz, rubies, etc. and . . . gingerbread, sassafras and castile soap.

Sarah Sutton described a grove of trees, "dressed in a brown petticoat, and green sack and vail with uplifted arms," while a similar scene along the Nebraska River reminded Ada Vogdes of *"green goats* hairfringe." Teresa Vielé rhapsodized over an oriole who "boldly lights on the flowering bushes, knowing no fear in these rarely interrupted soiltudes."[85]

Although some historians have asserted that men were more concerned with the mechanics of the westering venture than with the beauties of the country, men also wrote long descriptions of the land and its natural wonders. Women may have been more inclined to describe wilderness in religious metaphors, but men also remarked on the revelation of God in nature, and their comments on the landscape were often as romantic as those of women. Men's diaries and reminiscences were replete with references to "grand," "magnificent," and "romantic," and "wild and picturesque" scenery. John G. Bourke began his narrative of life in the Southwest with a comment that it was "a region in which not only purgatory and hell, but heaven likewise had combined to produce a bewildering kaleidoscope of all that was wonderful, weird, terrible, and awe-inspiring, with not a little that was beautiful and romantic." Traveling along the Platte, Vincent Geiger and Wakeman Bryarly noted that the bluffs near the river resembled "castles & old buildings" and "presented a truly grand & magnificent view, assuming many different shapes as we approached."[86] Men often included scientific, physical descriptions of the natural wonders of the country or described them in practical, materialistic terms. "Chimney Rock looked like a shot tower at a great distance," one wrote. "The whole hill and rock is composed of a very hard clay or soft stone and some rock." But such references are not missing from women's diaries. Mary Bailey also likened Chimney Rock to a shot tower, and she and other women carefully chronicled its circumference, height, and possible geological composition and recorded the physical as well as the aesthetic characteristics of the country through which they passed.[87] Even men intent on recording the topographical features, assessments of the minerals and soils, and rational explorations of geological phenomena could not resist a brief romantic aside from their objective reporting. Thus topographical engineer and army officer Randolph B. Marcy, viewing the canyons of the Red River, wrote "These stupendous escarpments of solid rock . . . were worn away by the lapse of time and the action of the water and the weather, into the most fantastic forms, that required but little effort of the imagination to convert into works of art, and all united in forming one of the grandest and most picturesque scenes that can be imagined. . . ."[88]

Immigrants also included descriptions of the new and varied plant and animal life on the plains and in the mountains and deserts. Margaret Carrington was so impressed with the wild life on the northern plains that she devoted the first two chapters of Ab-sa-ra-ka to a discussion of Western topography, flora, and fauna and became almost lyric in her descriptions of the "Home of the Crow . . . a region of the country which has no peer in its exhaustless game resources, and is rarely surpassed in its production of wild fruits." So many women wrote about the "great abundance" of prickly pears, "blooming cacti," and the "very rare and beautiful flowers" they saw that readers could believe that the plains and prairies were literally carpeted with "fine-looking flowers." Even in the barren desert areas there were the "curious round cactus trees," the famed giant saguaro, and the "romantic and mysterious" Spanish dagger.[89]

Animals, too, received a good deal of attention. Many women described the howling of the wolves, the coyotes that frequently "carried off any food left unprotected," the shy antelope, and the elk. Immigrants, both female and male, rarely failed to record their first sight of the great American bison and to comment on the "deafening, terrible noise" of the stampedes of these "mammoths of the plains." Prairie hens, ground squirrels, prairie dogs, tarantulas, even the "horrible tribe of Mosquitoes" and gnats furnished subjects for the journalists' pens. Not only real but mythical Western animals found their way into the women's accounts. The legendary hoop snake of the Southwest (that could put its tail in its mouth and roll across the desert like a hoop) and the mythical pendulum bird of the northern plains (whose thick, colorful wattle swung back and forth like a pendulum, keeping perfect time) came in for their fair share of attention, and attempts were made to explain these, and other, strange phenomena.[90]

The West could be desolate and violent as well as beautiful and entertaining. There was hardly an immigrant's diary which did not record a violent storm upon the plains, detail the terrible thunder and lightning, the giant hailstones, "big as hen's eggs," the vicious, wind-whipped rain which flattened tents, shook the wagons and soaked their contents, and made the travelers fear for their safety. Heat, dust, cold, bad water, barren spots, the fear of drowning in the rapid streams, or being delayed by overflowing rivers, the terrifying and difficult passes through the Sierras and the Cascades—all these were recorded. These less pleasant aspects of the West were the "elephants" of the trail, the dangers and terrors which had to be met and successfully overcome if one were to make it to the Promised Land. "We suddenly found ourselves in a desolate, rough country," Catherine Haun recalled. "I shudder yet at the thought of the ugliness and danger of the territory." In some places, the "abomination of desolation" was so complete that courage and spirits failed, and women, and men as well, broke down and wept.[91]

And then they arrived and settled in the lush, green valleys of Oregon, and on the golden slopes of California. The sense of awe and beauty did not disappear when they reached the Promised Land and had to contend with the everyday problems and vexations of frontier life. Amid the long days of labor in home-building, planting gardens, and establishing themselves, women still found time to enjoy the beauties of the natural scenery. "There is the most elegant and romantic scenery here that I ever saw in my life," one young woman wrote from Oregon. "The mountains are glorious and the forests elegant. I can't begin to describe it for it is beyond description." Women described the inexhaustible rich soil, the rivers teeming with fish, the woods abounding in game, the fisheries, mines, and other natural advantages of the new land. Once again women saw opportunities to turn this lush wilderness into busy, thriving communities of happy, prosperous, and contented men and women who would raise a "song of praise to God, where naught had been heard but the cry of the savage and the howl of the wild beast."[92]

During the closing decades of the century, the less desirable areas were opened to settlement—New Mexico, Arizona, Indian Territory, the far northern plains. The scenery was not as spectacular, but there was still much of interest in the new regions—new landscapes, new plants and animals, new opportunities. "This country was new then," recalled an Oklahoma settler, "and the grass was waist-high and there was lots of game. . . ." The South Dakota plains, Jeanne Wuillemin wrote, were covered with "lovely flowers, entirely different from those at home . . . and the birds along the road also attracted our attention, there being many varieties."[93]

Then came yet another gold rush, and it was on to Alaska and a last great journey to new and so-called grand areas. Once again, women described the beauties and the terrors of the wilderness, the "precipitous cliffs" with "barren and rocky slopes," the great mountains rising "almost perpendicular from the water's edge," the tall, dark spruce and cedar trees that "cast a myriad of shadows," the unexpected sea of wild flowers, "blue bells, paint brush, daisies, and buttercups," the huge glaciers, and twenty-foot-deep snows. The trip was wild and exciting and filled still with the "pleasing awfulness." As one young woman wrote of a particularly impressive scene, "Language becomes too poverty-stricken to express the awe and admiration which fill the soul at such a time."[94]

What French and Spanish-Mexican women thought of the wilderness and the new land on the frontier is more difficult to discern because they left fewer diaries, letters, and other written records. French women contemplating the journey to Canada could consult government reports and the Jesuit relations, and it is clear from the sixteenth-century letters of the missionary Marie de l'Incarnation's letters that she, at least, did so. It is also clear that her reading did not give her a very positive view of the New World wilderness which she described as "the depths of the most cruel Barbarism."[95] Most of the information about the lands north of Mexico available to potential Spanish immigrants was also in the form of government reports and journals and chronicles of earlier expeditions.

Common men and women, even if they could read, rarely had access to such material, but they undoubtedly had some preconceptions and expectations based on word-of-mouth and common knowledge about the new lands. The first Spanish women who came into what is now New Mexico with the Oñate expedition of 1598 were probably familiar with the tales of the Seven Cities of Cibola and had probably read or heard Garci Ordóñez de Montalvo's popular imitation of Amadis de Gaula in which California was pictured as one of the wildest islands in the world, made of bold and craggy rock, and inhabited by a tribe of black Amazons. Whether they believed such tales is something else again. Later Spanish frontierswomen in eighteenth-century Texas and California were probably better informed from published reports of expeditions and perhaps by folk plays such as *Los Comanches*, a favorite New Mexico drama about a great battle between the brave Spaniards and the Comanches. Whatever their preconceptions about the frontier areas, Spanish and Mexican women, like their Anglo counterparts, were generally pleased with the new lands. Señora Feliciana Arballo had such a good time on the trip from Mexico to California that she was dubbed the Merry Widow of the Anza expedition. Certainly Spanish frontierswomen recalled their pioneering years with pleasure. "No one need suppose that the Spanish pioneers of California suffered many hardships or privations," one wrote. "They came slowly, and were well prepared to become settlers." If it had not been for the Apaches, an Arizona frontierswoman reminisced, "we would hardly have known what trouble was." Although their memories of hardships were undoubtedly dimmed, those Spanish-Mexican women who left records of their experiences found the new lands generally productive and appealing.[96]

For Indian women, the frontiers were not wilderness but home, not strange and unknown lands but familiar ones. Whether one agrees with the modern authors who look upon the North American Indians as environmentalists, protecting and preserving the natural resources and the land, or with those who believe the Indians were as destructive of wilderness as whites (albeit in a different way), it is clear that Indians' religion, life-style, and tradition bound them closely to the land and forest. Yet when Indian women left their home areas and journeyed to unfamiliar lands, their descriptions of the country and their experiences were similar to those of other women. For example, a young Hidata girl, in words reminiscent of the first Illinois settlers, recalled, "Getting fuel in a prairie country was not always easy work." Lucy Young, a Wailaki girl, recalled her fear of the wilderness when she and her mother escaped from a government reservation and tried to make their way back home. "I 'fraid lost. Offus dark in redwoods." Catherine, a Nez Perce woman who later married a Scottish fur trader, described her 1841 trip from Idaho to the mouth of the Colorado River in words that would have done credit to the finest romantic writer:

> We were now bearing southwest to west daily the country becoming extremely barren of grass. . . . a country that appeared to possess no life; a big solemn silence prevaded the refused waste. I thought the Chief of ages denied it any gladness, yet I saw now and then a lonely flower, but whose face I knew not, stand up bravely from the deadlooking waste.[97]

Interesting as women's accounts of wilderness are, what is important is not the individual descriptions but the major themes they represent. Were women repelled by or attracted to the frontier and the physical wilderness which it represented? Were women's impressions of the wilderness substantially different from those of men or were they similar? How did women view the Western landscape, as Arcadia or desert, as a land for development and opportunity or as a frightening and inhospitable place filled with unknown dangers? It is clear from their own words that women approached the wilderness with many preconceptions and with both apprehension and optimism. Their diaries, letters, and reminiscences reveal both knowledge of and interest in the wilderness landscape. Despite the more disagreeable scenes and conditions on westward journeys they found much to admire and praise. Women's writings also reveal both realistic and romantic attitudes toward wilderness. Women, like men, evaluated the productivity and potential of the landscape, but, also like men, they were influenced by nineteenth-century ideas of sublimity in nature and the romantic wilderness cult. The better read made frequent allusions to classical and romantic literature and painting in their descriptions of the wilderness, but even poorly educated women made use of romantic terms and phrases in recounting their experiences. In regard to the physical wonders of nature, men and women experienced similar reactions.[98] Women were no more repelled by wilderness than were men. They saw beauty in even the most unexpected places—in the rocks, the barren spaces, the solitude of the open prairies. Women found wilderness both attractive and repelling, inviting and desolate, both Arcadia and desert.

3

"Land of Savagery/Land of Promise":[1]

Women's Views of Indians

During nearly two hundred years of westering, women confronted not only a physical but a racial frontier. The "unsettled" lands to the north of New Spain and to the west of the English and French colonies were occupied by peoples of other races and religions. Spanish, Anglo, French, and Indian peoples met, sometimes in friendship, often in conflict. Views of the racial frontier were as contradictory and ambivalent as views of the physical frontier, and different peoples at different times viewed each other in different ways.

The best known of the racial frontiers was the one between Europeans and Native Americans. It was, and is, one of the most misunderstood frontiers as it related to women. European women were consistently pictured as hating and fearing Indians whom they viewed as "irreconcilable enemies."[2] Various authors, from nineteenth-century writers like James Fenimore Cooper and Robert Montgomery Bird to modern Western novelists, described women's abhorrence of the "naked savage" and their fear of capture and physical and sexual abuse. "To the average woman," proclaimed one modern author;

> there was nothing more alarming than a threat of Indian attack. Death they learned to live with, but not the dread of captivity by male savages. In the present age of Freudianism, there is probably a ready explanation for the shivering ache of vulnerability that one finds expressed in letters and diaries of frontier women exposed to raiding Indians. . . .[3]

According to another writer, women's fears of Indians were closely linked to the development of American racism. Any captive woman must be rescued and the Indians punished, "for the sake of the captive and the values of society and Christianity" which she represented. According to this theory, men did not want to kill Indians, with whom they enjoyed a positive relationship, but they were forced to turn against their Indian brothers to protect white women from their fears and from their own sexuality.[4]

Yet it is interesting to discover that the opinion that all women hated and feared Indians was a view held primarily by men. What women said about Indians and whether they were to be "hated and feared" was much different. Citing impressive evidence to substantiate her conclusions, one historian pointed out that many male writers deliberately distorted women's opinions of Indians. Women, she asserted, were no more racist than were men. Rather, "men and women are very similar in their propensities to vice and virtue and neither is better than the others." More recently, another historian pointed out that nineteenth-century stereotypes of white women's interaction with Indians were heavily influenced by the above-mentioned cult of true womanhood and by societal perceptions of what constituted "real" Indians and "true" women. Because women, although "kind, gentle, pure, and refined" were also "helpless, childlike, non-assertive, indecisive and unable to protect themselves," they must, of course, fear Indians and be protected from them. This concept of "true womanhood" supported, in fact dictated, the portrayal of "fierce, rapacious Indians" and "weak, victimized white women." Unfortunately, these views were perpetuated by twentieth-century writers who did not bother to read what frontierswomen actually wrote about their feelings and reactions towards Indians.[5]

If we are to understand something of the truth about women's views of Indians, we first need to know something of the preconceptions women had about Indians and whether those conceptions came from actual experience or from literary, propagandistic, or other sources. Were women really frightened of Indians before starting westward, and what, if anything, happened along the way to change their minds? How did Native Americans, especially Native American women, view the Europeans? We also need to understand something of the context in which European women and Native Americans encountered one another. Were these encounters primarily hostile and tension filled or were they peaceful and relaxed? Each of the European nations viewed the Native Americans in a somewhat different way, and they evolved different policies for dealing with the Indians. Although these policies were primarily political and economic rather than social, still government policy did affect the ways in which common men and women viewed and interacted with the Indian populations along the frontiers of New Spain, New France, New England, and later the trans-Mississippi West. How did these policies affect women's preconceptions of Indians and did these preconceptions change when women and Indians met fact-to-face? These are questions which must be explored if we are to understand an important part of women's frontier experience.

From the first moment of contact between Europeans and American Indians in the fifteenth century, Europeans held ambivalent views of the New World's aboriginal population. Just as Europeans were both attracted to and repelled by New World wilderness, so, too, did they see the inhabitants of the wilderness in contradictory terms. During the first decades after the Columbian discoveries, Europeans tended to idealize the *tierra incognito* to the west and imagined a fabled Paradise peopled, in their view, by a "race of superior beings" who might serve as a model that would lead decadent Europe into "a better future of which philosophers dreamed."[6] The Indians were often pictured as a pleasant, physically handsome people, "capable of intellectual development," and characterized by "such traits as emotional restraint, stoicism, practicality, personal resourcefulness, individualism, and bravery." Seventeenth and eighteenth-century philosophers took this idealized portrait one step further and presented the Indians as superior to Europeans. They pictured the Indians as "noble savages" uncorrupted by all that was evil in European society, primitive innocents, living as nature produced them "in great simplicity and natural naivete."[7]

Such idealized people, like the imaginary Paradise of European fancy, were not consistent with the realities of the wilderness experience. The New World was no idyllic Garden of Eden but rather a land of savagery filled with barbarous Indians, "ugly of countenance, hostile, violent, murderers and torturers of innocent women and children." Increasingly in the late sixteenth and early seventeenth centuries most Europeans, and nearly all Englishmen, "saw the Indians as Satan-guided idolators standing in the way of industrious yeomen seeking to carry out God's will," the enemies of God and man who "deserved only extermination."[8]

By the eighteenth century, the image changed again. Caught up in the spirit of Romanticism, European writers again lauded the American natives as noble primitives "living in a state of natural goodness . . . strangers to oppression and conflict."[9] Such contradictory images of the American natives not only changed over time, often in cyclical patterns determined by the experiences and reports of erstwhile colonists, but these ambivalent views often existed at the same time and place. Prospective colonists were thus faced with opposing viewpoints about the nature of the land and peoples they would encounter. No matter what their expectations before they immigrated, their ideas were usually changed by the realities of frontier life.

Whether seen as "bestial savage" or "primeval innocent," the Indians also stimulated theological and philosophical discussions about European-Indian relations and the right of Europeans to occupy and rule the Indians and their land. If these beings were truly men rather than beasts, and an argument to that effect disturbed Europeans for several decades, then there was a Christian duty to convert them to the True Faith and to justify the Europeans' title to New World lands. Eventually, Europeans came to accept the idea that the Indians were indeed truly human although perhaps a step or two below the whites on the ladder of man. But because these red men had obviously reached the wrong conclusions on matters of social and religious concern, had not discovered the true religion, and had no "civilization," in European terms, they, "like immature children, required European tutelage in order to realize their full capacities."[10] The Indians must be converted to Christianity, and they must be taught to serve the Europeans and thus to aid in developing and exploiting the New World potential. Those who refused either conversion or labor must be removed from the path of European progress.

These views, as well as the economic realities of colonial development and European ambitions, were clearly reflected in the policies which the European nations evolved for their New World colonies and in the writings of the colonists themselves. Although most immigrants to the New World, especially women, had obviously not read the more learned treatises by such men as Juan Ginés de Sepúlveda, Bartolomé de las Casas, or Michel de Montaigne, there is little doubt that women's views of the Indians were influenced by these ideas which were a matter of lively discussion throughout Europe. Well-educated, upper-class women, for example Marie de l'Incarnation in New France, Juana Inés de la Cruz in New Spain, or Anne Bradford in New England, were certainly familiar with the prevailing theological and philosophical views of the natives, if not with the specific literature. Other women may not have been as knowledgeable about the contending theological and philosophical arguments, but they were well acquainted with the folk wisdom which pictured the Indians both as howling barbarians to be feared and dreaded and as noble savages, objects of interest and curiosity. They were also at least partially aware of the views taken by the European nations of the Indians both as a necessary tool for American development and as enemies and barriers to European civilization. Thus, the first meetings between Indians and women were set within a contradictory view of the Indians and within a context of government policy and intension.

Spain, the first of the European nations to meet the Indian problem, viewed the Native Americans as essential to the development of Spanish New World Empire. With a vast area to rule and with most of her already

inadequate population involved in European conflicts, Spain needed the
Indian's labor to work the mines, till the fields, and help defend the Spanish Empire against attacks from the French, English, and Dutch. At the
same time, the Catholic monarchs of Spain felt an obligation to save the
Indian's soul for the glory of God and the Church while preserving his
body for the building of the Empire. Thus, the Indians must be converted
to the Spanish Catholic faith, taught the essentials of European civilization, and made productive, taxpaying members of colonial society. To do
this, the Indians were congregated in pueblos and missions near the Spanish settlements and placed under the care of a Spanish landowner *(en-
comendero)* or a mission priest who were expected to control and discipline
the Indians, instruct them in the faith, and teach them the fundamentals
of European agricultural and industrial technology. In the Valley of Mexico
and other areas of New Spain, where the native peoples were sedentary
and agricultural, this system was reasonably successful in incorporating
the Indians into the new society. Intermarriage, although not actively
encouraged, was not condemned or forbidden, and Spanish and Indian
blood intermingled to produce a new people, the *mestizo* or Mexican—a
strong, proud race not particularly fond of either peninsular Spaniards
or full-blooded Indians.

Their experience with the Indians of central Mexico did not prepare
the Spaniards for the Indians of New Mexico, Arizona, Texas, and California. Although some of the tribes were semisedentary and agricultural,
they were far less amenable to conversion and exploitation. Moreover,
along the northern frontiers bitter disputes broke out between the mission fathers who viewed their charges as children to be taught and cared
for with love and gentleness and the *mestizo* settlers who wished to exploit their labor and treat them more as slaves than as children of God.
So bitter did this dispute become in New Mexico and so badly did the
government officials and settlers treat the Indians that a native revolt in
1680 forced the Spaniards to abandon the province for over a decade. There
were also occasional uprisings among the Texas and California Indians,
but they were quickly contained and rarely spread beyond one or two
missions. Eventually many of the Indians were pacified, converted, and
assimilated into Spanish colonial society, albeit in an inferior position.
They learned the Spanish language, accepted the basic tenets of the Catholic faith, tilled the fields, herded the sheep and cattle, worked as domestic servants, and lived in close proximity with their Spanish masters.[11]

Hispanic settlers, accustomed to the presence of the "reduced" (pacified) Indians, generally viewed them as the missionaries did, "simple of
nature, naturally peace-loving" although a "sly and crafty folk, unwill-

ing to work unless forced."[12] Some of the mission Indians, one young California woman recalled, were "the very perfection of silent, careful, unselfish service," who "could be trusted with the most important matters." However, some of the others, especially "the Indian vaqueros, who lived much of the time on the more distant cattle ranges, were a wild set of men." These peaceful Indians were neither an object of fear nor concern; rather they were viewed as inferior but generally friendly and gentle people who could be trained as reliable workers and servants. Thus Spanish frontierswoman Angustias de la Guerra recalled that when the French-Argentine filibuster Hipolito Bouchard landed at Monterey in 1818, the women and children of Santa Barbara were sent to a place of safety "under the care of the Mission Indians and also of some old and infirm white men." Although de la Guerra remembered the short-lived Indian revolt of 1824, it was clear from her reminiscences and from those of Juana Machado, who also recalled several Indian uprisings, that Indians were a familiar, recognized part of Spanish colonial life, more to be pitied than feared.[13]

Not all encounters between Hispanic frontierswomen and Indians were friendly, however. Centuries of conflict and warfare marked the relations between Spanish and Mexican settlers and the hostile Indians in New Mexico, Arizona, and parts of Texas. Women in these areas had little to fear from the few captive old men, women, and children who lived in the settlements as slaves or indentured servants, but the "wild Indians," the Apaches, Comanches, Kiowas, Yumas, and other groups were another matter. Frontier settlers viewed them as dangerous, perfidious, and untrustworthy. Mariana Díaz of Tucson spoke with considerable feeling about the many efforts that had been made to secure a peace with the Apaches, but, she said, "whatever promises they made but a few days would pass before they proved treacherous and commenced murder and robbery again." María Montielo recalled the horror of the Yuma uprising in 1781 when she and the other women "fled for our lives to the church" where they watched the Indians "burn our houses and belongings and kill as many of our people as they could." The language of Montielo's report, written in 1785, is calm and dispassionate, but she revealed something of her own emotions when she recorded, "That was the night my heart was broken, when my beloved husband was clubbed to death before my very eyes."[14]

Thus Spanish and Mexican women's experiences with Indians were as varied as the opposing images of the Indians in both literature and folklore. Relations between Hispanic frontierswomen and their Indian neighbors were sometimes friendly, sometimes violent. For most Hispanic women, Indians were both "amities" and "enmities," peaceful, childlike servants or dangerous and deadly enemies.[15]

Unlike Spain, France based her New World empire on commerce rather than colonization. France viewed her New World possessions as a vast commercial concession, and the development of a profitable trade in peltries and fish was the cornerstone of French imperial planning. The place of the Indians, from the French standpoint, was off in the wilderness trapping and fishing and then exchanging their harvest for goods of European manufacture at some convenient French outpost. As true sons of the church, the French also felt some obligation to care for the Indians' souls, but they could not afford the time to gather the natives into missions or settlements. Instead, the French sent missionaries to the Indian villages where they taught the gospel and baptized converts. Despite such concessions to the church, on the French frontiers trade took precedence over faith, and the *coureurs de bois* replaced the missionaries and settlers as harbingers of European civilization. From a very early period, French officials proposed intermarriage between the French and Indians as an alternative to large-scale emigration from France and to solve the problem of a largely male French population in Canada. Thus, intrepid French traders roamed from the Ohio to the Rio Grande, from Hudson's Bay to the Missouri, took Indian wives and created, as the Spaniards had, a new mixed race which became an important source of French settlers for the backcountry in Illinois and Arkansas.[16]

Because the French needed the Indians in the forests and not in the towns, they discouraged, and often prohibited, Indians from coming into the major French settlements, and French women colonists had little opportunity to come in contact with the native peoples. One exception to this generalization was the members of the teaching and nursing orders in Quebec and Montreal who taught and cared for many of the Indian children sent to them by French missionaries and government officials. The extensive correspondence of Marie de l'Incarnation, Mother Superior of the Ursuline convent and head of the French seminary for "savage girls" in Quebec, revealed both a mystical calling to convert the Indians and a practical assessment of the difficulty of the task. Before arriving in Canada, l'Incarnation had read the Jesuit *Relations* of 1634 which, among other things, described the bloody warfare between the Hurons and the Iroquois and the physical dangers and hardships suffered by the Jesuit missionaries. She envisioned the journey to Canada as a "pilgrimage of suffering and self-denial, perhaps of martyrdom." Yet she remained determined. "I shall cherish my little Savage girls more than if they were Princesses," she wrote.[17] Years of teaching and caring for the Indian girls did not dull the ardor of l'Incarnation or the other French sisters, but it did alter their opinion of the little "princesses." "When they give them to us they are as naked as a worm," l'Incarnation reported:

> it is necessary to wash them from head to foot, because of the grease with which their parents anoint their entire body; and whatever care we take, and although we change their linen and clothes often, it is a long time before we can rid them of their vermin because of the abundance of this grease.[18]

The Mother Superior also came to recognize the fact that not all of the Indians were amenable to conversion and acculturation. The Ursulines, as well as the other orders which ministered to the Indians, found that the children often became depressed and homesick and ran away or were taken home by their parents. It must have been a frustrating experience for these devout women.

The experiences of the Ursulines and the other female teaching and nursing orders with the Native Americans were not frontier experiences, of course. Whatever the earlier fears of l'Incarnation and her sisters about capture and martyrdom, they remained safely behind the walls of their convents and schools in Quebec and Montreal. Although the sisters from time to time urged that their schools be located closer to the Indian villages, the frontier was considered far too dangerous for French ladies. Although the French enjoyed generally good relations with most of the native peoples, the French alliance with the Algonquin-speaking tribes of Canada earned them the hostility of the Algonquin's traditional enemies, the Iroquois. Throughout most of the French colonial period, the Iroquois posed a threat to French settlements in the Great Lakes region. Unlike the friendly Algonquins, whom the French described in generally positive terms, the Iroquois were viewed as cannibals and savages "just one rank above the brutish beasts, but lower than the barbarians of the Orient."[19] Contact with such "brutes" was obviously inappropriate for French gentlewomen.

Very few Frenchwomen, other than the teaching and hospital nuns, went to New France, and most of those who did remained, like the sisters, in the established French settlements along the Saint Lawrence River. The few who did live on frontier farms or in small settlements in the interior had little trouble with Indians as neighbors with the exception of the Iroquois. However, Iroquois raids were a constant threat in some areas. A favorite story of Canada concerned Madeleine de Vercheres, a fourteen-year-old girl who, with the help of only two soldiers and a number of frightened women and children, held off an attack by the "cruel and cunning" Iroquois for more than forty-eight hours.[20] In 1660 Marie de l'Incarnation informed her son that it had been decided to wage a war of extermination against the Iroquois, a decision which she approved. If the perfidious Iroquois were not eliminated, she wrote, "all Christians and the Christianity of Canada perish."[21] Thus for all the friendship and concern expressed by the nuns for their savage charges, even they were ready to admit that not all Indians were worthy of their efforts.

The ambivalent views of Indians as both depraved brutes and noble savages were as common on the first Anglo frontiers as on the Spanish and French. Generally, however, English people more frequently stressed the negative rather than the noble attributes of the Indians' character. Some attempt was made to establish a profitable trade with the Indians, particularly in Virginia and later in New York. Strongly influenced by the earlier successes of the English trading companies, early English colonial planners suggested "trafficking" among the Indians "without challenging their possession of the land."[22] Such trade required a peaceful, and therefore positive, relationship with the Indians. This early Elizabethan mercantile approach to American adventure rapidly gave way to large-scale settlement and agricultural production, a colonization scheme which had no place for the Native Americans. Unlike the Spaniards and the French, who needed the Indians' labor, the English wanted only their land. The English had sufficient labor to build and develop their colonies, and they rarely wanted, or attempted to gain, the Indians' help.

Moreover, the English had special reasons for anticipating the darker side of the Indians' nature. English experiences in Ireland had convinced them "that indigenous peoples do not ordinarily accept graciously those who come to dominate them." In addition, English acquaintance with Portugese and Spanish literature led them to anticipate a hostile reception.[23] Thus Englishmen argued that the Indians' inhumanity justified the English in taking Indian lands:

> Although the Lord hath given the earth to children of men . . . the greater part of it [is] possessed & wrongfully usurped by wild beasts, and unreasonable creatures, or by brutish savages, which by reason of their godless ignorance & blasphemous idolatrie, are worse than those beasts which are of most wilde & savage nature.[24]

The English did not possess the Spanish and French obsession to convert and Christianize the Indians. The Spanish padres and French Jesuits and Ursulines saw their task as a divine mission and a means to personal salvation; the Puritan fathers, with the possible exceptions of John Eliot and Thomas Morton, saw both wilderness and Indians allegorically as

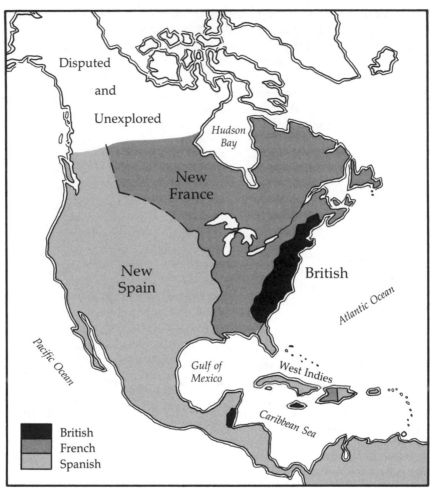

Map 1
The Frontiers of North America, 1700

Women lived on and wrote of their
experiences on all these
North American frontiers.

symbols of "worldly temptation, trial, and hardship" and the Indians specifically as the "instrument of the Devil."[25] Miscegenation, of the type encouraged, or at least condoned, by the Spanish and the French, was not only prohibited but looked upon as yet another manifestation of evil. Even the Quakers, who probably had the best Indian relations of any English group, had no missionary goals, and their message of love and friendship went little further than Puritan hostility in preventing Indian warfare and the eventual destruction of Indian culture and society in the English colonies.[26] Thus English women were even more likely to view the Indians with suspicion and fear than were the Hispanic and French frontierswomen.

The English attitude towards the Indians was well illustrated in *The Narrative of the Captivity and Restauration* [sic] *of Mrs. Mary Rowlandson*, written in 1682 by the wife of the minister in Lancaster, Massachusetts. In her description of the Indians' attack in 1675 and the events of her capture and subsequent sufferings, Rowlandson used all the invectives with which the English commonly described the Indians:

> Thus these murderous wretches went on, burning and destroying before them. . . . It is a solemn sight to see so many Christians lying in their blood . . . like a company of sheep torn by wolves, all of them stripped naked by a company of hell-hounds, roaring, singing, ranting, and insulting. . . . Little do many think what is the savageness and brutishness of this barbarious enemy. . . .[27]

Although later in her narrative, Rowlandson admitted that "not one of them ever offered the least abuse of chastity to me, in word or action" (and, in fact, one of her captors brought her a Bible), she did not interpret these actions as due to the kindness or humaneness of the Indians but rather as a sign of God's grace and mercy to her.

All English colonists did not take such vituperative views of the Indian character, of course. In a 1683 pamphlet, William Penn pleaded for justice for the Indians, "for it were miserable indeed for us to fall under the just censure of the poor Indian conscience, while we make profession of things so far transcending."[28] Benjamin Franklin, possibly influenced by Penn and other Quaker writers, also took a sympathetic view of the Indians, as did his fellow statesman Thomas Jefferson. But Rowlandson's and later captivity narratives and books of the Indian wars, such as Increase Mather's vindictive *History of King Philip's War*, carried as much or more weight with the average American citizen than did Quaker leaders and political figures.

The bloody colonial Indian wars of the eighteenth century also made a deep impression on the American mind. Chronicled in histories such as Joseph Doddridge's *Notes on the Settlement and Indian Wars of the Western Parts of Virginia and Pennsylvania* and supplemented by popular literature such as John Filson's immensely successful life of Daniel Boone, these accounts did little to produce a favorable picture of the American Indian in the popular mind. In the post-Revolutionary period, these negative images were reinforced by accounts of renewed Indian warfare in the Ohio country and along the Southern frontiers, by additional captivity narratives by both men and women, and especially by the stories of the "dark and bloody" soil of the Kentucky country. Robert M. Bird's 1837 novel, *Nick of the Woods or the Jibbenainosay* ranked second in popularity only to Cooper's *Leatherstocking Tales,* and the dark and evil portrait which Bird painted of the Indians' character had a powerful impact on the popular imagination.

> [T]here was a rushing out of men, women, and children, with the cracking of rifles, the crashing of hatchets, the lunge of knives, with yells and shrieks such as would turn the spirit into ice and water to hear. . . . I saw the weakest of them all—the old grandma, with the youngest babe in her arms, come flying into the corn. . . . when the pursuer . . . caught up with her and struck her down with his tomahawk. Then friend, . . . he snatched the poor babe from the dying woman's arms and struck it with the same bloody hatchet.[29]

Given passages such as these along with the captivity narratives and the bloodcurdling descriptions of the Indian wars, it is not surprising that women, and men as well, "suffered vastly more from fear of the Indians before starting," than they did when they actually reached the frontier and became more familiar with the Indians.[30]

Nineteenth-century literature, however, presented a contrasting view of the Indians. During the first decades after independence there was a shift toward a more positive portrayal of Indian life. The Indians might be savages, but they were American savages, and American national pride insisted that American savages be superior to other barbaric peoples. "At a time when barbarous nations elsewhere have lost their primitive purity," exhorted one textbook writer, "we find the American Indian the only true child of nature—the best specimen of man in his native simplicity."[31] In addition to American national pride, two strong European influences were at work here. Jean Jacques Rousseau and François René de Chateaubriad gave new vigor to the eighteenth-century myth of the noble savage and the morally superior nature of those "natural men . . . who lived in harmony with beneficent nature."[32] It was these views which so heavily influenced James Fenimore Cooper and other American purveyors of the noble savage in Romantic literature and provided a counterbalance to the dark Indian image portrayed by Bird and the captivity narratives.

Together with the rise of the "noble savage," Americans also began to take note of the "vanishing redskin" and to predict his eventual extinction. Even those writers who admired and mythologized the Indians saw them as members of "a dying race that must give way to American progress either through force or by acceptance of the true light of Christian ideals."[33] Such ideas, along with new government policies designed to remove the Indians to lands west of the Mississippi River and provide them with schools, agricultural implements, and technical training, at last gave rise to a strong missionary impulse. Even the poor barbarian might eventually see the light and be saved. This school of thought also gave rise to interest in a scientific study of Indian history and culture. That which was vanishing must be recorded. Careful, generally objective, although sympathetic works by men like John Heckewelder, Henry Rowe Schoolcraft, and Lewis Henry Morgan and the paintings and commentary of artist George Catlin provided yet another source of information about the American Indians and helped give rise to the new science of ethnology.[34]

Indians were one of the most popular topics for nineteenth-century literature, drama, and informational books. Novels, poems, plays, school texts, newspapers, and magazines all contained a great deal of information, and misinformation, about the Indians' physical appearance, intellectual capacity, morals, and character. There was endless speculation about their origins and early history, continuing interest in their aboriginal traits and customs. Thus by the 1820s and 30s westering Americans, who had little firsthand knowledge of Indians knew, or thought they knew, a great deal about them. As in the case of the physical or natural frontier, Americans went west with a number of preconceptions about the people who inhabited the area before them. As in the case of the physical frontier, their preconceptions were often contradictory. Just as Western lands were commonly conceived of as both garden and desert, Indians were seen as "savage, depraved barbarians," as "guileless primitives," and as "a once noble vanishing race." That westering Americans were aware of these stereotypes of the Native Americans was clear from the comments they made about them. Women and men approached the Indian frontiers with both caution and curiosity, fear and friendship—attitudes which they described in their journals and reminiscences.

Such attitudes were demonstrated in several women's narratives about the early Ohio, Kentucky, and Mississippi frontiers. One of the most famous was the account of Mary Jemison, taken captive in 1758. Her story, published in 1824, went through some thirty subsequent editions and was fictionalized in 1941 by Lois Lenski under the title *Indian Captive*. However, Jemison was not typical since she married an Indian and remained "exclusively within the Indian culture for the rest of her life."[35] A more traditional story was that told by Mary Smith in *An Affecting Narrative of the Captivity and Sufferings of Mrs. Mary Smith who with her Husband and three daughters were taken prisoners by the INDIANS, in August last (1814) and after enduring the most cruel hardship and torture of mind for sixty days (in which she witnessed The Tragical Death of her Husband and helpless Children) was fortunately rescued from the merciless hands of the Savages by a detached party from the army of the brave General Jackson, Now Commanding at New Orleans*. Smith had nothing good to say about her captors:

> I was reduced to the necessity of becoming a prostitute in order to prevent the most cruel death . . . to resign myself to the barbarity of the savages was a dreadful thought and to gratify the wishes of one of those vile monsters, was, I concluded, although shocking in the extreme, not quite so bad as to endure their savage torture.[36]

The trouble with accounts like Smith's was that they were consciously composed for publication and often written, as was the case here, by a second party who could and did distort the woman's recollections and words to suit what the writer thought the public wanted to read.

A different, and far less popular, picture of Indian warfare and captivity was presented in the narrative of Mrs. Margaret Helm whose husband was an officer at Fort Chicago at the time of the Dearborn Massacre in 1812. Helm survived the attack of the garrison and later told her story to a relative, Julia Kinzie, who included a part of the account in her 1856 book, *Waubun*. Despite the many terrible scenes which she witnessed and a good deal of personal suffering at the hands of some of her captors, Helm also recalled many incidents of kindness. She described one instance in which an old squaw, "infuriated by the loss of friends," seized a pitchfork and "assaulted one miserable victim." As Helm looked on in horror, one of the Indians "with a delicacy of feeling scarcely to have been expected under such circumstances . . . stretched a mat across two poles, between me and this dreadful scene. I was thus spared in some degree a view of its horrors. . . ."[37] Not only did Helm describe several other humane acts by individual Indians, but it is interesting to note that in the scene just described, she attributed some understandable motive to the old squaw. Helm's account was, in this and other respects, similar to a 1728 account by Elizabeth Hanson who also saw both cruelty and kindness and whose narrative implied some understanding of another culture.[38]

Helm's was one of the few firsthand accounts by women of their experiences in the Indian wars of the early nineteenth century. Aside from the captivity narratives, whose reliability was often open to question, most women who wrote about Indians in the trans-Appalachian West were generally curious and sympathetic. Lydia Bacon, who accompanied her soldier-husband to Indiana in 1811, admitted that she was frightened when the troops left Vincennes for the Battle of Tippecanoe. She wrote her mother that she rarely wandered too far from home, "for I do not like the thought of being scalped by our red Brethren"; but only a few months later she wrote again describing an Indian council she had attended, and prayed that "their condition be ameliorated by their becoming subjects to the meek & lowly Jesus." Another army wife, whose husband was stationed at Fort Snelling, Minnesota, also admired the local natives and pleaded for a more humane Indian policy. "We are allowing these people, with so much of the mysterious in their origin, to go into the annihilation which seems their inevitable fate . . . ," she mourned in 1849. She did not see the Indians as just noble vanishing red brothers. She reported they had vices, especially habitual dishonesty and stealing, but such was true of all people, and "the reader will find in the following pages living men and women, whose feelings are very similar to those of the rest of the world, though far less artfully covered up and disguised under pleasant names." Julia Kinzie, who recorded the Helm narrative, was consistently positive in her descriptions of the Indians she met in and around Detroit, Green Bay, and Fort Winnebago in the 1830s. She noted that contrary to "recent reports," the Indian women were virtuous and handsome, and she described the principal chiefs as "noble, dignified, and of striking appearance." Yet another woman, whose husband was an Indian trader and who lived among the Sac, Fox, and eastern Sioux for many years, generally thought the Indians a pleasant people. She wrote of many kindnesses provided to her by Indian women. Even after spending a hectic period with "our house full of drunken indians [sic] and squaws," she was able to conclude philosophically:

> they have divided their goods at last and are now starting to hunt, how glad I am to have peace and quietness again after so much howling in the wilderness, if we always had to live as I have for three weeks past I could not stay in the indian country, but I never was very much afraid of them.[39]

Not all women took such a laudatory view of the Indians. Harriet Bishop, who went to teach at a Minnesota mission school in the 1840s, found little to admire in the Indian character. "The world has been taught to admire him for his noble traits, his manly bearing, and his alleged remembrance of trifling acts of kindness," she wrote, but such a portrait, she continued, was incorrect. Indian habits, she recorded, were "disgustingly filthy," their dress "extremely unchaste," and their hearts "imbedded in moral pollution." Such comments by Bishop and others reflected both some prevailing opinions of the period and a failure to understand a culture different from their own. Despite her gloomy assessment of the Indians, however, Bishop remained at the mission for several years and admitted that there were exceptions. "From the first they were kindly disposed toward me, regarding me with apparent interest, and many a time since I have been glad to welcome some of these my earliest Minnesota friends." Mary Sagatoo, another missionary, also took a somewhat jaundiced view of Indian life despite the fact that she married a half-Chippewa, Joseph Cabay, and after his death married another Chippewa, Pete Sagatoo. Mary Sagatoo was particularly concerned about the way the Indians treated their women and about their lack of Christian background. "The Indians' ideas of the creation of the world were ludicrous and absurd," she wrote. "As a race they are more celebrated for preserving fable than facts; they are without any mode of denoting their chronology, without letters, without power of mind or hand to record truthfully events as they occur." Yet Sagatoo went on to relate these "ludicrous" stories in some detail.[40]

Sagatoo's problem, and Bishop's as well, was that despite their missionary calling and their interest in "this much abused and downtrodden race," they were unable to put aside racial and religious ethnocentrism and view the Indians objectively. For the missionaries and other white women, the American, Christian view of the world was right; the Indians' life-style and moral code were inferior. They did not hate Indians; they were not particularly frightened of them. Rather they adopted an attitude of pity and condescension:

> I cannot help feeling sorry for them, when I think of the many wrongs they have been compelled to endure from the white people. . . . In all their dealings with the white man, they had ever found him disposed to take advantage of their poverty and ignorance.[41]

Like Bishop and Sagatoo, other women missionaries viewed the Indians with both repulsion and romance. They were dismayed by what they viewed as "barbaric" habits of dress and conduct, appalled by their "non-Christian" practices, but they nonetheless spent a great deal of time and effort, in addition to their missionary duties, investigating Indian history and customs and describing the Indians' life-style in great detail.[42]

Settler women were less inclined to be interested in an in-depth investigation of Indian life than were army wives and missionaries. After the War of 1812 and the Indian defeats at Fallen Timbers and Tippecanoe, women settlers usually had only casual contacts wtih Indians, and after the Removal Bill of 1830 even these became less frequent. When Midwestern women did encounter Indians their experiences were usually similar to those described by Anna Shaw: ". . . the Indians were all around us," she recalled, "and every settler had a collection of hair-raising tales to tell of them. It was generally agreed that they were dangerous only when they were drunk; but as they were drunk whenever they could get whiskey, and as whiskey was constantly given them in exchange for pelts and game, there was a harrowing doubt in our minds whenever they approached us." Shaw went on to recount her own hair-raising experience when she unexpectedly met a group of drunken Indians in the woods near her home. The Indians followed Shaw home where her mother provided food and trinkets for them, and "they made her a second visit a few months later bringing a large quantity of venison and a bag of cranberries . . . later we became very friendly with them and their tribe, even to the degree of attending one of their dances. . . ." A similar incident was recalled by another woman settler who came home to find her kitchen "in possession of ten or fifteen Indian braves with as many squaws and papooses." She, too, provided them with food and gifts, and "this same band returned and I traded them meat and flour for parched squaw corn and hominy." A more forceful solution to her Indian problem was taken by an Illinois woman who, confronted with a drunken Indian trying to crawl through her cabin window, "cracked him on the skull with a wooden potato masher, pulled him on in, and barred the shutter." Some time later she pushed the "somewhat more sober Indian" out the door with his head wound neatly washed and bandaged. Thereafter she had no more difficulty.[43] Such experiences were fairly typical. For most Midwestern frontier women, Indians were a sometimes bothersome, but a not particularly frightening, part of the landscape. Women neither hated nor loved them; they simply accepted their presence. Indians, like the land, were a part of their lives to be improved if possible and, if not, to be tolerated or ignored.

The attitude of women toward the Indians in the trans-Mississippi area varied little from that of women on the trans-Appalachian frontiers. Although the lands west of the Mississippi were originally viewed as a perpetual homeland for the aboriginal inhabitants and the dispossessed Eastern tribes, Anglo-Americans soon began pushing into the region. By the 1830s, settlement in Arkansas, Missouri, Iowa, and Minnesota was well under way. The frontier experience in these areas was similar to that in the older territories; except for missionaries and army wives, there was only casual contact between women and Indians. Frontierswomen in these areas reflected attitudes towards the Indians similar to those of Midwestern farm women. Not until the 1840s and 50s, as men and women in increasing numbers joined the great overland migration to the Pacific Coast, did women begin to encounter large numbers of Indians in their native habitat.

Given the amount of misinformation about the Indians prevalent in nineteenth-century literature, it is small wonder that women on the overland trails were amazed to find that all Indians were not taciturn, stoical, brave, or independent; nor were they all childlike, filthy, treacherous, depraved, cunning, or any one of a hundred other pejorative terms which had been used to describe them. Such preconceptions were so deeply ingrained in the minds of westering Americans, however, that they were accepted as true even when the evidence proved contradictory. Exceptions to the stereotypes were often considered unusual or abnormal rather than indicative of the real nature of Indian character or culture. Yet despite their misconceptions and fears about possible encounters with the Indians, women were as curious about the natives as they were about the landscape and the flora and fauna of the vast interior of the continent. Almost every woman's journal of the overland trip included a reference to seeing "my first Indian," and thereafter the diaries were replete with references to and descriptions of the Indians.

Immigrant women's first contact with the Indians usually occurred in the outfitting towns in Iowa and Kansas. The Indians in these towns— Winnebagos, Pawnees, or an occasional Delaware—were often displaced and homeless and lived a hand-to-mouth existence by "begging and swoping" with the immigrants. Certainly they did not make a very good impression. Women generally considered them dirty and described them as being as "annoying as the mosquitoes and gnats" that buzzed about the camps. "From our first arrival at Council Bluffs," recalled Sarah Royce, "we had been annoyed by begging and pilfering Indians, male and female. To attempt to satisfy them was out of the question, for the most trifling thing bestowed on one, would bring a dozen more."[44] Moreover, these town Indians also had access to whiskey, and they were often drunk and disorderly, a fact which concerned many of the women and made them fearful of the Indians' possible conduct.

For many women, their initial reaction to meeting an Indian was one of fear. "They were the first Indians I had ever seen," Mary Jane Caples recorded of her meeting with the Pawnees, "and to my frightened vision, dressed in their long macinaw blankets with eagle feathers in their hair, they looked ten feet high—my thought was that they would kill us all, and take my baby in captivity." Young Allene Dunham remembered that her feet hung out of the wagon, and she was afraid that while she slept the Indians "would cut my feet off;" while another young girl confided, "I was afraid . . . because the Indians were crazy over my red hair and several times offered to trade a pony for me." This initial fear usually vanished rather quickly as the women discovered that the Indians, though bothersome with their constant begging, were generally friendly. "Indians came to our camp everyday begging," recalled Amelia Knight, and she reported that the members of the train soon got "used to them."[45]

As fear gave way to familiarity, women became increasingly curious and sometimes visited Indian camps or attended Indian dances. Some women gained a favorable opinion of Indian life from such visits. Angeline Cooper visited with some Indian women at the Kaw ferry and "found them very well fixed with household affairs, and very kind and sociable." Others were less impressed. "I visited the wigwams," wrote Harriet Clarke, "disgusting looking beings. . . . In one shady bower was an old squaw, one dog & four puppies & a calf, above hung cups and other dishes used for culinary [sic] purposes"; however, she conceded, "I do not wonder that squaws are so indolent for since we have been dwellers in tents I feel that to throw myself upon the ground is luxuriant ease free from restraints of etiquette. . . ." Once they found they had little to fear, many of the trail women took pity on these prairie Indians as "representatives of a once mighty but now fallen people." "The picture of the red men is indelibly impressed upon my memory," wrote one, "and sympathy for them still lives in my heart," for they had to leave "their beloved hunting land."[46]

Prairie tribes, who had long been in contact with white civilization were one thing. They might be pesky beggars and occasionally thieves, but they were generally regarded as friendly to the whites and more to be pitied than feared. The warlike Plains people were something else. It was common knowledge, accepted folk wisdom, that the Sioux were fierce warriors, feared by their Indian neighbors and a force to be reckoned with. "The Sioux and Shians . . . were the terror of the mountains," one guidebook warned,[47] and all accounts cautioned immigrants to take great care in passing through their country. Yet despite their warlike reputation and their disputes with the United States government over the building of forts and roads, the Sioux rarely caused the overlanders much trouble. In fact, with the exception of a brief skirmish in 1854–55, there were no major wars between Sioux and the United States Army until the 1860s. Even during the height of hostilities between army and Indians, immigrant trains were rarely harassed.

Many of the travelers thought the Sioux a handsome people, much more what they envisioned as a noble savage than the Pawnees or other tribes they had encountered. They were "the best-looking Indians I ever saw," wrote Lodisa Frizzell. "They are tall, strongly made, firm features, light copper color, cleanly in appearance, quite well dressed." Almost without exception, immigrant women described the Sioux as the "handsomest," "cleanest," and "best dressed" tribe of any they met. The Sioux seemed quite as interested in the immigrants as the immigrants were in the Sioux:

> They did not beg but, simply, were filled with curiosity over the strange ways of the white squaws. . . . We were surprised and pleased with this exhibition of goodwill and mannerly conduct. There was a degree of refinement in their actions which we had not expected to find among "just Indians" but we found that they were "just Indians" after all and nothing more, though in some ways more civilized than others.[48]

To some immigrants, of course, an Indian was an Indian, and they were all naked, dirty, and troublesome whether they were Pawnees, Sioux, or some other group. Sallie Maddox described them as "naked, disgusting, and dirty looking;" Frances Roe thought them "only painted, dirty, and nauseous-smelling savages." Some had expected to find noble redmen and were exceedingly disappointed. After a visit to a Sioux encampment Marie Nash remarked that she did not fancy the Indians' mode of living and had changed her mind "with regard to this class of people since I came on the plains very materially." Roe was blunter: "Almost all my life, I have wanted to see an Indian, a real noble redman. . . . Well I've seen a number of Indians but they are *not* noble redmen."[49] So much for James Fenimore Cooper and the Romantics' Indians.

At least in regard to the Sioux such negative comment constituted a minority view. Most of the trail women were fascinated by these people and wrote long descriptions of their dress, camps, and such of their customs as they observed. Moreover, as a recent study of overland immigration pointed out, there was a good deal of "beneficial interaction" between the Indians and the immigrants.[50] Indians occasionally served as guides and often assisted the travelers in getting their wagons and stock across dangerous streams. Immigrants paid for the Indians' services with sugar, coffee, biscuits, small items of clothing, and trinkets, or exchanged these items for moccasins, buffalo robes, horses, and other items. Some women, as well as many of the men, set out from home with various small items to use in bartering with the Indians.

Contrary to the modern mass media's portrayal of the beleaguered wagon train surrounded by hundreds of screaming savages armed with rifles and fire arrows, such attacks simply did not take place, particularly among the Plains tribes. Immigrants and Indians did not always interact in perfect peace and harmony, of course, and there were Indian-caused deaths among the immigrants; however, attacks were almost always launched against very small parties or stragglers. Despite the views of some nineteenth-century writers, Indians were neither stupid nor homicidal, and they were usually much more interested in the immigrant's livestock than his life. Moreover, Indians quickly recognized that attacks on large, well-armed trains would not only be dangerous but would bring immediate retaliation from the United States Army. Although they had a reputation for fierceness and hostility, and despite rumors of Indian attacks and massacres, the Plains tribes did not pose a major threat to the immigrants. One study suggested that between 1840 and 1860 perhaps 362 immigrants were killed by the Indians on the northern trails, and 90 percent of these killings took place not on the Plains but "west of South Pass, principally along the Snake and Humboldt Rivers."[51]

On the Plains, immigrant women remained cautious and suspicious, but most became increasingly reassured that the Sioux intended them no harm. "They appear to be perfectly harmless," Harriet Ward wrote her son, and "you would be surprised to see me writing so quietly in the wagon alone . . . with a great wild-looking Indian leaning his elbow on the wagon beside me, but I have not a single fear except that they may frighten the horses." As late as 1860, when the Sioux were becoming increasingly opposed to travel through their territory, Lavinia Porter and her husband, traveling alone and without protection, had no difficulty. "It truly seemed to us in our long journey traveling alone that the Indians watched over us," she wrote. "Perhaps our utter loneliness and unprotected position . . . awoke in their breasts a feeling of chivalrous protection. . . . Be that as it may, in our ignorant fearlessness we came through the many hostile tribes unmolested and unhurt. . . ." When finally forced to join a train at the insistence of a "Colonel Carrington," Porter found her "rough, uncouth, and ignorant" companions more frightening than the Indians and swore that she would rather "trust myself to the mercy of the Indians than to travel another day with these ruffians." Porter would probably have been reluctant to trust herself to the mercy of the Indians, but she and her husband did leave the objectionable train. Porter was not the only woman to decide that some Indians were indeed better than some of the whites they met. "These roads are infested with thieves all watching for a good opportunity to take emigrant cattle and horses," wrote one woman. "The indians are far better than whites in my estimation." Other immigrant women shared the opinion that they preferred the Indians to the meaner white element on the trails.[52]

The greatest Indian problems on the trail, both in terms of stealing and maiming of livestock and hit and run attacks on immigrant camps, came in the Snake River country and along the Humboldt. Immigrant opinion was virtually unanimous that the Shoshones, Snakes, Bannocks, and especially the despised "Digger" Indians were among the most loathsome of all the Indians along the routes. "They were a very low order of humanity, wretchedly poor and degraded, frequently coming to our camp in a perfectly nude state," recorded Margaret Hecox. "Sometimes they brought dried crickets which they tried to trade for food." They were also considered "the most thieving Indians on our route," as well as the most hostile.[53] Almost every woman who passed through their territory recounted some misadventure at their hands. These experiences ranged from attempts to stampede the stock to shooting arrows into the oxen, both serious threats to the immigrants whose already tired and worn-out animals were essential to the travelers if they were to make the last weary miles over the mountains to Oregon or California. In later years these same groups terrorized travelers on the Bozeman trail from Fort Laramie to the new gold fields in Montana. Furthermore the Indians of this region were not adverse to stopping wagons to demand food or payment of various kinds or even firing rifles or arrows into the immigrant camps. Helen Carpenter recounted a series of skirmishes between her train and the Bannocks and Paiutes, and she also went into some detail about various murders and scalpings attributed to the Indians along the Humboldt. In 1860 Indians attacked a train on the Snake River near Salmon Falls; several immigrants were killed and many others died of exposure and starvation before they were rescued by soldiers from Fort Walla Walla. Only in this region did women express an almost universal fear and hatred for the Indian peoples they encountered, and men's opinions were equally condemnatory.[54] Immigrants might take some pity on the paupers of the prairies, admire the noble horsemen of the plains, but in the opinion of most travelers, the peoples of the Plateau and Great Basin had few, if any, redeeming virtues. Many of these comments were unfounded, but it was indicative of the prejudices of the period that they were repeated in almost every overland diary whether written by a man or a woman.

There were fewer women on the southern trails and thus there were fewer comments by women on the Southwestern Indians than on those along the northern routes. Most of the immigrants never saw the elusive Apaches who were universally considered to be hostile and dangerous, and reports about them by immigrants were rarely based on firsthand encounters but rather reflected fear and distrust based more on rumor than on fact. A young girl from Grayson County, Texas, wrote that some Apaches stole her mother's dress, but those "were the only wild Indians that we saw . . . tho' there were plenty." Barsina French reported that their train had some trouble with Indians, probably Apaches, in New

Mexico. The Indians crept up on their camp during the night and ran off or killed all of their horses, but none of the family was injured. Susan Parish traveled in the same train as the Oatman family who were ambushed and massacred by Apaches about one hundred miles from Yuma; however, Parish recalled, the Oatmans had left the train and were alone when they were attacked, and Parish did not see any Apaches herself.[55] Again, as on the northern trails, there were far fewer attacks on immigrant trains than Hollywood and popular literature would have us believe. The story of the Oatman Massacre (in which Royce Oatman, his wife, and one daughter were killed and two other daughters were captured by the Apaches in 1851) was repeated so often that one begins to suspect it was the only example, or at least one of very few.

Although there were few firsthand comments on the wild tribes of the Southwest, immigrants did remark frequently on the friendly Pimas and Papagos. Maria Shrode, like most immigrants, was rather favorably impressed by them and complimented their house-building skills, as did Barsina French, though another young Texas girl was suspicious even of these supposedly friendly people. "There was a Peomore [sic] Indian here today," she wrote. "He was very friendly, but all he wants is a chance to steal our stock."[56] Thus, on the southern as on the northern routes, women's attitudes towards the Indians depended to some extent on whether the Indians were considered hostile or friendly. Women's comments about the Indians, like those of men, were ambivalent, expressing fear, distrust, and contempt on one hand and curiosity, admiration, and sympathy on the other.

Of course Indians as neighbors were something different from Indians as trail curiosities. It was one thing to visit an Indian camp or trade with a passing band of Sioux, and it was something else to settle permanently on the Indian frontier. Yet here, as with the encircled wagon train, the traditional picture of the relationship between women and their Indian neighbors does not reflect the complete reality. The picture of the frightened woman, huddled with her helpless children in the corner of the cabin while bloodthirsty savages lurk just outside the door was already deeply ingrained in American literature by the early nineteenth century. Schoolbooks and magazines printed lurid pictures of the embattled settler woman, and the story of the pioneer mother who "awoke amid the yell of the savage" and, overcome by overwhelming odds, "became his captive, was taken to his tribe, [and] treated most cruelly"[57] was familiar to every American schoolchild.

Such scenes did occur but with far less frequency than one might think. Indians did raid homesteads; they did kill and capture women; women were occasionally caught in the events surrounding the Indian wars. Women were directly involved in many of the outbreaks of hostility in the Pacific Northwest in the 1850s. The earlier, well-publicized, Whitman "massacre" involved not only the martyred Narcissa and the other missionaries but a number of settlers as well. The great Sioux uprising in Minnesota, the bloody border wars in Texas, Cheyenne and Arapaho raids in Colorado, all involved settlers more directly than the later military campaigns which are such a familiar part of American history. Most women's diaries for these places and periods at least mention the Indian problem, and many relate from firsthand experience the terrors and horrors surrounding these events. During the Washington Indian wars of 1854–55, for example, Sarah Hartman recalled her family huddled in their cabin under the watchful care of friendly Indians while the hostiles surrounded their cabin and threatened at any moment to burst in and murder them. During the same outbreak, Caroline Sexton fled from her home on horseback "squaw fashion" to Fort Levens where she "took her gun and stood at a porthole and fired upon the indians [sic] all night" while "her little daughter Mary . . . died at her feet."[58] Other Washington women "forted up" in their homes or with neighbors, never sure what the next day, or night, might bring. Texas women shared similar experiences. For example, Susan Newcomb's diary for 1865–66 told of the difficulties encountered at Fort Davis, a temporary, stockaded community near Weatherford in north central Texas:

> We often hear of our friends or relatives being killed and scalped by the wild Indians. They are continually roving through our country killing our comrades here and yonder. . . . Weather warm and dreary— Water scarce and bad—The stoutest hearts grow weary—And merriest hearts grow sad.[59]

Other women recalled even more frightening experiences. Texas settler Matilda Jane Friend and two other women attempted to fend off an Indian attack on the Friend cabin while the men were away. Her two companions were killed, and Mrs. Friend was "shot twice with arrows and partly scalped." She survived, and two weeks later was safely delivered of a baby, but the family, "anxious to put the scenes of so much unhappiness behind them," soon moved to Kansas. Helen Tarble and Minnie Carrigan were both captured by the Indians during the Sioux outbreak in Minnesota in 1862, and both wrote about their fears of death before they were finally rescued. Another Minnesota woman described her suffering as she hid in the grass with her two small children without food and with very little water. Josephine Meeker, daughter of the Indian agent at the White River Agency in western Colorado, was captured, beaten, and raped by her father's killers.[60]

Obviously these were terrifying and frequently loathsome experiences, but in the accounts of the women who underwent them, there were few of the quivering, quailing pleas to leave the frontier, little of the vitriolic diatribe against all things Indian which might be expected. Most of the accounts were rational, fairly objective reports of what happened. Often these women, while not excusing the Indians' actions, found some justification for their behavior. "History tells us the Indians were bring [sic] on war because of their jealousies of the whites taking their lands," wrote a Washington woman, "but we old settlers know many other causes, one among the many was the treatment of their women [by the whites]." Matilda Delaney, a survivor of the Whitman massacre in which most of her family was killed, "became a benefactor of the Indians" and tried to alleviate the sufferings and hardships of their women and children. Most of the captivity accounts included at least one comment on friendly or kind treatment from one or more of their captors. Typical was the statement of Josephine Meeker. "It must not be supposed," she wrote, "that all the Utes are like Douglass and Jane. There are among them, both men and women who in their rude, wild way, are as tender-hearted and really noble in disposition as white people. . . ."[61]

Despite the wide publicity given to Indian attacks on settlers and the captivity reports, Indian scares were far more common than actual Indian raids. "We had several Indian scares, but were never molested, and I suppose never in actual danger," recalled one Oregon woman. "We got up a little excitement about the Indians," a Texas woman recalled, "but it did not amount to anything, only to frighten Leslie, and us women folks."[62] Many women conceded that a number of the Indian scares were false alarms. Newcomers to the West often misinterpreted the howls of wolves or coyotes as the whooping of Indians on the warpath, and traces of camps made by hunting parties or travelers were sometimes attributed to Indian raiders. Sometimes the circumstances surrounding such incidents became a matter of community humor. One young woman reported her entire neighborhood had forted up for several days only to discover that the scare was started by a young man "getting a new hat with feathers on it and he come home wearing the hat and his mother thought he was an Indian and started running and screaming to a neighbor's house and her son saw it would scare her so bad to try to overtake her so he let her go on and that is how the Indian scare started."[63]

Unwelcome visits from Indian neighbors also caused frontier women some alarm. Who, male or female, would not be upset, even frightened, by the appearance of one or more armed strangers in the front yard or at the door? Yet women generally handled such occurrences with presence of mind and often turned potentially dangerous situations into friendly encounters. One young woman, "without stopping to think," raised her broom and threatened to strike one Indian if he did not leave her yard. Sometimes the offer of food or a trinket was enough to send the visitors on their way peacefully. Other women kept a revolver, knife, or other weapon handy to discourage unwelcome guests.[64] Sometimes these encounters had their amusing aspects. One Comanche Indian tried to trade his clothes to Ella Bird-Dumont for a rifle he wanted. She understood no Comanche and he understood no English, and the confrontation was becoming embarrassing when Bird-Dumont's husband returned. Later, as she recounted it, "everyone had a good laugh" about the misunderstanding. Ellen Throop remembered the story of her grandmother Johnson who discovered some Indians stuffing watermelons into their blankets. Mrs. Johnson fled to the house where she was chided by her husband for leaving the Indians to "take what they wanted." Indignantly Grandmother replied, "Do you think I would stay there, after the Indians took their blankets off?"[65] Indeed, many women were embarrassed by what they considered a lack of properly modest dress, but most became accustomed to their Indian neighbors, dressed or not.

Less well known than the always popular stories of Indian raids are the peaceful and often helpful encounters between women and Indians. Although these stories are not nearly as sensational nor as exciting as burning cabins, mutilated bodies, and violated women, they more nearly represent the reality of interactions between women and Indians on the frontier. Just as immigrants and Indians worked out mutually beneficial relationships along the overland trails, so, too, did settlers and Indians find ways of assisting each other. Frontier women often pictured Indians as helpful friends and a welcome and necessary aid in adjusting to wilderness living. Often Indians supplied fish, game, and wild fruits and berries to supplement meager pioneer diets or traded baskets, buffalo robes, or moccasins to the hard-pressed frontier housewife in exchange for flour, sugar, coffee, or other supplies. In the Southwest, Indians taught pioneers how to build adobes and in other parts of the country helped them find shelter until their cabins were built.[66] For some women, the Indians' knowledge of the surrounding countryside and the uses of various wild plants were an almost indispensable aid. Sarah Hartman recalled that her family lived on "Indian food" for many months until they could clear ground and harvest their own crops. "We children learned to like the Indian food so well," she remembered, "that we thought we could not exist without it."[67] In many frontier homes, Indian women worked as domestic servants, cared for the children, helped with the household chores, and provided a sympathetic ear for the complaints of the frontier housewife. Indian men often worked on farms and ranches and became valued employees. Given the shortage of hired hands in some areas, it is doubtful that some settlers could have worked their land and herds without Indian assistance.[68]

Many settler women recalled small acts of kindness from Indians. A group of Arkansas women fleeing the Union forces during the Civil War were given temporary food and shelter in the cabin of a Cherokee family, at some risk to the Indians. Another woman recalled that her baby was saved from falling into the fireplace by the quick action of an Indian woman. Many women struck up friendships with Indian women, tried to learn some of their language, and exchanged recipes and household hints. Indian women, Eva Dye recalled, often served as arbiters and diplomats between whites and Indians.[69] Even during outbreaks of violence, friendly Indians often came to the assistance of their white neighbors, warned them of possible danger, and sometimes assisted them in fleeing from the hostiles or in spreading the alarm to other white settlers.[70]

Many women, curious about their Indian neighbors, visited their camps and villages and investigated their way of life. Perhaps because they felt more secure and better protected than their settler sisters, army women were especially fascinated by the Indians, and they spent a good deal of time visiting Indian camps or entertaining them in their homes. Army wives' journals and reminiscences were filled with discussions of Indian clothing and customs and descriptions of individual Indians. Often, their preconceptions and prejudices vanished as they observed and studied Indians firsthand. Eveline Alexander was surprised to find that Indians were not the stolid, humorless people often pictured in books and newspapers. On a visit to a Pueblo village she commented that "one little fellow . . . laughed like a white baby." As she became more familiar with the Indians she observed, "Any one who had been at the ration distribution today would have had their ideal of 'Jo's' [Navajos] stolidity rudely shaken." Another army wife reported that she was pleased by the ease with which her Indian servants learned English and "white men's ways." Rather than being "idle, ignorant savages," most proved conscientious and willing workers.[71] Many settler women had similar experiences and came to regard at least some Indians with admiration and respect.

In some cases friendly encounters led to close friendships. "The buffalo-hunting Indians came as usual and Chief Joseph took dinner," Mary Hopping noted in a matter-of-fact way. "Everyone was glad to see them." Ellen Fletcher also reported that she frequently entertained Indian visitors in her home as did Phoebe Judson. Matilda Delaney had a number of friends among the Indian women. They often visited her kitchen, laughing and talking over the events of the day. "Her living room," observed one of Delaney's friends, "was the only place I have ever seen

Indian women and girls lighthearted and chatty."[72] Missionary women particularly became deeply attached to some individual Indians and regarded them as close relatives, and some settler women and Indians formed similarly close relationships. Caroline Phelps wrote that when their Indian servant was killed, "we felt his loss very much, my children cryed [sic] for poor John as much as though he had been a relative." In her memoirs of her life at various Western army posts, Maria Kimball recalled that the Indians were "first curios, then neighbors, then friends,"[73] and many Western women would have agreed.

Of course, some women never became accustomed to Indians, even friendly ones. "Many were the frights I got from Indians until I grew to hate the sight of them," recalled Mrs. Jacob Stroup, an early Idaho settler. Yet it is clear from her memoir that she was never seriously threatened. To Stroup and women like her, however, an Indian was an Indian, and they were all "dirty, vermin-covered," and "untrustworthy, thieving, and treacherous." Shooting was too good for them. "Oh the rascals," declared one woman, "they ought to be butchered, every one of them."[74] Others were openly sympathetic to the Indians' plight and mourned the passing of their way of life. Frances Carrington, whose first husband was killed by the Sioux at Fort Phil Kearney, still sympathized with the Indians and admired their attempt to protect their homes and lands "with a spirit akin to that of the American soldier of our early history."[75]

To some extent, women's attitudes towards the Indians depended on the particular part of the country where they lived and the experiences which they had in their relationships with them. Some despised all Indians; others found much to admire in the Indians' culture. Some regarded them with pity, others with condescension. A survey of one hundred settler women's diaries and reminiscences revealed that while some women expressed strongly positive views of Indians (16 percent) and an almost equal number (18 percent) expressed equally strong negative views, the majority of women (66 percent) held both positive and negative views. Most women recognized that there were "good" and "bad" Indians just as there were good and bad whites. Some Indians were friendly and could be trusted; others were hostile and treacherous. Most women neither hated nor loved, despised nor respected Indians, they simply accepted their presence as a part of the wilderness experience.

It is equally clear that the terrified woman living in constant fear of capture, torture, and rape was more a creature of the sensational captivity narratives and "penny dreadfuls" than of fact. No matter what their preconceptions of Indians before going West, most women found the reality far less frightening than they had supposed. Few women lived in terror of their lives and chastity, and even those women who continued to dislike and even fear Indians rarely saw them as an excuse to abandon the frontier for civilization. In the settlements, as on the trail, friendly contact and "beneficial interaction" were more common than violence and bloodshed.[76]

It should also be noted that men, like women, were both apprehensive and curious about the various Indian peoples they encountered. Men, too, had read the guidebooks, school texts, histories, captivity narratives, newspaper articles, and other accounts of Native Americans, and their preconceptions were similar to those of their womenfolk. Men's diaries, like those of women, included long descriptions of the various Indian peoples they met, and these descriptions did not differ significantly from those of women. Men, too, were concerned about the possible dangers from Indians. Most were reluctant to voice their feelings for fear of being labeled "unmanly" or dubbed cowards by their fellows, though their brave words often betrayed their underlying fears. A few men indirectly acknowledged their anxiety. According to one woman, her husband's "fear of Indians was well established . . . the country was surrounded by different tribes of Indians and he saw many of their barbarous tricks." One young man wrote that he was terrified by his first sight of Indians (who turned out to be friendly Pawnees) and ran to get his old revolver, although he sheepishly admitted that it was "more dangerous to the shooter than to the shootie."[77] Others were more circumspect. "We are now in the Pawnee country—the most *hostile* [italics mine] of the tribes," wrote one man of his first venture into Indian country. He made similar comments about other Indian peoples along the way. "We are now in Indian country (*The Sioux*) they boast that they can bring 10,000 braves into the field," reported another overlander, adding defiantly, "I don't believe it."[78] To cover their own fears, men often attributed their misgivings to their companions. After providing a long account of an altercation between two immigrants and a group of Indians near Independence Rock, Vincent Geiger concluded, "This taught them, however, never to stray too far from home." After describing the panic in camp following a false Indian alarm, Byron McKinstry opined, "I don't expect that the [women] poor souls will get over their fright in a month, and I am not sure that all the men will."[79]

Despite their fears, men were more feisty and aggressive in their reaction to possible Indian problems than were women. Men's response to possible danger was to arm themselves and take a defiant stance or attack the enemy before he had a chance to attack them. Women preferred the more peaceful path of conciliation and negotiation. This attitude is clearly illustrated by the refusal of one woman to follow her train captain's orders to circle the wagons and prepare to fight as a group of Indians approached. Pointing out that the immigrants knew little about firearms and that armed confrontation could only lead to dangerous conflict, she convinced the captain to greet the Indians in a friendly manner—a tactic which proved successful in preventing a fight.[80]

Although men were certainly more aggressive in their response to and in their dealings with Indians, women could be provoked to direct action. Threats to their safety or to that of their children usually elicited an immediate and violent response. Women armed themselves with rifles, revolvers, and knives and stood ready to defend themselves and their families when they felt it was necessary. Occasionally, women's ire was aroused by Indians who annoyed them with their incessant begging or whose curiosity invaded their privacy, and they struck out in anger with brooms, hot pokers, boiling lard, or anything else close at hand. Despite such occasional flares of temper, women usually eschewed violence and sought peaceful solutions to their Indian problems.[81]

We know a great deal about what white women thought about Indians. Most pioneer diaries and reminiscences have some comment about them. Less well known is what Indian women thought about white people, especially white women. Unfortunately, when ethnologists and anthropologists invaded the Indian reservations in the late nineteenth and early twentieth centuries and attempted to record the memories of what was generally conceded to be a dying race, they concentrated their efforts on Indian men. The life of Indian women was of interest to them only as it reflected matrilineal inheritance patterns or matriarchal social structures or unfamiliar customs related to menstruation, marriage, and childbirth. Even when the interviewers did talk with Indian women, they were more interested in the old ways than in the women's perceptions of the white man's world.[82] Yet from the few sources which are available, it would appear that Indian women regarded white women much as white women regarded Indians, with a strong sense of their own superiority and a mixture of fear and curiosity.

Indians, like whites, regarded different peoples as inferior to themselves. Most Indian groups called themselves by a name which meant "The People" or "The Chosen Ones" and which thus implied that others were not only different but inferior. In other words, Indians "had their own somatic norm image and considered themselves aesthetically superior."[83] Just as whites often regarded Indians as a subhuman species, so some Indians regarded whites as something other than human. When Sarah Winnemucca's father first saw white men, he reported to his family that "they were not like 'humans.' They were more like owls [a bird of bad omen to the Paiute] than anything else." Some Indian women openly expressed their belief that white culture and white ways were inferior to those of the Indian. "We have learned, as a race, very little from the white people that has been helpful," declared Annie Lowry, a half-Paiute. "Sometimes I wonder at the white people who are so smart and think they know so much. They do things as dumb as Indians in spite of all their high falutin' talk." Even white food was inferior to that of the Indians. "I think it has no strength," Papago woman Maria Chona told anthropologist Ruth Underhill; "my grandchildren make me gruel out of wild seeds. That is food."[84]

Whites criticized Indians for failing to make the land productive, but Indians criticized whites for not knowing how to live off the land or how to preserve it. Delfina Cuero, a Dieguneo woman, described how her mother and grandmother taught her which roots to gather and how her people had always been self-sufficient until the white man came. Then they had to go "farther and farther from San Diego looking for plants." White men also destroyed the game. "Ah my heart fell down when I began to see dead buffalo scattered all over our beautiful country," recalled Crow woman Pretty Shield, "skinned and left to rot by white men, many, many hundreds of buffalo." White men and women had no understanding of nature's spirit, Indian women reported:

> The tree says, 'Don't. I am sore. Don't hurt me.' But they chop it down and cut it up. The spirit of the land hates them. . . . The Indian never hurts anything, but the white people destroy all. . . . How can the spirit of the earth like the white man? That is why God will upset the world— because it is sore all over. Everywhere the white man has touched it, it is sore.[85]

To the whites, Indian women noted, nothing was sacred. The whites treated the Indians as "barbarians" and "half-wits," one Indian woman charged, and they "said we couldn't run our business." Moreover, Indians were often the target of indiscriminate cruelty, not just in the Indian wars, but sometimes as a result of a "jest" or a "lark." Sarah Winnemucca recalled when she was a young child, whites, for no discernable reason, burned her people's entire winter food supply. Indian women were well aware that some whites wished to destroy them. "White people want our land," Lucy Young, a California Indian girl mourned. "Break and burn all our basket, break our pounding rock. Destroy our ropes. No snares, no deerskin, flint, knife, nothing." Even the graves of Indian ancestors were not safe. "If the white people learned where a grave was," Annie Lowry wrote, "they would dig it up for curiosity or profit."[86]

Just as white women were often frightened of Indians, Indian women were afraid of the whites, and with good reason. From the time of the first Columbian voyages, Indians had been kidnaped and sent back to Europe to be paraded through the cities as curiosities of the New World. The Spaniards frequently sent captive Southwestern Indian women and children south into Mexico to live out their lives in the cruel slavery of the *obreros* and textile mills. Later the Mexican government offered bounties for Indian scalps, and women and children were often the victims. Although the Anglos did not openly condone scalp hunting, some of the best-known figures in the trade were from the United States. The United States government did not openly enslave the Indians, but Indian children were sometimes forceably adopted or simply impressed. As late as the 1860s in California, Indian children were taken from their parents and indentured as servants, a practice permitted by the state law.[87] Moreover, whites considered Indians promiscuous, and Indian women were far more vulnerable to sexual abuse by white men and had more to fear from them than did white women from red men. Many Indian women were forced into common-law marriages with white men or simply raped. Sarah Winnemucca wrote that white men tried to take her sister and "abuse her" in front of her mother and sister. Years later, when she was lecturing and writing on behalf of Indian rights, Winnemucca still recalled her sister's words: "I hate everything that belongs to the white dogs. . . . Oh I hate them so badly." Lucy Young's sister was taken by a white man, and she never saw her again. Young was also taken by a white man, and although it appeared from her story that she was kindly treated, it was clear that he used her sexually. "I hear people tell 'bout what Inyan do early days to white man," Young declared. "Nobody ever tell what white man do to Inyan."[88]

Whites also brought disease into the Indian camps—new deadly attacks of smallpox, measles, and pneumonia against which the Indians had little or no immunity. Understandably, the Indians were frightened by these strange new plagues with which they were unfamiliar and against which Indian medicines had little effect. A Canadian Indian woman gave eloquent testimony of the effects of white diseases:

> It is the black Robes who make us die by their spells; listen to me, I prove it by the reasons you are going to recognize as true. They lodged in a certain village where everyone was well, as soon as they established themselves there, everyone died except for three or four persons. They changed location and the same thing happened. They went to visit the cabins of the other villages, and only those where they did not enter were exempted from mortality and sickness. . . .

Many believed that the white men were deliberately trying to kill them. During a cholera epidemic, Annie Lowry reported, the Indians were sure that the white men had "not only poisoned the river but had bewitched the whole country." When Sarah Winnemucca became ill from eating too much cake, her mother was sure that she had been intentionally poisoned by whites. Sioux woman Susan Bettelyoun wrote that her people, too, believed white food was poisoned.[89]

Indian women, like white woman, had heard all kinds of horror stories about members of the other race and the destruction and danger they represented. Many Indian women reported that their initial reaction to the first white person they saw was to run and hide. An Oklahoma Indian woman, for example, recalled that she and her sister "ran to the bushes" when they first saw a white man. "At that time," she remembered, "the older people told the younger that some time there would be no Indians, that eventually they would merge into the white race." Another Oklahoma Indian woman, Sally McKillip, revealed to her white friend that she was terrified of white people because of the stories she had heard about the terrible things that happened on the Trail of Tears. Winnemucca's grandfather told her of a dream in which he foresaw the destruction of the Paiute people. He had tried to be friendly, he told her, but "they do not seem to think we are like them." In his dream he saw "my men shot down by the white people . . . and I saw the blood streaming from the mouths of my men that lay all around me." Little wonder that Winnemucca—and other Indian women—were frightened of the whites.[90]

Despite their fears, however, Indian women, like the white women, were also curious. Annie Lowry recalled going to a trading post near the Humboldt River. Here the Indians would "sit on the ground in the evening and watch the pale faced emigrants climb in and out of the ox wagons and prepare their food." It was a mutually curious crowd, Lowry noted. The Indian women would sit "without changing expression, weaving baskets or grinding food . . . while these strangers gawked as they walked around them." Many accounts by white women also remarked on the interest of Indian women in the whites' habits and dress. Alice Baldwin described the interest of the women near Fort Wingate in her hair style of "waves and crimps." Finally Baldwin agreed to show them how to do their hair, and "such an array of giggling, crimpheaded squaws had never before been seen in all the history of Fort Wingate." Indian women's curiosity about white women extended well beyond hair styles to many facets of white life—food, clothing, religion, even the most intimate details of women's lives. Noting that she had never seen white women segregate themselves each month, Maria Chona confided, "that thing finally happened to me which happens to all our women though I do not know if it does to the Whites. I never saw any signs. It is called menses."[91] Such curiosity, of course, also revealed something of the misunderstanding of each other's cultures which developed between white and Indian women. They saw and frequently attempted to understand each other through eyes clouded with misconceptions and prejudices from their own backgrounds.

As the Indians were pushed farther and farther from their homes and finally confined on reservations, many Indian women's fears and curiosity about whites gave way to a sense of frustration over what they considered their exploitation by the whites. Some, like Sarah Winnemucca's sister, came to hate all things white. Others accommodated as best they could to the new ways, but they continued to look with nostalgia on what was gone. "I cannot forget the old ways," one told her interviewer. "I don't hate *anybody*, not even the white man," said another. "But he changed everything for us, did many bad deeds before we got used to him." An Oklahoma woman best summarized their feelings: "I have seen many changes in this country since my childhood, but with the majority of Indians, I think, it lacks a great deal of being an improvement."[92] Some Indian women, like Winnemucca, the Osage sisters Susette and Susan LaFlesche, and Sioux Susan Bettelyoun, convinced that they would have to adjust to the ways of the dominant white society, acquired an education and often took to the public platform to plead for justice for their people. The whites, Susette LaFlesche wrote, were like a "huge plough" which had turned down "into the darkness of the earth every hope and aspiration which we have cherished." Only citizenship and equality with whites, she pleaded, could restore Indian dignity and hope.[93]

Many Indian women, however, neither embraced white society nor rejected it. Like the Winnebago, Mountain Wolf Woman, they came to recognize that there were "categories of whites on the basis of class and personal character."[94] They were open and friendly with those they considered their friends and distant and withdrawn with others. Like white women, Indian women were both frightened of, and curious about, members of the other race, and, like white women, they gradually accepted the presence of a people different from themselves as a part of their lives. Like white women, they differentiated between good and bad members of the other race and determined friendship or hostility on an individual basis.

Like their Indian counterparts, white women approached the racial frontier with apprehension and suspicion and a good deal of curiosity based on many, often contradictory, sources of information. As women and Indians came into contact with each other, first on the overland trails and later on frontier farms and ranches or in frontier settlements, their preconceptions were modified and changed by their personal experiences. Curiosity overcame fear, and women filled their diaries and journals with detailed descriptions of the various native people they encountered and began to make distinctions between different groups. Indians, they realized, were not all alike. Despite the prevailing images of "howling savages" and "cowering women," most relationships between women and Indians were peaceful and often mutually beneficial. White women continued to consider their own culture as superior, but as they came to know and understand something of Indian culture, they usually eschewed the prevailing stereotypes of Indians for a more realistic assessment of the Native Americans. Like Indian women, white women also judged members of the other race as friendly or frightening, helpful or hostile on an individual basis.

4

The Savage Within:

Women, Race, Religion, and Class on the Frontier

Racial prejudice, which is the subject of this chapter, is an extremely complex pattern of behavior that includes both conscious and unconscious attitudes. Racism has existed, in one form or another, in all periods of history and in all cultures, and one of its most frequent manifestations is the use of the psychological device of projection. As one modern analyst has suggested, unconscious desires, inadmissible to the conscious mind, are projected onto others so that they can be criticized and dealt with. Thus by projecting our own evil or sordid desires, by perceiving them in other people, we are able to deal with "The Savage Within."[1]

The ethnocentrism and prejudice which prevailed in nineteenth-century America and colored and confused intercultural relationships between westering Americans and Indians also affected relations with other so-called minority groups. Just as westering women's ideas and attitudes about Indians changed as they came to know the Native Americans, so, too, were their preconceptions about other peoples altered by their frontier experiences. This was particularly true in regard to the Hispanic population of California and the Southwest. Almost two centuries elapsed between the English settlement of North America and their penetration into the Spanish lands to the southwest. During that time, the area remained a *terra incognita*, a fabled land of fantasy and fancy, "as fabulous as the old Spanish story that romanced about an Amazonian realm on 'the right hand of the Indies . . . very near to the Terrestrial Paradise.' "[2] Yet despite the mystery surrounding the Spanish lands, Americans of predominantly English background had some preconceived ideas about the Hispanic people and some deep-seated racial and religious prejudices about the "devilish Papists" and the "cruel, bloodthirsty conquistadors" which went back to the time of Elizabeth I of England and Philip II of Spain. Books critical of Catholic Spain and the Spanish conquest by English interpreters such as Thomas Gage, Richard Hakluyt, and William

Robertson did much to color attitudes towards the North American Spanish population. Robertson's influential *History of America,* published in 1777, pictured the Spaniards as "rapacious and daring adventurers," men whose deeds were "so atrocious" and reflected such "shocking barbarity" as to have brought "disgrace upon their country." According to Robertson and other English writers, the "Spanish government was authoritarian, corrupt, and decadent," and the "Spaniards were bigoted, cruel, greedy, tyrannical, fanatical, treacherous, and lazy."[3] Moreover, predominately Protestant North Americans were zealous anti-Catholics, and they viewed the Spaniards as the "most superstitious and intolerant" Catholics in Europe.[4] From the time of Cotton Mather and Samuel Sewell, New England clerics emphasized the need to drive out the "numerous and parasitic" Catholic clergy from Spanish America and convert the people "away from Satan to God."[5] Such attitudes presaged nineteenth-century nativism and prepared the way for the expansionist ambitions that a later age would label Manifest Destiny.

Together with the violent anti-Spanish propaganda of seventeenth and eighteenth-century North America was a growing interest in the lands, people, and resources of Spanish America. Americans sought to learn as much as possible about the Spanish dominions, and they began to cast covetous eyes on the Spanish-held lands to the southwest. As early as 1751, Benjamin Franklin expressed an interest in the acquisition of Spanish Louisiana, and as American frontiersmen poured through the Appalachians and out into the Mississippi Valley, geographer Jedidiah Morse confidently predicted that the Western country would not long remain under Spanish rule. "The Mississippi," he proudly declared, "was never designed as the western boundary of the American empire."[6]

The Louisiana Purchase further stimulated interest in the Spanish lands and led to new prejudices and misconceptions about the nature of the inhabitants. After 1803, Americans avidly read reports, books, and articles about the lands beyond their new western boundaries, and Spanish California and the *Provincias Internas* of New Spain (including Texas, Arizona, and New Mexico) became objects of Yankee interest and enterprise. The journal of Capt. William Shaler (a well-known trader whose ships visited the California coast), published in the Philadelphia *American Register* in 1808, and the published reports of army officer and explorer Zebulon Montgomery Pike of his experiences in Santa Fe, Mexico, and Spanish Texas did much to increase interest in these territories as possible fields for future endeavor. At the same time, these reports intensified Americans' poor opinion of the Spanish-Mexican population. The people were generally hospitable, Pike admitted, but they were nonetheless morally degenerate, their government was corrupt, and they lacked any skill for mechanical operations. It was clear to Pike that nothing would "prevent the enterprising spirit of the Americans penetrating the arcanum of their rich establishment of the new world." In a similar vein, Shaler informed his readers that the "mixed breed" of California were of an "indolent, harmless disposition, and fond of spiritous liquors." Still, Shaler wrote, California had many resources, and "under a good government, the Californias would soon rise to ease and affluence." To both Pike and Shaler it was clear that the Spanish lands had great productive potential and both felt sure that the corrupt government and general indolence of the people would assure an easy conquest. The Spanish army and government were both weak, Shaler assured his readers, and would "fall without an effort to the most inconsiderable force."[7]

Shortly after the publication of Pike's and Shaler's reports, Mexico won her independence from Spain. Although some Americans hailed Mexico's "emancipation from the Spanish yoke" and "from their priesthood hierarchy" as an opportunity for the establishment of a new industrious nation, "which in principles and features much resembles that of the United States," others believed that independent Mexico had even less to recommend it than Spanish Mexico.[8] Mexico was inhabited by a mongrel race with "all of the bad qualities of the Spaniards from whom they are descended, without that courage, firmness, and patience which makes the praiseworthy part of the Spanish character." Clearly, "the marriage of 'cruel and treacherous' Spaniard and 'savage' Indian had produced lazy, degenerate people."[9] North American writers were quick to point out that despite Mexican independence and a republican form of government, "the true principles of liberty are but imperfectly understood; and Christianity has acquired but a limited and imperfect influence."[10] Such opinions set the tone for Americans' conceptions of Mexicans during most of the first part of the nineteenth century.

Shortly after Mexican independence, frontier merchants began trading with Spanish Santa Fe and California, and Stephen F. Austin opened Texas to Anglo colonization. Between 1820 and the beginning of the Mexican War, a number of accounts of Mexican life in Texas, New Mexico, and California helped to convince Americans that the Mexicans were unworthy to occupy such fertile and potentially productive territories. Like the Indians, the Mexicans were "incapable from their character of appreciating its resources."[11] James Ohio Pattie's popular narrative of his adventures in New Mexico and California (first published in 1833), Richard Henry Dana's best seller, *Two Years Before the Mast* (1833), Josiah Gregg's widely acclaimed *Commerce of the Prairies* (1844), and George Ruxton's *Life in the Far West* (1849), first published serially in *Blackwood's Magazine*, along with articles, reports, and letters from Santa Fe traders, California merchants, and Texas colonists all painted a negative picture of the Mexican character. To some degree all of these writers agreed with Dana's assessment of the Mexicans as wanting "in industry, frugality, and enterprise, lacking in godliness and cleanliness, and immoral, violent, and brutal in their domestic relations."[12] About the only thing Mexican that American men could find to compliment were the Mexican women, who were often described as kind and hospitable and physically attractive. At the same time, however, the writers dwelled on the women's provocative dress; their propensity for *cigarillos*, liquor, and gambling; their devotion to the "superstitious" teachings of the Catholic priests; and their "lasciviousness" and lack of modesty.[13]

Given such comments, it was not surprising that many women were hostile toward Mexican Americans. Yet, despite their initial animosity, women found much to admire in these people, and their opinions were often ambivalent, even contradictory. Women's preconceptions and prejudices, like those of men, were based on a number of cultural and ethnic differences including color and religion. At the same time, both men and women perceived differences between the wealthy, upper classes and the often impoverished peóns, and their comments reflected these differences.

Two women played an important role in shaping the early stereotypes of the Mexicans. Mary Austin Holley's widely read *Texas*, published in 1832, supported the prejudices of most westering Americans. The Mexican settlers in Texas, Holley wrote, were "very ignorant and degraded, and generally speaking, timid and irresolute," and their soldiers were both brutal and cowardly. She thought the Indians far superior as a race. Even the savage Comanches were "distinguished for two prominent virtues—fidelity and hospitality," she informed her readers, and they were "more amicably disposed towards Americans than towards Mexicans" and were "certainly braver." Another woman writer of the period, Jane Cazneau, was somewhat more favorably impressed. "Filial love is a deep enduring trait in the Mexican character," she wrote, ". . . and throws its light on some of its darker shades." Cazneau expressed great sympathy for the peóns and Indians, but she, too, criticized the church for exploiting the people, and she had no use for the government or the privileged classes whom she described as "cowardly, cruel, and defiant of our laws."[14]

As Americans learned more about the Mexican territory and its people, they cast greedy eyes on the land and justified their attempts to obtain it by further vilification of the Mexican people. The wide coverage of the Texas Revolution, and especially such Mexican "atrocities" as Goliad and the Alamo, yielded new evidence of Mexican "perfidy," "callousness," "cowardice," and "violence." Robert M. Bird's novels, *Calavar, or the Knight of the Conquest* (1834) and *The Infidel, or the Fall of Mexico* (1835) (which were as blatantly anti-Mexican as his later *Nick of the Woods* was anti-Indian) plus a series of Texas postrevolutionary "romances" with provocative descriptions of Mexican "treachery" and "brutality" added to the negative literary picture of the Mexican character. As war between the United States and Mexico came closer, newspapers and popular periodicals, especially in the Midwest and the South, besieged their readers with anti-Mexican propaganda. Much of the flavor of these articles was continued throughout the 1840s and 50s. Even the guidebooks warned prospective immigrants of the defects in the Mexican character. One of the most popular guides devoted an entire chapter to exposing Mexican "ignorance," "superstition," and "barbarity," implied that most Mexicans were drunkards and gamblers and probably thieves, and pronounced, as did most of the other guides, that the Mexican population was "scarcely a visible grade . . . above the barbarous tribes."[15]

Thus by the time American women came into contact with Mexican-Americans in any substantial numbers, there was a good deal of literature which had shaped their thinking and which presented anything but a positive or reassuring picture. Given what they had read, it is hardly surprising that westering women tended to view their first contacts with Mexicans with much the same mixture of fear and curiosity with which they viewed their first Indians. As in the case of the Indians, most of the criticism was unjust and the stereotypes unrealistic, but they were indicative of the strong nativist and racial prejudices of the period. It is surprising that in the face of such seemingly overwhelming evidence of Mexican "ignorance and perfidy" that American women found anything good to say about the Hispanic people.

As might be expected, women who lived in Texas during the Revolutionary period were not particularly charitable in their remarks about the Mexicans. Mary Helm, who was forced to flee her home in Matagorda as the Mexican army approached, wrote of the Mexicans' "barbarism, butchery, and cruelty." According to Helm, Mexicans were "weak, cowardly, and lazy [and] the very antithesis of the Anglo American." Reflecting the then current attitudes, she went on to describe Mexicans as

the debris of several inferior and degraded races; African and Indian crossed and mixed and even the old Spanish blood was mixed with the Moorish and demoralized by a long course of indolence and political corruption. . . .[16]

Of course, like many American colonists in Texas, Helm lived in segregated surroundings, and it is doubtful that she had an opportunity to meet, much less get to know, a Mexican. Women who lived in closer proximity to their Mexican neighbors tended to take a more charitable view, even under sometimes hostile conditions. Mary Maverick, for example, lived in San Antonio de Bexar and, unlike Helm, had a number of Mexican friends and neighbors. According to Maverick, the Mexican ladies "dressed nicely and were graceful and gracious of manner." She also described a number of her Mexican neighbors in sympathetic terms, although it was clear that she felt herself superior to them. Still, like Helm, Maverick reflected many of the common prejudices of the period and described the Mexican soldiers as men who "burnt and plundered and committed all kinds of outrages."[17]

Outside Texas, contacts between American women and the Mexican population were conducted in a somewhat more peaceful atmosphere. Susan Magoffin, who accompanied her husband on a trip over the Santa Fe trail in 1846, expressed a generally positive opinion of the Mexican population. Magoffin learned Spanish, helped clerk in her husband's store, and made many friends among the Mexicans whom she found a generally charming and delightful people. It seemed clear to Magoffin that many of the prevailing ideas about Mexicans were wrong. "What a polite people these Mexicans are," she wrote in her diary, "altho' they are looked upon as a half-barbarous set by the generality of people." Furthermore, the charge of cowardice was incorrect. "What a strange people this. They are not to be called cowards; take them in a mass they are brave. . . . Take them one by one and they will not flinch from danger." Even when her brother-in-law was jailed in Mexico and the Magoffins were under threat of attack from Mexican forces, Magoffin's assessment of the Mexican people remained balanced:

My knowledge of these people has been extended very much in one day. There are among them some of the greatest villains, smooth-faced assassins in the world and some good people too.

Margaret Hecox, who arrived in California in October 1846, after the outbreak of hostilities between the United States and Mexico, was equally sympathetic. The Americans were greeted with tales of Mexican hostility, she recalled and were warned that "the natives might attack us." Such was not the case, she continued; rather "the Mexicans with whom we met treated us most kindly. . . . Never will I forget the kindness of the Spanish people. . . . particularly the Spanish women, who came to us as we traveled along . . . bringing us offers of homemade cheese, milk, and other appetizing food." Later, Hecox learned Spanish and seemed fond of her Mexican neighbors "whom I learned to love like sisters."[18]

Comments like those of Magoffin and Hecox presaged a change in American attitudes towards the Mexican population. The annexation of

Texas, the successful conclusion of the Mexican War, and the acquisition of California and New Mexico made the Mexican population seem more American. They were still strange, ignorant, and not quite honest barbarians, but, like the Indians, they were our barbarians, interesting examples of a dying culture. As a modern commentator pointed out, "Alien ways begin to appear more charming when they are no longer a barrier or a threat."[19] By the post-Civil War period, most of the Mexican-directed jingoistic propaganda of the 1830s and 40s had disappeared. Popular writers like Bret Harte, Robert Louis Stevenson, and Helen Hunt Jackson sentimentalized the old Mexican ways and created a never-never land of beautiful senoritas, gallant caballeros, and kindly padres. The real Mexicans, deprived of their property and many of their civil rights, like the Indians, were simply accepted as a part of the land to be improved if possible and, if not, to be ignored or suppressed, condemned to a second-class citizenship.[20]

This changing point of view was reflected in the writings of a number of women who came in contact with Hispanics in California and the Southwest during the 1850s and 60s. Many of these women were the wives of army officers and had both the education and time to write about their impressions of the land and the populace. Generally, they were favorably impressed. They were fascinated by the old style Spanish architecture, local customs, and the "delightful society both Spanish and American." They attended fiestas and *bailes*, went sightseeing, and visited Mexican homes.[21] Some tried to learn the Spanish language, and a few adopted at least some of the ways of the people. Several found Mexican food delicious and learned to make tortillas and other specialties. One young wife, initially shocked by the "immodest" dress of the Mexican women, soon came to appreciate their adaptation of life-style and dress to the vagaries of climate and viewed her Mexican neighbors not as dirty, half-dressed barbarians but as a "scrupulously clean and modest" people.[22] Several of the army women also commented on the warmth and hospitality of the Mexican people. One declared them an "amiable, smiling, innocent race of people." They were particularly known, she continued, for:

> the feeling of sympathy in misfortune which pervades all classes of Mexicans. So universal is this sentiment that the bitterest enemy, in the hour of trouble, will receive care and attention. The well-known devotion of the Mexican women to the sick and wounded of our army during the war finds no parallel in history.[23]

Other women were similarly impressed with some of the characteristics of Mexican life, so different from their own and from what they had been led to expect. "A new sensation seized me when I saw, for the first time, a *Mexican* . . . ," wrote a young New England schoolteacher who hoped to convert the Mexicans to the Protestant religion. "I did not feel, as many others have expressed, that the sight of a Mexican was enough to disgust one with the whole nation." Others, like Anna McKee of Illinois, were surprised to find "This class of people are different from our 'Greasers.' I was surprised to see such elegant dresses—silks, satins, and velvets and what beauties some of the girls were. The men are handsome, too." Women who took up residence in predominately Mexican towns such as Tucson, Santa Fe, or one of the smaller towns and villages found the Mexicans to be active and helpful or at least "harmless and inobtrusive" neighbors. A young New Mexico woman recalled her Mexican neighbors with pleasure and warmth—a "people so different in many ways from the Americans that I never tired of studying them." Even though her father was engaged in a legal dispute over his land title, Mary Ronan wrote, she was welcomed as a friend by her Mexican neighbors, and "any trace of ill-feeling toward me as a squatter's daughter was entirely dispelled. . . ."[24]

Of course, some women retained their preconceived prejudices about the Mexican people and especially about their religion. Despite their "well deserved reputation for . . . sympathy in misfortune" and their "mild and inoffensive" manner, Teresa Vielé declared, "they have enough Spanish blood left in their veins to be occasionally raised to deeds of desperation and bloodshed." Moreover, the peons were "lazy," the priests "a dissolute, carnal, gambling, jolly set of wine bibbers," and the better classes only a faded "relic of the departed glories of their line." The beauty of the Mexican women was decidedly overrated, wrote another, ". . . and I have the first really pretty Mexican women yet to see." Rather, in her opinion, their reputation rested on their skillful, and probably underhanded, use of "their dark eyes, which they knew how to use on the poor deluded men." One young girl recalled her mother's loathing of the "wicked acts" committed by the priests and people who would "flock to the Church for morning Mass and in the afternoon . . . would go to the Bull and bear fight."[25]

Women who traveled the southern routes to California also considered the Hispanic population lazy and untrustworthy. For example, it was commonly accepted trail lore that the Mexicans were thieves. As one woman confided to her diary, "One Mexican tried to get one of our cows yesterday. O, how mad he got when he found his lies would not get the cow." Another woman remained suspicious of a Mexican woman who insisted on doing her washing in return for a favor. "My mother had her doubts as to her motives," her daughter recorded, "and each week sent me to the river with her to watch the clothes." American women failed to understand Mexican culture and criticized the Mexican life-style. "They do not care as to houses, just so they have shade," one overlander declared. "Their corn and gardens have no fence around them and therefore our loose stock was much trouble." Another woman traveling the southern trail also noted the lack of fences. "their fields are all out of doors and some of their houses look like potatoe houses," she noted. Moreover, "most of them can talk a little broken English but will not. . . . They pretend like they can't talk any till they find not one to talk Mexican and then they can talk."[26]

Despite the strongly nativist and racist tone of such comments, they were usually tempered with curiosity and interest. As with their attitudes towards Indians, most women expressed ambivalent views of the Mexican people. Despite their "idle ancestry," "viciousness," and "indolence," army wife Mrs. Orsemus Boyd declared, the Mexican people were truly hospitable and "made us welcome and yet exacted no reward for time and attention bestowed." Lydia Lane thought the Hispanic women less than beautiful, but she admired their national dress, "which suited them much better than the half-American and wholly bad style recently adopted by them." The young overlander who stated that the Mexicans did not "care as to houses," was nonetheless intrigued by the people, and after a visit to one of their homes noted that they were "very nice-looking people, white as anybody. . . . Their house looked so nice and clean inside." Susan Wallace wrote at some length of the "empty, aimless, and joyless" life of "these sitters in the sun," but she also complimented their fighting spirit (as "the United States, France, and Austria may testify") and their " 'grand air' of Old Spain, descended to all who have a dash of her blood."[27]

A few women were openly sympathetic to the plight of the Mexicans following the American occupation. "This [is a] *most unfortunate race,*" wrote one. "I say unfortunate because they have been ill treated by our people. Possessing natural refinement of manners, their *diffidence* we entitle ignorance." Another woman, noting "the different styles, in which the generality of the Americans talk at the unfortunate Spaniards," went on to criticize the poor manners of her countrymen while lauding the patience of the Hispanic population.[28] Few women were so perceptive, however, and most treated the Mexican population with derision, scorn, or open animosity or, at best, with the same condescension reserved for Negro slaves and poor white servants.

In addition to race and religion, color and social and economic class were important factors in American prejudice (just as they were among the Mexicans themselves). American women made a clear distinction between the "Spanish," and usually lighter-colored, people of the upper classes and the "black Mexicans" of the poor peón families. Describing the Californios, one women wrote that "some of them are full of Spanish blood, and are intelligent and meritorious citizens [and] soon win the high esteem of the English-speaking Americans;" however, she continued, "the lower orders of Mexicans are exceeding illiterate . . . [and] in a religious sense elevated not far above its Indian ancestors."[29] Women who visited the great *ranchos* of California or stayed in the homes of the *ricos* of Texas or New Mexico were more inclined to find virtue and grace in the Mexican people than those whose acquaintance with Mexicans was limited to *mestizo* servants or who saw only the *jacales* of the poor.

Such distinctions reflected the realities of Mexican society. Mexican culture was far from homogenous. Not only was there a difference between *ricos* and *pobres*, but here was a considerable difference in the nature of Mexican frontier society from one province to another, and these differences had a major effect on the nature of Mexican-American relations in the frontier provinces. In New Mexico, the oldest of the northern Mexican settlements, a small class of landowners and *patrons* dominated the poverty-stricken, illiterate peasantry (many of whom were held in debt-peonage). Having anticipated the wave of the future, some of the *rico* families educated their children in Eastern cities and joined in partnerships and business alliances with the Santa Fe traders who began moving into the area in the 1820s. After the American occupation, they formed matrimonial as well as business alliances with the Americans, and together they continued to exploit the lower classes. Thus, at least some of the *rico* families continued a prominent role in politics as well as in business and enjoyed fairly cordial relationships with the newcomers.

In Texas, the situation was quite different. The deep-seated animosities which developed during the stormy years of the Texas Revolution and the ensuing unrest during the years of the Texas Republic and the Mexican War left a heritage of bitterness and misunderstanding between Mexican residents and American invaders. The Spanish-speaking population of Texas was much smaller than that in New Mexico; and although some areas, especially south and west of San Antonio, had a numerically superior Mexican population, they were quickly overwhelmed by the Anglos and reduced to a second-class status only slightly better than that of the Negroes. Even the few *rico* families who formed marriage and business alliances with the Americans and supported the Texican cause during the Revolution lost their economic power base and thus political as well as social influence during the turbulent post-Revolutionary period.

In Arizona, only the Tucson area had a significant number of Mexican settlers. During the 1850s, a bicultural society emerged which, although dominatedly by the numerically fewer Americans, had a decided Mexican flavor and appearance. As a modern historian pointed out, throughout the nineteenth century Tucson "was decisively 'Spanish' in appearance, language and customs." Here, as in New Mexico, Mexican businessmen were able to retain a hold on both political and economic power, and, as in New Mexico, intercultural marriages were frequent not only between upper-class Spanish-speaking women and American businessmen and merchants but between peón girls and soldiers, miners, and adventurers. Few American women went to Arizona before the Civil War, but after they began to settle in the Territory, the number of intercultural marriages, particularly among the upper classes, decreased.

California presented the most complex interrelationship between the two ethnic groups. The early years of contact between Californios and Americans were peaceful and followed patterns similar to those of the early years in New Mexico. A few American business men and merchants established themselves in California, married girls from good families, and quickly became acculturated into the dominant Hispanic society. The gold rush ended all that. Hundreds of thousands of Americans of every age, class, and condition poured into California and buried the Hispanic population beneath a floodtide of alien ways. In northern California, the Spanish-speaking population was completely engulfed. Clever Yankee lawyers and unscrupulous government officials stripped them of their lands, pushed them from political power, and occasionally physically drove them from the area. In southern California, where many of the old Anglo-*rico* alliances still existed, some California families were able to hold onto at least a part of their land and form a new and prestigious society made up of the old Spanish elite and the better elements of the new American population. They never attained the political power of the New Mexico families, however, and a number of natural disasters in the 1860s ruined many of them financially. Thus, despite differences from one province to another, "it is hard to see that in any of the Southwestern states, Spanish-speaking cultures proved resilient or resourceful in meeting the challenge of the aggressive, acquisitive Anglo-Americans." This situation was clearly reflected in the writing of both Americans and Hispanics, both men and women, who visited or lived in the Southwest in the nineteenth century.[30]

Just as American women were suspicious of and curious about the Hispanic population of the Southwest, so, too, were Hispanic women fearful of but interested in the American newcomers. Unfortunately, few Hispanic frontier dwellers, male or female, could read and write. Thus few women recorded their reaction to the influx of American settlers, and there were no extensive oral history projects of the type which were so helpful in studying the American Indian past. Nineteenth-century anthropologists and ethnologists were interested in Indians, not Mexicans;

they made no attempt to interview the people whose families had lived in the Southwest for over two hundred years.[31] The few Mexican women who did leave records of their views of the Americans, however, expressed their fear of and hostility toward the newcomers. "It is necessary, for the truth of the account," wrote Guadalupe Vallejo, "to mention the evil behavior of many Americans before, as well as after, the conquest." Many feared that the Americans meant harm to them or their families. When the Mexican troops left Tucson in 1853, Doña Atanacia Santa Cruz related, many of the Mexican families went with them because ". . . it was rumored that as they advanced the American troops were seizing all that had formerly belonged to Mexico, abusing and even killing families." Mexicans especially feared *los diablos Tejanos*. "Living in ranches meant constant fear," wrote Arizonian Doña Jesus Moreno de Soza. "There was a saloon nearby where the Texans occasionally visited. My husband had a narrow escape once. . . ." A New Mexico woman recalled in detail the climax of the feud between the Hispanos and the Texans on the Llano Estacado in which the Hispanos were "pushed further on, or completely out, as the homesteaders began to take up land."[32]

Most Hispanics believed that the Americans were underhanded and untrustworthy. A young California girl related how frightened she and her mother were when a Yankee ship captain asked her father to board his vessel. "Mother was much afraid to let him go," she recalled, "as we all thought the Americans were not to be trusted. . . . We feared they would carry my father off and keep him a prisoner." Several other California women recorded their suspicions of American behavior as being unreliable and not inspiring confidence. Some were thieves and murderers, they noted. "Our cattle were stolen by thousands," Vallejo wrote. "Men who are now prosperous farmers and merchants were guilty of shooting and selling Spanish beef 'without looking at the brand,' as the phrase went." Other Americans used legal devices to defraud the Mexicans of their property. Carrie Lodge related that her mother, Martina Castro Lodge, was "totally unprepared for the problems that came with American rule. Not only was the language foreign to her, but also the concept of property taxes, mortgages, and land title regulations." Partly because of this, Lodge continued, her mother lost most of her property and "her mind broke." Many Mexican families had similar experiences. Doña Merced Williams de Rains, whose husband was murdered and whose property was systematically looted by her Yankee brother-in-law, was clear in her assessment of most of the Americans she knew. "It is imposibel for me," she wrote a trusted American friend, "to be amongest so many theapes and murders. I wish and hope to settel my business. I wish to cleir everybody out of this place. [sic]"[33]

Even Americans who were not thieves and murderers were less than acceptable to some of the women, however. Mexican women were as appalled as the American women by the customs, manners, and morals of the other race. Ysidora Bandini Couts, who married an American, was so upset by the bad manners displayed by General Ulysses S. Grant that she "politely but firmly asked the 'Hero of Appomattox' to leave her home." Another Mexican woman, also married to an American, was convinced her husband's actions had caused her daughter's death. "Study has killed my daughter," she wrote. "My husband kept her too long indoors, to read in English and French and do silly sums. . . . It is because of Don Perfecto and his learning that she died." The Americans had no regard for the environment, recalled another California woman who pointed to the destruction of a sycamore grove by an American squatter. "The Spanish people begged him to leave them, for the shade and beauty," she recalled, "but he did not care for that." Even the human environment seemed threatened by strange American customs. "[U]ntil the arrival of the Americans," Dorotea Valdez told an interviewer, "our population increased very rapidly . . . but since the Americans have taken possession of this country, sterility has become very common, because the American women are too fond of visiting doctors and swallowing medicines. *Este es un delito que Dios no perdona.*"[34]

Despite the mutual hostility, suspicion, and frequent misunderstandings between Mexicans and Americans, there was a good deal of intercultural mixing. Mexican women tended to consider Americans somewhat socially, and certainly culturally, inferior (a feeling shared by Americans in regard to Hispanic culture), but there was nonetheless a good deal of visiting back and forth at least among upper-class families and attendance at the same social functions.[35] American men found Mexican women attractive both physically and socially, and Mexican women were likewise attracted to American men. As one woman wrote, "The conquest of California did not bother the Californians, least of all the women," and she and many of her friends married American men.[36]

Intercultural marriages were fairly common occurrences in early California and throughout the Southwest. Although, as some historians have suggested, the Americans' motives were at least partially self-serving, other factors were involved. American men valued Hispanic women as "helpmates, and as mothers, companions, and lovers" as well as links to powerful Hispanic families or as a means to gain control of land. Although many of these marriages were contracted between American men and upper-class Mexican women, intercultural marriages existed at all levels of society. For some Hispanic women, marriage to an American brought an improved social and economic status and started the process of assimilation between the two ethnic groups. Although some wives clung tenaciously to traditional patterns of language, religion, and home life, others adopted new ways while still retaining some of their old customs and became truly bicultural. Marriages between American women and Hispanic men were much less common, but they did occur from time to time, primarily among women and men of elite families. Children of mixed marriages often spoke English as a first language, attended American or mixed schools, and became completely assimilated into the new society.[37]

Westering women's prejudice against Mexicans was based on a number of factors including race, color, and religion; prejudice against Negroes was based on race and color and on their social and economic status as slaves or former slaves. Although Negroes were part of the westward migration rather than a native people encountered on the frontier, they were most often regarded, like Indians and Mexicans, as an alien influence. Patterns of discrimination, developed in the early years of African slavery, were unfortunately not discarded by Western immigrants but were transferred to the frontier areas along with other racial and social prejudices.

In the pre-Civil War period many Western immigrants held strong exclusionist views and attempted both to prevent new Negro immigration and to remove blacks already in the West. Following the Texas Revolution, the Congress of the Republic passed a number of laws intended to reenslave or expel the free Negroes within her borders. Similarly, in 1851, Indiana prohibited all Negroes from entering the state as did Illinois in 1853. Throughout the Midwest there were a number of colonization groups anxious to get rid of local free Negroes by sending them somewhere outside the United States.[38] Negroes were also excluded by many immigration companies. The articles of incorporation of an 1843 Oregon company declared, "No Black or Mulatto person shall, in any case or any circumstances whatever, be admitted into this Society, or permitted to emigrate with it."[39] Similar clauses appeared in the charters of other westward-bound groups as well.

As a result of such exclusionist sentiment and legislation, and more important because most lacked the mobility, capital, and skills needed for such a venture, few blacks went West. In fact, one of the outstanding features of black life in the West was the small number of Negroes, especially Negro women. Even after the Civil War, when increasing numbers of blacks migrated West in search of new freedom and opportunity, they made up only a small percentage of the total population. In 1870, Colorado had 436 blacks; Minnesota 759; Nebraska 789; New Mexico 172. Only in the former slave states and in Kansas, where freed slaves built a number of communities in the post-Civil War years, did blacks constitute even a small minority of the population. Black women made up only a small portion of this population. As late as 1920, black women constituted less than one percent of the female population in the Mountain and Pacific states.[40] So rare were Negroes in the West that many immigrants commented on the fact. "I have not seen a darkey since I have been here," one woman wrote her family from Iowa in 1856, and her statement was not unusual.[41]

When westering women did confront blacks, their views were colored by existing racial and class prejudices. "These Negroes of the Fifty-seventh Regiment are indeed the most hideous blacks I have ever seen," commented a young army wife. "There is hardly a mulatto among them; almost all are coal black, with frightfully bad places [sic]." A young overlander also made a number of derogatory remarks about the Negro soldiers and noted with amazement, "Here we seen the colored troops standing around among the yankees regardless of color or grade." Elizabeth Custer spoke with more kindness and affection of her black servants, but her descriptions of their physical characteristics and her caricatures of their speech reflected the stereotypes and prejudices of the time.[42]

That black women were well aware of the prejudice and discrimination against them was clear from their own recollections. "In the earliest days after the opening each family was grateful for the help of each other family and 'we were all on a level'," one Oklahoma woman recalled. "However later differences arose and sentiment against Negros developed to such an extent that Mr. Davis sold out and went to Emporia Kansas."[43] In most Western states and territories black women and men faced various forms of legal restriction and denial of civil rights. Westering might provide new opportunities for blacks, but it did not bring an end to discrimination.[44]

Prejudice in the white community and the small number of black women in the West increased Negro women's sense of isolation. "There were but few of our own people in Seattle when we came," one wrote, "and at times I got very lonely." Yet aside from this sense of isolation and the problems posed by legal restrictions and social discrimination, black women's Western experiences were very similar to those of white women. The few reminiscences by black women of life on the frontier mention many of the same problems as do those of white women, and they also record many of the same small triumphs in homemaking and caring for their families.[45] Moreover, the small number of Negroes in the West and their frequent segregation in all black communities such as Nicodemus, Kansas, and Boley, Oklahoma, mitigated strong anti-Negro sentiment. Most blacks encountered much less racial prejudice and violence at the hands of whites than did other Western minority groups.[46]

Prejudice against Hispanics and blacks was based primarily on race and color, but enmity towards the other large group of different people confronted in the West was based on religion. The members of the Church of Jesus Christ of the Latter-day Saints, or the Mormons as they were commonly called, were primarily of English and northern European stock, but their religious doctrines and political and economic organization quickly earned them the reputation of being the most despised sect in nineteenth-century America. Organized by the Prophet, Joseph Smith, in 1830, the Mormons, almost from the beginning, faced hostility and persecution. Driven from place to place by non-Mormon, or Gentile, opposition, they moved from Ohio to Missouri to Illinois seeking a refuge where they might establish their new Zion and practice their religion free from interference and intolerance. In 1847, under the leadership of Brigham Young, the Saints began to gather in the valley of the Salt Lake in Utah, and by 1852, over twenty thousand Mormons were strongly entrenched in Salt Lake City and the surrounding area.[47]

Despite their physical separation from the mainstream of American society, the Mormons were the target of an increasingly virulent propaganda campaign in the East. Although many Mormon doctrines were basically conservative and did not differ significantly from those of most Protestants, the Mormons' exclusivity and political and economic organization and especially their preaching and practice of plural marriage made them the objects of suspicion and alarm. Anti-Mormon writers, who were both ignorant of Mormon beliefs and prejudiced against any non-Protestant sect, condemned the Mormons as "pagan, despotic, and undemocratic." Mormon theology, they charged, contradicted the separation of church and state; Mormon economic practices undermined the system of competitive free enterprise, and the practice of polygamy subverted the ideals of family and true womanhood. According to some, America faced an "irrepressible conflict" with Mormonism because "it was said that either free institutions or Mormon despotism must ultimately annihilate the other."[48]

Although anti-Mormon sentiment existed in the 1830s and 40s, the public acknowledgement by the Mormon leadership of the practice of polygamy in 1852 increased both the volume and the intensity of anti-Mormon literature. Editorials, newspaper and periodical articles, travelers' accounts, and a growing number of popular novels and plays created an increasingly negative image of Mormon society in the American mind. These works depicted Mormon men as drunken, abusive husbands who often beat and even tortured their wives; as white slave procurers and kidnapers of innocent young girls; and as seducers, libertines, and lecherous old "bearded patriarchs who continued marrying young girls as long as they were able to hobble about." The writers described the Mormon Church as a "sinister secret society" and Salt Lake as a "sinful fallen city."

They charged that the Mormons were as immoral and corrupt as the "debauched Turkish infidels with their slave markets and harems," and they compared polygamy to the abhorrent system of Southern slavery.[49] "Repulsive as slavery appears to us," wrote one particularly vehement Mormon critic, "we can but deem polygamy a thing more loathsome and poisonous to society and political purity." Another described Mormons as "the apostles of a religion built upon a foundation of lust and blood, and the annals of the people they led are black with the records of deeds that disgrace humanity. . . ." Some of the Mormons' deeds, yet another writer noted, were too horrid to record out of sensitivity to the emotions of the readers.[50]

No charge was too wild or ludicrous to escape the critics' venom-laden pens. One writer reported that 40 percent of all children of polygamist families died before the age of eighteen, while others declared that the children of polygamous homes were ill fed, ill behaved, malformed, mentally retarded, and prone to disease. An assistant surgeon in the United States Army asserted that the Mormon system of marriage produced physical and mental defectives with yellow, sunken, cadaverous visages; greenish colored eyes; thick, protuberant lips; low foreheads and lank, angular bodies, while another "scientific" observer noted that in Utah one found a great number of people with "deformed eyes, limbs, hands and feet, by-products of their polygamous heredity."[51]

Mormon women were a special target of the church's critics. Although not all Mormons practiced polygamy (some investigators think no more than 10 to 15 percent of Mormon families were polygamous[52]), Mormon women were almost always pictured as plural wives, brutalized by their husbands and degraded and corrupted by the Mormons' "false religion." According to the critics, some Mormon women were as cruel, brutal, and depraved as the men. It seemed obvious to the writers that women who voluntarily entered into plural marriages were either "insane, mentally deficient, or debauched." Any woman who believed in this "abominable system," which was the "ruin of domestic peace" and the "destroyer of all household affection" was undoubtedly immoral. Mormon women were thus no better than "harlots" and "dull-witted hussies." They were "prostitutes and concubines, totally lacking in all noble and righteous instincts." Indeed, one propagandist asserted, polygamy was worse than prostitution for "Prostitution only degrades its victims . . . but where polygamy is the rule all women are essentially degraded."[53] Polygamy destroyed women's "true nature" and made them "jealous, conniving, deceitful," and unfit to fulfill their role "as moral guardians."[54]

Some writers depicted Mormon women in a somewhat more kindly light as the victims of economic and sexual exploitation. However, the image remained primarily a negative one that pictured Mormon women as impoverished, uncultured, and unsightly.[55] The female victims of polygamy were described as being uniformly homely, poorly dressed, and illkept, overworked and seemingly incapable of helping themselves to escape their demeaned and degraded status. According to the writers, these women rarely smiled or spoke; they had a weary, repressed look; dull care-worn expressions; and an unhappy countenance and dejected bearing. Moreover, they were "subdued, reticent, reserved, and elusive," although whether due to their own ignorance or the repressive measures of their jealous husbands was left unclear in these accounts.[56]

Some of the most violent antipolygamy literature was written by women. Of the fifty anti-Mormon novels published after 1852, twenty were attributed to women.[57] These novels, which were especially popular among Eastern middle-class audiences, carried provocative titles such as *In The Toils; or, Martyrs of the Latter Days; Elder Northfield's Home; or, Sacrificed on the Mormon Altar* and *The Fate of Madame La Tour: A Tale of Great Salt Lake.* In vivid, explicit language, which frequently bordered on the pornographic, the women novelists depicted scenes of torture, abduction, rape, and murder as lurid as any modern-day detective novel. One novelist, for example, described the punishment meted out to a wife who criticized polygamy:

> [She] was taken one night when she stepped out for water, gagged, carried a mile into the woods, stripped nude, tied to a tree, and scourged till the blood ran from her wounds to the ground, in which condition she was left till the next night. . . .[58]

Such passages were so common in these novels that one writer suggested they might have been entitled "Utah as the Torture Chamber."[59] All the novelists stressed the idea that Mormon society was dangerous and vice-ridden and that Mormon women were both psychologically and physically degraded by the terrible practices of polygamy.

Most of the novelists were Eastern women who had never been to Utah and, most likely, had never met a Mormon, but the books by two apostate Mormon women were as sensational as the novels and equally popular. Like the books by the non-Mormon "critics in crinoline," Fanny Stenhouse's *A Lady's Life Among the Mormons* (1872) and Ann Eliza Young's *Wife No. 19, or The Story of a Life in Bondage . . . Revealing the Sorrows, Sacrifices and Sufferings of Women in Polygamy* (1876) stressed the evils of polygamy and the sorrows and degradation of women trapped in plural marriages. Stenhouse, a young English woman who migrated with her husband to Utah, accused the Mormons of cruelty, brutality, and duplicity. Many young immigrant girls, Stenhouse charged, were forced to enter covenants "too dreadful to repeat," and once in Utah "there was no possibility of escape." Mormonism, according to Stenhouse, not only destroyed homes and families but "true" religious feeling as well. Women who refused to accept polygamy were subjected to terrible psychological and emotional pressures, she wrote, and threatened with Divine vengeance. "So repugnant has this teaching been," she concluded, that many women in Utah "have the utmost disgust for religion and care as little about 'the Lord' as they do about their husbands." Young, who had been "sealed" in marriage to the head of the church, was even more passionate in her denunciations of both her former husband, Brigham, and the church. Young, himself, she charged was coarse, miserly, vulgar, profane, and devious and "his own practice is entirely at variance with his teachings." She accused Young and other Mormon leaders of being thieves and swindlers and of committing all kinds of crimes including the murder of apostates and Gentiles and those who "were suspected by, or disagreeable to, Brigham Young." "Incest, murder, suicide, mania, and bestiality are the chief 'beauties' of this infamous system," Young wrote, and she illustrated her points in some detail in a 605-page tome which, along with her public lectures, attracted national attention.[60]

Not all observers of the Mormons were as critical in their discussions of the Saints. Several travelers who visited Utah and observed the Mormons at firsthand found much to praise. They were impressed by the hard work and industry of the Saints and their achievements in building an attractive and productive community in the barren desert terrain. Although none of the travelers approved of polygamy, they attempted to be objective and open-minded and to understand the religious justification of the practice. Most found polygamy degrading to men as well as women, but they did not find women abused or downtrodden or depraved. Unlike the anti-Mormon propagandists, these writers found Mormon women "clean, wholesome, pious, chaste, and virtuous." They complimented the clean, neat Mormon homes and remarked that Mormon women, rather than being homely and unkempt, were generally "attractive and neat." They also noted that the women did not appear to be subdued, weary, unhappy, or repressed. Rather, as one wrote, Mormon women were as "cheerful, industrious, and charitable" as any other women.[61]

Although the more objective accounts of Mormon life attracted a reading audience, they could not begin to counteract the more lurid tales of Mormon atrocities and dark deeds which poured from the presses. Thus, by the time non-Mormon women began traveling through Utah on their way to the West Coast or settled in the Mormon territories, they had an image of the Mormons which was in some cases even more negative than the images they had of Indians, Mexicans, or other minority groups. Westering women had read or heard so many horror stories of Mormon kidnaping, murder, and robbery that it is little wonder that some were concerned about traveling through the Mormon territory and believed that the Mormons were more to be feared than the Indians. Lavinia Porter had been told that "the Mormons never allowed a young woman to leave their borders," and she admitted that she felt "decidedly uneasy" until she was well beyond the Mormon settlements. Others feared that they might be attacked. This fear was especially prevalent in the years immediately following the 1857 massacre of a non-Mormon emigrant company by a combined Mormon and Indian force. This so-called Montain Meadow Massacre received wide publicity in the States, and women's diaries and journals reflected their knowledge of this event. Wrote one in 1859, "This is the noted Mormon range where most of their deeds of horror have been transacted." Another woman recorded that "Fearful tales had been told us of how whole trains emigrating from Missouri were surrounded and captured by Mormons disguised as Indians, the women and children kept in bondage, and the men put to death." Even women who had little fear of physical danger believed that the Mormons would try to steal their livestock and supplies and that they would be deliberately overcharged for goods and services in Mormon settlements. As one women put it, "They made it a business to steal from Gentiles." Some feared no more than the necessity to have to associate, however briefly, with these unsavory folk who were "a treacherous lot and sect." Some were so concerned about Mormon price-gouging and so disgusted by what little they had heard about Mormons that they deliberately bypassed Salt Lake City and the opportunity to rest their teams, repair their wagons, and purchase needed supplies. "I had such an aversion to the Mormons that I did not want to go to Salt Lake," wrote Roxanna Foster, and she did not. Another young woman wrote that she and her party did not want to go to Salt Lake for several reasons and left the main wagon train to take another route.[62]

Those who overcame their fears and revulsion and visited Salt Lake found much to interest them. Most were impressed with the physical appearance of the city. "It was a beautiful city even at that time," recalled an overlander of 1852. "Every block had a little stream of clear, sparkling water running around it." Another wrote that the city had a number of neat, pleasant homes built of sun-burnt bricks, "and could you divest yourself of the idea that they were inhabited by Mormons, would in some instances be truly beautiful."[63] Most travelers went to visit Brigham Young's house, the Tabernacle, and many public buildings. Some had the opportunity to see or hear Young himself. One young woman described him as a pleasant man while another related a good portion of Young's sermon (which she seemed to approve), complimented the singing, and noted that "the people seem to be poor but very well disposed."[64] Other immigrants found the people "not as black as they were painted," and a few gained a favorable impression. "I thought the inhabitants were fine people," wrote one woman. "Setting aside their peculiar doctrines I believe as a community they are as good as are usually found."[65] Such accolades were rare, however. Most visitors complimented the industry of the Saints but lamented their religious beliefs and condemned their marital arrangements. Few were as honest as Sister Monica of the Order of St. Joseph who noted that the Mormons were "a degraded-looking set of people" but admitted, "perhaps it is prejudice that makes me think so."[66]

Among non-Mormon women who settled in Utah or stayed some time there, there was a wide divergence of opinion. Two wives of territorial officials who spent several months in Salt Lake City were strongly anti-Mormon in their sentiments. Sarah Harris, the young wife of the territorial secretary Broughton D. Harris, lived in Utah in 1851 and was impressed with the industry and honest labor of the people which "were apparent on every hand," but she also recorded that "Flagrant cases of murder and other crimes occurred constantly, people disappeared mysteriously . . . the band of Danites were much in evidence . . . and suspicion was rife on every hand." Harris was so appalled by the practice of plural marriage that she finally refused to visit in polygamous homes. "My pent-up feelings of disgust, indignation, and horror, found vent in a severe attack of hysterics. . . . This was the end of our social visiting among the Saints." Mrs. B. G. Ferris, whose husband served in the territorial government during the winter of 1852–53, was even more condemnatory. Ferris, who may, in fact, have written the Maria Ward novels, had not a single good word for the Mormons. "We are unquestionably in the midst of a society of fanatics who are controlled by a gang of licentious villains," she wrote in her popular book, *The Mormons at Home.* According to Ferris, those who praised Mormon industry and did not condemn polygamy were simply passing through the settlements and had not "penetrated the veil that conceals the true deformity of Mormonism. . . ." She repeated most of the stereotypical views of the anti-Mormon writers, and she must have serached the dictionary to find new epithets with which to condemn her neighbors. Nor was Ferris willing to waste any sympathy on the Mormon women whom she described as "poorly dressed, poorly fed." Most, she wrote, exhibited "a sense of degradation" while the other were simply "good-natured, stupid fools."[67]

In contrast, Elizabeth Wells Cumming, wife of Utah's first Gentile governor, thought the Mormons a "peaceable and well-disposed" people. She saw little intoxication or public violence, and she believed the people devoted to their religion and the Mormon leaders generally agreeable. Cumming had no use for polygamy, of course, and she felt that in respect to their religious beliefs, the Mormons were "ignorant, fanatical, super-stitious & possessing a profound disdain for the religious belief of the rest of the world." However, she continued, "all these last qualities are their own business, not mine." In a somewhat similar vein, Rachel Fra-zier, who spent several months in Salt Lake City in 1866, also pointed out the peaceful nature of the city and its inhabitants. Moreover, she noted, the incidence of polygamy had probably been overdramatized, for although "some Mormons marry from two to seven wives," she had "observed many who had not entered into plurality of wives." Sarah Kane, whose husband had long been a friend to the Mormons, was also generally im-pressed. Like many other non-Mormon visitors, she felt that plural wives deserved pity and sympathy, but she also noted that they did not seem unhappy with their lot. "I got rid of more than one preconceived idea," she wrote during a tour of the Mormon settlements in 1874. "I began at once to seek for the 'hopeless, dissatisfied, worn' expression travelers' books had bidden me read on their faces. But I found that they wore very much the same countenances as the American women of any large rustic and village congregation."[68]

Whether passing through or residing in the Mormon settlements, most westering women had very decided ideas about these people and their peculiar institutions. Their strong, preconceived opinions were sometimes modified by closer acquaintance, and some were warm in their praise of all but polygamy. As with the Indian and Mexican frontiers, westering women approached the Mormon territories with apprehension and cu-riosity, and they were often pleasantly surprised by what they saw and learned.

Unlike the Indians and Mexicans, the Mormons were vocal in their own defense. Mormon women were well aware of the criticism of their reli-gious and social institutions, and they were quick to answer the charges against them. "[I]f you wold listen to mormonism," one wrote her non-Mormon brother,

> I colde tell you many things. . . . it is plaine and all on natural prinsapel you must not believe all you heare tha are some as good pepele heare as enny whear. . . . many falls [false] reports is out.

Other, more articulate, women also defended the Mormon way of life. In letters and speeches and through the pages of the *Woman's Exponent*, published every two weeks by the women of the Church, they pointed out the high moral character of their community, their strong beliefs in their church's teaching, and their commitment to the growth of Zion.[69]

Although a number of Mormon women privately admitted their dissatisfaction with some aspects of polygamy, they were quick to defend the practice publicly. According to Mormon doctrine, polygamy was a divine ordinance, essential for salvation, and even women who initially had difficulty in accepting the teaching testified that after a period of questioning and prayer they received a powerful and irresistible message of the sanctity of plural marriage which they "dared not refuse to obey . . . lest peradventure I should be found fighting against God." They pointed out the Biblical precedents for polygamy, citing the examples of Abraham, Isaac, David, and other patriarchs and argued that it was clear from the Scriptures that the practice had been sanctioned, indeed commended, by Christ and the Apostles.[70] In addition to its religious aspects, Mormon women also argued that polygamy offered a workable solution to many social ills. By making it possible for women to be free from masculine demands during gestation and at other times when nature "dictated that a husband should remain apart from his wife," polygamy provided for better-spaced and healthier children and led "directly to chastity of women and to sound health and morals in the constitutions of their offspring." According to its female defenders, polygamy eliminated the need for marital infidelities and did away with prostitution. Monogamy, on the other hand, led to prostitution and illicit affairs and thus to "murder, infanticide, suicide, disease, remorse, despair, wretchedness, poverty, untimely death, & c."[71]

Mormon women also attempted to refute the charges that they were drudges and slaves. On the contrary, they claimed, Mormonism provided everything a woman could want—security, freedom, purpose, and opportunity for self-development. Mormon women, they pointed out, had a better chance for gainful employment and many more opportunities than the monogamous wife to pursue intellectual and financial interests. "The women of Utah today," proclaimed an editorial in the *Woman's Exponent*, "occupy a position which attracts the attention of intelligent and thinking men and women everywhere." According to the *Exponent's* writers, Mormon women were individuals of "character, intelligence, and high aspirations," dedicated, self-confident, and contented. "If the women of Utah are 'slaves,' " exclaimed another writer, "their bonds are loving ones and deeply prized." Even those Mormon women who were less than happy with plural marriage still had a deep commitment to the other basic tenets of Mormonism and to the Mormon community. They had been through persecution and trial, and they felt a part of a close-knit society which they believed superior.[72]

Most anti-Mormon sentiment was religious and political in nature while anti-Mexican sentiment was both religious and racial, but in both there were also elements of class prejudice. Most Americans made a clear distinction between the upper-class Hispanic population and the darker Mexicans or *mestizos*. Anti-Mormon critics often claimed that Mormon converts were made among the most degraded and ignorant classes of Europe and the East. Thus it is not surprising that lower-class people of predominantly English ancestry were also the target of a good deal of class prejudice on the part of westering women. People of a certain cultural and economic background, later typified by the term Missourian or Piker, had almost as bad a reputation as peóns, Negroes, and Mormons. They were characterized by the journalists as generally being "of a 'backwoods' class," profane, hard drinking, rude, and occasionally dangerous. Their women were pictured as lazy, slovenly, pipe-smoking crones whose filthy houses and filthier personal appearance characterized their mental and moral make-up.[73]

Early literary travel accounts by women reflected the Eastern prejudice against the backwoodsman and his consort. Although not always as vicious in their descriptions of the tobacco chewing, profane, uncouth folk who lived in indecent poverty, as the famous English visitor Francis Trollope, several Eastern women who traveled or lived briefly in the Midwest criticized the homes, manners, dress, and general behavior of the frontier's poorer classes. Most of Caroline Kirkland's *A New Home* and *Forest Tales* were stories which took good-natured pokes at her frontier neighbors. Kirkland described the strange speech and rude manners of the Michiganders and was particularly shocked by one of her "helps," a "sallow damsel" who

> arose from her seat, took a short pipe from her bosom (not 'Pan's reedy pipe,' reader) filled it with tobacco, which she carried in her 'work-pocket,' and reseating herself began to smoke with the greatest gusto, turning ever and anon to spit at the hearth.

Other women took a similarly jaundiced view of the backwoodsfolk's speech and behavior. According to most of the writers, the men of this class abused their women who were little better than domestic slaves. One recorded a long conversation with a "hopelessly benighted and brutified" young man who badly mistreated his young bride, a girl who "possessed little of that strength of mind and bold thought, which characterize most of these rudely-bred women." Eliza Farnham blamed much of the lower class "refusal" to improve itself on the women. Describing one home of the "meanest description," she pointed out that the farmer was "not all that poor," but that their living arrangements were the result of "the incapacity of the mistress . . . to appreciate a better condition or help to create one." And, she continued, she "afterward saw many cases of a like mode of living" where "the credit was due in nearly every one to the females."[74]

No doubt the opinions of many of the Eastern women writers were influenced, like those of their British counterparts, by their economic and political philosophy.[75] Many feared that the relaxed tone in the manners and speech of frontier America presaged a breakdown in the social and political order of the nation, but it was also clear that the prejudices against economic, and thus cultural and social, "inferiority" were deeply ingrained in middle and upper-class Americans in the nineteenth century. Certainly these attitudes were reflected in the diaries and reminiscences of frontier women. Many of their comments about the dirty cabins "perfectly infected with bugs," "broken and unclean" eating implements, the "vacant faces of the filthy children of the poor white trash," and the "many singular expressions . . . right smart, I reckon, I allow" which characterized the speech of some frontier dwellers were very similar to those of European and Eastern tourist-journalists.[76] Several of the diarists also made it clear that they did not wish to associate with such people. "These new folks," wrote one overlander of a family which had recently joined their train "seem not the class I care to mingle with, so we shall keep to ourselves and our wagon."[77]

Westering Americans took a good deal of their cultural as well as their physical baggage with them as they moved westward, and prejudice, whether based on race, religion, or class, was, regrettably, part of that baggage. Indians, Mexicans, Mormons, poor whites, and the few Negroes who went West were all targets at one time or another of the racial and religious prejudice which characterized much of nineteenth-century American life. Both men's and women's diaries, journals, letters, and published books reflected many of the racial and nativist sentiments of their day, and there is little evidence that women were any less, or more, vehement in their feelings and statements than were men.[78] Moreover, it should also be noted that frontier conditions often attenuated strong prejudicial and intolerant thoughts and actions. Many of the irrational myths and stereotypes which formed an important part of racist and nativist sentiment in the East and South were also present in the West, but the status rivalries—the face-to-face confrontations and political, religious, and economic conflicts—which were also an important part of nativism did not occur as often in frontier areas or in the new Western communities as they did in the older and more crowded Eastern cities.[79] As a modern immigration historian has pointed out, intolerance was less pronounced in the West than in the East or in the South, at least during the frontier years.[80] This is not to maintain that discrimination and intolerance did not exist in the West, for as the material in this chapter indicates, it is clear that they did. Westering women packed many of their prejudicial myths and stereotypes with them, but often these ideas were modified or sometimes discarded, along with other prized possessions, when they confronted the frontier and its inhabitants.

5

Westward Ho!

Women on the Overland Trails

Perhaps no mass movement in history has been better recorded than the great migration of Americans across the continent during the 1840s, 1850s, and 1860s. Beginning with the first explorations of the Louisiana Territory, gaining momentum with the opening of Oregon, swelling into a rush with the California gold discoveries, thousands of Americans followed the major routes westward. Yet until recently little was written about women on the trails. Westering was supposed to be a male enterprise, full of hardships, unsuitable for the "weaker" sex. But women, too, were a part of the westward migration, and their experiences, recorded in diaries, letters, and reminiscences are an important part of the trail literature.

Unfortunately, our perceptions of westering women have been shaped by male writers who did not read what women themselves wrote about the West. Or, if they did read the many journals and reminiscences written by women, they chose to ignore them in favor of more dramatic legends and myths. Westering women became the protagonists of a stereotyped version of the West as false as that of the Hollywood Indian. Pioneer women were neither the sunbonnet saints of traditional literature nor the exploited drudges of the new feminist studies. Women's lives on the trail, and their impressions of the journey, like those of men, varied with the circumstances of their backgrounds, family, education, and the problems and pleasures encountered on the trip.

There is no such thing as a typical overland journal. Each writer had different experiences; each noted different things along the route. Each started with different preconceptions of the trip, and these ideas changed during the course of the journey. There is a pattern to the journals, however, whether written by men or women. Most described the preparations for the trip, the sorrows of parting from friends and family, the excitement of "The Start." Each noted at least some of the firsts along the way—the first night of camping out, the first Indians, the first buffalo. There were usually comments on the weather, the scenery, and the availability of grass and water. All writers documented something of the pleasures and hardships of the trip. Some found it exciting and generally pleasant, while others saw it as a grueling and difficult journey with few pleasantries or diversions. Individual women experienced different conditions, and reacted in varying ways to the westward journey.

Although diarists recorded different impressions of the trip and their experiences, men's and women's descriptions were generally quite similar. Understandably, women's diaries included more details of family life, care of children, and their own camp work. Men's accounts more frequently concentrated on their trail labor, details of train organization, and disputes over decisions made by the captain or other leaders. Men were also more likely to discuss fights and violence, hunting, defense, and possible attacks by Indians or outlaws. Despite these differences, one recent analyst of trail diaries pointed out that over two-thirds of the content of men's and women's diaries concerned three broad themes—"practical matters, health and safety, and natural beauty."[1]

There are many misconceptions about women's lives on the overland trails. Far too often women have been pictured as reluctant immigrants, trudging mournfully after the wagons, constantly turning around to gaze homeward. Of course, some women were reluctant to accompany their husbands or fathers West. Some simply refused to go as was the case with Julia Dodge whose husband's pleading letters from Fort Lyon, Colorado, made clear Julia's adamant refusal to join him at any post west of the Hudson River.[2] Others faced the prospect of westering with fear and trembling. They dreaded the journey, the dust, the heat; they were terrified of Indians and wild animals. One wife admitted that she "shuddered" at the idea of the long overland march, but she finally agreed to go. Another, after reading a number of guidebooks and accounts of the California trail, decided that there were "no very flattering accounts" and that her reading had certainly not "improved my ideas of the pleasure of the trip."[3]

Many dreaded leaving civilization. "I do remember my emotions after we were all landed on the Indian Territory side of the river. I felt as if we had left all civilization behind us," wrote a frightened Margaret Chambers,[4] and her sentiments were echoed by many others, both men and women. Men, as a matter of male pride, were supposed to look forward with anticipation to entering the uncivilized wilderness, but there is evidence to suggest that their words were bolder than their hearts. "Should any one of my readers ever be impelled to visit the prairies," cautioned traveler Francis Parkman, "A dreary preliminary . . . awaits him before he finds himself fairly upon the verge of the 'great American desert' . . .

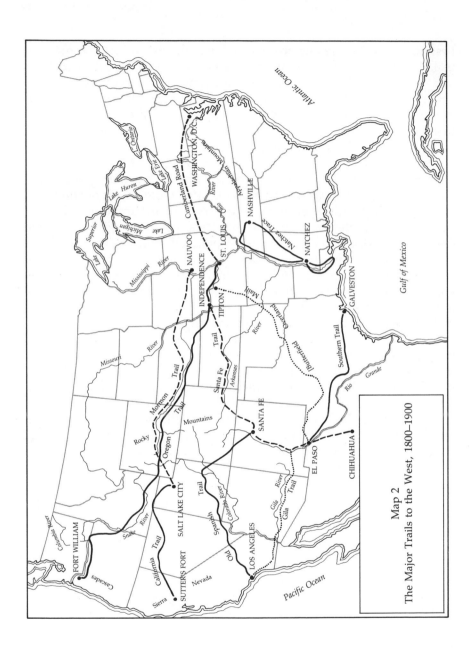

Map 2
The Major Trails to the West, 1800–1900

where the very shadow of civilization lies a hundred leagues behind him."[5]

Some never made it to the edge of civilization. The first look at a frontier tavern or their first introduction to frontier society was sometimes enough to convince the erstwhile immigrants to turn around and head for home.[6] Many others who started a westward journey in reasonably good spirits became discouraged by bad roads, storms, disagreeable traveling companions, or other vexations of the trip and wanted to turn back. "Almira says she wishes she was home," wrote a discouraged Amelia Knight, "and I say ditto." Lucy Cooke and her mother-in-law were both sorry that they had started by the time they reached the Missouri River and agreed that, given the opportunity, they would return home.[7] Such statements would seem to reinforce the stereotype of women as reluctant pioneers, but it should be noted that these were not strictly feminine sentiments. Men's journals and letters reflected the same "regret we ever started for the golden prize."[8]

Of course, some women went West because they had no choice in the matter. One woman began her overland journal, "Agreeable to the wish of my husband."[9] Some wives grimly agreed, in the spirit of Ruth, "Whither thou goest, I will go," but there is little evidence that women were coerced by their men into undertaking the journey. As one historian pointed out, women could see the worn-out land, the poor health of family members, or the richness of the West as well as their men could. Many were anxious to go West and joined wholeheartedly in the words of a favorite trail song:

> Farewell's a word that breaks my heart
> And fills my soul with woe
> But the fertile fields of Oregon
> Encourage me to go.[10]

Perhaps it was the heart-rending scenes of leave-taking and the admitted homesickness so prevalent in women's diaries that led historians to conclude that women did not want to go in the first place. Yet men, too, suffered from pangs of homesickness and the leave-taking of loved ones. One young man admitted that he hurried behind the barn before his grandmother saw his tears when he bid her farewell.[11] Many men's diaries mention the "painful departure." The only difference between Margaret Irvin's plaintive, "I remember it was awful sad and I didn't know whether I wanted to go or not" and John Clark's, "I was leaving all that was near and dear to me for a 'wild goose chase' " was a matter of Clark's more restrained language.[12] Women probably felt freer to express their emotions than men, but once out on the prairies and plains men, too, felt the solitude and loneliness and conjured up pleasant pictures of the folks back home. Firsthand observers like overlanders Charles Gray and J. G. Bruff made it clear that men as well as women felt the effects of the long distances which separated them from their homes and all that was familiar.[13]

Many women were as enthusiastic as their men about a move to the frontier. Some, like the Iowa farm wife who, according to her daughter, "was always ready and willing to go," obviously enjoyed frontiering.[14] Wilderness held perils to be sure, but these could be overcome. A survey of 159 women's trail diaries and reminiscences showed that only a small number, about 18 percent, were strongly opposed to the westward journey while 32 percent were strongly in favor of the trip. Their comments ranged from the exuberant Helen Carpenter's joyous, "Ho for California . . . We are off to the Promised Land" to the more practical Sarah Sutton's, "I do not in the least regret leaving the sickness and cold, sand-piles and lakes."[15]

Reluctant or enthusiastic, women did journey westward. Some opted for the faster, and generally more comfortable, sea routes, either via Panama or the longer trip around the Horn, but since sea travel was expensive, and little baggage could be taken, this method of westering was impractical for large families. Most chose one of the overland routes, and along the way they began to acquire or refine many of the skills that they would need once they reached their new homes. The trails west were the transitional link between the old settled patterns of women's lives and their lives on the frontier. The trail experience was not just a prelude to the frontier; it was the first chapter of frontier life. During the weeks and months on the trail, women, and men, had to learn and master new skills and adapt to new ways of daily life if they were to gain their desired goal of a new life in the West. First, of course, they had to move themselves physically to their new homes and find ways to perform the chores connected with daily living while on the move. At the same time, they had to begin "reshaping their mind-set from looking back East to looking westward," adapting emotionally and psychologically to the new environment while they learned and perfected the new skills which they would need for frontier living. If these lessons were not successfully learned on the trail, the immigrants' chances of success in their new homes were considerably lessened.[16]

Of course, women moving from New England and the Atlantic seaboard to the trans-Appalachian and Midwestern frontiers had a much shorter distance to travel than the later overlanders, and they thus had less opportunity to acquire trail and frontier skills. Moreover, there were usually inns or empty houses where they could spend the night and farmhouses where they could purchase fresh vegetables, milk, and eggs. Still, most of them experienced at least a night or two of camping out and cooking over a camp fire, and they learned to care for their family's needs under less-than-ideal conditions. Thus, even during shorter trips, women began to acquire new housekeeping skills.

Some westering women came from rural environments where they had already had substantial experience in meeting new and difficult conditions. Some had previous trail experience, for some of the immigrants were perennial movers, and many had moved at least once or twice and some three or more times. One analysis of Midwestern male heads of households on the overland trails showed that 78 percent of them had made at least one previous westward move.[17] One can assume that women probably followed similar patterns. A surprising number of westering women, however, not only had no trail experience, they had very few skills in basic homemaking. They came from comfortable, middle-class homes where they had domestic servants to carry out most of the duties, and they had never learned to do these things for themselves. Virginia Ivins, for example, had been married for four years, but she had "never kept house" and did not "even know how to bake bread." Lavinia Porter admitted that "like many other Southern girls" she had never "tried to cook a meal." She eventually learned, but the lesson was a difficult one. Many of the younger women, untrained in the domestic arts, were at a loss as to where to start. "I was too young, being only eighteen, and inexperienced and fearful, to have much faith or comfort in anything," mourned Arvazena Cooper; many another young bride felt the same sense of inexperience in her new role not only as wife but as immigrant.[18]

Some of the wealthier families took servants to do the trail chores, but such help was often unreliable. Hired hands left one company to join another, hired on with a new master or mistress, or decided to turn around and go back home. For example, one young woman reported that their servants disappeared, along with most of the family's money, and "the comfort with which my father had surrounded mother was swept away" and "the hard labor of cooking and washing had fallen on her shoulders." Catherine Haun's husband provided her with help, but they "lost the cook in only a few days" and Haun, who had "never made even my first cup of coffee," had to learn rather quickly how to prepare meals for herself and the six men who made up the rest of the party.[19]

Inexperience was not confined to women. Many men did not have pioneering skills either. Lavinia Porter wrote that her husband "knew nothing of manual labor . . . nor had he the training to make a living on the plains of the West or the crossing of the continent in an ox team a successful venture." Agnes Stewart noted that the men of their company had difficulty in yoking the oxen for "some of them scarcely ever saw cattle before they started on this journey." Yet another woman noted that their men were so inept in handling the stock that the women "walked nearly all the way" for the first week of the trip because "We were afraid to ride, as the men were unaccustomed to driving oxen." Other women commented on their menfolk's lack of expertise in repairing wagons, fording streams, and setting up camps.[20] Contrary to the picture of the frontiersman as experienced hunter and Indian fighter, many of the men had little or no skill with firearms. According to one analyst of the trail, mutilation or death from accidental shootings was fairly common. Trail journalists often noted men's lack of experience in the use of weapons. "Yesterday evening we killed a beef," Maria Shrode recalled. "The boys shot at it about 50 times before they got it." Another woman commented, "I should say we had some mighty men of valor with us. The Indians would die of fright as soon as they saw them! These mighty men could fire forty shots out of their wagons without reloading!" So much for the skill and prowess of pioneer fathers.[21]

However inexperienced, men could turn to the guidebooks which offered all kinds of advice and helpful hints to male immigrants. Most of the guides included instructions for purchasing and breaking stock, on selecting and outfitting a wagon; they discussed what clothes would be needed, what tools to take, and where and how to arrange camp grounds and corral livestock. No such advice was provided for immigrant women. Some guides, in fact, were detrimental to women's interests. One guidebook writer informed his readers that although men would need special clothing for the trip, women needed nothing "other than their ordinary clothing at home." Most of the guidebooks provided a list of provisions necessary for the journey—flour, bacon, beans, salt, coffee—but they had no hints for the homemakers on how to build a fire with buffalo chips or how to add variety and spice to the monotonous daily fare. Some guidebooks included a list of essential cooking utensils, but these were designed for a small company of men, not for a woman trying to cook for her family and possibly equip a kitchen in her new home. "Very few cooking utensils should be taken," advised one guide; "a baking kettle, frying-pan, tea-kettle, tea-pot and coffee-pot are all the furniture of this kind that is essential." The selection was hardly adequate for most women no matter how limited their culinary skills, although many of them managed with even less. The guidebooks offered no advice to women on washing, sewing, or keeping track of wandering children on the journey. There were no instructions on how to make a bed in a wagon or arrange a tent for sleeping quarters. None of the guidebook writers included instructions on how to clean dishes, not to mention clothes, how to make a dry camp, or how to keep infants reasonably dry and clean when there was no water for washing.[22] Women either learned these things from other women or figured them out for themselves, just as they would have to do later in their new homes.

On the trail, men's and women's work was divided and assigned by sex. Men generally tended to the stock and wagons, selected roads and camp grounds, provided game, and were responsible for the safety of the train. Women's duties included cooking, washing, and caring for the children—all familiar household tasks, but tasks altered and complicated by the stress of the trail environment. Women on the trail had to overcome their initial revulsion and learn to appreciate the need to gather buffalo dung for their fires and for smudge pots to keep off mosquitoes and gnats. They had to learn to cook over an open fire and to provide tasty, attractive meals with limited provisions. They had to master the onerous chore of keeping the family clothing clean and repaired—a major challenge given the hard alkaline water, lack of usual home laundry aids, and the dust and heat of the journey. It required a great deal of ingenuity to make a wagonbed and tent seem homelike, just as it would require skill and imagination to set up housekeeping in a mining camp shack, a tiny log cabin, a soddy, or a dugout. Many women gained their first practice with frontier housekeeping problems during the trip West and learned to make the adjustments and accommodations to difficult circumstances and new conditions which would also be useful in their new homes.

One of the most frequently mentioned adaptations frontier women had to make was to set aside their squeamishness and learn to cook with buffalo chips. Along most of the trails, wood was scarce, sometimes completely unobtainable, and dry buffalo or cow dung was the accepted plains' substitute. According to one informant, a man could "gather a bushel in a minute; three bushels makes a good fire." Generally the task of gathering this fuel was assigned to the women and children who walked along beside the wagons with large sacks and secured enough for the evening fires. According to Sarah Cummins, this practice "caused many ladies to act cross and many were the rude phrases uttered, far more humiliating to refined ears than any mention of the material used for fuel could have been." However, she continued, necessity soon overcame revulsion, and "ere long each member of the various households were busily employed in the search for fuel." Once women got over their initial aversion, they found that chips made a good fire and "were much more satisfactory than one would think who had never tried them." Helen Carpenter wrote that not only were chips "not at all offensive" but that they made an excellent mosquito repellant. One or two lighted buffalo chips placed in the wagon, she reported, soon smoked the mosquitoes out, and "we can stand it longer than they can."[23]

Along the Southwestern trails both trees and chips were in short supply and mesquite roots substituted for fuel. "This is the greatest country for firewood to have no timber growing on it that I ever saw in my life," declared one Southwestern woman immigrant. "There is mequit [sic] brush growing everywhere. Some of it is dead and we dig the roots for firewood which makes the best coals of anything. They are not hard to get." Another woman disagreed with this optimistic assessment. As she climbed down from her wagon after filling her pail with water from the water barrel, she cried in disgust, "Oh, God, how I hate a country where you have to climb for water and dig for wood."[24] Whatever their assessment of chips and roots, women whose permanent homes were in areas where wood was scarce continued to use these and other substitute fuels, such as tightly-wrapped twists of grass, for many years after they arrived in the West.

Whatever the source of fuel for their fires, women found that trail cooking required a good deal of resourcefulness and imagination. Many had never cooked over an open fire, and they found it difficult to "get my kettle to stand upright . . . [and] keep the smoke out of my eyes and ashes out of the food . . . ," as one woman complained. Some immigrants took along small sheet-iron stoves especially designed for camp cooking, but these were often broken or lost, and some found them more of a "nuisance than a help." Many women learned to prepare a trench "about one foot deep and three feet long" and then "hung the crane over the trench with the coffee pot and camp kettle"—a device which one woman praised as "a very good substitute for a stove."[25]

However convenient stoves or trenches may have been for cooking, they were of little assistance against the vagaries of wind and weather which made trail cooking an adventure. "You had better believe it [made] me cross when I had to get out and spat around in the mud to cook," complained Catherine Bell. Another woman recalled a dinner just set on the table when a sandstorm hit the camp:

> After it was over our most intimate friends could hardly have recognized us—so dirty were our faces. And our dinner! Who would have eaten it? We could not tell what it consisted of, although before the storm it looked very tempting. So we had to cook another.

Iowa immigrant Jane Gould recalled a similar instance in which, driven inside the wagon by rain, she returned to her fire to find her beans had burned and "nothing was left for me but to cook more."[26]

W. H. D. Koerner, *Madonna of the Prairie*. Koerner's often reproduced and always popular portrait graphically shows the romantic ideal of the Westering woman—the Madonna of the Prairie. (Courtesy Buffalo Bill Historical Center, Cody, Wyoming.)

Harvey Dunn, *The Homesteader's Wife*. Although not as well known as Koerner's painting, Dunn's piece shows another popular view of Westering women. (Courtesy South Dakota Memorial Art Center.)

Calamity Jane. One of the "bad girls," she represents yet a third common stereotype of Westering women. (Courtesy Library of Congress.)

Above: Peter Moran, *Cliffs Along the Green River*. Scenes such as this inspired Westering women to see the relationship between man and God reflected in Nature and to expound on the beauty of the wilderness. Wrote one woman of this spot, "Some of the most romantic scenery I ever *saw*. . . . What a theme for the novelist." (Courtesy Amon Carter Museum, Fort Worth.)

Pioneer Woman. This frequently reproduced photograph probably depicts more accurately the life of women on the frontier than the popular stereotypes. Westering women quickly learned to "make do" as portrayed by the wheelbarrow full of buffalo chip fuel. (Courtesy Western History Collections, University of Oklahoma Library.)

Women dancing on the Sierra Nevadas. Two women kick up
their heels on Overhanging Rock, Glacier Point, Yosemite
National Park, in a photograph taken by George Fiske in the late
1890s or early 1900s. (Courtesy U.S. Department of the Interior,
National Park Service, Yosemite National Park.)

Family camping trip. Even after long months on the journey West, women continued to enjoy the beauty of the natural wilderness, and sightseeing and camping trips were a favorite frontier recreation. (Courtesy Colorado Historical Society.)

Carl Wimar, *The Abduction of Boone's Daughter by the Indians.* Nineteenth century literature often portrayed women as the victims of "cruel and rapacious" redmen. (Courtesy Amon Carter Museum, Fort Worth.)

Mrs. Bozarth defending her dwelling. Frontier women were also
frequently portrayed as the brave defenders of home and
children. (From John Frost, *Thrilling Adventures Among the
Indians*, New York, 1854.)

Entertaining Indian visitors, Anadarko, Oklahoma. More typical of contacts between women and Indians were friendly, and often helpful, encounters. Women often visited with Indian neighbors and sometimes came to be good friends. (Courtesy Western History Collections, University of Oklahoma Library.)

"Spanish Beauties." Despite unfavorable preconceptions such as that pictured above, Westering women often found Mexican towns attractive, enjoyed the *bailes* and fiestas, and came to know, and often respect, their new Mexican-American neighbors. (Courtesy Library of Congress.)

A first view of polygamy. Mormon women were the target of prejudice throughout the nineteenth century. They were usually portrayed as "depraved participants" in a polygamist conspiracy or as pitiful, helpless victims. (From Samuel Bowles, *Our New West*, Hartford, 1896; Courtesy Amon Carter Museum, Fort Worth.)

Frontier family, Brewster County, Texas. Black women were an almost invisible part of the Western scene. But black women often accompanied families to new Western homes, and some helped to establish all-black communities in Kansas and Oklahoma. (Courtesy Southwest Collection, Texas Tech University.)

F. O. C. Darley, *Emigrants Crossing the Plains*. This romanticized view of the overland journey by a New York illustrator and artist depicts a common Eastern concept of Westering families. (Courtesy Denver Public Library, Western History Department.)

Joseph G. Bruff, "Struggling Emigrants, Fall of 1849." Fortyniner Bruff presented a very different view of women on the overland trails from that of Eastern artists who often romanticized the journey. (Courtesy Henry E. Huntington Library, San Marino, California.)

Prairie schooner, Sheridan County, Kansas. This photograph of families on the overland journey is a more realistic visual record than many artistic renderings. (Courtesy Kansas State Historical Society, Topeka.)

Culinary efforts were also hampered by the lack of suitable utensils and the kinds of provisions available. Part of the problem stemmed from the fact that equipment and supplies were often selected by men. Trail kits with a kettle, skillet, coffee pot, and tin plates and cups were available, but many women complained about both the quality and the assortment. Spanish and Mexican expeditions into Texas, New Mexico, and California were usually government financed and planned, and women had little to say about the equipment and supplies which were provided. On one such government-planned journey the immigrants discovered they could not prepare their frijoles because someone had forgotten to include the pots in which to cook them. For an overland expedition to California the company's leader thoughtfully included "eight frying pans, ten copper camp kettles, [and] twelve large chocolate pots"—intended to meet the needs of 175 men, women, and children! On other frontiers, army wives experienced a similar problem with the oversized pots and pans provided by the quartermaster's department. "I was surprised," recalled one young army wife, "to find nothing smaller than two-gallon tea-kettles, meatforks a yard long, and mess-kettles deep enough to cook rations for fifty men!"[27]

Finding ways to cook in rain and dust storms with inadequate equipment and still prepare a palatable meal tested women's skills as cooks. One woman invented a method for cooking beans to a jelly and then forming them into a loaf "which was fine for sandwiches." Many of the women gathered wild berries and fruits such as the famous service berries and wild currants and made pies and tarts to add variety to the usual monotonous diet of beans, bread, and bacon. Some women had been well advised before they started and had included pickles, vinegar, and dried fruits or citric acid in their list of supplies to aid in warding off scurvy, but many did not and suffered from this disease before the end of the journey. Other women included dried fruits or preserves in their trail provisions to be cooked as special treats. Some added a few luxury items for special occasions—canned oysters, a few eggs carefully packed in flour or corn meal, molasses, and tomato catsup to help season the plain fare. Most immigrants supplemented their dull diet with game and fish, for as one young woman explained, "We got tired of our home cured hams and bacon . . . and fresh meat and fish was greatly relished." But no matter how ingenious women might be, much of the time the food was plain and unvaried: "one does like a change and about the only change we have from bread and bacon is to bacon and bread," wrote Helen Carpenter, and her experience was reflected in many other women's journals.[28]

Occasionally women cooperated in preparing special dinners. One woman described a difficult fording of the Green River where "all the ladies went in together and got dinner for the men." Another recalled a Fourth of July celebration near Independence Rock which featured "canned vegetables, fish, rice cakes and other little dishes." In some families, meal preparation was a cooperative enterprise in which men assisted with the cooking chores. Helen Carpenter described one such arrangement:

> The old gentleman Farmer is very good to help "Mother" in the culinary arrangements. He makes the fires, gets out the pots and kettles and the eatables and helps generally while "Mother" makes the bread and coffee. "Sister" is too small to do more than be in the way. When the four sons and men are ready for a meal each for the time being becomes his own cook so there is no occasion for anyone to grumble. Willows are sharpened and slices of bacon speared and held in the fire ad lib. It looks quite amusing.

Other women also reported that their menfolk assisted with the cooking, but according to Lucy Cooke, the results were not always satisfactory. "It's so nice to have women folks manage the cooking," she reported. "I don't know that they have any better food or more variety . . . but it looks better." Most women did handle the majority of cooking chores and would have agreed with Margaret Chambers that "None but those who have cooked for a family of eight, crossing the plains, have any idea of what it takes."[29]

Clothing posed as many problems for immigrant women as cooking. Although guidebooks frequently recommended suitable clothing for overlanding males—trousers made of strong, durable goods; woolen shirts; sturdy, well-made boots; work gloves; and broad brimmed hats—they did not offer similar, practical advice for women and children. The government-equipped Spanish expeditions of the seventeenth and eighteenth centuries included prescribed clothing for women as well as men. For example, women immigrants traveling with one expedition received three chemises, three white Puebla cotton petticoats, a serge skirt, and a baize skirt as well as underskirts, jackets, shoes, and a hat. In addition each was provided with two pairs of "fine Brussels stockings . . . and six yards of ribbon," undoubtedly welcome but impractical luxuries for the long desert crossing from Sonora to California. Immigrant women in the nineteenth century quickly discovered that items of fashionable ladies' dress were not well suited to overlanding. Hoop skirts proved particularly cumbersome, and, according to one woman, required "a good deal of manoeuvring" to get them in and out of wagons. Helen Carpenter's party had a good laugh at the expense of a young bride who wore hoop skirts and was promptly dubbed "Miss Hoopy." Carpenter declared that she "would not recommend them for this mode of traveling," since "the wearer has less personal privacy than the Pawnee in his blanket." One army wife, who considered herself "an old campaigner," suggested a simple calico frock, "plainly made" and "without hoops" for Western travel. "I must have looked outlandish to my young friends just from New York," she recorded, "but there was not a husband who did not commend my commonsense dress, urging their wives to adopt it." Other women complained that without hoops their long skirts dragged the ground, attracted sand burrs and dirt, and interfered with many of their activities.[30]

To overcome these difficulties, women tried various kinds of adaptations in dress. Helen Carpenter's aunt and sister, bothered by the high winds which "switched" their dresses about their ankles and made walking "precarious," decided to pin some rocks in the bottom of their skirts. Unfortunately the rocks blew against their shins and turned them black and blue. "Their invention was not a success," Carpenter lamented, "and so was never patented." Some women attired themselves in what they considered proper emigrant clothing—a simple homespun or cotton dress, large apron, and a sunbonnet. Lavinia Porter scorned a neighbor's advice to take dresses of linsey-woolsey because "these fabrics were worn only by the negroes in the South"; however, Porter soon discarded her blue cloth dresses with white collars and cuffs, put on some "short wash dresses . . . tied my much betrimmed straw hat up in the wagon, put on my big shaker sun-bonnet and my heavy buckskin gloves and looked the ideal immigrant woman." A number of immigrant women opted for some type of bloomer costume, not as a political statement but as a practical dress. Although there was occasional criticism of these women, most thought the dress "very appropriate." Cora Agatz described a group of young ladies who wore grey wool gymnasium costumes. "When compared to the long, slovenly soiled calico gowns worn by the other women of the train," she noted, "these simple costumes elicited many favorable remarks." Once in their new homes, many women discovered that bloomer costumes or men's pantaloons under a short skirt were much more practical for carrying out farm and ranch chores. Although they dressed "appropriately" most of the time, some continued to wear pants when doing outside chores.[31]

Whatever their choice of clothing, the most troublesome of all camp chores for women was the always arduous task of doing the family wash. This job was never easy, even under the best of circumstances, and on the trail the problems were compounded by lack of water and proper facilities and clothes that were dirtier than usual. The long, hot, dusty days, unusual trail chores, and outdoor life ground dirt into every fiber. Women who took pride in having their families clean and neatly dressed were often discouraged and frustrated by their inability to preserve the amenities of civilized life in trail dress. As Lodisa Frizzell complained, "this Gypsy life is anything but agreeable, it is impossible to keep anything clean, & it is with great difficulty that you do what little you have to do." Some women recommended taking special trail linens, "pillows covered with dark calico and sheets colored" instead of the usual white, and plainly made clothing in dark colors which would not show dirt and which could be spread out to dry and look fairly neat without ironing.[32]

Most trains "laid over" a day at fairly regular intervals to wash and catch up on other chores that could not be completed at the brief "nooning" or during an evening in camp. "About every two weeks it was necessary to have a family wash day," Elizabeth Warren explained. "This was quite a chore as all the water had to be heated in camp-kettles." Much of the usual equipment for washing had to be left behind or was lost or abandoned along the way, and women had to "make do" as best they could. Myra Eells and her companions dressed in their nightdresses and waded out into a creek where they build a fire on some flat stones:

> We would have got on well had the water been soft, but being so hard, it took all our strength and a great portion of our soap, besides our clothes would not look well, which spoiled our anticipated merriment, but we found we could heat water, wash, boil and rinse in the same kettle.

Often washdays became community affairs. "Prepared for a general washing in the train," recorded Mrs. Hockensmith. "All washing around a spring, cheerful and lively." Noted a more laconic Maria Shrode, "All went to washing. Men and women and children all went to washing." Men and boys usually assisted the women with at least the hardest part of this work, but even with assistance washdays were difficult and tiring. Washing was a task most women dreaded, and as one weary woman commented, "The sooner it is done the better."[33]

Not only was washing hard work, it could also be hazardous. "May and I did our washing," recalled Missouri Bishop Moore. "I blistered my hands and arms. So much for my first experience." An even more painful accident befell Catherine Bell when she hung her baby's clothes "on some poison oak not knowing what it was and poisoned him very bad." Most women learned to make the best of the situation and were usually successful in their efforts. "I cannot imagine how the washing was ever accomplished," Caroline Dunlap remembered, "but I do know that our little dresses and trousers off the same piece of dark blue goods came to us fresh and clean . . . and I remember, too, seeing father and mother washing away by moonlight one night."[34] Thus, women learned yet another lesson in adapting to circumstances that would serve them well in their new, poorly equipped homes.

In addition to cooking and washing, there were other general trail chores. Equipment had to be repaired, wagons aired out, supplies repacked. Many of these chores, like the washing, were reserved for layover days. Many women's trail diaries describe such occasions. "When we found a good camp with good water and grass," Lizzie Sisk recorded, "we often laid over for a few days for rest and repairs. Our blacksmith was busy shoeing oxen and mending wagons. The women washed clothes and baked light bread." Maria Shrode described a typical day in camp:

> While we was laying over some washed, some watched the camps, some fished, some visited, and some of the boys herded cattle. Some went hunting and some went in bathing and looked like somebody else when they came in they was washed off so clean and looked so fresh.

Layover days were also used to clean and air the wagons, dry bedding and clothing that had been soaked by one of the frequent rain and hail storms, and repack provisions. Cecilia Adams reported that she took advantage of a layover to make "dutch cheese" and then "took everything out of the waggons [sic] to air." Another woman "rearranged the loading of the wagons for employment" while others used the extra time to reorganize their provisions and supplies and discard unnecessary items. Such periodic house cleanings, according to Catherine Haun, "freshened up our train very much, for after a few weeks of travel things got mixed up and untidy. . . ."[35]

Sundays were often chosen for layover days, but the amount of work which had to be carried out was resented by the more devout Christians, both men and women. After a few weeks, however, most immigrants recognized the necessity for either traveling or working at least a part of the Sabbath and resigned themselves to a more practical approach. "If we had devotional service," one woman reported, "the minister—protem—stood in the center of the corral while we all kept on with our work." Another practical woman was described by Ellen Fletcher:

> One of the men washed his clothes today [Sunday], and one of the women . . . did her washing. She is an Oregon woman, and has been there fifteen years. She says that she has crossed the plains before and shall wash when she gets the opportunity.[36]

Such changes in normal home routines reinforced the lesson of adjustment and accommodation necessary for frontier living.

Whether in camp or on the trail, another regular part of women's work included child care. While this task was less physically demanding than other trail chores, it was certainly the most worrisome of women's duties. Initially, some mothers harbored deep-seated fears that their children might be kidnaped or killed by the Indians or suffer some other misadventure at the hands of the "red savages." Although such fears generally dissipated following actual contacts with the Indians, other more realistic concerns remained and added to women's emotional and psychological burdens. Children became tired and impatient and cross and were a sore trial to their already overburdened parents. "I am going to get some switches as the boys are crying. They have driven me almost crazy," cried one distracted mother. "But for the trouble of attending to the children," wrote another, "I should enjoy the trip so much." And later this weary mother explained:

> I sit so much in the wagon and walk so seldom—for I cannot leave the baby and it is no pleasure to walk and carry him, that I am almost growing double and my limbs feel so cramped and tired that I can hardly sleep at night. The children too are getting tired of the monotony of our life and are sometimes very cross and fretful. . . .

Sometimes older children, especially girls, helped with the younger ones, but the burden of responsibility and fears for their children's safety led to many a sleepless night and uneasy days for the mothers.[37]

Even at home children had accidents, but on the trail there were additional hazards. Children fell from wagons, were knocked down and injured by loose livestock, or drowned in swift streams. "Jennie fell out of the little wagon and both wheels ran over her arm and hand and one knee and bruised them considerably but did not brake [sic] any bones," reported a worried Maria Shrode. Such accidents were not uncommon, often with more serious consequences. It was difficult to keep track of toddlers and young children, and their natural curiosity and unaccustomed freedom got them into all kinds of mischief. "[M]y dear little baby Belle was just learning to walk," Arvazena Cooper recalled, and "if left to herself would get into things, her favorite pursuit was washing the dishrag in the water bucket, which proved a rather serious matter." A much more serious consequence of childish curiosity was reported by Lucy Henderson Deady whose little sister died after drinking an entire bottle of laudanum.[38]

Sometimes children wandered off from the trains. Elisha Brooks recalled one such instance in which a three-year-old boy wandered away and was not found until the next morning "nearly dead from exposure." Other children went off to play with friends, climbed into the wrong wagon, or were simply forgotten in the hustle and bustle of starting. Amelia Knight reported her little sister was left behind because everyone thought she was "in someone else's wagon." Fortunately the child was found by another train and quickly returned to her family, but Amelia remembered with a sigh of relief, "It was a lesson to all of us."[39]

Mothers not only feared kidnaping by Indians, accidents, and lost children, they also had to guard against illness. Wet bedding, chilling winds, severe heat, and constant exposure brought on chills, fevers, and frequent colds which could quickly turn into pneumonia or "lung fever" and other illnesses. Trail children were prone, as well, to the usual childhood diseases—measles, chickenpox, whooping cough, and scarlet fever. They were also exposed to more deadly diseases such as cholera, smallpox, and dysentery which were endemic to the trails. Most families carried a medicine chest which included such staple remedies as "physicking pills, castor oil, rum, peppermint essence," and usually something recommended by friends "to ward off the cholera." Sometimes a doctor was available, but more often worried mothers had to cope alone. "I know how worried my mother was when any of us got sick," Margaret Irvin recalled:

> There were no doctors in the party and all we had to doctor ourselves with were the few medicines we brought along and the home remedies we knew about, such as tying a strip of bacon around our necks when we had a sore throat or blowing sulphur down our throats.

Sometimes another woman was available to help a tired mother with the nursing chores, but many anxious women had to get along as best they could without medical advice, adequate medicines, or the usual facilities for child care. Many children, as well as adults, sickened and died as a direct result of the trail experience. Those who did survive, however, were often better able to withstand the rigors of life on a new frontier, and their mothers certainly were more experienced in managing family sickness without medical assistance.[40]

A number of women bore children on the trail without the benefit of medical advice and often without adequate care. Sometimes a train was able to lay over a day or two while the new mother rested, but other times there was nothing to do but stop briefly for the birth and then hurry on to find grass, water, or a safer campground. Surprisingly, many women did very well under the circumstances and were soon "up and around" taking care of their usual camp duties. Commenting on a birth along the Humboldt River in Nevada, Lydia Waters noted: "The mother and child did well, could not have done better anywhere else." Another woman maintained that women with doctor, nurse, and servants did "not do as well" as some of the trail mothers, but it is doubtful many of the new mothers would have agreed. The problems of feeding and caring for new-born infants under trail conditions increased the mothers' burdens and taxed their imaginations.[41] Some women found that they were unable to nurse their newborns, and if another nursing mother could not be found to help out, the women had to try various, and not always satisfactory, substitutes. One woman, suffering from sore and bleeding nipples, tried various artificial means to nurture her child. A bottle and cow's milk were easily obtained, but a suckling device was more difficult. "Have obtained a mare's tit," she reported. "Hope to succeed in using it." Even such an ordinary and seemingly simple task as keeping the baby clean and dry became a major challenge. Many women did not have enough spare cloth for little shirts, sacques, belly binders, or even diapers. Even if they were able to provide suitable clothing for their babies, lack of water or time to wash often meant that even the best-intentioned mothers often were unable to provide dry, sanitary clothing. Diapers posed a special problem where water was scarce. Some women may have used grass or soft mosses, if these were available, but most evidently resorted to the common, although frequently criticized, practice of simply drying, scraping, and airing the diapers and reusing them.[42]

Despite the additional problems posed by childbirth, most women took it in their stride and "made do." They named their children Humboldt, Sierra Nevada, La Bonte, or Idaho Montana; they did the best they could to keep them nurtured and clean and dry and prayed they would survive, along with the rest of the family, to reach the new Promised Land. A surprisingly large number did. One Spanish train began the trip from Sonora to California with 115 children and arrived at San Gabriel with 118.[43] A survey of one hundred trail diaries revealed fourteen births and only three reported infant deaths.

In addition to the adaptations they had to make in cooking, cleaning, and child care, trail women had to adjust to changed social and sexual mores. Conditions on the trail, one declared, "were a great leveler," and many social customs and restraints were discarded, or at least temporarily abandoned. Moreover, on the trail, everyone pitched in to do what had to be done, and distinctions between men's and women's work became blurred. Men helped with the cooking and washing, helped to pack and unpack the tents and bedding, and prepared the sleeping quarters for the night. Women, by necessity or choice, took over a number of duties which were considered to be in men's sphere. For example, a number of women drove the wagons for at least a part of the trip. Sometimes this was by choice, but other times there was simply no one else. "My husband was taken sick and I had to drive the team," one woman wrote. "At that time there were nine women who were driving—not well men enough in the company to drive the teams. Well, that was a sad day for me. I had never done anything in that line and was very awkward." Undoubtedly, other women, too, were awkward at these new tasks and resented the manual labor involved, but others were obviously proud of their newly acquired skills. Lydia Waters, who learned to drive an oxteam on the trip out the Platte, boasted of her ability to drive the heavy wagon. Women helped to scout the trail, find good campgrounds, and yoke the oxen; a number of women and girls helped drive loose livestock. Many women enjoyed this kind of work because it gave them something to do besides sit in the wagon and watch the often monotonous scenery.[44]

However, not all of this extra work was pleasant, and some women openly resented the added responsibility. "One of the new hands was sick," recorded Mrs. Isaac Moore, "so I had the pleasure of driving myself. It is very tiresome to drive and hold the baby." The weary Mary Powers recalled that she had to help carry heavy stones to brake the wagon wheels on steep hills and "carry and pull along the children at the same time." At length she was so exhausted that "I shook and trembled" and "it was almost impossible to get my breath." The trail, noted one woman, was "a good place to study human nature," and there were both the selfish and those who bore adversity with good grace and patience. In the face of difficulty some women open rebelled and refused to go on. Elizabeth Geer recalled a woman in their train who got so mad at her husband's refusal to return home that she burned their wagon. A woman in Emma Tate's party "refused to help the other women at cooking and camp work, in fact would not even comb her children's hair." She persistently sat on the wagon tongue and nagged her husband while he did both her work and his own.[45]

Other women obviously enjoyed their newfound freedom and cheerfully joined their menfolk in doing what was necessary. In one party, the women stood guard while the men enjoyed a Fourth of July feast; others joined their husbands to keep them company during the long hours on night guard or took their own turn when the men were ill or otherwise occupied. Some women were considered good shots and were called on to help out in potentially dangerous situations. Mary Hopping told of a woman in her company who "intimidated a Pawnee chief into helping rebuild a bridge" the Indians had destroyed. In the face of an expected

Indian attack, Mary Catharine Vineyard reported, her mother and several other women were elected to shoot while other women and young boys loaded the rifles. "She was an excellent shot," Vineyard recalled, "and had acquired greater proficiency by killing wolves and coyotes along the way." Many women and girls helped supplement the family larder by fishing, and a few skilled outdoorswomen joined the hunting parties. The most unusual of these "dead eye Dianas" were four young Southern women who joined Thomas Potter's overland company "for the purpose of hunting large game such as buffalo, elk, and antelope." Dressed in bright red bloomer suits, these remarkable young ladies "kept the train well supplied with antelope meat" and even put on a shooting demonstration for a band of Snake Indians. Their extraordinary ability was quickly recognized by the men of the party who agreed the women should have a voice, along with the men, in the party's organization and governance.[46]

The Southern huntresses were quite exceptional young ladies, of course, and few women would have joined in their sport or even envied them their prowess. As a recent historian pointed out, even with their new skills and enlarged responsibilities, frontier women were essentially conservative, and few of them abandoned their conception of women's nature or ceased to value "female culture." Adrietta Applegate Hixson recalled that her mother "was particular about Louvina and me wearing our sunbonnets and long mitts in order to protect our complexions, hair, and hands." Mrs. Applegate likewise "was always reminding Louvina and me to be ladies," but the daughters were more flexible than their mother and thought "the requirements were too rigid." Other women rebelled against conventions of suitable female behavior, demanded consideration of their opinions and openly challenged male decisions. Disgusted by the unsanitary conditions of a male-selected campground, Lavinia Porter refused to stay and forced her husband to move to a cleaner place she had picked out. "The other women," she recalled, "looking on my daring insubordination with wondering eyes, and envious of my cleanly quarters, at last plucked up courage to follow my example, and with much profanity the camp was moved." Cora Agatz's mother refused to obey an order to circle the wagons and prepare to fight an approaching party of Indians. "Captain Hill," she told the surprised train leader, "I know you are the master of this train, but I refuse to obey you for you know as well as I that we are in no condition to fight these Indians." The surprised Captain Hill agreed she was right and bluffed his way through. The Indians passed peacefully on, and a possible tragedy was averted.[47]

In recent years, feminist historians have made much of the unusual pressures placed on women on the overland trails. They have presented trail women as drudges, reluctant companions, and overworked helpmates following wearily after the wagons. Preoccupied with death, resentful of male-imposed rules, they maintained, the women performed unaccustomed tasks, gathered buffalo chips, and cooked and washed while their strong male companions lolled before the fires, smoked their pipes, and made bets on "how many miles we had covered during the day." Or, as one trail woman phrased it, somewhat less directly, "There were meals to prepare, washing and mending, and many other duties to perform the same as at home. My hands were full, I assure you."[48]

Women might have had their hands full with trail chores, but there is little evidence to support the contention that most women were simply trail drudges. In fact, some chores were easier on the trail. There were no floors to scrub, no iron stoves to be cleaned and blacked; most women did not bother to iron trail clothing. Food preparation was simpler and occasionally easier. Almost every woman's diary describes the "nice butter churned by the motion of the wagon." Immigrants milked their cows in the morning, hung the churn from the wagon bows, or fastened it in some other convenient place and by lunch time had "little balls" of butter and "cool buttermilk" to supplement their midday, and later the evening, meal.[49] Much of the day women had little to do in the way of physical labor. They sometimes gathered buffalo chips for the evening fire, but just as often they gathered wild flowers or little stones that struck their fancy or wandered with a friend to a high point along the road for a better view of the countryside. They wrote long letters home, to be mailed from the next fort or sent with a returning traveler; they kept journals; they visited back and forth with other women. "During the day," wrote Catherine Haun, "we womenfolk visited from wagon to wagon or congenial friends spent an hour walking, ever westward, and talking over our home life back in 'the states' . . . voicing our hopes for the future and even whispering a little friendly gossip of emigrant life." Sewing was a favorite pastime as were tatting, crocheting, knitting, "exchanging recepts [sic]," and "other feminine occupations and diversions." Maggie Hall reported that her mother "knit all the way across" because "it took lots of knitting to keep us all in stockings." One woman became so adept at trail sewing that she reported she could knit or tat while driving the oxen. Other women spent their time in "reading and meditation" or "alternatively drove, and dozed, talked and meditated."[50]

Some women did, indeed, have a hard and difficult time on the trail and "went through a great deal of suffering and trial." However, most of the women so described belonged to a class of people contemptuously referred to as "Missourians" or "Pikers." These were the poorer immigrants, often from the Appalachian region. The men cursed, drank, and abused their livestock and their women. The women were often dirty and slovenly, and their trail life was not much different, in terms of hard work and male abuse, than it had been in Kentucky, Tennessee, or Missouri.[51] According to Lavinia Porter, the Pikers were "the roughest, most uncouth, and ignorant people I had ever come in contact with. Perfectly lawless, fighting and quarreling among themselves, using language terrible to hear. . . ." Among such people, Mary Ann Morrison reported, "The women helped pitch the tents, helped unload, & helped yoking the cattle. Some of the women did nearly all the yoking; many times the men were off." According to Helen Carpenter, "Some women have very little help about the camp being obliged to get wood and water (as far as possible), make camp fires, unpack at night and pack up in the morning, and if they are Missourians they have the milking to do if they are fortunate enough to have cows." But, Carpenter continued, "I am lucky in having a Yankee for a husband, so am well waited on."[52] Carpenter's experience seemed to have been the more common one. To a great extent, of course, the degree of women's difficulty or comfort was determined by how much their menfolk were willing to help or hinder their efforts, but in most companies, trail chores were shared by the entire family, and everyone pitched in and did his or her part, whether yoking the cattle or doing the family wash.[53] The trail women themselves seemed to have harbored far less resentment about their lives than that with which modern writers have burdened them.

The degree of women's comfort on the trip was also influenced by the kind of equipment and provisions the party had. Trail outfits ranged from the most meager to almost luxurious. The Mormon migrants between 1856 and 1860 often traveled in handcart companies pulling either open or covered carts loaded with provisions, bedding, extra clothing, and a tent. Designed to be pulled by the men and boys of the family, the carts were also hauled along by the women. Many of the Mormon families were quite poor, and their provisions were often as scanty as their outfits. One woman in such a company recalled that after the first few weeks of travel they had only little cakes of flour and water to eat. "During this hard journey," she recorded, "I was expecting my first baby and it was very hard to be contented on so little food." Mormon handcart pioneers were not the only ones who traveled under less-than-comfortable circumstances. A Mexican-American woman traveled to her new home on horseback with her small children encased in sacks hung on either side of her saddle. Maggie Hall reported seeing one party with "a man & boy each a gun on shoulder—one horse, a feather bed tied on it & woman sat upon it and tied on horse were pans, kittle [sic] & little bags, etc." A Texas woman described her own similarly sparse outfit with acerbic humor:

we put all *ouer rament* and things on the old horse. . . . after the most
delicate part of the Pack was put on first then ouer pervishan then
ouer little kittle which was hardley large enofe to cook a boiled dinner for three person. then the Skillet and lid was put on top then my
spining wheel was put on top.

When yet another burden, a lame pig, was added to the pile, the horse
rebelled and "run off and made a compleet stampeed and kept picking
and kicking untell he got everything off and the result was the pigs brains
was smasht out and the dinner pot broke all in bits."[54]

Other women traveled in style. According to Rebecca Woodson, one of
her traveling companions had her tent "fixed just so. It was like stepping
into a parlor to go into her tent." Virginia Ivins described another party
with three spring wagons with "folding beds inside, leaving room for small
chairs and sewing tables, work baskets, bird cages, and pretty knick
knacks around." The women in this party had "a good girl to do the cooking" and "an elegant marquee tent and camp equipages." One young
army wife included a rubber bathtub in her luggage so that she could
bathe "before dinner," and another young woman reported that her father had fixed a small "privy" in the back of their wagon.[55] Such luxuries
were as uncommon as abject poverty. Most women traveled in large but
crowded wagons sitting and sleeping on top of their household goods. It
was good practice for "making do" in their often less-than-commodious
frontier homes.

Whether their outfits were simple or elaborate, whether they had help
or not, women's lives on the trail were not always easy. There were difficult days when everything seemed to go wrong, tempers flared, men
shouted, women wept. In the evenings, there were meals to prepare,
dishes to wash, plans to be made for the next day's travel, and much of
this was women's work which had to be carried out under less-than-ideal
circumstances. "Although there is not much to cook," Helen Carpenter
wrote, "the difficulty and inconvenience in doing it amounts to a great
deal. So by the time one has squatted around the fire and cooked bread
and bacon, made several trips to and from the wagon, washed the dishes
(with no place to drain them), and gotten things ready for an early breakfast, some of the others already had their night caps on." Margaret Irvin
recalled that after supper "the men folks lounged about the fire resting,
swapping yarns and talking about the happenings of the day" while "the
women folks busied themselves washing clothes and getting things ready
for setting out early the next morning." But men, too, had evening chores
to perform. "The women are having a good time visiting back and forth,"
wrote Mary Mahoney of an evening camp, "but the men have to rush

and hurry." Another woman recalled that in the evening, "the women would sit around the fire and visit while the men would take the oxen to grass and water."[56]

Once the chores were done, both men and women enjoyed a brief hour or two of "socializing." "We have had a long and tedious day," wrote Harriet Ward, but in the evening, she reported, everyone relaxed:

> Some of our company have been out hunting, some fishing and some playing Euchre. This evening is truly delightful . . . I have learned that the real wants of life are very few indeed. . . . Frankie [her daughter] seems just as happy sitting upon the ground playing her guitar as she was at home.

Immigrants carried an amazing number and variety of musical instruments—fiddles, guitars, harmonicas, even melodeons, and they enjoyed frequent impromptu concerts and "sing-alongs." Occasionally there were parties, dances, and celebrations to mark special events. A priest who accompanied one of the Spanish expeditions reported the people held frequent "fandangos" at which there was much "singing and dancing" and entertainment by "a very bold widow" who "sang some verses which were not at all nice, applauded and cheered by all the crowd." Although usually not so ribald, similar celebrations occurred on most trips, and there was often singing and dancing and "general good times." "The young people of our company are having quite a merry time this evening," one woman reported. "The dancers raise such a dust that it is a hard matter to see the fiddler. Mr. E. Fish is master of cermonies which ceremony consists of raising all the dust they can without choking."[57] Such activities gave the young people opportunities to make new friends and engage in a little "courting." Some met, fell in love, and married, either before the journey's end or shortly after their arrival at their new homes. Sometimes lifelong friendships were made in the course of the journey, and a few families even changed their plans in order to settle near friends they had met on the trail. A wagon train was somewhat like a small, mobile community, and many community activities were available from time to time. In addition to concerts and dances, there were baseball games, hunting and fishing parties, and sometimes spelling bees or debates. Some played chess or checkers or simply "enjoyed the hour around the campfire." Then it was time to go to bed in order to get a good night's sleep and be ready for an early start.[58]

Westering was not all dances and pleasant evenings around the campfire, of course. The journey was a difficult one, and it placed severe strains on interpersonal relationships. There were often family disputes which resulted in hurt feelings and harsh words. "This afternoon I was annoyed by something very unpleasant & shed many tears & felt very unhappy," one woman recorded. Another took more direct action. When her husband refused to "go off the trail a half mile for wood," she "retired to my bed and let them cook their own supper." The supper was not a success, and thereafter "my men folks . . . made quite commendable efforts to keep me supplied with fuel." Sometimes family problems were more serious. Mary Power's husband became temporarily deranged in the course of the journey, and she was forced to turn to strangers for aid. "If there is anything that makes a brute (Yes and worse than a brute . . .) of man, it is a journey from Council Bluffs across the Plains," she recorded. "I felt as though myself and my little ones were at the mercy of a mad man."[59]

Disputes often went beyond family quarrels. Almost every overlander's diary or reminiscence mentioned at least one "split up" when unhappy train members left to join another, more agreeable company. There were often disputes over the terms of contracts or agreements, quarrels over train leadership or simply which trail to take or who was to drive at the back of the line and "eat dust." Sometimes, disagreements were even more serious. As in any community, there were occasional outbreaks of violence, robbery, and even murder. A typical outburst was described by one young woman:

> A dreadful occurance took place. A wicked man who had whipped one of his men overheard Ben Farewell say that no man could make him run by whipping. He came into our camp, took an ax & felled him like a beef. We thought he was killed. Will not describe the excitement.

Such incidents, fortunately, were not usual; but they were dangerous to the safety of the train, and if the perpetrators could be apprehended, they were swiftly tried and punished. Westering Americans carried a sense of law and government along with them, and strict rules of conduct were preferred and usually enforced. As a legal analyst of trail behavior recently concluded, "To a greater extent than has been thought, the habits, actions, and values of nineteenth-century American society were formed by a behaviorism based on law," and nowhere was this more apparent than on the overland trails.[60]

Contrary to the many misconceptions about overlanding fostered by Hollywood, television, and novelists, the trip was not one long series of fights, Indian raids, prairie fires, and armed desperados. It was neither one "great adventure" from beginning to end, nor was it the "perfect pleasure trip" described by one young woman. Most of the days were long, the scenery dull and uninteresting. "It is refreshing to see even the mail coach away out here in these vast plains," one woman recorded. "Even an old broke down ox or a flock of snipes will break the monotony of the plains." The overwhelming impression of the trip was one of monotony and a desire to reach the journey's end. "I am getting impatient for our journey to come to an end," one woman wrote from Tucson, "yet it cheers me to think that every day finds us nearer our destination." Another summed up the trip in a few succinct sentences: "Most of the train have lost the day of the week. . . . Still pressing onward. It is a long & tedious journey."[61]

Generally, then, trail life was a combination of monotony, hard work, and both pleasant and painful, and occasionally violent, experiences. There is no evidence that the trail was harder on women than on men. Both were concerned with the responsibility of safely completing the journey and making plans for their new homes. Both were subjected to physical and emotional stress. As one woman recorded:

> During the week our men had been very busily employed driving their oxen, yoking and unyoking their cattle, standing guard at night, unloading and reloading the wagons at the ferries, and swimming the stock. Saturday night found them very tired and much in need of physical rest, so they lolled around in the tents or under the wagons out of the sunshine. . . . But the women, who had only been anxious spectators of their arduous work, and not being weary in body, could not fully appreciate physical rest, and were rendered more uneasy by the continual passing of emigrant trains all day long. . . . To me, much of the day was spent in meditating over the past and forebodings for the future.[62]

Women's cares and duties were frequently less arduous than men's, but their tasks tended to increase mental and emotional strain which led to psychological rather than physical exhaustion. Because everyone was expected to "lend a hand" which "might mean anything from building campfires and washing dishes to fighting Indians, holding back a loaded wagon on a downgrade or lifting it over boulders when climbing a mountain,"[63] the trail experience often blurred distinctions between the sexes and demanded great adaptability. Women on the trail soon learned that they would need great flexibility and not a little humor if they were to meet some of the challenges presented by frontiering.

According to a nineteenth-century verse, "Ladies have the hardest time,/ That emigrate by land." For some the physical and emotional strain of the trip was too much. Some did not survive the journey or succumbed soon after their arrival from disease or exhaustion. But many women, like Margaret Frink, "never had occasion to regret the prolonged hardships of the toilsome journey."[64] Most arrived at their new homes better prepared not only to endure but to triumph over the new tests imposed by frontier conditions. New skills acquired on the trail and the practical experience of mastering the problems of daily living under new, and often difficult, circumstances were extremely useful on frontier farms and ranches, especially when the men were absent or ill. More important, the lessons of flexibility and adaptability learned under the conditions of trail life helped women to cope with new conditions and new problems.

6

New Home—Who'll Follow?[1]

Women and Frontier Homemaking

Whatever the pleasures or perils of the trek westward, everyone was anxious to get to the journey's end and cease his or her "gypsy" existence. As the long days on the road drew to a close and Iowa, or Texas, or California, or Oregon drew closer, women's thoughts turned toward the future and how they would make a home and reestablish family life. They could hardly wait "to sit at a table and eat like folks and sleep in a house on a bedstead." Yet anxious as they were to arrive, women still could not help but be apprehensive about the future. As Katherine Kirk approached her new South Dakota home, she remembered, "With a sinking feeling I realized that I was entering a new kind of life, as rough and full of ups and downs as the road over which we traveled. Would I have the courage and fortitude to stick it out?"[2]

The first look at their new homes certainly tested women's courage and fortitude. Crude log cabins without doors or windows; mining shacks with dirt floors and canvas ceilings; dark and dreary dugouts; flimsy tar paper homestead shacks; dirty brown soddies—the sight of these unfamiliar dwelling places was enough to discourage all but the most optimistic or foolhardy. Anna Shaw vividly recalled her mother's reaction to her first glimpse of their log house on the Michigan frontier:

> I shall never forget the look my mother turned upon the place. Without a word she crossed its threshold, and standing very still, looked slowly around her. Then something within her seemed to give way, and she sank upon the ground. . . . When she finally took it in she buried her face in her hands, and in that way she sat for hours without moving or speaking. . . . Never before had we seen our mother give way to despair.

In a similar vein, a "gently reared" Southern woman saw her Texas "pioneer cabin'' and broke into tears. A young bride of seventeen took one look at her mud roof and dirt floor and indignantly announced, "My Father had a much better house for his hogs!" Another compared her new home to a stable. One young homesteader was quite proud of her acumen in buying a claim with buildings already up—until she saw the house which reminded her of a "none too substantial packing-box tossed haphazardly on the prairie. . . ."[3]

At least these discouraged and disappointed women had a roof, however unsatisfactory, over their heads. Until a home could be built, many pioneer women were faced with the prospect of little or no shelter for themselves and their weary families. Often the most important thing was to clear and break ground and get in a crop, and families continued to live in tents and wagons until there was time to begin building a cabin, a soddie, or a dugout. Many families continued to camp out for many weeks after their arrival. "A settlement old enough to boast a log cabin," Johnaphene Faulkner remembered, was "an improvement upon a tent which in its turn [was] an improvement upon the camp which 'newcomers' usually erected [of boughs and poles] in the first day of arrival upon a chosen site." Cedenia Bagley, like many Mormon women sent with their husbands to found new settlements, "wintered in wagon boxes;" Mary Rabb spent her first weeks in Texas "spinning under a tree," with only "a quilt and a sheat [sic] for a tent."[4] And these experiences were not unusual. When the Pilgrims landed at Plymouth, they "burrow(ed) themselves into the earth . . . under some hillsides, casting the earth aloft upon timber." Two and a half centuries later conditions were little improved, as one Kansas pioneer recalled. "We had expected to find a thriving settlement," she wrote, but instead "we find the families living in tents of cloth, some of cloth and green bark . . . and some wholly of green bark stuck up on the damp ground without floors or fires." In the face of such conditions, it is not surprising that some erstwhile pioneers "were not sure" they were going to stay, or like Exoduster Malinda Harris, wrote discouragingly, "dont study a Bout coming away. if I knowed what I know no Body could not Pull me a way . . . Pray for me for I kneed Prayers."[5]

Even when the first crude homes were completed they were often less than satisfactory. "Really I had thought a sod house would be kind of nice," recalled Luna Kellie, "but the sight of the first one sickened me." May Avery remembered that during her first summer in a Nebraska home "the roof leaked something awful [and] we killed a snake or two in the dugout and several centepedes [sic]." Hasty construction often led not only to leaky roofs but to leaky walls as well. Mary Jennings lived in one cabin "built of lumber and every crank or cranny the snow came through and made mounds [of] snow by the walls." Another family found a similar situation in their new Texas home. According to the oldest daughter, "We had no furniture, no stove, not even a fireplace. . . . The mud daubing between the logs had dried and fallen away [and] one morning we found we were covered with snow that had drifted in." Most women gritted their teeth and prepared to make the best of it. As one young woman wrote of her new home, "It does not look much like home right now but no one said a word."[6]

Frontiering, like overlanding, required many skills, and contrary to popular opinion, not everyone knew how to go about building a log or a sod house. Johnaphene Faulkner told a hilarious story about her two young Virginia uncles trying to build a cabin. Neither knew the first thing about house construction, and their trials and tribulations in getting up the walls were exceeded only by their chagrin when they discovered they had left no openings for doors or windows. Sarah Martin's "tender-foot" father-in-law built his house too near an undercut bank, and the whole thing slipped off into the river. Another woman recalled that her father "tho't he knew more about building with sod than he did." The walls of his structure collapsed before the roof could be added. "I am afraid that some of our houses will fall in upon us this winter," wrote a young Texas woman. "The cross piece of the widow Sutherlin's house broke this morning and I tell you that makes me afraid of mine." Obviously pioneer women needed a good deal of patience, and a sense of humor, as they tried to adjust themselves to frontier conditions and hoped for a better future. Indeed, wrote one, given the "sparse comforts [and] meagre advantages," women "possessed little else than hope."[7]

And hope they did. Despite the dirt floors and canvas ceilings, the snakes and centipedes, the sagging roofs and leaning walls, women described their first frontier homes with a sense of accomplishment in their ability to cope with unusual situations. In fact, the variety of living arrangements almost defied description. In the Southwest, Spanish families took over Indian dwellings or built temporary *jacales* of brush or small adobes with "doors fashioned on rawhide stretched on sticks," floors of "native soil," and peeled poles "for roof beams." In parts of Texas, "pole houses," constructed of vertical limbs stuffed with moss and grass to fill the cracks were popular. On the plains, baled hay houses and rammed earth structures sometimes substituted for soddies and dugouts. In the Mormon settlements, house construction had to be adapted to the needs of multiple families, and "an architecture of equal comforts" was developed to provide accommodations for two or more families. The necessity for shelter called forth all kinds of innovative solutions to the frontier housing problem. To be near her husband, Mary Maverick spent several weeks living in a corn crib. At a later date, Rena Mathews refurbished a

"box-car or outfit car" so that she could follow her engineer husband
from one job to the next. Ella Bird-Dumont and her husband spent a
Panhandle winter in a house built from "dried buffalo hides [with the
legs tied together] and put around the walls." Bird-Dumont was proud
of her unusual dwelling and firmly declared that "a more clean and comfortable little home you could not find in any of the Eastern cities." One
of the most unusual wilderness homes was that occupied by Sarah Hartman's mother. Determined to remain with her husband while he worked
some new land far distant from their cabin, she had her husband clean
out two large tree stumps and put on a roof. She then moved in with her
six children. According to Hartman, her mother found the tree stump
home to be "very comfortable indeed. She used the burnt out roots for
closets and cupboards."[8]

Not all frontier dwellings were so unusual or primitive, of course. And
not all families went into rural areas. Some moved to frontier towns where
accommodations were often fairly comfortable, if not luxurious. Until they
were able to find quarters of their own, some families (especially young
couples) "boarded out" or rented one or two rooms in established resi-
dences. Although some women found such arrangements satisfactory,
many complained of the crowding and inconvenience. Margaret Murray,
for example, had two rooms. "In our large room," she reported, "we
cooked ate & sat. [I] carried our water from a well in the back yard &
washed down stairs in land ladies kitchen same day she did."[9] Most
boarders and renters were anxious to have homes of their own, and as
soon as possible they tried to secure private quarters. New construction
was expensive, however, and in many frontier towns single-family dwellings were difficult to find. Some enterprising pioneers bought prefabri-
cated houses (sometimes called balloon houses) in the East and shipped
them to Kansas and Iowa towns along the Western waterways or around
the Horn to California.[10] Sometimes living and business space was combined. "We have bought us a house, at last," wrote Sara Hively; "paid
two hundred and fifty dollars for it. We intend to keep cigar store in the
front part and live in the back room." An Arizona bride, Aggie Loring,
wrote her mother from Phoenix that although her home and store were
in one building and she had only one large room, "the place [is] much
more pleasant than I expected."[11]

Although town homes were often more commodious and luxurious
than rural dwellings, not all farmhouses were uncomfortable or primitive.
Once the first crops had been made and the family's economic condition
was more secure, improvements were added—an extra room, a new kitch-
en, sometimes an entirely new house was built, usually frame or brick.
Margaret Murray recalled with great pride the two-story frame house her

father built to replace their log cabin. It had "5 rooms 3 down & 2 up stairs . . . & a cellar size of house. mother got a cook stove for the first time." But even without such improvements most women did not seem to think that they suffered unduly. Joanna Haines made it clear that she thought writers like O. E. Rölvaag had exaggerated the privations of frontier life. "We lived in a log cabin, of course," she informed an interviewer, "but we were always comfortable." Many women shared her feelings. "We have a good house, Built of hewed logs one story and a half high," Fanny Adriance wrote her brother from Golden, Colorado. "I trust we shall be contented here." A black Oklahoma woman remembered when she moved from her one room log house into a new addition with "2 frame rooms" and she "thought we had lots of room." Most frontier women, like Lizzie Sisk, recalled their frontier homes with great fondness and described in detail "the bunks to sleep in" and the "stakes driven in the ground and rough boards placed on poles that were fastened with pegs to the stakes [which] made our table."[12]

It was easy, of course, once women moved into new frame houses with a few modern conveniences to forget the difficulties and frustrations of life in those first tiny cabins and dugouts. A good deal of nostalgia prevailed in their reminiscences of pioneer life, and they saw the past through a golden haze of blessed forgetfulness. As they looked back on the first years of settlement, they tended to remember more of the pleasant than the painful, more of the happiness than the hardship. "With the strange contradictoriness of the human mind," so well described by a young army wife, the hardships and deprivations they had endured "lost their bitterness when they become only a memory."[13] Dirt floors, small rooms, smoking chimneys, and cold sod privies were more attractive to remember than to live with.

Even allowing for nostalgia, women still remembered their first frontier homes with affection and proudly recalled their accomplishments in making them more homelike. Despite the scarcity of materials, women found ways to "make do" with what they had and added little touches to brighten their homes. One girl recalled how her mother made mirrors by "taking an old black shawl and tacking it smoothly over a board" and placing a pane of "some of the presious [sic] window glass" in front of the shawl. Another woman, "longing for a change from the look of the grey sage brush," set up a small willow branch outside her front door and "used artificial flowers that I happened to have to make blooms on the little tree." Mary Hallock Foote used her husband's geological survey maps to decorate her cabin, much to the amusement of the other engineers who "thought it peculiarly feminine . . . to stick up old Silurian and the Tertiary deposits for the sake of their pretty colors!" Other women made curtains for the windows (often of paper when cloth was unavailable), whitewashed the walls or covered them with muslin, canvas, or newspapers, braided rag carpets for the floors, and stretched clean canvas across the ceilings. As one Oklahoma woman described the homemaking process:

> I had 58 yards of new rag carpet and we used that to put up around the walls on the inside of the house to make it more comfortable in the wintertime; we also sewed sheets together & tacked up to the joists as a ceiling for the house. . . . We used dry goods boxes for a cupboard & for a bureau, and used newspapers for window curtains.[14]

Making a new house more "homelike" was only one of the many jobs with which frontier women had to contend. Whether they lived in tents or cabins, temporary shelters, soddies, or dugouts or had fairly comfortable houses, there were still meals to be cooked, the washing to be done, clothes to be made and mended, children to be cared for, and a myriad of other chores which had to be done and done under new and unfamiliar circumstances. Housekeeping on the frontier, like housekeeping on the trail, required a good deal of ingenuity. Just as men struggled to learn new farming techniques and modified existing economic institutions to meet new conditions, women had to devise new domestic techniques to meet the challenges of frontier living. Moreover, they had to do this with few of the basic tools and conveniences to which they were accustomed.

Only the most essential household goods could be carried West by wagon, and women had to leave behind many of the housekeeping utensils found in most Eastern homes. Even those that were packed were often discarded before the end of the journey to "lighten the load." Of course, families who moved to less remote areas could have goods shipped by boat or later by railroad, but costs were high, and most frontier women learned to "make do" with very little in the way of kitchen utensils or other household equipment. "When I went to housekeeping," Mary Minto recalled, "I had just one stew skettle [sic] We had 3 butcher knives [and] just two sheets & when Mr. Minto started to the Cayuse war I cut up the sheets to make shirts for him." Phoebe Judson's first Oregon home was only a little better equipped, although in addition to her camp kettle, frying pan, and Dutch oven, she managed to arrive with "three stone china plates, as many cups and saucers, and one glass tumbler . . . the only one on the prairie." Similarly, most Mexican frontierswomen "got by" with a kettle, a *metate*, and a soapstone griddle or a substituted flat stone for baking tortillas. Women invented all kinds of substitutes for missing items. Effie Wiltbank recalled churning in a square gallon can with a lid and dasher her father carved. It served until they finally were able to buy a churn, but "the can was so small it kept one churning most of the time." A Kansas woman rolled out her pie and cookie dough with a bottle which had once held "Lyman's Effervescence," much to the amusement of her husband who frequently called for "another dose" of pastry.[15]

Very few frontier homes had cook stoves. The small emigrant stoves sometimes used on the journey West were not very substantial and were usually demolished or discarded by the end of the trip. Large metal stoves of the kind common in Eastern homes after the 1830s were far too heavy to carry in a wagon or ship any considerable distance. Until stoves and ovens were available, women cooked in an open fireplace or over an outdoor campfire. This entailed a good deal more dexterity than the pictures of rosy-cheeked pioneer mothers cheerfully stirring up a tasty kettle of soup would imply. Moreover, all frontier women were not experienced in or particularly adept at this chore. Many Mexican women were accustomed to outdoor cooking and could manage meals on a *hornilla* with some ease, but many women were taken aback by the prospect. Guadalupe Callan's mother, faced with the unexpected necessity of preparing meals over an outside fire, broke into tears and then retreated to the house where she "picked up an ostrich fan, a relic of past grandeur, and fanned herself," and left her daughters to cope with the unfamiliar food preparation. Most women could not afford the luxury of Mrs. Callan's retreat from reality. They simply gritted their teeth and learned. Miriam Colt reported that she managed to cook over an open fire, but it was not very satisfactory. Trying to bake bread for a family of seven in a Dutch oven "with the wind blowing" took "all day" and then produced only "two small loaves." Besides, her long skirts kept brushing the fire and soon "the bottoms of our dresses were burnt full of holes." She and her friends eventually solved the skirt problem by donning bloomer costumes, but they continued to have difficulty in preparing enough bread to feed their hungry families. Fireplace cookery caused similar problems as Ellen Pennock reported:

> It was a whole day's job to bake a panful of cookies and a few pumpkin pies, as only four cookies or one pie could be baked [in the bake kettle] at one time. The lid had to be lifted and the hot coals removed often. If your hand should suddenly lose its grip, or someone jostled your elbow, down the lid would come and the coals more often land inside the kettle. The fronts of my dresses would be scorched, the toes of my shoes, burned, and my face blistered in the process.[16]

Trying to fix meals in such circumstances with meager equipment was difficult enough, but finding something to cook was sometimes an even greater challenge. Families who arrived at their new homes in the fall or early winter could not get in gardens or crops until the next spring, and the cost of supplies was often prohibitive. In some areas, there simply was nothing to buy even if the money was available. During the first years in Spanish California, the colonists found themselves near starvation. The women supplemented their meager supplies of beans, corn, and dried meat with wild greens, seeds, and roots; the men staged a bear hunt to help the colony survive until the relief ship arrived. In later years, Oregon immigrant women recalled the first hard winters when they survived on "boiled wheat and boiled peas" and what fish and game their menfolk could provide. Even such basic needs as matches or a tinderbox were sometimes lacking, and several women wrote of going to a neighbor's to borrow coals for a fire or shooting into a pile of shavings and kindling to start a fire to cook the meal. One army wife wrote that at Ringgold Barracks, Texas, "post stores usually consisted of 'mouldy flour and rancid pork' and a few beans," while Chestina Allen recalled that during their first winter in Kansas they ran out of flour and "could buy none in Juniatta."[17]

Given the shortages of supplies and utensils, the variety and tastiness some women could add to their meals was remarkable. "Mother was clever at making good meals out of nothing," recalled Carrie Shive Dunn. During their first months in Montana, Mrs. Shive fed her husband, four sons, and little daughter on well-balanced and substantial meals of "potatoes, beans cooked with a ham bone (a relic of the trip), and pigweed greens (she was always gathering greens of one kind or another)." Women substituted and tried to "make do." They learned to use "shorts" instead of flour, made ersatz coffee from browned wheat or corn, concocted "vinegar" pies, rendered watermelon syrup for sugar, substituted biscuits for bread, and vied with each other to see who could make the best cakes without butter or eggs.[18] It is doubtful if Lydia Child, Catherine Beecher, or Sarah Hale, the formidable arbiters of American domestic science, would have approved of many of the frontier's culinary inventions, but Child, Beecher, and Hale did not live on the frontier, nor did their very popular books on housekeeping include advice for the Western housewife. Beecher might inveigh against the "green, clammy, acrid substance called biscuit, which many of our worthy republicans are obliged to eat" and call upon the "daughters of our land" to revive "the old respectable mode of yeast-brewing and bread raising,"[19] but Beecher did not have to substitute for half the ingredients because they were unavailable or to bake her bread in a Dutch oven over an open campfire. Women who were short of salt and flour and baked in the fireplace or went several miles to borrow a neighbor's oven might understandably be excused from the additional job of brewing yeast and making proper bread instead of biscuits.

Women not only managed to feed their own families in often primitive circumstances, but they also cooked for visitors and neighbors, for occasional boarders, or for work crews who came to help with the plowing or the thrashing. Women who were particularly good cooks often prepared meals for the single men in the community in order to earn money or baked pies and bread for sale. Some, it seemed, cooked for the multitudes. On army posts, officers' wives frequently prepared meals for the junior officers and welcomed transient families into their homes for days at a time. A Colorado lawyer's wife reported she had baked "15 loaves light bread," and "51 pies" on Tuesday and twenty-three more on Wednesday in preparation for Court Day and an expected influx of visitors. One young bride of sixteen recalled she had twenty ranch hands to "cook and do all the work for," while another woman reported "washing and cooking for ten men I find I do not get much time for fine needle work."[20]

Not only were women responsible for feeding their families, they had to clothe them as well. Most girls learned to sew and knit and some learned to do embroidery, tatting, crocheting, and other fancy work as well. In the East, many women had a seamstress or dressmaker who helped to keep the family in well-made clothing, but such luxuries were not available to frontier women who not only had to make and mend the clothing but often produce the material for it as well. Spinning and looming of flax, wool, and cotton cloth was a regular part of the work of many Western housewives until well after the middle of the nineteenth century when machine-made cloth became generally available. Even after dress goods and other materials became common at Western stores and trading posts, some women continued to economize by looming at least a part of their cloth or produced surplus materials to be traded for other goods. "I have been spinning flax all my spare time thru the winter," wrote Kitturah Belknap. "Made a piece of linen to sell. Got me a calico dress for Sunday and a pair of fine shoes and made me one homemade dress for everyday." This was only the beginning of Belknap's cloth manufacture; on the same day that she wrote of her new clothes, she continued, "It is now May and the sheep are sheared and the wool must be washed and picked and got off to the carding machine. So my summer's work is before me." Like other women who made their own cloth, Belknap invited a few women over for the afternoon to help her "pick wool." Wool-picking parties were popular in frontier communities. Like quilting bees and corn huskings, they provided an opportunity for women to get together for a neighborly visit while continuing important chores. The cleaned and "picked" wool, cotton, or flax was then sent to the carding machine and made into rolls and then spun and woven into either a coarse jeans material or a finer flannel or cotton cloth. Often the women did the coloring of the spun thread or the finished fabric as well, using various kinds of native or natural dyes to add some variation to their homemade garments. On the plains and in areas where game was available, women also used tanned hides or buckskins to fashion durable work garments such as shirts, pants, gloves, and riding skirts.[21]

If one had a large family, the task of looming fabric and making all the family clothes took a good deal of time. Even if the family could afford and had access to finished cloth, the time involved was still considerable. And the results were not always satisfactory. "I had never learned how to make dresses or to fit garments," mourned one young Western wife during her first attempt at dressmaking, "and the result was something like a bag."[22] Others, however, were considerably more adept and took great pride in their needlework.

On the Mormon frontier, women often turned the production of clothing into a cooperative enterprise. In polygamous households each wife contributed her special skills—one would spin, another loom, another sew. On other frontiers, spinning, weaving, sewing, and mending were often evening tasks carried out after supper when the children were in bed and husband and wife sat companionably together discussing the events of the day or making plans for the future while the wife worked at some piece of sewing or mending and her husband repaired equipment or fashioned various essential tools and utensils from bits of wood and metal. Kitturah Belknap recalled many such evenings while her husband read aloud and she prepared the clothing for their trip to Oregon. Other women also recalled similar, companionable times.[23]

Women found time not only to do their essential sewing but to do some fancy work as well. Mormon wife Martha Heywood made caps and hats to supplement the family's income; Ella Bird-Dumont earned extra money making gloves and vests for local ranch hands and "had many more orders than I could fill." Other women enjoyed making things to decorate their homes or adding special touches to their clothing. "I have been making Towels [and] fixed my gown," wrote Henrietta Embree. Like many other women, she also "read Godeys Ladies book nearly thru," undoubtedly to get some idea of the latest Eastern fashions. Except during the first very difficult months in a newly opened area, frontier women were not nearly so poorly dressed or out of style as they were sometimes pictured. Many took at least one "good dress" with them or had fine goods and patterns sent to them after they arrived. In addition to their government-issued Brussels stockings and ribbons, many Spanish women included a silk or fine cotton dress and an embroidered or painted shawl in their luggage. For example, the clothing listed in an eighteenth-century New Mexican woman's will included ten *baras* of silver lace, a blue silk damask cloak lined in red Chinese silk, a hoop skirt of pekin silk, and several strings of black pearls. Another woman of the same period had four shawls, "1 *pintados* (painted), uno bordado (one embroidered)," and a taffeta cloak. Anglo women, too, tried to have at least one "Sunday best" and to keep up with changing fashions. "People are generally . . . not half so heathenish as many imagine," Harriet Carr wrote from Kansas in 1858; "people expect taste and tidiness in dress, at least in ladies, just as much as in the East." A Colorado mining community resident recalled, "The boys wanted to see the ladies with clean dresses, white collars and cuffs on, and their hair waved." And the "ladies" seem to have obliged, at least when they were in public. They poured over such popular women's magazines as *Godey's* and *Ladies Repository* and copied the latest styles or at least adapted them to available materials and frontier living. *Godey's* even offered a mail order shopping service for braids, laces, and other ornaments for their rural (and Western) readers who could not obtain such finery in their local stores or trading posts.[24]

Despite the amount of time and labor involved, women seem to have taken a good deal of pride and pleasure in their needlework. A favorite pastime for women was quilt making, fashioning the intricate and colorful patterns into the warm covers that were both practical and beautiful. Quilt patterns were passed from mother to daughter and copied down in books so they would be remembered. Moreover, quilting parties offered another opportunity for women to combine recreation with useful work. Perhaps most important, quilting and other fine needlework provided an avenue for artistic and creative self-expression on the part of the maker. As one woman so eloquently phrased it:

> And then you're just given so much to work with in a life and you have to do the best you can with what you got. That's what piecing is. The materials is passed on to you or is all you can afford to buy . . . that's just what's given to you. Your fate. But the way you put them together is your business.[25]

Cooking and sewing, no matter how difficult or under what circumstances, did have some rewards. Not so with what was probably "the most trying" of all household chores, East or West, town or country—the "always dreaded" wash. No satisfactory mechanical aids for laundry were developed until after 1900, and women universally despised the long hard hours spent over wash tubs and soap barrels. One woman's "receet" for washing clothes gave a good idea of the labor involved:

1. bild fire in back yard to het kettle of rain water.
2. set tubs so smoke won't blow in eyes if wind is peart.
3. shave 1 hole cake lie sope in bilin water.
4. sort things. make 3 piles. 1 pile white, 1 pile cullord, 1 pile work briches and rags.
5. stur flour in cold water to smooth then thin down with bilin water [for starch]
6. rub dirty spots on board. scrub hard. then bile. rub cullord but don't bile just rench and starch.
7. take white things out of kettle with broom stick handel then rench, blew and starch
8. pore rench water in flower bed.
9. scrub porch with hot sopy water
10. turn tubs upside down
11. go put on a cleen dress, smooth hair with side combs, brew cup of tee, set and rest and rock a spell and count blessings.

Just reading the account is enough to make one long for a comfortable chair and a "cup of tee." Little wonder that women who could afford it sent their laundry out or that taking in washing was a good, although strenuous, way to make money.[26]

As with other household tasks, washing was complicated by frontier conditions. "A full supply of all conveniences is needed for good washing," advised Catherine Beecher in her *Housekeeper's Manual*. Unfortunately, most frontier women did not have "all conveniences." They counted themselves fortunate if they had more than one tub, a scrub board, and a battling stick. Before they could even begin washing, they first had to make soap. Some frontier women purchased their lye,[27] but more often they made their own by pouring water and lime through fireplace ashes carefully preserved for this purpose. Then the lye was combined with the leftover household grease, also carefully preserved in a barrel or can. The two ingredients were boiled together and had to be constantly stirred until the soap "came" and could be dipped into the soap barrel. This odiferous task was usually done outdoors in the blowing wind, while the nauseous steam assaulted the cook's nostrils, ashes clung to her arms and hair, and sparks threatened skirts and bare skin.[28]

Once the soap was made, water had to be hauled, often from some distance. In early homes, wells and cisterns often had not been dug, and frequently the water supply was several miles from the house. "As we've no cistern and no well very near," wrote one Illinois housewife, "we wash just as it happens." Often the men would haul the water for the wash, but when they were engaged at other tasks or gone from home, the women had to do the best they could. Leola Lehman recalled that her mother hauled water for several miles in a little wagon in which she pulled her youngest child and four gallon syrup buckets. Another disgusted house-wife, whose husband had not found time to dig a well, lamented that it took so long to haul water "I do not get much else done. Burt gets mad because I complain." Some women found it easier to take their clothes to the water. A young Mexican girl happily remembered washdays when the clothes and children were bundled into a large *carreta* and driven to a distant hot spring where "columns of white steam rose among the oaks, and the precious waters, which were strong with sulphur, were seen flow-ing over the crusted basin."[29]

Once the soap was made and the water hauled, the real work began. As grandma's instructions suggested, the clothes had to be sorted, the dirtiest put to soak, the white clothes boiled over a hot fire, and all scrub-bed on a washboard. In addition, as one woman wrote, "every one had the battleing stick an heavy bench. very dirty clothes were wet an soped [sic] good put on the block beat & battled & turned over an over. then rubbed some on the wash board, they were really cleaned." Some women preferred "a large barrel with a big shug stick" to the "battling stick," but no matter what tools and tricks women devised to help with the wash, they must have appeared like instruments of torture to the weary laun-dresses. Once clean, the clothes still had to be rinsed, wrung out, blued and starched (if such niceties were available), and hung on the line or spread out on the grass and bushes to dry. Small wonder that women described washday as "the day I detest above all others" or that one pro-nounced herself as feeling "worse than a stewed witch" after a day over the laundry tub.[30]

Doing the family laundry was a day-long chore which had to be fitted into a whole myriad of other household tasks. Women's days were a con-stant round of cooking, baking, sewing, cleaning, ironing, mending. A typical entry from a frontier housewife's diary is tiring just in the read-ing. "Burt digs in the well," Julia Hand recorded in November, 1872. "I cook, clean house & sew a little. after dinner we go over to Salt Creek after water." Or Sarah Price's entry for January 18, 1879: "Washed a large wash, baked my bread and scrubbed and ironed a little & all my house-work besides." Such tasks, too, were complicated by frontier conditions. Bugs and vermin were a constant problem, particularly in soddies and dugouts, and there were frequent mentions of general scrubbing and cleaning to get rid of these pests. "We were kept awake so much by fleas & bed bugs," wrote Myrtle Hopper, "that first thing after breakfast was to tear everything up & clean them well." Another woman recalled help-ing her grandmother take down the canvas tacked over their ceiling "each spring & fall," to get rid of the accumulation of dirt and vermin, while "the carpets were also taken up, beaten & tacked back down."[31]

Always interspersed with women's daily tasks was the constant care of children. Although there was a declining birth rate in the nineteenth century, many frontier women continued to bear large numbers of children.[32] It was also clear that women were not always happy about their numerous pregnancies and some tried to do something about them. Various books of medical and marriage advice offered contraceptive information, and some women obviously read them and attempted to follow their instructions. The most widely circulated and read tracts on birth control included Charles Knowlton's *Fruits of Philosophy: or, The Private Companion of Young Married People,* published in various editions between 1832 and 1891 and Frederick Hollick's *Marriage Guide, or Natural History of Generation* which also went through numerous editions during the 1850s and 60s. Knowlton and Hollick, like English socialist Robert Owen who inspired Knowlton's work, all stressed the positive social benefits of birth control. Other tracts, such as A. M. Mauriceau's *The Married Woman's Private Medical Companion,* pointed out the benefits to personal health and happiness:

The happiness as well of husband, of wife, and children will be enhanced by the preservation of her health, by lengthening the intervals between the periods of pregnancy, making the interval between the births, three, four, or more years. . . .

Among the most common methods of contraception suggested by these writers were spermicidal douches, the vaginal sponge, condoms, and coitus interruptus. However, the latter was often criticized as psychologically and possibly even physically damaging to both partners. Pessaries were also used, and after 1864 a vaginal diaphragm was available. An increased knowledge of the menstrual cycle led to the publication of several books on the rhythm method of birth control during the 1870s. This method was particularly advocated by feminists who stressed that it "neither violates physical laws nor involves moral degradation" and put women in control of their bodies.[33]

Although there were few explicit statements about birth control in nineteenth-century women's diaries and letters, the few extant references suggest that women were aware of contraceptive techniques and that the topic was more openly discussed than modern historians have assumed.[34] Lizzie Neblett's correspondence with her husband is full of references to her difficult pregnancies and deliveries and her desire to find a safe and effective method of birth control. "I know no doom that would horrify me," she wrote, so much as to know or believe that, 12 years to come, could add five more children to my number. I had rather spend the remainder of my life even tho it were 35 years in the Penitentary or in solitary confinement for the same length of time, either of which would be ten thousand times worse than death.

She went on to urge her husband to procure some "preventitives" for her:

Let me say right here that if you apply and get your wine detail this summer don't start home without a good quantity of pulverized Ergot and as good a syringe as you can find, Richardson's No. 1 that I described to you long ago is the best I know of.

Then turning to folk medicine, Neblett promised, "I don't think I'll even wean my babe and that will help to ward off some danger." In a similar vein, another Texas woman wrote her sister, "And so you are going ahead of me in the multiplication line. Am I *free* yet? Yes!! No more babies for me. . . . But I must not exult too much I might be *caught* yet; but I'll try not."[35]

Abortion was also readily available during the middle decades of the nineteenth century, and several recent studies have suggested that upper and middle-class married women as well as unmarried and poor women used abortifacients such as ergot, oil of tansy, and black hellebore or engaged the services of abortion practitioners. It would have been strange indeed if women had not been aware of both contraceptives and abortifacients. Newspaper and magazine advertisements (some in religious journals), broadsides, and private cards announcing such services and information appeared throughout the United States in both urban and rural areas. In addition to advertised commercial remedies there was also a good deal of folk wisdom concerning both contraception and abortion. It was generally believed, as Neblett mentioned, that nursing mothers would not become pregnant, although several women's journals implied reliance on this method was not always effective. Strong purgatives and various douches were widely recommended as abortives. According to one source, indigo or calomel and turpentine were widely used by Texas black women who wanted to "unfix" themselves. "In them days," one informant said, "the turpentine was strong and ten or twelve drops would miscarry you." Again, the few surviving sources suggested that women were aware of ways to terminate unwanted pregnancies. It was also clear that although women were rather circumspect in their discussions of pregnancy and childbirth, many of them would have been happy with fewer children and some took measures to prevent or to terminate their pregnancies.[36]

Even women who used contraceptive measures or had one or more abortions or miscarriages usually bore at least two or three children, and most women looked forward to their confinements with both anticipation and dread. Childbearing was often fatal to the mother or brought on a long period of general malaise and weakness. Women developed sore breasts or got milk fever. Others, delivered without aid or by inexperienced assistants, suffered vaginal tears, childbed fevers, prolapsed uteruses, or painful hernias in the pudendal area. Women in remote frontier areas without access to skilled assistance or even to the comforting presence of another woman often suffered increased psychological strain. Martha Summerhayes, recalling the birth of her first child at Camp Apache, Arizona, wrote, "So here I was, inexperienced and helpless, alone in bed, with an infant a few days old. . . . I struggled along, fighting against odds; how I ever got well at all is a wonder. . . . I had no advice or help from any one."[37]

Even when safely delivered, women held great fears for their children. Infant mortality rates in the nineteenth century ran as high as 25 to 30 percent, and epidemics of measles, scarlet fever, influenza, and similar diseases often wiped out whole families. "I feel perfectly careless and indifferent," wrote one woman, "My Babes all snatched from me one by one. it is hard to bear." "I lost my little baby," another wrote her mother; "it was borned three days after I taken the fever and lived twenty-four hours and died." Many women who mentioned the birth of a child also mentioned a child's death.[38]

Children who survived the dangers of infancy were still susceptible to all kinds of diseases and accidents, and worried mothers in frontier areas without doctors or other medical aids simply had to do the best they could. "At last we were visited by that terrible Foe, chills and fever," wrote an Iowa woman, "which attacked ourselves and baby Lucien everyday with grim vengeance; and as we had no one to wait upon us, our suffering and loneliness was hard to bear." The frontier medicine chest was often limited; many home medical books tended to be more circumspect than helpful, and some of the treatments suggested undoubtedly would have done more harm than help. One popular medical treatise, William Buchan's *Every Man His Own Doctor,* included an "Appendix Containing a Complete Treatise on the Art of Farriery with Direction to the Purchasers of Horses; & Practical Receipts for the Cure of Distempers incident to Horses, Cattle, Sheep, and Swine . . . ," but the good doctor offered no advice on the treatment of snake bite, the setting of broken legs or arms, or the care of seriously ill children.

This lack of discussion of common frontier medical problems was typical of many of the books of medical advice for women, including those by the two directoresses of women's domestic life, Lydia Child and Catherine Beecher.[39] Most women relied on simple home remedies, careful nursing, and prayer. One woman recalled their home medicine chest included peppermint, which "would cure anything that ailed you—from colic in newborn babes—to aches and pains accompanying old age." She also recommended yarrow for coughs, colds, and for women who cramped "during monthly periods." These universal medicines along with senna and Epsom salts for purgatives, mustard plasters, and various "spring tonics," rounded out most frontier medical supplies. Occasionally desperate mothers would seek advice from Indian medicine men or Mexican *curanderos*, but most tried to get along with what they had or invented remedies based on their limited experience and medical knowledge. One Texas woman, for example, trying to save the life of her very weak infant daughter, bathed the child "in beef soup (made with lean meat and the bone left in) [and] not wiping her but wrapping her in blankets and putting her to sleep." Fortunately, this mother also procured a goat and put the child on a mixture of boiled water and goat's milk, and the baby survived. Under such circumstances, some women became skilled nurses and healers and were frequently called on by their neighbors in times of medical emergency. Mexican women were often responsible for the health of ranch and farm hands as well as that of their own families. Fabiola Cabeza de Baca recalled that her grandmother "was called every day by some family in the village, or by their *empleados*, to treat a child or some other person in the family." In the Mormon settlements, the church leaders encouraged women to practice the healing arts, and some received special training in nursing and medicine.[40]

Frontier mothers not only had to contend with the usual childhood diseases and accidents, they also had to worry about rattlesnakes, centipedes, scorpions, and other poisonous insects. Some worried that their small children might wander off on the prairies and plains and become lost. Many of their diaries and journals reveal their fears about the danger from wild animals, fires, and other natural hazards. Frontier mothers were well aware of the additional hazards to their children that their living conditions imposed, and they did their best to protect their offspring. One such mother, trying to keep her children warm during a raging blizzard, dressed them in their hats and coats and tried to keep them amused in the poorly heated kitchen, because "I was afraid to trust them alone in the papered room which a sheet-iron stove made very comfortable, they might fall against it or tip it over they had so little room to play in there."[41]

For some mothers, the worry over their children and the burden of child care in addition to their other duties was almost too much. "My children make me a great many steps as well as stitches," one weary woman wrote her father. Another confided to her diary, "Weary days of labor and pain. Have made 175 loaves of bread and 450 pies. Taken care of the children and done all the housework but the washing." Another harassed housewife who was trying to run the family farm and care for her house and children lamented to her husband, "It is no pleasure for me to visit with that crying baby of yours. I wish I had more patience with her. I think you ought to pay me liberally for raising her."[42] But other women obviously took birth and child care easily in stride and were almost casual about their children. "Very pleasant this morning," one wrote in her diary. "We have a nice little girl this morning before Cal came home," while another commented that she had "learnt to take it quite easy giving myself very little trouble about my juveniles." Some mothers enjoyed their children and found child care a pleasure rather than a burden. "I don't see as two babies are any more trouble than one," noted Kitturah Belknap. "I put them both in their little cradle and the little girl amuses the baby till he gets sleepy." "My babies were no trouble to me," another recalled. "They helped me too." Martha Crumbaker wrote that when she was left alone the "children are lots of company for me." But even the most adoring mothers must have had their bad days and cried, like Mary Mahoney, "I am going to get some switches as the boys are crying. They have driven me almost crazy."[43]

Aside from the daily tasks of cooking, sewing, mending, cleaning, and child care, women had special chores. In addition to preparing daily meals, they also made jams and jellies, dried many fruits and vegetables and preserved foodstuffs for the long winter months, and even canned some things in jars or tin cans sealing the tops with paraffin or a soldering iron. Most also planted and tended gardens, raised chickens and other livestock, and made their own butter and cheese. Many frontier women made their own candles and some fashioned part of their household furnishings. In all of these activities, they learned to improvise and to substitute for materials that were not available. "We put up jelly in tomatoe cans," Mary Hopping remembered, "but for jam we found a way to break the necks from beer bottles to make glasses for the jam; dishes were scarce and we found many uses for the beer bottles after the necks were broken off." Doña Eduarda Osuna Foxen found herself without candle molds, but she was able to form her candles by pouring the melted *sebo* (tallow) "upon strips of rolled tape hung from a horizontal bar."[44]

There were also a number of seasonal jobs which added to women's duties. During planting and harvesting some women helped in the fields, and others cooked extra meals for plowing and threshing crews. At hogkilling time, as one woman recalled, there was "lots to do." Men did the slaughtering and butchering, but the preparation of the meat was woman's work. Mary St. John reported that in one afternoon she had "cut up the pork, cleaned the souse, tried the lard," and still found time to churn and mop! On just one page of her diary, Kitturah Belknap inventoried a list of time-consuming seasonal jobs which would have defeated many women before they even began. During the winter, she spun "flax and tow to make some summer clothes." In the spring, at shearing time, the wool had to be "washed and picked and sent to the carding machine and made into rolls, then spun, colored and wove ready for next winter." Then came harvest time, and while her husband was in the fields, she busied herself "tending the chickens and pigs and making a little butter. . . . Butter is 12½c a pound and eggs 6c a dozen," she reported. "I think I can manage to lay up a little this year." Then the whole wearying round began again. "The work of this year will be about the same," Belknap noted. Yet in the midst of all this activity she still found time to keep her house, cook meals, and take time off to chaperone a group of young people attending a camp meeting.[45]

For some the multiplicity of tasks seemed overwhelming, as one young bride wearily reported.

I am feeling in an ill humor with myself and everybody tonight. I have just finished supper where there was nothing right. . . . I felt vexed in the first place about my chickens. Some of my neighbor's . . . chickens have taken up here and some of my hens gone. The chickens always mixin, 'tis vexatious and don't think that I'll be able to raise a single fowl and then at table I had to put so many things on that had been left off, found the meat fly blown, turned the milk over on the table indeed everything went wrong. Will sat and ate complacently as if there was no one on Earth saving and excepting himself. . . .

But other women were able to take things in their stride and even laugh at the situation. "Just done the chores," one wrote to a friend. "I went fence mending and getting out cattle . . . and came in after sundown. I fed my White Leghorns, and then sat on the step to read over your letter. I forgot my wet feet and shoes full of gravel and giggled joyously."[46]

In addition to their own chores, a number of women did extra work such as raising chickens or making butter to sell. Others did additional baking or sewing to supplement the family income. For example, when her husband fell ill, Mary Caples sold pies to the miners. "I sometimes sold a hundred a day," she wrote, "and not even a stove to bake them in, but had two small dutch ovens." Some women, like Keziah Finley, ran a small dairy operation. Irene Corder's mother "baked pies, bread, cakes and sold to the miners," while Sarah Baldwin's mother "made sunbonnets and sold them in the store." Matilda Delaney recalled a preacher's wife who carded and spun wool and knit socks to "sell to miners at a dollar a pair." Other women took in a boarder or two or did extra sewing or washing for single men in the neighborhood. Sometimes the money earned from such activities was used to purchase little luxuries or traded for extra supplies, but in other cases women's produce was needed "to help make the living."[47]

Women were also called upon to help with men's work. The frontier, like the trail, tended to blur sex roles. Everyone was expected "to lend a hand," and this often led women to perform tasks ordinarily considered outside their sphere. In more settled areas, hired hands, neighbors, or other family members might have been called in to help, but on the frontier, hired labor was not only expensive but often unavailable; friends and family were far away, and neighbors had their own work. Thus, from the earliest colonial frontiers, women worked beside their men to help clear the land, fell trees, construct a shelter, and plant and harvest crops. In seventeenth-century New Mexico, the women did much of the planting, irrigating, and harvesting and knew how to butcher and skin animals. In South Carolina, women helped their husbands grub the land, fell trees, and operate the whipsaws. According to a contemporary observer, women on the Vermont frontier in the eighteenth century were "often found in the fields assisting to secure the crops of hay and grain and not unfrequently were employed in piling logs and brush when their husbands were clearing the land." The same patterns were repeated on successive nineteenth-century frontiers. Although women were more accustomed to cooking, weaving, sewing, and similar household tasks, most realized, as one Oklahoma woman remarked, that "in those days the wife had to help do everything," and they joined their husbands in a number of traditionally masculine tasks.[48]

Many women helped to construct their first homes. "The girls soon learned to chink and daub and strip off the bark from the inside walls," Johnaphene Faulkner related. When the fireplace her uncles had built refused to draw and scattered sparks and ashes into the room every time the wind blew, making cooking impossible, the aunts fell to and built a cookhouse. "It was not exactly plumb," Faulkner noted, but "it served the purpose very well." Oklahoma pioneer Mary Edmonson recalled, "While John was building a place for us to live, I was digging a storm cellar and a place to keep the milk." Other women helped to "chink and daub," haul timber, drive nails, and generally made themselves useful. Maria Cable helped her husband with the crosscut saw, and she and her daughter also helped dig "the first well that was Dug on the prairie."

The indomitable Eliza Farnham did all the carpenter work for her elaborate two-story house in California. "Let not ladies lift their hands in horror," she admonished. "I laughed whenever I paused for a few minutes to rest, at the idea of promising to pay a man fourteen or sixteen dollars per day for doing what I found my own hands so dexterous in."[49]

Women not only helped build frontier homes, they also helped defend them. Prairie fires were a constant threat in many areas, and men, women, and children had to be prepared to clear firebreaks near houses and planted fields, to keep a sharp eye out for windblown sparks, and to help set back fires. As one young Kansas girl remembered the experience, "We all went out and set fires all around the ploughing . . . kept [them] burning until night and made out to save the premises. We were tired." From time to time, frontier women also had to help fight, or at least watch for, Indians. Many, like Margaret Hecox, found this a frightening experience, but they rarely allowed their fear to overcome a sense of duty. "I was always timid," Hecox recalled, but "I couldn't stand idly by, when danger threatened and my services were needed. . . . I put on my husband's hat and overcoat, then grasping our old flintlock between my shaking hands I went forth in the darkness to the corner of the wall assigned to me." A Texas woman, who admitted her fear of Indians, became so angry after one raid near her home that she set out to track the culprits and report their location to the then absent menfolk of the family. "Aunt Peggy and me and ouer [sic] children tract [sic] them Indians half a mile," she proudly proclaimed. And, she continued, "I have went many times and took my gun and lay in the corner of the fence and helped your Pa wach [sic] for Indians."[50]

On almost every American frontier from the Rio Grande to Hudson's Bay, from the Atlantic to the Pacific, there were stories about gallant women who shouldered their rifles and joined the men in defense of home and family. A chronicler of New Mexico wrote with great admiration of the display of valor of Doña Eufemia Peñalosa who rallied the women of Pueblo San Juan to "man" the housetops and assist in the defense of the village. In Canada a favorite story was told of the defense of a fort by the young Madeleine de Vercheres. Almost all readers were familiar with the various tales of bravery and courage of Anglo-American women in Kentucky or Minnesota or on the plains where women were "victors in hand-to-hand fights with savages . . . transforming them from gentle matrons into brave soldiers." Often these women seemed larger than life, like some of the men in the stories of deeds of frontier bravery. But most often women's encounters with Indians were not in pitched battles with marauding hostiles but with an occasional small party bent on begging or stealing food, horses, or other supplies. One pioneer wife, alone with her children, handled such a situation with determination. As one of the Indians approached her children, she picked up her water bucket and "started toward them saying: 'You-ca-shee' meaning in Indian 'Go away'. . . . it had the desired effect. They all scrambed to their feet and left at once. . . . After that I always shouted You-ca-shee as soon as an Indian approached." Most women handled their Indian problems in similarly firm, but non-violent, ways.[51]

Despite the many tales of women as Indian fighters and home defenders, their duties were more often associated with the plow than the rifle. Women and girls frequently joined the men in the fields to assist with planting and harvesting. As one woman recalled, "The thing you learn on a farm is that the cultivating of crops and the butchering is man's work, while everything, including cultivating the crops, is woman's work, except the butchering." At busy times of the year women "lent a hand" to plow and plant, cut and shock the wheat, pick the corn, or keep an eye on the livestock. Some became quite adept at these tasks. One woman noted that when she herded the cattle, "I often took my knitting or some other hand work along with me." One man bragged that his wife could plow as well as he could and since he was fond of baseball, "[I] sometimes left my wife home plowing while I went away for a game." Some frontier girls grew up more accustomed to field work than to kitchen chores. "I had learned to ride when I was almost a baby," one boasted. "I began to help herd the cattle at the age of 10. When I was in my early teens I began riding the 'line'." Another girl recalled that her older sister "Had to play the part of a son to father as well as a daughter to mother. She helped with the milking, drove cattle to pasture, and drove the teams for hauling hay."[52]

When their husbands were ill or absent, women often took over the entire burden of farming. When her husband was incapacitated by an accident, Rebecca Burlend wrote that she had succeeded in reaping, carrying, and stacking "our whole crop of wheat, consisting . . . of three acres, with no assistance other than that of my little boy under ten years of age." Burlend's experience was by no means unique. Frequently men were away from home for long periods of time fighting Indians, trying to earn extra money, or just "wandering." Mormon women often had the sole responsibility for farms and crops, and as Mary Ann Hafen somewhat bitterly recalled, it was difficult to oversee both home and farm chores and care for the children as well. Moreover, as another plural wife recalled, Mormon women who lived in the country received less monetary support from their husbands because they had "free" produce and foodstuffs. On other frontiers, too, women were left to carry on the farm work, often with no help other than that which the children could provide. As one such woman recalled, "My husband had taken his horses & arms & equipments & joined Capt. Lindsay Co. & left me to take care of the farm & effects." Her husband was gone so often that it became her responsibility to "live on the land until we made our final proof." Lizzie Simons, whose husband joined the Texas forces during the Civil War, wrote out a long list of the "unladylike jobs" she had to perform. She had the horse and buggy to harness and unharness, she complained, and when she "undertook to take the calf down to the lot it almost jerked me to pieces." Moreover, she found she had to become a cooper and caulker to keep her tubs and barrels in order, and she also "put in window glass— swung a gate" and "put new fossit [sic] in cistern." Mrs. W. O. Bishop recalled that her mother and the children "did a large share of the breaking of the ground and raised all the crops they could as my father spent much time working away from home to earn as many dollars as possible to supply some of the needs of the large family." Yet another woman took over the farming chores so that her preacher-husband could devote all his time to his scattered congregation.[53]

Like Simons, some women resented the necessity which forced them to assume "men's" work. Others enjoyed and took pride in their abilities and often boasted of their prowess in driving teams, planning and constructing improvements to their homes and farms, and fighting prairie fires, grasshoppers, and the elements. "I was said to be a good driver of horses," said one woman. "At any rate, when in my buckboard my husband who was on horseback, unless I wanted him to, could not pass me." Bragged another, "The men folks never doubted my ability to do most anything." Other women, too, spoke of their men's pride in their accomplishments, and it is clear that many of them enjoyed their outdoor work. "I have tried every kind of work this ranch affords and I can do any of it," wrote Elinore Stewart. "I just love to experiment, to work, to prove out things, so ranch life and 'roughing it' just suit me." Some women preferred outside chores to housework. Carrie Dunn remembered of her mother that "She was a neat and efficient housewife, but repairing fences, searching for livestock or hunting were always legitimate excuses to take her out."[54]

There is no doubt that a number of frontier women, particularly those on isolated farms and ranches, were often overburdened and even exploited by uncaring, or unconcerned, husbands. Amelia Perin's husband spent so little time on their farm that "Amelia saw to everything." Yet the ungrateful Sam Perin spent most of his time with the widow McCarthy and "gave away and/or sold many pieces of her jewelry." Abigail Scott Duniway wrote in indignation of the women she had known whose husbands took their butter and egg money to pay the taxes without so much as a "by your leave." Even women whose husbands did try to provide sympathetic understanding and help often found the burden of keeping home and children more than they could take. "I, mama, fully intended writing or commencing to write a year ago a brief sketch of our day to day life," mourned Ella Gale, "but getting settled in our new home took sometime, then Teddie had scarlet fever, then little Jessie made her appearance which caused the cook to leave and by that time I was so worn out and nervous that papa had to take me away to Granma Barstow." Other women were simply not suited to frontier life and, like the gently reared Southern woman described by a hardier pioneer, "she was dashed and buffeted by the winds of western life until her frail body broke."[55] Yet an amazing number of women managed their own work, helped with farm and ranch chores, and still found time to read, sew, visit, and add special touches to their homes.[56]

Recently feminist historians have emphasized the drudgery of frontier wives, particularly on the farms, and the failure of men to appreciate women's efforts. Although these writers acknowledged that men occasionally helped out, they still contended that women "regularly performed certain details of what were men's responsibilities" while "men only rarely took over women's work." Moreover, they asserted, men were singularly inept—and they implied deliberately so—at women's work. Women's diaries and reminiscences, however, clearly disputed this interpretation. Most women suggested that men frequently helped with heavier household chores and could and did take over child care and cooking duties when women were indisposed. According to Texas pioneer Willie Lewis, "men knew how to do the homely chores, like cooking and washing, as well as the female folk did." Harriet West remarked that her male ranch hands "did the cooking and did it well." Not only did these men "Make delicious biscuit and bread of all kinds," but they were also "well up in the preparation of all the dainties and finishing dishes." Other women also remarked on the skill of menfolk in baking bread, a sort of measure of a cook's skill. A number of women mentioned that their husbands became "chief cook and bottle washer" when the women were ill, although one admitted "only 2 meals when the man cooks." There was mention in many of the diaries of men helping with churning, washing, cleaning, "fetching and carrying," and other housework.[57]

Some historians have also emphasized that "the work women performed and the mental anguish they endured . . . was not repaid by a bond of inclusion in what was essentially a male-directed undertaking," and women were excluded from the decision-making process and often became "alienated and disheartened."[58] Yet it is clear from women's diaries that in many families women's work was respected; their role in the family's fortunes, and therefore in the decision-making process, was an important one. Many women's writings revealed a deep understanding of both the mechanics of the farm or business and the family's economic position. One woman wrote that "The women talked among themselves of chickens, gardens, sewing, housekeeping, the care of children and such . . . [while] men had more important matters to discuss such as stock, farming, the crop outlook and prospective prices." Yet this woman, like many others, was obviously familiar with "crop outlooks and prospects," and she, like other women, discussed these topics with her husband, if not with her female friends. Many women considered theirs a cooperative rather than a competitive enterprise, and they certainly did not view their position as "second class."[59]

Some feminists have suggested that the new household arrangements and the changed nature of women's work on the frontier represented compromise with, even subservience to, a male-dominated world. But rather than a surrender to male expectations, women's adaptation to frontier life was a realistic adjustment to physical and psychological realities. Men obviously realized that a period of change and accommodation was necessary if the frontier were to be conquered and civilized, and so did women. Within the new and often unfamiliar sphere of activities imposed by frontier conditions, women compromised few of their Eastern-dictated goals, but they did find new outlets of expression and new fields for personal development and satisfaction.

Were frontier women sometimes disappointed? Of course they were. Did they become discouraged, disallusioned? Of course they did. Did they cry into their pillows, rail at their husbands, fuss at their children? Of course they did. Their diaries and journals were filled with comments such as "am very blue today" or "feeling very discouraged" or "madder than a stewed witch" or "wish I was back at home."[60] These were ordinary women, often tired, ill, cramping, or pregnant. They laughed and cried; they were alternately happy and sad, optimistic and pessimistic. They had their good days and their bad ones, too. Some gave up the continuing battle to overcome frontier conditions as well as the usual problems of daily life. Most endured, indeed prevailed, and discovered a resilience, an inner store of courage and the means to overcome the obstacles presented by frontier living. Like other westering Americans, frontierswomen did what had to be done, under less-than-ideal circumstances, and they did it well.[61] In the process, they learned new ways of doing things and new things about themselves. Despite the increasingly narrow sphere of "woman's place" in nineteenth-century America, women on the frontiers, or at least on most of them, occupied an important place within the family. Their skills as artisans and producers of domestic goods were valued "in a society which judged a person by immediate results rather than by wealth, family name, or social class."[62] Women's knowledge of business and the economics of frontier life often stood them in good stead when their menfolk were absent or when they were left widows. In some instances their increasingly important role within the home and in the family's business brought them new opportunities to participate in community affairs and an enlarged sphere of social and political activity as well.

7

A Pioneer's Search for an Ideal Home[1]

Women, Family, and Community on the Frontier

A familiar image in Western American history is that of the lonely frontier woman, solitary, separated from home and companionship, a victim of the isolation, the wildness, of the frontier. Her story has been told in hundreds of books of both fact and fiction, and her likeness gazes from numerous prints, lithographs, and canvases. We recognize her, and her sisters, in the "Homesteader's Consorts," who,

> . . . longing to catch a glimpse of one of their own sex, swept their eyes over the boundless prairie and thought of their old home in the East. They stared and stared out across space with nothing to halt their gaze over the monotonous expanse. Sometimes the burning prairie got to staring back at them and they lost their courage.[2]

Certainly loneliness and isolation were a part of life on some frontiers. In the first days of settlement, homes were scattered, neighbors often miles away. Women, tied to home and hearth by a variety of tasks, often found themselves tired and lonely, filled with longing for familiar places and the faces of friends and family. "[H]ave not sean a wagon in tow month," wrote one ranchwoman in New Mexico, "Jest think of that and hardly unbody. I have [not] sean a woman in tow month only what is on the Ranch. [N]o one passes here a tall o my so very lonsome it is bad." "O How lonely, lonely, I feel from day to day and from week to week," recorded another. "How long must I remain in this isolated spot. . . ."[3]

Yet usually women's isolation was more perceived than real. The physical isolation imposed by distance or weather soon came to an end; new settlers arrived; the comforting sight of smoke from a neighboring cabin could be seen on the horizon; the long winters ended; spring came again. But isolation and loneliness were not the same thing. Frontier women were rarely isolated from people; they were surrounded by husband, children, hired hands, often Indians or other native people; but they still were lonely. They missed their old companions and family members. They gazed out across the seemingly endless stretches of prairies and plains and recalled the green, well-watered valleys of the East; they stared at the great mountains and virgin forests and remembered the New England villages, the gentle rolling prairies of the Midwest. Without rejecting their new homes and new friends, they longed for the old and familiar. As one reads their letters and diaries, one is struck by the frequency of comments about new friends, new delights in Western life juxtaposed with sad yearnings for home and family and bitter cries of loneliness, homesickness, and depression.[4]

Most of all, frontier women missed the company of other women. "Give a woman a chance to talk to a sympathetic listener about the things that interest her," one wrote, "and she will be happy."[5] But often a sympathetic listener in the person of another woman was not readily available. On those frontiers where men outnumbered women by ratios of five or six to one, women often lived for months without seeing another woman. "There were few settlers in the valley at that time," an Arizona woman recalled, "and it would be two or three months at a time that Mother and I would not see another white woman."[6] Wives of army officers frequently found themselves the only woman at a small Western garrison, and they looked forward to the occasional trips to a larger post or a settlement so that they might enjoy a brief visit with other women.[7] Even in the burgeoning towns, women were often as lonely for female companionship as on isolated farms and ranches. In Colorado, one woman recorded, there were twenty men for each woman in the settlement, and "I was the 8th white woman in Denver." Another commented of her first impression of San Francisco, "men were to be seen everywhere, nothing but men, not a woman—nor a child." Men were fine, in their place, but they were not the same kind of companions and friends as women. "If men was company to me like friends at home," one wrote, "I would never get lonesome."[8] These women were not isolated, but they were lonely.

For some women the lack of female companionship and the constant demands of their home duties were more than they could bear. One woman, constantly surrounded by male hired hands and boarders, contended that she was getting "very near the jumping-off place." Another filled her diary with mournful longings for other women's company. "I feel quite lonesome & solitary," she confided to her diary; "my spirits are depressed. I have very little female society, consequently feel lonely after a social visit. . . ." Another recalled her sense of abandonment when her husband "went north to teach school," and in addition to her loneliness, she faced "the hard work and inconvenience of managing the home on her own." Some broke under the strain of hard work, worry, and loneliness. Like the heroine, Beret, in O. E. Rölvaag's well-known novel *Giants in the Earth*, they grew "more sober . . . more locked up" within themselves while "a heavy heart lay all the time" in their bosoms. Rölvaag's Beret was fictional, of course, but her story was not different from those of some real women on the prairies and plains frontier. One, for example, confined to the house and farm, nursing a sick husband, throughout a "dreadful," "gloomy," and "long, dreary winter" lapsed into a severe state of melancholia and tried on several occasions to "destroy herself and the children." Fortunately, her story was unusual.[9]

Other women, however, managed to take their social isolation fairly well in stride. Some almost gloried in the solitude and quiet. Snowed in during the long Montana winter, Mary Ronan recalled, "I was conscious of no hardship, of no monotony. Outside was the endless variety of hills. . . . Inside was warmth and congeniality. . . ."[10] Others found alternative ways to deal with their homesickness and loneliness. Frances Reed recalled that her mother took over the task of making the three-day trips to town for supplies in order to enjoy "the company of other women." Another wrote to a solicitous friend that she was far too busy on her ranch to worry about being homesick. She admitted that when she thought of her friends, she felt "very lonely," but, she wrote, "I am not homesick. . . . I would like to see my friends, but would rather they come here."[11] Women also worked out new ways of neighboring over the long distances between isolated farms and settlements. They visited back and forth, usually for the entire day, taking their small children and some mending or other handwork with them to occupy their hands while they chatted and visited with a woman friend busy with her cooking or washing. The next week the visit was exchanged with a reversal in the type of work to which each woman attended. Women often exchanged services as well as visits. One Iowa woman, for example, exchanged her fine needlework with neighbor women who came to her home to help wash and clean, and they visited together at the same time. Quilting bees and wool-picking parties were frequent events which provided women with opportunities to enjoy each other's company while they attended to important tasks.[12] The tendency of Mexican-Americans to cluster in small villages rather than scattering "higgledy-piggledy" across the landscape made the problems of neighboring easier for these women. But Mexican-American women living on outlying ranches in Texas and California experienced the same feelings of loneliness and need for female companionship as did Anglo women.[13]

For some frontier women, no female society at all was preferable to "unsuitable" companions. "Interned," as it were, near Boise, Idaho, Mary Hallock Foote eschewed the society of the local ladies whom she declared "had ridiculous social pretensions and showed bad taste in their attempts to imitate what they conceived to be the latest Eastern fashions." One might understand the reluctance of a literary figure like Foote to mingle with "the locals," but ordinary women, too, had standards of proper society; and many were willing to endure the longing for female friends rather than "lower" what they conceived to be their own status. Writing to her mother-in-law in 1839, a young Illinois housewife mourned her lack of "Friends neighbors books papers. Here we have non [sic]," she reported,

> for the present inhabitants cannot be called civilised beings. They want no society nether are they fit for any but enoughf of this complaining. Such is my lot and I will be contented. I did think we should have some of our eastern people here but I have about given up that any will ever com [sic] to Ill. . . .

Almost four decades later Ann LeGrand sent a similar letter to her mother from the Texas frontier. "[W]e have some near neighbors," she wrote, "but they are beneath my notice if i cant keep good company I don't want any."[14] Such self-imposed social isolation was also common on army posts where women generally observed the required social distance between the officer's quarters and the laundresses' huts on Suds Row and in Mexican-American communities where *ricos* and *pobres* carefully maintained the correct relationships between masters and servants.[15]

Women were not the only frontier dwellers who experienced pangs of homesickness and loneliness, of course. Men, too, were sometimes lonely. They, too, left behind friends and family; they, too, were isolated from neighbors; they, too, were restricted by chores or bad weather to the narrow confines of house and farm. "Although I am making money here," one man wrote from California, "yet I am one of the most unhappy human beings on earth, and shall continue to be till I return to my family." A young Dakota homesteader described his physical isolation in terms of the distances to town and neighbors and concluded, "My claim was a lonesome place until I got used to it."[16] Men were customarily more restrained, less voluble about their feelings, but they, like women, suffered from the emotional traumas of separation from traditional family and friendship systems.

Men, however, frequently had more freedom of movement than women. "A woman does not see much satisfaction in this country," a Texas frontierswoman lamented:

there husbands are never with them much. . . . The men are always with a croud [sic], they see people nearly everyday. [T]hey hear news while they are gone and they are gone so long that they forget it before they get home or it is so old they think that everybody knows it.

Men were often gone from home for long periods of time, chasing Indians with the local militia, hunting and fishing, making trips to the nearest settlement for supplies, driving stock to market, or working at other jobs in order to earn money to support the family while they were "proving up" their homesteads. "[I] was alone most of my time," one woman wrote, "as my husband being a good carpenter & miner & prospector & Indian fighter . . . I [had] to live on the land untill we made our final proof."[17] Mormon women had a particularly difficult time. Their men were often gone on missions for the church, sometimes for as long as a year or two at a time. Mormon women whose husbands practiced polygamy and whose "sisters" did not share the same household were also often alone on isolated farms and ranches for long periods of time. Mary Ann Hafen recalled with some bitterness the difficulty of her first years in the new settlement at Bunkerville. Her husband had a number of church duties and three other families to care for while she had to care for her seven children, "mostly by myself." Her husband "provided us a house, lot, and land and he furnished some supplies. But it was a new country and we had a hard time to make a go of it."[18]

Even women whose husbands were theoretically at home often resented their spouse's freedom to come and go at will. "Burt is off to town early," Julia Hand complained. "I churn & mend, attend to cattle. . . . it is impossible for him to get home before dark any more & I am getting so tired attending to stock. indeed! it is midnight this time."[19] Women's work, closely tied to house and children, was indeed more confining than that of men. This was not, of course, a frontier phenomenon, but one which could be found in any predominantly rural area in nineteenth-century America. The separate worlds of men's and women's lives had been carefully shaped along the Atlantic seaboard and in the trans-Appalachian Midwest, and these patterns of family life were only modified, not discarded, by further Western migration.[20] However, pioneering brought changes, sometimes temporary, sometimes permanent, in the relationships between the sexes. Men and women worked together to meet and solve the problems and challenges posed by wilderness living. Men sometimes had to enter woman's sphere at least briefly to help with normal women's tasks, such as washing and child care, which required assistance under frontier conditions. More frequently, women had to help with or take over chores ordinarily considered men's work. Such role reversals plus the problems and anxieties of building a new home and trying to provide greater economic security and opportunities for themselves and their children placed strains on even the most compatible marriages. During the nineteenth century, family structure underwent "a wrenching transformation" under the multiple impact of industrialization, urban growth, and the breaking up of traditional family patterns as young people moved to the city or across the continent to a new frontier.[21] Women often found themselves without traditional support systems and had to develop new ones. In the process, marriage relationships changed as well.

Some women clung to traditional patterns of love and marriage and seemed to have been both happy and fulfilled. "I often reprimand myself severely for wishing to hurry the moments," Margaret Lea Houston wrote her often absent husband, "[but] my husband is so inexpressibly dear to me that I can not be happy without him." Another woman remembered her twenty years at an Indian Agency, isolated from civilization, with great affection:

> Keeping my household organized, attending to the needs of growing children, the insistent demands of a baby . . . counseling my husband when, in our mutual concerns, we felt that two heads were better than one, all combined to keep me in the midst of enthusiastic activity and burning with a sense of quickened and multiplied consciousness.

Other women, too, related the growing sense of partnership and mutual sharing of concerns necessary for frontier living. Carrie Strong Robbins, embarking on a new marriage and a new life in the West, confided some of her fears for the future to her diary, "but," she concluded, "we love each other so dearly, I know we shall be very happy."[22]

The optimism of the first years of marriage did not always result in a happy future, of course. Many frontiering families were successful in securing a better life for themselves and their children, but others were not. Leaving her first Nebraska home because of their inability to pay off the mortgage, Luna Kellie's usual optimism failed her. "We both realized," she wrote, "that in leaving our first home we had left not only our youth but most of our hope there. While one has youth and hope or either of life, life is not a burden, work is not a drudging but without them it becomes almost unbearable." Some women blamed their husbands, at least partially, for such failures. Recalling the way in which her husband had been cheated on some loans, Olive Brown wrote to her children: "He was so good and trusting. It doesn't pay to trust any body or go on anybody's note." Another woman whose husband had drifted from job to job was more circumspect in writing about her married life for her children. " 'The wise forget' many things," she advised, "and refuse to listen to recollections that come to haunt them, so I will not enter into the disallusions and disenchantments that cloud the life of every mortal." Others, however, were more open in expressing their dissatisfactions. Writing to her absent husband, one woman berated, "I do not know but I will die of fear and lonliness [sic]. You have plenty good company & are differently situated. . . . I sometimes think that men's stern nature is not so susceptible as the wife's." "[M]y companion is at Bill Hoovers store playing drafts," wrote another disgusted young wife; "it seems to me that he would rather be their [sic] playing them than to be at home with me and his little boy . . . I don't guess that he is thinking or caring how long and lonesome the hours are to me here alone in this old cabin."[23] Such complaints were not exclusive to frontier women, but they were exacerbated by frontier conditions and the lack of usual female support systems.

Some women feared that the long years of pioneer deprivation and worry and their own physical changes brought on through childbearing and hard work had diminished their husbands' affections. Writing on the eve of her wedding anniversary, a young Texas woman mourned:

> I think you have undergone a gradual change and that the present finds you a far different man from what you were eight years ago. . . . and that the wife of day [sic] is a far different creature from the bride of eight years ago, that she has not the same call upon your love, and sympathy that she had then.

Another, grieving the loss of her infant daughter, was sure her husband blamed her for the child's death. "Oh God," she cried, "thou who readest the heart knowest—my husband and the father of my children *loves me not* alas—I fear me he even looks upon me with disgust. Why? O Why?"[24] Most women were more inclined to berate their husbands than themselves, however. "My man came home about half mad," one wrote, "but he can't scare me much. He will have to scratch his mad place and get in a good humor." One South Dakota woman became so angry at her husband that when he and another man were chased by a small party of Indians while out cutting hay, she clapped her hands together and shouted, "I hope they kill him, I hope they kill him!" and calmly walked back into the house. Others took more direct action. Rena Mathews recalled that her mother "followed her husband, with a growing family of five— from one end of the state to another. . . . After seventeen years of these wanderings, Mother obtained a separation and settled in Sacramento. . . ."[25]

Separation and divorce were increasingly common in the nineteenth century. As part of the general plea for reform of laws relating to married women, divorce laws were revised in a number of states. Western states were the most liberal in admitting new grounds for divorce and in simplifying the divorce process. Indiana in the 1850s and South Dakota in the 1880s both preceded Reno, Nevada, as the mecca for discontented spouses.[26] Even in Mexican California where the Church's strong injunction against divorce was upheld in the civil law, annulments ("a process by which putative spouses were returned to the status of single persons") and judicially granted separations were permitted. Both appear to have been used fairly freely by both Mexican and American residents prior to the institution of American law in the area.[27]

Despite the relative ease of divorce in the Western states and territories and the appearance of divorce mills in some Western towns, most frontier marriages remained conservative and traditional. Women generally accepted the idea that they, more than their husbands, were responsible for creating the climate and conditions for a satisfactory relationship. "You have . . . in your power all the essential ingredients of domestic happiness," one mother advised her newly married daughter.

> The first maxim which you should impress deeply upon your mind is never to attempt to control your husband by opposition, by displeasure, or any mark of anger. . . . If he be a good man, he expects from you smiles, not frowns. . . . Besides, what can a woman gain by opposition or indifference? Nothing; but she loses everything. She loses her husband's respect for her. She loses his love, and with that all prospect of future happiness.[28]

Most women who found themselves in less-than-happy marital circumstances simply made the best of the situation. A few, like an unhappy Texas woman overburdened by childbearing, illness, and her husband's frequent absences, retreated into melancholia, alcoholism, or an opium-induced euphoria.[29] Most, however, simply devoted themselves to their children and a flurry of domestic activities or turned to the solace of religion or community work.

Whatever their marital or familial relations, Western women, unlike many of their Eastern sisters, participated actively in many phases of community life. Given the supposed isolation of frontier families, the discussions of dances, parties, visits, and other entertainments found in women's diaries and reminiscences seems surprising. However, as noted above, complete physical isolation was relatively rare on most frontiers. As soon as the first difficult months were past and there was a small nucleus of settlers, frontier residents found many ways to provide opportunities for social intercourse. Frontier amusements, although simple, were numerous and frequent.

Dances were an especially popular form of socializing, and they varied in size, kind, and custom from one area to another. In some areas only square dances or folk dances could be held since conservative families frowned on more modern forms of dance. As one young woman remembered, her parents were very strict and would not let her waltz or "round dance."[30] In the larger settlements formal balls and cotillions were held in suitably decorated halls with an exclusive guest list, elaborate gowns, and skilled musicians.[31] In the county seats, court week was usually the occasion for a good deal of entertainment, including dances and parties and much visiting among families who had come from the surrounding countryside to attend to legal matters, marketing, and other business.[32] In most areas, however, the dances were informal, neighborhood affairs. Everybody was invited; clothing as well as decorations and refreshments were simple (although everybody donned their Sunday best). Often the entire family attended. The babies were put down to sleep in charge of one or more teenagers, and the younger children played games or watched the dancing until they nodded off to sleep. Occasionally other adults were pressed into service to watch the children while their friends enjoyed the dancing. Idaho pioneer Mary Hopping remembered a woman with a baby who was asked to dance. "A bachelor was sitting nearby," she recalled, "and the lady plumped her baby down in his lap and said, 'yer—Hold this youngin' while I dance and if he cries you wallop 'im.' This lady believed in making a bachelor useful as well as ornamental." Often these dances lasted all night or at least until three or four o'clock in the morning when first light allowed the sleepy participants to find their way to their distant homes. Another Idaho woman wrote, some came "from thirty to forty miles to attend the dance. They served a sumptuous supper at midnight and all stayed for breakfast, enjoying themselves immensely visiting as well as dancing." Of course, the participants often felt the effects the next morning. "Feel worse than a stewed witch," one woman wrote. "I say farewell to dances for me. . . ." But the next week or the next month they were off to another one. "They never tired of dancing," summed up one woman. "The host furnished a house; the guests did everything else. . . . [They] danced the whole night through. When the east was grey with dawn, they returned . . . to morning chores and a day of farm work."[33]

In areas where church members frowned on dancing or where there were no musicians or musical instruments, the play-party substituted for the all-night dance. The play-party, like many other adaptations made by pioneer settlers, was a frontier institution, a way of providing entertainment with the means at hand. It required "no organization, no management, no dancing-floor, no musician," only a group of enthusiastic participants and a room in a hospitable home. Young men on horseback spread the word that there was to be a play-party, and about dusk the guests would begin to gather at the appointed place. The host and hostess cleared the party room of all furniture, took up the rag carpet, and placed makeshift benches around the walls. When enough guests had assembled someone would begin to sing one of the play-party songs and lead the players through familiar steps and actions. Everyone knew the words and the motions, and leadership passed from one to another of the participants as they played Snap, Pig in the Parlor, Bounce Around, Skip-to-my-Lou, We'll All go Down to Rowser, or one of the other party favorites. Later in the evening the more daring might join in a reel-like Weevily Wheat, frowned on in more conservative communities because of its similarity to "real dancing." At midnight refreshments were served and, like the dances, most participants stayed all night or until dawn provided enough light for them to start for home. "We played games until 12 o'clock," one young woman recalled, "when we had a supper, then played until morning." Play-parties were popular throughout the late nineteenth and early twentieth centuries and persisted in some remote rural areas of the Midwest until after World War I. As other forms of entertainment—concert halls, theaters, dances with musicians—became available, the play-party usually disappeared along with the other "make-do" aspects of frontier life.[34]

Parties, fiestas, and dances or *bailes* were also popular on the Hispanic frontiers. Like other pioneer entertainments, these were usually community affairs in which everyone participated and which often lasted for several days. Any occasion—a wedding, a baptism, a major saint's day—provided an excuse for a fiesta and dance. So frequent were such occasions among the *rancheros* of Southern California that one woman remarked that "dancing, music, religion, and amiability were the orthodox occupations" of the area. A favorite custom at Mexican-American festivals and dances was the breaking of *cascarones*, egg shells filled with gold and silver confetti and cologne or different colored liquids. Often, as a young Mexican woman remembered, "the ladies' dresses and faces suffered, but we all took it in good part." Cockfights, bullfights, rodeos, and bear hunts, often followed by bull and bear fights, were also popular forms of amusement along the Spanish and Mexican frontiers as were more sedate entertainments such as the staging of traditional secular and religious plays such as "Los Comanches" (a particularly popular New Mexican drama) and "Los Pastores," described by a California woman as "kind of a religious comedy in which appeared various characters, among them an Angel, the Devil, a Hermit, a Bartelo."[35]

The variety of frontier amusements and entertainments was seemingly endless. Many were variations of familiar Eastern activities; others were unique to the time or place. In the towns and small settlements there was a good deal of visiting, both formal and informal. In the larger, more settled communities, these visits often followed the protocol of Eastern social calling. "There is a great deal of Fashion & Style here," a California woman wrote her sister. "We ladies visit only in the afternoon and rarely ever stay untill [sic] after Tea." A Denver woman recalled, "Every woman knew when her friend's day at home came, and afternoon calls formed a part of every woman's plan of life and a schedule . . . [was] carefully observed."[36] Usually frontier visiting was a good deal less formal, however. "If your friends are coming to see you, they don't wait for ceremony, but come whenever they feel like it," an Oregon woman informed her mother. "I think it just suits me for I don't put myself out any and I have a good deal of company." Not only friends, but total strangers came to call. An Illinois woman recorded that in her small community visits were paid on Sunday when

> there would be a tremendous knocking at the door accompanied by the sonorous demands of . . . a loud drawling, "h-o-u-s-e-k-e-e-p-e-r-s!" and when the door was opened a backwoodsman would walk in with a big baby on his arm, following by his wife with the youngest in both her arms, would introduce his lady and let us know they had come for a day's visit.

Often a woman had barely arrived in a frontier community when her neighbors, some from many miles away, hurried to bid her welcome and get the latest news from the East. "We had visitors from the first day we started housekeeping," an Oregon woman recalled. Sometimes frontier housekeepers had so much company that they were glad of some time to themselves. After the departure of a series of short-term boarders and a round of visits from travelers and neighbors, Chestina Allen noted in her diary, "A happy day because we are alone once more."[37]

The custom of visiting was not confined to any one frontier or to one sex. On the Hispanic frontiers, the paying of calls was so popular that a special verb, *jacalear*, was coined to describe the custom of visiting from house to house. Formal, as well as informal, calls were made by men as well as women. Sometimes these were courting calls—opportunities for young men and women to get to know one another, but men, both single and married, often called on women and spent a pleasant hour or two in conversation. As with calls between women, such visiting might be very formal and carried out according to a strict protocol or simply a "drop-in" visit in the evening or on Sunday afternoon. Especially in mining camps and other areas where there were few women, lonely men took advantage of any opportunity to spend some time in a familiar homelike atmosphere.[38]

Musical evenings, both formal and informal, were enjoyed throughout the West. Although Bach and Mozart were not particularly popular outside the larger cities like San Francisco and San Antonio, frontier settlers enjoyed music and looked forward to the arrival of a talented musician and musical instruments. Local historians recorded the arrival of the first piano or the first parlor organ with the same enthusiasm as the first school and the first preacher. In fact, it is rather surprising how many families managed to take pianos, small organs, and melodeons with them to their new Western homes. Mrs. Isaac Moore, for example, took her piano with her from Kentucky to Denver, and army wife Emily Andrews had hers shipped by boat from Boston to Galveston and then taken by Army wagon to Fort Davis, Texas. The Tansill family arrived at Menard on the Texas frontier with "no furniture . . . no stove, not even a fireplace," but the beloved piano was hauled from the railhead near Houston and provided many happy evenings of entertainment for the family and the ranch hands who came from miles around to listen to the girls play and sing. Those who were unable to bring pianos or organs with them ordered them from the East just as soon as transportation facilities were available, and letters filled with elaborate instructions as to size, make, and wood and shipping arrangements went to families and friends from frontier dwellers. Immigrants also carried violins, fiddles, guitars, and a variety of other instruments with them, and many a frontier community soon had a local band which played for dances, parades, and patriotic occasions and gave evening or Sunday afternoon concerts.[39]

Town dwellers could also take advantage of occasional visiting lecturers or traveling troupes of players or musicians. One young woman recorded in her diary that she had attended an astronomy lecture and the following week another given by a balloonist. Town women enjoyed musicals, teas, and card parties including the popular "Salamagundi progressives" where the guests moved from house to house to enjoy refreshments and various games such as "Muggins, Loto, dominoes, checkers, and Pigs in Clover." A young Washington girl recalled that help was hard to get so the girls had ironing parties in the evening. "While we ironed the gentlemen prepared supper. They were experts at baking clams, oysters on the half shell and mixing innocent drinks. Thus we turned work into play and obliterated hardship."[40]

Army wives whose husbands were stationed at Western garrisons devised a number of ways to combat the tedium and monotony. At the smaller posts they spent their days riding, hunting, tending their gardens, or took up botany, painting, or other hobbies to help while away the hours. Frances Roe, for example, stationed at many small posts in Colorado and

Montana, soon developed "a real passion" for hunting and fishing and noted sanctimoniously that "only stay-at-homes complained of the days being long and tiresome." At the larger posts the wives planned picnics, parties, and "hops," held amateur theatricals, attended colorful parades and band concerts or gave fancy dinners for visiting dignitaries or helped with an occasional wedding or special holiday celebration. Often they had to borrow or improvise to provide the proper accoutrements. Katherine Gibson recalled a party at Fort Lincoln where "a long table was set up, and a rubber bucket containing wild flowers marked the joining of each set of carpenter's horses. Handkerchiefs served to cover the bare planks in lieu of doilies, which gave something of a festive touch, the men gallantly declaring the effect to be ravishing."[41]

In more isolated or rural areas, the pleasures were simpler but equally varied. Settlers in the Pacific Northwest enjoyed clamming while frontier dwellers throughout the West participated in berrying and fishing parties. These recreational activities served a practical purpose as well. As one woman wrote, "we enjoyed very much . . . going to the mountains for thorny gooseberries, or down into the canyons along the river for wild grapes. . . . Soon after the middle of August parties were organized and men, women, and children could be seen heading for the mountain or down the canyon to gather our winter fruit." In the Midwest and on the Northern Plains sleighing was a popular winter amusement which allowed settlers an opportunity to get out of the cabin or dugout and enjoy the fresh air and socialize a bit with the neighbors during the long, often dreary winters. In the summer sleighing gave way to horseback and buggy rides. Ingenious prairie residents took "slicker" rides. As described by a Kansas woman, "A cellar door would make a good one or a low flat sled with a ring in front to which we hitch a horse. Then we go first gliding over the prairie. Some of the people fasten a spring seat on it. But Cephas and I put a chair on and then lay a board on that. The only trouble with that arrangement is that we must sit down together and get up together, or we will be likely to sit down (on the ground) separately." Other seasonal activities included harvest dances and husking bees. During threshing season women often worked together to provide the huge meals for the crews. At hog-killing time in the South and Midwest several men worked together to slaughter and clean the animals while their wives made sausage and packed down the meat for the winter while the children made "candy stew" (a kind of cooked molasses that was pulled like taffy) and salvaged the hog bladders for "Christmas guns." In the later part of the nineteenth century, meetings of the Grange, and later the Farmer's Alliance, provided opportunities for rural folk to socialize as well as to discuss economic and political problems, and such activities became a regular part of the Western social scene.[42]

Camping and sight-seeing trips were also a favorite recreational activity. Even fairly recently arrived overlanders hitched up the horses to a buggy or wagon, reloaded the camp equipment, and went off on long trips to see the local natural wonders. Yosemite held special charms for California pioneers. In 1855 James M. Hutchins led the first party of sight-seers into the valley, and the following year three women—a Madame Gautier, a Mrs. Thompson, and Mrs. John Neal of Mariposa—became the first women tourists in the area. Thereafter camping parties and groups of eager sightseers entered the valley in increasing numbers. So popular did the area become that in 1858 William C. Ralston, a San Francisco banker, and his bride Elizabeth Fry, invited their entire wedding party to share their wedding trip to Yosemite. A hotel was built near present Four Mile Trail in 1858, and another was opened in 1859, but many visitors continued to camp out rather than avail themselves of the hotel facilities.[43] Women also visited Mount Hood, climbed Pike's Peak, and explored the Grand Canyon. Scenic wonders, however, were not the only attraction. Summer camping trips to the mountains and fishing and camping trips to various rivers and streams offered a welcome respite from the heat and the monotony of daily life.[44]

Families who were far from neighbors and who could only rarely attend social functions also found ways to occupy their leisure time. They, too, took trips to visit distant friends or to see the local scenery or spend a pleasant day or two hunting and fishing. Reading was a favorite pastime in many frontier families, and they looked forward to receiving new books, magazines, and newspapers which were read and reread from beginning to end. Some women occupied their spare hours in teaching their children, but they also attempted to improve their own education. Some studied French or Spanish or attempted to learn the local Indian language. Others, like the army wives, took up hobbies such as painting, guitar, fancy sewing or, where it was impossible to obtain special materials for such activities, concentrated on learning about the local flora and fauna. For example, Emma McIntyre and her husband, who for several years were the only whites at St. George in the Pribilof Islands, made a careful study of the natural history of the region. Emma made a collection of plants and flowers of the island and kept detailed climatic records while her husband stuffed birds and collected boat models. Fortunately for later historians, a few women like Mary Hallock Foote and Elizabeth Custer wrote articles about their Western adventures for Eastern magazines while many others kept detailed journals and diaries or wrote reminiscences and recollections about their pioneer life for their children and grandchildren.[45]

At holiday times even the most isolated families attempted to organize some kind of social activity or at least to provide a "little something special" for the children. Frontier mothers popped corn and "boiled molasses candy for the babies" and made little gifts for birthdays, Christmas, and other special occasions. In most frontier communities, holidays provided a convenient excuse for a party or dinner or a recitation or play at the schoolhouse followed by a community Christmas tree, singing convention, dance, or other activities. An Illinois woman remembered a special New Year's dinner given by the local tavern owner with "cornbread, backbones and ribs with gravy and coffee" which was enjoyed by the entire neighborhood. A Colorado woman wrote that although their social life was "quite limited," they had been entertained by the "nearest neighbors" at Christmas time and "had a fine dinner." Halloween parties and dances, Thanksgiving dinners and Fourth of July picnics, frequently with political oratory and patriotic music, provided other opportunities for women to visit and socialize and to break the monotony and tedium which were a part of the hard work of making a frontier home.[46] Men enjoyed these activities and chances to visit as much as women, and in some communities men, rather than women, took the initiative in planning social affairs.[47] More often, however, the women planned, organized, and coordinated social events and in the process learned a good deal about participation in community life.

Women were interested in more than homemaking and socializing, however. Just as women tried to make their frontier home more homelike so they also attempted to civilize raw Western communities. On the trails West women, and men, longed for the familiar manifestations of civilized society—churches, schools, established law and order—but these had to be subordinated to the pressing need for getting there. Where possible, they improvised with temporary services and meetings, but these institutions were generally unsatisfactory substitutes. Once their homes were established, pioneers looked to the building of schools and churches, as the necessary next step in banishing wilderness and taming the frontier. Women's diaries contained frequent references to the establishment of schools and churches, and their reminiscences were replete with descriptions of the first school, the first Sunday school class, the first preacher, and the first church building. In fact, Western progress was often measured in terms of the development of these important institutions. "The country is settling up very fast," one woman wrote. "There is no school nor church as yet in this place. There is preaching once in three or four weeks at private houses." Another noted, "Society was organizing itself faster than we could keep up with it. Churches, schools, clubs, and companies were formed on every side."[48] Obviously wilderness had been partially overcome when churches and schools were available, and just as women played an important role in establishing new homes on the frontier, so they also participated actively in the development of new communities and social institutions.

Until a community was large enough to support new social institutions, pioneer families had to improvise. In the early days in a new frontier area, mothers, and sometimes fathers, with sufficient time and education tried to teach their children at home. This added to the cares and duties of already overburdened parents, but the importance of education made it seem worthwhile. "It makes me feal sorry to See them growing up in ignorance," wrote a Texas frontier mother; "Mollie can Spell & read a little but Julie dount no her letters. I am going to get them some books and try to learn them at home." Sometimes literate parents agreed to help instruct the neighbors' children as well. An Iowa girl noted with some pride that "During two winters school was conducted in our house; and father taught the school. . . ."[49]

Some parents were concerned that their children would not receive a proper education in distant frontier areas and sent them "back East" to school. Sometimes both husband and wife agreed to give up pioneering for life in a town or settlement where there were more advantages for growing children. "Mother did not let any of the unusual life about us interfere with our bringing up," a young Arizona girl recalled. "Except for the desire of giving us a more extended education than we could get in the state at that time, I am sure my father and mother would have remained . . . instead of removing to New Mexico."[50]

The usual solution to the problem of the children's education was not to send the children East or move to town but to establish a local school. Settlers were anxious that their children not only learn to read and write but that they be inculcated with the social, economic, and political values which represented civilized society. Schools were perceived as civilizing agencies, and their appearance in a newly settled area represented a first step in dispelling the wilderness and opening the way for a progressive, orderly community. As soon as there were enough families in an area, attempts were made to organize a regular school and hire a teacher. "Mothers with their children, though they did not count a dozen all told, felt the necessity of some kind of schooling," one woman remembered. Another young woman recalled her father's efforts to "round up" enough "scholars" for a school. The area where they lived had only five children of school-age and six were required to "hold school a full term," so her father traveled about the countryside until he found four children "who didn't have access to another school" and brought them home to board during the school term. Even single men often realized the need for schools in a new community. Lucia Darling recalled her encounter with a rough, old man she hoped would rent her a room for a school. " 'Yes, glad of it,' he said, 'D——d shame, children running around the streets, ought to be in school. I will do anything I can to help her, she can have this room.' "[51]

In some areas the first schools were church related. This was especially true in New Mexico, Arizona, parts of Texas, California, and Colorado where the Roman Catholic parochial schools were the only educational institutions during the Spanish and Mexican period. Even after these areas became part of the United States, the Church continued to dominate the educational field until the latter part of the nineteenth century. At first most of these schools were taught by priests or friars from one of the missionary orders, but after 1850 several orders of teaching nuns came into the area to establish both Indian and non-Indian schools. Some of the *rico* families sent their children to Mexico City or later to Saint Louis to school or hired private tutors, but many Hispanic children, especially among the poorer classes, received little or no education unless they had access to the church schools. As a young California girl recalled, "Owing to . . . the great difficulty of obtaining teachers, most of the girls of the time had scanty education."[52] After 1850 Protestant missionaries also founded schools in New Mexico and Arizona and later in Indian Territory. The various Protestant denominations also established a number of colleges and seminaries throughout the West.[53]

In other areas the first schools were private, housed in homes, rented rooms, or whatever facilities were available. Many of these were established by young, educated Eastern women or by husband-and-wife teams seeking new opportunities in the West. Private schools required tuition payments, however, and although the costs were small, they were often more than frontier families could afford. "At that time we did not have public money," a California girl recalled, "and we had to pay our tuition . . . so we did not get as much schooling as we would have liked." Thus citizens tried as soon as possible to organize a public school district and erect a permanent school building. The buildings were usually modest structures of logs or sod, often built by the settlers themselves and furnished with plain benches and tables for the scholars and the most meager pedagogical equipment. An Iowa girl's recollection of her school was fairly typical of other frontier schools:

> it was 2½ miles north west to our log school house with puncheon benches to set on no backs to them no desks in front had a table up where the teacher sat there we went once a day to write in our coppy-books our studies were reading writing spelling & a little arithmatic.

Even these simple structures were often built at great cost and effort. In Trempealeau County, Wisconsin, building costs for the schools in 1855 were $100 to $150, but by 1869 costs had risen to $1500. Even when the men joined together to build the schools themselves, the cost in time and effort were considerable. A Texas woman recalled an incident near Marble Falls when some neighbors decided to build a school house. "[T]he crude building took much of their time and energy," she wrote. "These pioneers had dreams of educated children, but alas! In a few weeks after the completion of their dream school . . . it was burned by Indians."[54]

Although many Western states and territories provided for a public school system, they did not provide state financing, and funds for local schools had to be provided by the local community. In frontier areas where there was little cash and a reluctance to tax, money was often raised by public subscription or by various benefits and socials. In one Oklahoma community, for example, the Ladies Aid Society raised the money to pay the teacher. In other communities women put on box suppers, theatricals, and other entertainments to raise funds for schools. Sometimes they also pitched in and helped with the building. The school board "took up collections and bought rough lumber," one woman recalled, "and they and the pupils and I built that school house with our own hands."[55]

Western women also took an increasingly active role in formal school activities. During the eighteenth and early nineteenth centuries, few women had sufficient education to teach, and most school boards believed that men were better disciplinarians, particularly with older, rowdier pupils. In the 1830s and 1840s, however, the number of women in the teaching profession increased. The post-Revolutionary generation witnessed a rapid growth in educational opportunities for women,[56] and the establishment of graded schools created a demand for more teachers. The evolution of the primary school also opened the door a bit wider for women since educational leaders reasoned that younger children could be "more genially taught and more successfully governed by a female than by a male teacher."[57] On the more practical level, women could be hired for less money. Although some states attempted to legislate equal pay for male and female teachers, it was generally understood that female teachers would work for less than their male counterparts. All of these factors contributed to an increase in the number of women teachers; and although most school districts were organized and administered by men, by the 1870s, the majority of the teachers were women. This was especially true in the Western states.[58]

Western communities often had difficulty finding teachers. Frequently they turned to the wives and daughters of local men who were willing to teach a term or two in order to earn extra money for little luxuries or to supplement the family income. A number of teachers were single women who hoped to earn money to furnish their "hope chest" or to provide for their basic needs until they married. Many were little better educated than their pupils, and some did not particularly like teaching; but teaching provided one of the few economic opportunities for women outside the home and domestic sphere.

In order to meet the increasing demand for properly trained teachers for the rapidly growing Western communities, the Western states took the lead in providing equal educational opportunities for men and women in the new state universities. When the first class entered the University of Iowa in 1856, it included eighty-three men and forty-one women. Two years later the board of education provided that both men and women would be admitted to the University on equal terms. Gradually other Western universities followed Iowa's lead. By 1870 Wisconsin, Kansas, Indiana, Minnesota, Missouri, Michigan, and California all admitted women to their state universities, although not always on equal terms with men.[59] Although some conservative school boards preferred male teachers, especially for the winter term when the older boys were most often in attendance, more and more women were accepted as equal, if not superior, teachers.[60] Women, after all, were considered the cultural censors and moral guardians of nineteenth-century society, and it seemed appropriate that they might transfer some of their teaching of social, cultural, and religious values from the home to the schoolroom. So important was women's role in this area believed to be that during the 1830s Catherine Beecher, backed by the American Lyceum, began a campaign to send as many as 90,000 female teachers to the West to "civilize and Christianize" raw frontier communities.[61]

Although women did not often receive equal pay for their teaching, they did have opportunities for professional advancement. When the franchise was opened to Western women, elective school offices such as county superintendent or even statewide posts were also opened to them. In Colorado, for example, by 1906 thirty-four of the fifty-nine counties had women superintendents. In other Western states, as well, women served as principals, superintendents, and sometimes on state boards of education. It was also significant that states that did not grant full suffrage voted school suffrage for women at a fairly early date.[62]

Since the teacher was a prominent and very public figure in small Western communities, her role as both civilizer and community leader could be an extremely important one. In Eastern towns (with the possible exception of New England) and throughout the rural Midwest and South, women did not participate in public affairs. Women were systematically excluded from public life and, as a modern historian phrased it, "remained in their domestic spaces, in a mild kind of rural American purdah."[63] In Western communities this tradition of women's nonparticipation in community affairs was changed and modified. As women began to participate in public affairs as teachers and as voters on school issues, Western residents could clearly see for themselves that public life need not cause the defeminization of women or change their basic domestic instincts, and women could enter public life in other areas as well.

Education and religion were considered the twin harbingers of civilization, and women participated in community life through the churches as well as through the schools. Since women were viewed as moral guardians of family and domestic life, their devotion to and role in church life was consistent with prevailing social and religious theory. Even in rural societies which excluded women from most public events, churches and religious meetings were an exception.[64] Moreover, serious religion was woman's work. Women, most Americans believed, were "happily formed for religion" by means of their "natural endowment, . . . modest, superior delicacy, . . . natural softness and sensibility . . . and imagination." Men must, of necessity, concern themselves more with the worldly affairs of politics and economics attendant upon daily life, but women, "because they were above and beyond politics and even beyond producing wealth," were free to seek God and ensure moral and religious virtues in the home and in the education of the children.[65]

Women might be seen as the guardians of morality and virtue in the home and as the more serious believers in religion, but men and women worked together to bring religion as well as education to the West. Americans saw the untamed wilderness as immoral and irreligious, and men and women alike decried the lack of churches and other suitable moral and religious institutions.[66] "The Sabbath is greatly desecrated *here*, and religion is at a very low ebb," reported Julia Lovejoy from Kansas. "There was no church in town today so we have according to custom spent the holy day in idle chit-chat," complained a Texas woman, while a Wisconsin man exclaimed, "Today is the Sabbath! O that the Lord would raise up a people in this valley who will delight to do His will. O that we might have Sabbath and sanctuary privileges once more."[67]

Pioneers were not the kind to wait for the Lord to build churches and bring ministers to the wilderness. Until a community was prosperous enough to build a church and pay a preacher, frontier settlers relied on Sunday schools, singing meetings, and other informal, lay-led activities supplemented by itinerant preachers and camp meetings to fulfill their religious needs. The arrival of an itinerant or circuit-riding minister for one or two days of preaching or, better yet, to hold a camp meeting, were occasions to which frontier dwellers eagerly looked forward. "Our outside pleasures were few," one woman remembered; "we were too far from Yuma to have church services. As I remember, only three or four times a year, a wandering preacher would stop in Palomas for one meeting. But what a sermon it would be." If an expected preacher failed to arrive, his potential congregation was understandably disconcerted. "Had an early dinner and went to Saratoga hoping to find ministers there according to appointment," an Iowa girl confided to her diary, "but lo, it is again a disappointment. We had a season of prayer, 15 present."[68]

Boxcar "home" in Cochise, Arizona. Frontier women found many diverse
solutions to their housing problems as shown by this unusual Arizona "home."
Other women reported living in tents, wagon boxes, and even burnt out tree
stumps until suitable housing could be found. (Courtesy Arizona Historical
Society.)

Preparing a meal, Oracle, Arizona. Preparing meals for their
families posed many problems for frontier women. Many cooked
in an open fireplace or over an outdoor fire using a tripod and
Dutch oven. (Courtesy Arizona Historical Society.)

Quilting party. A favorite pastime of nineteenth century women, quilting and other communal activities allowed women an opportunity to combine recreation and productive work. (Courtesy State Historical Society of North Dakota.)

Family wash day. The always dreaded wash was a difficult job under the best of circumstances. Women on the frontier learned to make do with what they had at hand. (Courtesy Western History Collections, University of Oklahoma Library.)

Oklahoma women and their families. Despite the difficulties of keeping house and caring for children under less than ideal conditions, many women looked back on their pioneer days with affection and nostalgia. (Courtesy Western History Collections, University of Oklahoma Library.)

Dance at a frontier army post. Dances and parties, which frequently lasted all night, were a favorite form of frontier entertainment. At this outdoor dance, a stretched piece of canvas substituted for a dance floor. (Courtesy Christian Barthelmess Collection, Miles City, Montana.)

The David Hilton family and their organ. Musical instruments were popular on the frontier, and families proudly boasted of having the first piano or organ in a new community. (Courtesy Solomon D. Butcher Collection, Nebraska State Historical Society.)

Public School House, Teacher and Pupils, in Live Oak county, Texas, 1887. Photo by Brack.

Brush Arbor school, Live Oak County, Texas. Schools were an important part of new Western communities and served as centers for many activities as well as educational institutions. Until permanent buildings could be erected, frontier settlers made do with temporary quarters. (Courtesy Western History Collections, University of Oklahoma Library.)

Camp meeting. These and other religious services quickly sprang up on the Western frontier as women and men attempted to re-create the society from which they had come. (Courtesy Library of Congress.)

Votes for Women   Votes for Women

Equal Suffrage Map of the United States, 1909

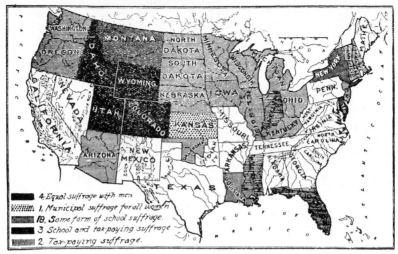

For the Long Work Day
For the Taxes We Pay
For the Laws We Obey
We Want Something to Say.

Men and women vote on equal terms for all officers, even for presidential electors, in **4** of the United States.   In **25** other states women have partial suffrage.

California Women have no Votes

Printed by California Equal Suffrage Ass'n   Price, one-half cent each
Address: Votes for Women, 611 Gilman St., Palo Alto

Equal suffrage map of the United States, 1909. Maps like this one were frequently used by suffrage associations to publicize their cause. This one is from stationary used by the California Equal Suffrage Association. (Courtesy Henry E. Huntington Library, San Marino, California.)

Above right: First women voters in Guthrie, Oklahoma. Women in the Western states quickly proved their ability to vote and hold office without losing their femininity or destroying the political process. (Courtesy Western History Collections, University of Oklahoma Library.)

Below right: Sara Bard Field presenting the Western Suffrage Petition to Congress. In 1915, Western women sent Congress a petition urging them to enfranchise their "suffering sisters" in the East. (Courtesy Library of Congress.)

196

First Lady — Voters in Guthrie Ok. Jinnggo

A Western house of prostitution. For a few women, prostitution was a highly successful and lucrative business. For most, however, it brought only poverty, disillusionment, and often illness and death. (Courtesy Amon Carter Museum, Fort Worth.)

Women ranchers, San Luis Valley, Colorado. A number of Western women successfully managed their own farms and ranches. (Courtesy Colorado Historical Society.)

Women prospectors in the Klondike. No field of endeavor was considered too new or too difficult for some Western women. (Courtesy Library of Congress.)

Dr. Bethenia Owens-Adair. A few Western women were able to
enter previously all-male professions such as medicine and law
and, like Oregonian Bethenia Owens-Adair, prove that women
could successfully compete in these professions. (Courtesy
Oregon Historical Society.)

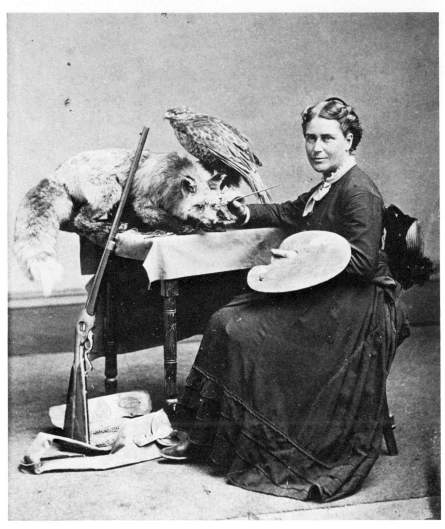

Zoologist Martha Maxwell. Greater educational opportunities for Western
women allowed them to enter a number of new fields of economic endeavor.
Coloradoan Martha Maxwell earned a national reputation as a zoologist and
taxidermist. Other women entered such fields as ethnology, anthropology, and
botany while some turned to technical work in photography, telegraphy, and
surveying. (Courtesy Amon Carter Museum, Fort Worth.)

Itinerant or circuit-riding ministers and the camp meeting were institutions developed specifically to meet frontier needs, and they served an
important social as well as a religious purpose. Camp meetings, particularly, provided a means for scattered frontier dwellers to visit together
and enjoy a variety of mutually enjoyable activities and thus refresh both
their spiritual and social lives. An Oregon woman recalled that, "We
looked forward to the camp meetings in June. . . . I think they were pretty
nearly our only salvation from entire stagnation." An Iowa woman described with obvious delight a quarterly meeting held at her home in January 1844:

> We had a good time and the house was packed every night. Good
> sleighing, and everybody seemed to be interested . . . The meeting
> lasted for ten days. Had over twenty conversions, and I thought that
> was about the best time I ever had. I cooked by the fireplace and our
> one room served for the church, kitchen, dining-room, bedroom, and
> study for the preachers. Sometimes we had three or four as they came
> from adjoining circuits to help us thru the work.[69]

Just as education became increasingly feminized, so too did religion.
Men directed and administered the local churches as well as denominational organizations, but women were in charge of an increasing number
of auxiliary activities. Although few women became preachers (Olivia
Brown and Anna Howard Shaw were notable exceptions),[70] they directed
many aspects of church-related work. It was usually the women in the
community who urged their sometimes reluctant husbands to attend the
preaching or the camp meetings, and some Western congregations were
made up almost entirely of women. Women organized and taught Sunday schools, conducted prayer meetings, planned church socials and fairs,
and participated in a variety of organizations such as the Home Missionary Society, the Foreign Missionary Society, and various other benevolent
associations. Often, too, it was the work of the minister's wife that enabled him to follow his difficult, and usually underpaid, calling. One Texas
minister's daughter recalled how her mother declared that "she did not
propose to live on charity" and invested her inheritance in a farm for herself and her children and "left her minister free to evangelize." The letters of another frontier clergyman, Gershom Day, and his wife Elizabeth,
showed clearly that his wife was the money earner in the family as well
as the overseer of their farm and finances.[71]
    The variety of pioneer women's church activities was somewhat aston-
ishing considering their many other duties. One Kansas woman wrote,
for example, that she had organized a Sunday school, been chosen assistant

missionary, and had entertained eighteen people at dinner after a meeting conducted by a circuit-rider minister. An Illinois woman's diary revealed that in a three-day period she had attended a "female prayer meeting," a "church conference meeting" followed by a "meeting of the session for business," and regular church services. During the following days she planned to participate in "a meeting of the society to consult upon hiring Mr. Gale as a regular preacher," an "antislavery prayer meeting," and a "Church conference."[72] Mormon women were equally as active in church work as their Protestant and Roman Catholic sisters. They attended church meetings, instructed the younger children, raised money for various church programs, and participated in the many activities of the Relief Society.[73]

Just as women contributed to the organization of schools and sometimes assisted in their construction, so, too, they worked to organize and build churches. Until funds were available for a church house, religious meetings were often held in private homes or in the school. Women volunteered their parlors or other facilities and often undertook the task of seeing that the quarters were swept, a fire laid, and that other provisions had been made for the comfort of the congregation. Women were anxious, as one wrote, that "moral education privileges were also available," and they helped raise funds to erect church buildings and were often the members of the community who took the initiative to establish a regular church to replace the irregular services of an itinerant minister or circuit rider. Church building, like school building, was often a community activity. As one Washington woman described it:

> The settlers from the surrounding country, all with one accord, cheerfully turned out and felled the mighty monarchs of the forest, to be converted into lumber at the saw mill. To help prepare the dinners for the volunteer workers who were wielding the axe and the saw, was my part of the free will service.[74]

Once a building had been erected, women helped raise money to pay the minister's salary, and they often aided in providing church furnishings as well. For example, a Kansas woman wrote at length of the fair the women organized to "aid in providing means for lighting and warming the church." Another wrote, "I presented our minister with a cash donation which I done the begin [sic] for, and I was given the work of selecting and buying an organ for our sunday school." Given the variety of their activities, it seems clear that women's role was essential to the founding of religious as well as educational institutions in frontier areas.[75] Moreover, church work, like school work, gave women opportunities to participate in community activities and gave them an increased sense of their own worth in the eyes of both man and God. As one modern historian pointed out, "organizational experience could be obtained in many reform groups, but only religion brought with it the heightened sense of who you were and where you were going."[76]

Churches and schools were more than religious and educational institutions, however; they also served as the center for social and cultural activities in most frontier communities. Church meetings and camp meetings gave people a chance to get together and visit with friends and provided opportunities for young people to go courting. Box suppers, church dinners on the grounds, community singing conventions, fairs, bazaars, and other socials designed to raise money for various school and church projects also provided opportunities for settlers to meet and enjoy themselves. Often such socials took the form of a picnic or community dinner followed by singing or a prayer meeting. Schools frequently served as community centers for parties, for special programs at Christmas and other holiday seasons, and as the site for amateur theatricals, recitations, spelling bees, debates, and other community activities. Most frontier women fondly remembered these simple pleasures as a welcome break in the humdrum routine of daily life. "[W]e always in winter time [had] spelling school one night a week at the schoolhouse," one Midwestern woman recalled; "old & young went & all took part it was fun for the children to spell down their parents. . . ."[77] Others wrote of debates, political speeches, and discussions of community problems which frequently took place during school or church-sponsored activities.[78]

Women's participation in community affairs went far beyond social and school and church-related activities, however. Once their homes were fairly well established, their farms and businesses underway, and the schools and religious institutions (which they insisted upon as a first step toward transforming the gloomy wilderness into a satisfactory new community) were built, settlers turned to other activities designed to bring some culture and a more genteel atmosphere to the raw frontier towns. In their search for "an ideal home," as Oregon pioneer Phoebe Judson phrased it, they undertook all kinds of projects for personal and civic improvement. Many of these activities were carried out by informal groups of interested men and women. An Oklahoma woman recalled that "the neighbors organized a literary society and these were held every two weeks at different homes." In other areas, reading clubs, literary and debating societies, and amateur musical and dramatic groups were also popular. Often both men and women participated, and the meetings combined both social and educational functions. Such gatherings also gave women opportunities to learn about new topics, gain new interests and skills, and to speak before mixed gatherings.[79]

The first such organizations in a frontier community were often informal and included both men and women, but usually as soon as enough
women were available in an area, they established some kind of formal
organization exclusively for women and undertook various benevolent and
philanthropic activities for the development and betterment of the community. Volunteerism and the formation of voluntary societies and associations increased throughout the late eighteenth and early nineteenth
centuries. As the well-known French traveler Alexis de Tocqueville observed, voluntary organizations substituted in a democracy for the stable
institutions and status relationships of Europe. "The Americans," he
commented:

> make associations to give entertainments, to found seminaries, to
> build inns, to construct churches, to diffuse books, to send mission-
> aries to the antipodes; in this manner they found hospitals, prisons,
> and schools. If it is proposed to inculcate some truth or to foster some
> feeling by the encouragement of a great example, they form a society.[80]

Spurred by the evangelical revivals of the late eighteenth and early nineteenth centuries to participate more actively in such associations, American
women entered into a number of benevolent activities including "abolition, prison reform, Sunday schools for poor children, and other causes."[81]
    Such associations were also quickly established in new Western com-
munities. The ladies of Galesburg, Illinois, for example, immediately
formed a Moral Reform Society as well as "two female prayer meetings
. . . a maternal association and sewing society." No sooner were the "first
white women over the Rockies" settled in their Oregon homes than they,
too, had formed a Maternal Association similar to those they had known
in the East. The group, Mary Walker confided to her diary, was "to meet
on the second and last Wednesday of each month. . . . We are to hold
meetings at each Station, and report to the Recording Secretary as often
as is practicable." A young army wife, concerned by the plight of the
Navaho Indians on the Bosque Redondo reservation, urged her mother
to organize the ladies of upper New York state into a society to help provide missionaries and other workers for the reservation. In other communities the Ladies' Aid societies distributed Bibles and missionary tracts,
charitable associations of various kinds helped care for orphaned children
and widows, and other women's groups held bazaars and fairs to raise
money for various civic projects. In the early days on the frontier, such
projects were often undertaken by individuals or one or two families, but
as the areas became more densely populated, these activities became increasingly a part of women's responsibility.[82]

After the Civil War, Eastern women who had been active in the Sanitary Commission, the Freedman's Bureau, and other activities began to organize clubs specifically for women. Caroline Severance, one of the first club women, wrote in her memoirs that in the course of the war "many women who had discovered their own capacity for public effort . . . were prepared and inclined to put the same features to use in other urgent special ways." They envisioned their organizations as both personally stimulating and rewarding to their members and as forces for social improvement. "Its plan," Severance wrote, "involves no special pledge to any one form of activity but implies only a womanly interest in all true thought and effort on behalf of women, and of society in general. . . ."[83] Such organizations spread rapidly from New England and New York and were soon to be found in communities, both large and small, in the West as well as in the East.

Some women's groups were principally study groups intended for the edification and enjoyment of their members, but others undertook extensive programs for civic improvements. In many communities literary and reading clubs helped organize libraries and free public reading rooms. Sometimes these were individual or informal efforts. "[A]s we had brought a good supply of books with us," a Denver settler wrote, "our room became a sort of free reading room to all who wished to avail themselves." An early Washington resident remembered that "Everyone ordered some of the newest and best publications . . . so we had an informal circulating library." Using such temporary organizations as a base, women's groups turned them into public activities. "We have a Literary Association," an Arizona woman wrote her mother. "We are to use the funds for a Public Library. They have decided to have the library in our store and have chosen me for Librarian." In Houston, Texas, the Ladies Reading Club shared rooms with the Houston Library and later helped pay the library's moving expenses to its new building.[84] Another women's group in Florence, Arizona, "conducted a system of sanitation having the streets and habitations that were repulsive thoroughly cleaned, erected signs for marking the streets . . . [and] also were influential in efforts being made for incorporating of the town." In Texas, women's clubs took the lead in lobbying for improved schools and increased funding for public education. They also worked to establish county libraries, raised money to provide scholarships and loan funds for women, and helped bring pressure on the legislature to create a state department of education and pass a compulsory school attendance law. In many Western states, women's clubs were also active in the women's suffrage movement. In 1890 many of the women's clubs joined together to form the National Federation of Women's Clubs which included Western as well as Eastern women. These organizations, like the community activities in which women participated, allowed them to fulfill what they believed to be their civic and Christian duty to their family and community and at the same time to gain a good deal of organizational and leadership experience.[85] Black women, who formed similar organizations in their own communities, viewed them as a means to improve the education and position of their race as well as their sex. In many Negro communities women were particularly active in all kinds of civic and philanthropic organizations. As one Colorado woman pointed out, the men were often away from home attempting to find work, and women "were the backbone of the church, the backbone of the family, they were the backbone of the social life, everything."[86]

Civic activities were not without their problems, however. For women accustomed to a domestic role and confined within the home, the move into a public sphere was not always easy. Women lacked experience in organizing and directing activities outside the home, and they had much to learn about public life. Women's groups often lacked direction and leadership, and there was a good deal of petty bickering and occasionally bitter, acrimonious argument. Western women, although more accustomed to public activities than Eastern women, faced special problems in attempting to organize and carry out various programs. The long distances between homes made it difficult for women to meet together, and the transient nature of the population in many Western communities caused difficulties in establishing a stable group and an on-going program. One young Western woman, frustrated in her efforts to organize the women of the community, wrote her mother:

> Everyday parties are leaving. . . . I often ask myself what shall be my course of conduct, how shall I live in such a community. . . . One's best friends leave them in a day and pleasant acquaintances prove mere gossip. . . . Shall I too selfishly address myself to money getting and ignore the claims of society upon me, or shall my influence be used to bring about a better state of things and beget a little public spirit.

In a similar vein, Susan Wallace wrote of New Mexico, "There never has been a woman's meeting in this territory of 207,000 square miles; and, in consequence, the weak-minded creature is not aware that men are great rascals, rob women of their rights, and bar the avenues to wealth and fame against them." For other women, the frontier population lacked the virtues of civilized society, and they longed for the day when "men began to wear white shirts in the place of hickory." "Society is rough, coarse & low as a general thing," complained a young Colorado settler, and her sentiments were frequently echoed by other well-bred and educated women who decried the lack of manners and the uncivilized behavior of many of their neighbors. Sometimes such problems had an amusing aspect. When the women of Newcastle, Wyoming, decided to organize a women's study club they placed a notice in the local newspaper inviting "*any* and *every* woman" to attend the initial meeting. Much to their surprise and chagrin the local dancehall girls and "ladies of the evening" took them at their word and arrived at the appointed home for the meeting. It took a good deal of work and diplomacy for the organizers to develop a program requiring homework and preparation which the dancehall girls could not possibly find time to complete.[87]

Despite such problems, women continued to form both temporary and permanent organizations and to participate actively in community life. Increasingly their activities involved them not only in social and cultural affairs but in political reform movements as well. "Good" men and women abhorred the violence and vice which was typical of some frontier areas. Most blamed the roughness of society and the lawlessness in their communities on the "primitive conditions" and "godlessness" which they felt was inherent in the wilderness setting. When men left "civilization" and entered the wilderness, they believed, they frequently allowed the "darker," "evil" side of man's nature to prevail over their better instincts. "It is well said that on this road the bad passions of men show themselves," wrote one young Western immigrant, and her comments reflected those of other westering Americans. Others pointed out that men and women freed from the constraints of established society, engaged in practices they would never have considered appropriate "back in the States." "You know that at home it is considered vulgar for a gentleman to swear," wrote a California mining camp resident,

> but I am told that here, it is absolutely the fashion, and that people who never uttered an oath in their lives while in the "States," now "clothe themselves with curses as with a garment."

Such behavior, many frontier residents believed, encouraged lawlessness and threatened established social values. "Iniquity abounds much in this place; gambling, drinking and frolicing are practiced in by many," a Chicago physician wrote, and religious leaders in the young town were "scandalized by the villainy" which the community tolerated. In a similar vein, Julia Lovejoy portrayed Kansas City in the 1850s as a place where "the inhabitants and the morals, are of an *indescribably repulsive* and undesirable character."[88]

Some frontier residents doubted whether there was any more drinking and carousing going on than in their Eastern towns, but they were nonetheless appalled by the lack of Sabbath observances and the large number of saloons, gambling halls, and billiard parlors which they believed were the major cause of social disorders. "Of course the saloons were the center of gravity in all camps," wrote a California woman:

> The men had already been innoculated with the virus of evil. . . .
> Whiskey created antagonisms and their faces would remind one of a
> personified day of judgement, untempered by mercy. Then they were
> ready for anything—robbery or murder, but above all they loved to
> fight.[89]

Women's diaries indicated that fistfights, shootings, stabbings, lynchings, and outlawry were fairly common events in some frontier communities.[90] Although they usually reported these in a matter-of-fact way, it was also clear that they were appalled by such behavior, and many applauded the efforts of vigilance committees and similar extralegal organizations to establish some kind of law and order.

Frontier residents viewed vigilance committees, like many other frontier institutions, as necessary, temporary expedients to be utilized until more normal forms of social control were established. Beginning with the South Carolina Regulators of the 1760s, such groups operated on most American frontiers. One modern investigator estimated that, excluding lynch mobs, there were over five hundred such organizations in American history. In the trans-Mississippi West, alone, he identified two hundred and ten vigilante movements.[91] These informal groups of citizens were expected to clean out the bad elements in frontier communities, mete out justice to wrong doers, and enforce the law as they interpreted it. Often they were formed because there were no effective law enforcement organizations or because citizens suspected that law enforcement officials were in league with the criminal elements. Vigilante methods were as violent as those of the criminals they intended to punish, and they often were as dangerous to peace and good order. Although frontier dwellers recognized the occasional need for such groups, they longed for the day when more familiar, stable institutions would replace the legal violence of the vigilance committees.[92]

Women were particularly ambivalent about methods used by the vigilantes. A female editor of the Durango, Colorado, newspaper penned a grim description of the body of a victim of vigilante justice as it swayed from a tree branch and the moonlight "clothed the ghastly face with a ghastlier pallor." It was not a pleasant sight, but she added, "Thus the Powers that Be . . . have proclaimed to the world that good order, peace, quietude and safety must and shall prevail in Durango." Louisa Clappe applauded the work of the San Francisco vigilance committee, but she severely criticized the actions of a similar group in the mining camp at Indian Bar. She firmly believed, she wrote, that the sentence (death by hanging) in the case she observed exceeded the crime and concluded:

> It seems to have been carried on entirely by the more reckless part of the community. There is no doubt, however, that they seriously *thought* they were doing right, for many of them are kind and sensible men. They firmly believed that such an example was absolutely necessary for the protection of the community.[93]

Whatever their beliefs about the merits of vigilante committees, frontier residents, both men and women, were anxious to transform their crude pioneer settlements into well-organized, peaceful communities, and they poured a good deal of their energy and precious time into the reform and reorganization of frontier society. Reaching for a new future, they kept their ties to the past. More adventurous, perhaps, or more motivated by new opportunities than their stay-at-home Eastern cousins, frontiersfolk, both men and women, remained conservative creatures. They were willing to seek adventure, but they also longed for the familiar—the school bell, the church spire, and the reassurance that God was in his heaven and that all was right with the world, even on the edges of civilization. They joined voluntary associations such as the Independent Order of Good Templars, the Women's Christian Temperance Union, and the Young Men's Christian Association or local groups such as the Pale Noses of Lake City, Colorado, or the Union Church and School Society of Ruby City, Idaho, in an attempt to bring peace and good order through the elimination of the twin evils of the saloon and gambling hall. When these voluntary efforts failed to reform frontier society, they organized political pressure groups and lobbied for Sunday closing laws, antisaloon bills, taxes on gambling and dance halls, and other measures designed to bring about their desired ends.

As suggested by some nineteenth-century proponents of the role of women as civilizers and culture bearers, women did help to bring some measure of civilization and refinement to Western communities. Their activities in these areas often far exceeded the limited sphere of woman's place as it was so carefully defined by the cult of true womanhood. In community activities, as in other areas of their lives, westering did not radically change women's views of themselves and their role in society, but the frontier did offer many new opportunities for women and an expanded definition of "woman's place." Increasingly women who participated in community building and community activities believed that their influence must be extended beyond the informal powers of moral persuasion and exercised more directly through the ballot.

8

Suffering
for Suffrage

Western Women and the Struggle
for Political, Legal,
and Economic Rights

Women keenly felt their disadvantage in not having a legal voice in the decisions which affected the institutions in which they invested so much time and energy. If women could help establish schools and teach in them, why should they not have a voice in selecting school board members and determining school taxes and bonds; if women could help to establish communities and work for municipal improvements, why should they not vote in municipal and county elections; if women's work could help to provide the tax monies for local, state, and national programs, why should they not participate in decisions as to how these monies were to be spent? Many women were not happy with the roles into which they had been forced by the cult of true womanhood. Pedestals were not for them, and they intended to do something about it. Throughout the nineteenth century women lobbied for enfranchisement, reform of restrictive legal codes, and new economic opportunities. Although the women's rights movement started in the East, it was on the frontiers that the first significant gains were made.

The question of political and legal equality for women was not a new one in the nineteenth century. During the colonial period there were a few instances of women participating in local elections, although generally women were denied the vote. But in a society where a number of men were also denied the ballot, the question of voting rights for women was hardly a central question. Legal rights were important, however, in the English colonies where the common law prevailed and severe restrictions were placed on the rights of married women. In the Spanish colonies, where community property rights were established, married women had considerable control over their property and could hold property and make contracts in their own name, and, under certain conditions, exercise governmental authority. But under English common law, married women, in theory, lost their separate identity and became "one unity with the husband" for purposes of law. Thus, as the great English jurist William Blackstone explained in his *Commentaries on the Laws of England*, "By marriage, the husband and wife are one person in law; that is, the very being or legal existence of the woman is suspended during the marriage, or at least is incorporated and consolidated into that of the husband; under whose wing, protection, and cover, she performs everything. . . ." Married women could not sign contracts, they had no title to their own earnings, they had no property rights (even when the property was their own by inheritance or dower), nor could they claim guardianship of their children in cases of separation or divorce. As it was sometimes said, in marriage women suffered civil death: "the husband and wife are one and the husband is the one." Remedies were available in equity law, but they were generally known to and used only by upper-class women or when there was extensive property involved.[1]

Different economic and social conditions in colonial America brought a number of modifications in the English common law either by statute or in equity. Men were often absent from home, and women needed more legal freedom in order to care for the family business. Colonial women also frequently participated as partners in their husbands' businesses or conducted business in their own name. In addition, many colonial women were landowners and heads of families. Thus changes were made in the laws which increased women's proprietary capacity and modified other legal restrictions. According to one modern historian, such provisions were one of America's important contributions to the legal status of women.[2]

Despite the fact that colonial laws were less restrictive than in England, women had no political rights and far fewer legal rights than men, and they often found their narrowly defined limits oppressive. Anne Hutchinson's revolt against the Puritan leadership is well known. Of course, Hutchinson's revolt was primarily theological rather than strictly political and legal, but given the important role of religion in New England life and the theocratic nature of the Puritan state, religious rebellion was tantamount to political protest. In other colonies a few women specifically protested the narrowness of women's political and legal sphere. Margaret Brent of Maryland, who was executrix of Leonard Calvert's estate, demanded two votes in the Maryland Assembly—one for herself as a landowner and one as Calvert's attorney. This was denied, but the outspoken Mistress Brent "protested against all proceedings in this present Assembly unless she may be present and have vote as afors[d]." A group of New York women, who described themselves as "she merchants," wrote the New York *Journal* that as householders and taxpayers they felt they were entitled to greater political and social recognition, "as we in some measure contribute to the Support of Government."[3]

By the time of the American Revolution, the more militant and vocal women expressed the hope that independence of the colonies would bring greater independence for women as well. As one Southern woman wrote, "I won't have it thought that because we are the weaker sex as to bodily strength . . . we are capable of nothing more than . . . domestic concerns. . . . Surely we may have sense enough to give our opinions to commend or discommend such actions as we may approve or disapprove. . . ." During the Revolution, women contributed to the war efforts, sometimes in active roles, such as the legendary Molly Pitcher, but more frequently in supportive roles such as organizing antitea leagues or soliciting funds for the hard-pressed Continental Army. At the end of the war, women believed that they were entitled to a fuller share in the nation which they had helped bring into being. "In the new code of laws which I suppose it will be necessary for you to make," Abigail Adams wrote her husband,

> I desire you would remember the ladies and be more generous and favorable to them than your ancestors. Do not put such unlimited power into the hands of the husbands. . . . If particular care and attention is not paid to the ladies, we are determined to foment a rebellion, and will not hold ourselves bound by any laws in which we have no voice or representation.

Such changes as women like Adams, and her friend Mercy Warren, advocated did not occur, however. Well-educated, upper-class women who were consciously aware of the need for change were few, and groups like those described by Eliza Wilkinson in which "none were greater politicians than the several knots of ladies who met together" were not exactly commonplace.[4]

The Revolution brought no immediate change in women's political and legal rights. In fact, one modern American historian asserted that the Revolution, rather than bringing increased recognition and rights for women, actually narrowed their sphere, both domestic and political. The changing nature of the family structure and the modernization of the economy which placed less importance on women's production plus other subtle psychological and social factors, she argued, resulted in changes which brought actual losses in legal and political status rather than any gain in or even maintenance of the status quo. The Revolution, she concluded, resulted in "conscious neglect of female rights combined with subtle educational and economic exploitation."[5]

If such a gloomy assessment was correct (and much of the data are subject to a different interpretation), a change was on the way. During the early years of the Republic a few voices were raised both in England and in the United States against the legal and political restrictions on women. Mary Wollstonecraft's *Vindication of the Rights of Women*, published in 1792,

Hannah Crocker's 1818 *Observations on the Real Rights of Women,* and Frances Wright's militant speeches in the 1820s, along with the educational reforms advocated by Emma Willard, helped to publicize the need for change. By the 1830s, agitation for increased rights for women had become, along with abolition of slavery and the temperance and peace movements, a part of the reform program of the period. As one historian reminded us, "Reform is based on the gap between generally accepted ideal and actual fact."[6] Thus, women became increasingly interested in redressing the gap between ideal and fact in relation to education and women's legal and economic rights. By 1848, when the first Woman's Rights Convention met in Seneca Falls, New York, a small but vocal group of men and women had dedicated themselves to a new and vigorous movement for increased legal and political rights for women.

During the first years of the movement, the lack of a formal organization and the dual role of the leading women advocates of reform in both the women's rights and the antislavery movements prevented many positive gains from being made. Additional conventions were held in Rochester, New York; Salem, Ohio; and Worcester, Massachusetts, and after 1850 a national women's rights convention was held each year (except 1857) along with smaller gatherings in Ohio, Indiana, New York, and Pennsylvania. Legal reform legislation was passed in several states beginning in New York in 1848, but often these changes were made less because of women's agitation for them than because of the generally accepted need for legal reform. Aside from such radicals as Elizabeth Cady Stanton, few of the women's rights advocates in the pre-Civil War period were interested in suffrage. Of more immediate interest were control of property, guardianship, divorce laws, and increased opportunities for education and employment. Many of the early feminists considered the right to vote far too radical a measure—it was in fact the only resolution of the Seneca Falls convention which was not passed unanimously. Nonetheless, in a few areas the question was raised.

During the pre-Civil War decades much of the attention of the women's rights advocates was centered in the newer Western areas where the leaders hoped that a freer, more egalitarian society might be more willing to accord rights to the women who had helped to open and settle the country. Moreover, in the newly settled areas laws inimical to women were not as firmly entrenched or had not been included in the legal codes. As a Vermont woman who moved to Kansas in 1854 to "work for a government of equality, liberty, [and] fraternity" noted, "It was a thousand times more difficult to procure the repeal of unjust laws in an old State, than the adoption of just laws in the organization of a new State."[7] The reformers saw an opportunity to lobby territorial governments for better laws relating to women in the territorial constitutions and in the constitutional conventions for new states.

The first attempts were made in the top rank of territories just west of the Mississippi. During the late 1840s and throughout the 1850s, Eastern middle-class women toured the Western territories and states delivering public lectures on behalf of women's rights and attempting to gain favorable discussion of such provisions in territorial legislatures and constitutional conventions. These early efforts met with some limited success. In Wisconsin, the 1846 constitutional convention adopted a strong married women's property law, and the members somewhat facetiously debated women's suffrage. When the constitution was rejected by the voters, the women's property provision was dropped, but it was reinstated by the legislature shortly after statehood and in 1853 and 1855 several women visited the state to "scatter suffrage seed." In 1855 Amelia Bloomer addressed the Nebraska territorial legislature on the question of women's rights, and in response to her plea that women be given "all the rights guaranteed by the Constitution," the lower house passed a suffrage bill. The upper house, however, embroiled in a controversy over county boundaries, adjourned without taking action on the bill. Four years later Clarina Nichols presented a series of petitions to the Wyandotte, Kansas, constitutional convention demanding equal political and civil rights for women. She received a friendly hearing and the question was debated at some length, but the suffrage provision was rejected for fear that a constitutional provision granting women's suffrage would be used "as a pretext by congress to keep Kansas out of the Union." Mrs. Nichols, however, was able to persuade the delegates to extend the elective franchise to women in school district elections and to secure legal protection for women's property rights and equal guardianship of children.[8] At about the same time, the Iowa legislature provided for women to control their own property and also passed improved divorce legislation. According to one observer in Iowa:

Pioneer life fostered independence and equality. Women who settled here have been, for the most part, intelligent and educated, while the lawmakers and judges have been responsive to the demand for reform when once their attention has been called to unjust treatment of women.[9]

Although the reformers also attempted to gain support in the older states for legal and political reform, most of their early successes, aside from the New York reform bill of 1848 which had been introduced before the Seneca Falls convention, were in the Western states.[10] The lack of more than very modest success was hardly surprising. As one historian pointed out, most pre-Civil War advocates of women's rights were married women who spent most of their time looking after their husbands and children. They had no experience in political affairs, and they had no national organization; in fact most thought that an organization would be unnecessary and unduly cumbersome. Their campaigns were therefore largely the uncoordinated work of a small group of dedicated men and women who attempted to interest legislators in their program. Although women's suffrage was mentioned from time to time, it was still considered somewhat radical, and most of the pre-War efforts concentrated on legal reforms and other less controversial changes which were more widely accepted than votes for women. The women themselves were not of one mind; they were still unsure of their program, especially as it related to suffrage. They still had not decided what they wanted to achieve nor had they developed an ideology and strategy to accomplish their goals once they had been determined.

During the Civil War, women left active campaigning for women's rights and turned their attention to the national struggle. As one Wisconsin woman recalled, women frequently "managed the farm, the shop, the office, as well as the family" while the men were at war. Some, including Dorothea Dix and Clara Barton, were active in recruiting and training of nurses while Susan B. Anthony and Elizabeth Cady Stanton headed the National Women's Loyal League to help secure passage of the Thirteenth Amendment. Many women in the North worked to raise funds or participated directly in the work of the Sanitary Commission to provide hospital and medical services. Although nominally headed by men, the work of the Sanitary Commission was carried out almost entirely by women. Such activities helped women gain experience in new areas of endeavor; it helped them clarify their post-War goals, and it changed their opinion of the need for organization as a means to accomplish their ends.[11]

Many of the women believed that once the war ended they would be enfranchised as a reward for their work in the antislavery crusade and the Loyal League. However, it soon was apparent that the Republicans were more interested in Negro suffrage than in women's suffrage. This became clear when the language of the proposed Fourteenth Amendment specifically limited the franchise to male citizens. Believing themselves betrayed by their friends in the American Equal Rights Association, which had been organized to further the interests of both women and Negroes, the leaders of the feminist movement moved to form their own organization to work for women's suffrage. In the meantime, however, personality conflicts and rival strategies developed among the leaders of the movement. The New England group, led by Julia Ward Howe and Lucy Stone, preferred a moderate course which stressed a male-supported campaign and hoped to secure the vote through a series of referendum votes in the various states. The more radical women in Midwestern cities and small Western towns rallied behind Susan B. Anthony and Elizabeth Cady Stanton who believed that women, without male participation, should head the movement and preferred an aggressive campaign to secure a federal constitutional amendment granting women the vote. In 1869 two separate suffrage organizations were formed—the National Woman Suffrage Association, established by Anthony and Stanton, and the rival American Woman Suffrage Association.[12]

Before the split between the women leaders, however, a new attempt was made to secure the vote in the Western states. In Wisconsin a constitutional amendment to provide women's suffrage passed the legislature in 1867. However, an amendment still had to be approved at two successive legislative sessions, and in 1868 the bill failed by a vote of thirty-six to forty-six. According to one observer, the loss was due as much to "the general apathy on the subject" as to active opposition to the proposal.[13] An attempt was also made to raise the suffrage issue in the 1866 Nebraska constitutional convention, and the following year the Nebraska legislature did extend school suffrage to women.[14] Iowa legislators also debated women's suffrage in 1866 and again in 1868, but votes for women was an issue whose time had not yet come; and in Iowa, as in Wisconsin, Nebraska, and Kansas, it was inextricably tied to the issue of votes for Negro men. The most vigorous 1860s campaign was carried out in Kansas where the legislature approved a referendum on both women's suffrage and Negro suffrage. Sam Wood, who had introduced the bill in the legislature, formed the Impartial Suffrage Association, which included both the governor and the lieutenant governor, to work for the passage of both amendments. Lucy Stone and her husband came to help campaign followed by Stanton, Anthony, and the charming Anna Dickinson. Despite the effort and the optimism of the suffragists, the amendment was defeated by a majority of 10,787 votes. Negro suffrage failed as well, although by a smaller margin.[15] These campaigns were only the first in a long series of unsuccessful attempts to gain the vote for women. Between 1870 and 1910 there were seventeen state referenda held in eleven states— all but three of them west of the Mississippi. Yet by 1910 only four states had extended full suffrage to women.[16]

During most of the early suffrage campaigns, the impetus for change came not from the women in the Western states but from male leaders in Western state governments and Eastern women who came to campaign on behalf of women's rights or who, like Amelia Bloomer and Clarina Nichols, had moved from Eastern cities where they already had experience in the women's movement. Women on Western frontiers did not have the time or the means of organizing their far-flung neighbors in order to become an effective lobby.[17] Nowhere was this more clearly illustrated than in the first successful Western suffrage votes.

In December 1869, the Wyoming Territorial Legislature passed a bill providing for the enfranchisement of women—the first full suffrage legislation to be enacted in any state or territory. Yet this was done without any suffrage association, without any suffrage campaign; in fact no suffrage petition had been addressed to the legislature. There had been some discussion of the issue, of course. In September 1869, Eastern suffrage speaker Anna Dickinson had spoken briefly in Cheyenne and made a good impression as an entertaining and graceful speaker. In November the "beautiful Redelia Bates" also presented a well-received suffrage lecture. Both the Wyoming *Tribune* and the Cheyenne *Leader* gave the speeches full and fair coverage. The *Tribune* was openly supportive of the women's issue, and the *Leader* occasionally reprinted articles from Susan B. Anthony's *The Revolution*. Nowhere in Wyoming before or during the legislative debate over women's rights was there the frantic activity and high emotion that marked the suffrage movement in the East or which had characterized the Kansas campaign two years before.

Why then should a provision which had failed in other states during the previous two decades be accepted in a territory where there was little or no agitation for votes for women? Part of the answer lay in the fact that there were few women in the territory (the 1870 Wyoming census showed 1,049 females over ten years old as compared to 6,107 males), and therefore there seemed little danger that they could do any great harm at the polls. As a writer for *Harper's Weekly* suggested, "Wyoming gave women the right to vote in much the same spirit that New York or Pennsylvania might vote to enfranchise angels or Martians. . . ."[18] Part of the answer lay in the fact that the bill was introduced, debated, and passed before vigorous, effective opposition could be organized. Several months after the legislative action many of the antisuffrage arguments were presented in the territorial press, but at the time of the legislative debate the usual arguments against suffrage—that homes and families would be ruined, women unsexed, and divine law disobeyed—were not raised. In that regard, the lack of a suffrage association or suffrage campaign may have been a great advantage.[19] Part of the answer lay in the fact that the chief proponents of the bill—Territorial Secretary Edward M. Lee, who probably wrote the legislation, and legislator William H. Bright, who introduced the bill—were able to convince the legislators that women's suffrage would be a good thing for Wyoming. One of the arguments used by the proponents of the bill was that it would help to attract stable family immigration to the territory. "I am sure that up to that time not a score of suffrage disciples could be found within the Territorial limits," Lee wrote in an 1872 article. "Even the women themselves did not appear as petitioners . . . but the suffrage was conferred, as has been said, solely for advertising purposes."[20] There were also those who supported the measure out of the conviction that it was the "right and just" thing to do. This was probably true of Bright himself whose wife was a supporter of women's rights and whose opinion he valued. Possibly suffrage supporter Mrs. Esther Morris, who was a friend of the Brights, influenced Bright's vote and that of some of his friends as well.[21] That some of the legislators voted for suffrage out of real concern for women's rights was suggested by the fact that the same legislature that voted suffrage also provided for equal pay for teachers and passed legislation giving married women control of their separate property and the right to carry on business in their own name. At least a few men in the all-Democratic legislature hoped to use the suffrage issue to embarrass Republican Governor John A. Campbell whom they believed would veto the bill. Esther Morris later told a newspaper reporter that she believed "the whole matter of the adoption of Woman Suffrage in the Territory was the result of a bitter feud between the existing political parties, and it was done in a moment of spite—not out of any regard for the movement. . . ."[22] Whatever the reasons—advertising, conviction, or political jealousy—the suffrage bill passed by a vote of six to two in the upper house and by seven to four in the lower house.[23]

The Wyoming legislation also permitted women to hold office and serve on juries. In February 1870, Esther Morris was named a justice of the peace and held court for eight and a half months, long enough to prove that women were capable of holding such offices. In March 1870, the first jury to include women as members convened in Laramie, and in September 1870, Wyoming women went to the ballot box for the first time. Although women were later removed from juries and did not fully realize full political and economic equality, territorial residents, including the women, were generally pleased with the results of their "great experiment." In 1871 some disgruntled Democrats, unhappy over the election of several Republican legislators, attempted to repeal the suffrage provision, but the effort failed, and thereafter women voted regularly in Wyoming elections. In 1889, the all-male constitutional convention included a suffrage provision in the proposed state constitution, and in 1890 Wyoming entered the Union as the first state to extend the franchise to women.[24]

In Utah, the next territory to extend women the vote, there was as little debate over the measure as there was in Wyoming, although for very different reasons. Again, in Utah, as in Wyoming, women did not actively campaign for suffrage. In fact, the question of women's suffrage in Utah was first raised by an Indiana congressman and suffragist, George W. Julian, who introduced a bill in Congress in December 1868 to give women the franchise in all of the Western territories. In the course of the hearings, another suffragist, Hamilton Willcox of New York, testified that in his opinion such a measure would attract women to the territories (an idea quickly expropriated by Wyoming's Edward M. Lee). He suggested,

in addition, that if the women of Utah could vote they would surely abol-
ish the terrible system of polygamy. The bill died in committee, but the
Willcox argument led Julian to propose a "Bill to Discourage Polygamy in
Utah" which provided for the enfranchisement of Utah women. Again
Julian's bill failed (in fact it never came to a vote), but the Utah Territorial
Delegate, William H. Hooper, and other Mormon leaders seized on the
idea of women's suffrage in Utah as a good thing. During the hearings
on Julian's bill in March 1869 several articles appeared in the *Deseret Evening News* supporting the idea of women's suffrage. "Our ladies can prove
to the world," proclaimed an editorial, "that in a society where men are
worthy of the name, women can be enfranchised without running wild
or becoming unsexed."[25] Sure that Mormon women would support, not
abolish, polygamy since "to do so would require repudiation of their religion, cause disruption of many families, and engender the term 'illegit-
imate' for thousands of children," the Mormon leadership determined to
implement women's suffrage.[26] When the territorial legislature convened
in 1870, the House instructed its Committee on Elections to look into the
matter of extending the voting franchise. The Committee reported favorably on February 2, and three days later the lower chamber unanimously
approved the bill and sent it to the Council which, after suggesting some
amendments which the House refused, also approved the bill unanimously. The bill was signed by Acting Governor S. A. Mann on February 12,
and two days later women in Salt Lake City went to the polls for the first
time to vote in a municipal election. Six months later they cast their bal-
lots in the territorial elections.[27]

Although one historian of Western suffrage concluded that Utah women
did not go to the polls as enthusiastically as Wyoming women, another
pointed out that neither did they "simply rest with their newly won freedom." The Relief Society sponsored a program of civic education for the
women of the territory which included organized classes in government,
history, and parliamentary law, and the *Woman's Exponent* published regular articles on women's rights and responsibilities. Unlike the Wyoming
bill, the Utah legislation excluded women from holding any but minor
offices, but Utah women did serve on school boards and juries.[28] Moreover, although Utah women certainly did not initiate the suffrage action or
speak in its behalf in the territorial legislature, many of them had some
interest in and influence on the matter. William Godbe and his wives
Annie, Mary, and Charlotte, and Franklin Richards and his wife Jane, along
with their son and daughter-in-law, were all early advocates of women's
rights and convinced some of the Eastern suffrage leaders to speak in
Utah. Several wives of prominent Mormon leaders, including Sarah M.
Kimball, Eliza Snow, and Emmeline Wells, were also strong women's
rights advocates. Once suffrage was passed in Utah, they continued to
be vocal and effective spokeswomen for the cause.[29]

Historians of the suffrage movement disagree on the reasons why suffrage came so easily in Utah. Some point to the fact that the railroad was completed to Salt Lake in 1869 and suggest that the Mormon leadership wanted a reserve force of Mormon votes to prevent any Gentile takeover of Utah politics. Mormon historians tend to downplay this idea and credit "progressive sentiment" among the Mormon leadership. They also point out that women voted on church matters, were encouraged by church leaders to participate in public affairs, and were held in high esteem. Other historians point to a combination of factors, both external and internal, including the antipolygamy legislation pending in Congress, the need to dispell the image of enslaved, downtrodden Mormon women, and a desire to gain the support of Eastern suffrage groups to counter attempts by Congress to suppress polygamy. Some have also suggested that the granting of suffrage was an attempt by the leadership to gain political solidarity against a growing liberal schism within the church.[30]

Whatever the motives of the Mormon leadership, once suffrage was granted the idea took firm hold. Seventeen years later Utah women lost their voting privileges, along with polygamist men, with the congressional passage of the Edmunds-Tucker Act. When the question of restoring the franchise came up in the constitutional convention of 1895, it was placed in the proposed document despite the fears of some delegates that a women's suffrage provision would endanger congressional approval of statehood. Almost 70 percent of the male convention delegates voted to include women's suffrage in the constitution which was approved by the male voters of the territory by a comfortable majority. Utah entered the Union in 1896 as the third state to grant women full suffrage.[31]

While the Utah Territorial Legislature quietly and quickly enfranchised women, a bitter debate raged over the question in Colorado. There was some discussion of women's suffrage in both the 1868 and 1869 legislative sessions, and in 1870 Republican Governor Edward H. McCook recommended adoption of a suffrage statute in his January 3 address to the legislature. A women's suffrage bill was reported to the House on January 19 where debate and discussion continued off and on until February 10. The legislature invited outside speakers to address the assembly, Colorado newspapers gave the subject and debate extensive coverage, and several groups presented petitions favoring suffrage. Proponents argued that it was unjust for Negro men to be allowed to vote on matters which affected a white woman's property when she could not vote. They also suggested that women would have a purifying effect on politics. Borrowing the Wyoming argument, they asserted that the passage of a women's suffrage bill would "speedily fill up the waste places of [the] valleys and mountains with a teeming population."[32] Opponents used many of the counterarguments that had become familiar in other debates. They declared that politics would destroy the symmetry of woman's character and undermine the home and family. One Democratic legislator declared that he certainly would not give "negro wenches the right to vote." Others testified that women did not particularly want the right to vote. Although the upper house or Council approved a suffrage bill by a narrow margin of seven to six, the House, after further debate, voted fifteen to ten to postpone the bill indefinitely, thus effectively killing it. Part of the reason for the defeat may have been the antagonism between Republican Governor McCook and his Democratic legislature. One observer suggested that "it must be remembered that any measure publicly approved by Governor McCook at this time was bound to meet with opposition."[33] There were also some adamant antisuffragists in the House; and there were some members who, not convinced one way or the other, preferred to dispose of the controversial measure by tabling it. Whether owing to politics, timidity to follow the lead of their Wyoming colleagues, effective opposition, or a combination of factors, the issue failed to carry and was not brought up again until the constitutional convention in 1876.[34]

When the Colorado constitutional convention convened in December 1875, suffrage proponents were fairly optimistic that they might be able to gain passage of a women's suffrage provision. The members of the convention faced a number of controversial issues, however, including taxation of church property, allocation of part of the school funds to parochial schools, and regulation of railroads. All the delegates were anxious to have the constitution ratified by the voters and approved by Congress before the end of 1876, so that Colorado might enter the Union as the Centennial State. In order to avoid alienating large blocks of voters and possibly defeating the constitution, they sidestepped as many controversial issues as possible, including suffrage. They declined to provide full suffrage, but they did give women the right to vote "in all elections for district school officers and in voting upon questions relating to public schools within such district." The convention also provided for future referenda on the suffrage issue and made it binding on the first legislature to hold such an election.[35] However, when the referendum was called in 1877, suffrage was soundly defeated—14,053 against and only 6,612 for. Anthony, who had campaigned extensively in Colorado, blamed the failure of the vote on the Mexican population in the southern counties; others blamed it on corruption in the voting. Suffrage leader Margaret Campbell blamed it on the women themselves. The desire of women to participate in politics was not high enough, she maintained. "The fact which was the slogan of the antisuffragists still remains: the mass of women do not want it."[36] Whatever the factors involved, it was sixteen years before Colorado voters again considered the question of votes for women.

In the meantime, suffrage had become an increasingly lively issue discussed in many state and territorial legislatures. In addition to Colorado, six other states passed bills calling for a suffrage referendum—Michigan in 1874, Nebraska in 1882, Oregon in 1884, Rhode Island in 1886, Washington in 1889, and South Dakota in 1890.[37] All failed. Washington briefly extended suffrage to women in 1883, but revoked it in 1887 under rather peculiar circumstances.

In fact, the entire Washington suffrage story was somewhat strange. Women's suffrage had been discussed in Washington Territory before the Civil War, and in 1854 Maine emigrant Arthur A. Denny introduced a suffrage bill which failed by the narrow margin of eight to nine. Denny did not follow up on the question, and thus no further legislative action was taken until 1869. The question was not entirely out of the public's attention during this long drought, however. In 1858 Drs. Gideon A. and Ada M. Weed, practitioners of hydropathic medicine and reform, arrived in Salem, Oregon, to set up their practice. For the next two years the Weeds toured the state giving public lectures on hydropathy and women's rights. Ada's lectures particularly engendered the anger of Asahel Bush, editor of the Oregon *Statesman,* and the two exchanged frequent verbal blows in the editorial columns and on the front pages of the paper.[38] Although the Weeds did not extend their lecture tours into Washington Territory, some of the news items were reprinted by the Washington papers and served, along with speeches by a few firmly committed suffrage advocates, to keep discussion of women's rights before the public. Shortly after the Civil War, the Washington Territorial Legislature passed a new election code which gave suffrage to all white citizens. Mary Olney Brown, backed by legislator Edward Eldridge, attempted to gain recognition for the principle that women were citizens and were therefore entitled to suffrage under the election code. When legislation for women's suffrage failed in 1869, Mrs. Brown convinced election judges in two precincts to allow women to vote, a maneuver which excited considerable public discussion. This opened the way for a more vocal and militant campaign.[39]

In 1871 lawyer Daniel Bigelow introduced another suffrage bill. Abigail Scott Duniway of Oregon, who started her women's rights paper, *The New Northwest,* in May, went to Washington and helped organize an Equal Rights Association. She also persuaded Susan B. Anthony to address the legislature on the topic of women's suffrage. Anthony and Bigelow made well-reasoned and well-received appeals for passage. Anthony, borrowing the successful Wyoming gambit, suggested, among other things, that suffrage would bring "the most gratifying of results—the immigration of a large number of good women to the Territory."[40] Despite the oratorial skills of Anthony and Bigelow, the legislature tabled the bill by a vote of sixteen to eleven and in its place passed a bill which cleared up the ambiguity in the 1866 election code by specifying that "hereafter no female shall have the right of ballot or vote at any poll or election precinct in this

Territory. . . ."[41] Still suffrage proponents remained undaunted. Duniway, through her newspaper and a number of lecture tours, continued to speak out for suffrage.[42] In 1873 Edward Eldridge again tried, unsuccessfully, to get the legislature to approve a suffrage measure. This was followed by new campaigns, and failures, in 1875, 1878, and 1881. However, in 1881 the suffrage bill lost by only two votes, and the legislature did pass a liberal married women's property bill. Finally in 1883, perhaps weary of the whole topic, the legislature finally approved a suffrage bill by a vote of fourteen to seven in the House and seven to five in the Council.[43]

Washington women immediately took advantage of their new power at the ballot box—with disastrous results. Many women's rights advocates had also come out strongly in favor of prohibition, and the two issues were often tied together. Duniway realized that liquor interests and drinking men would not look favorably on women's rights as long as prohibition and suffrage were so closely related in the public's mind. Although Duniway was a temperance advocate (as opposed to complete prohibition), she believed that the two issues should be kept entirely separate. When Washington women won the vote she feared that if immediate changes were made in liquor laws, suffrage would be blamed. She warned that women must maintain "a low profile" until men had become accustomed to their participation in politics, reminding them that just as it was easier to approve suffrage in a territory, so it was also easier to rescind it. Therefore she urged Washington women to downplay the prohibition issue. Unfortunately, most did not follow her advice.[44]

No sooner had women been granted the ballot than a series of successful local option campaigns were carried out throughout the territory. At about the same time, voters installed a new reform government in Seattle and turned out the Republican delegate to Congress in favor of a Democrat. Although there is little evidence that women's votes were primarily responsible for these changes, they received the credit—or the blame—for them, and antiprohibitionists and antisuffragists banded together to deprive women of the vote. This was accomplished through a series of legal maneuvers. The 1883 suffrage bill opened the way for women to serve on grand juries, and this provided a convenient means to test the entire bill in the courts. A man named Jeff Harland was indicted on charges of conducting a swindling game. The grand jury which indicted Harland included several married women, so when Harland was tried and convicted, his attorney appealed to the Territorial Supreme Court charging that the grand jury indictment was flawed because women were not legal jurors. Judge George Turner, a former Alabama attorney and a political appointee of President Arthur, concluded in the majority opinion that the legislature had intended only to grant suffrage and not the obligation of jury service, "which for centuries had been restricted to men."[46] Moreover,

Turner ruled, the act which had granted the franchise was invalid, since its entitlement did not conform to the provision of the Organic Act of the territory which required the purpose of each bill to be clearly stated in its title. Thus the suffrage act was void, and women, not being electors, were ineligible for jury service.[47]

The legislature quickly reenacted the suffrage act and retitled it to conform to Turner's ruling, but opponents again took the question to the courts. In 1888, Mrs. Nevada Bloomer, a saloonkeeper's wife, challenged the new law. The court ruled that the act was void, because "Congress had not intended to give the territories authority to enfranchise women."[48] When the constitutional convention met shortly thereafter, the delegates decided not to include a women's suffrage provision in the proposed document but instead provided for a separate referendum on the issue. The result was as devastating as the 1877 Colorado vote; suffrage failed by 35,527 to 16,613. A second attempt to gain suffrage through a constitutional amendment failed in 1898 although by a considerably smaller margin. Soon after the first Washington defeat, two other states—Colorado and Idaho—approved suffrage amendments. Nonetheless the two defeats at home broke the spirit of the suffragists. Mrs. Duniway thereafter concentrated her efforts on Oregon, and Washington women gave up their fight.[49]

Shortly after the initial Washington defeat, the suffrage issue was again raised in Colorado. In January 1893 a bill to amend the state constitution to "extend the suffrage to women of lawful age, and otherwise qualified," was introduced in the Colorado House; a similar measure was brought before the Senate.[50] After extensive debate in both houses, the legislature voted to submit the amendment to the electorate at the 1893 general elections. This enabling legislation also stipulated that the amendment was to be approved by a simple majority. Suffrage proponents quickly began planning a public campaign. Working through the Non-Partisan Equal Suffrage Association, they solicited the aid of Populist Governor Davis H. Waite and other prominent men and women who supported the idea. The Association carried out a widespread educational campaign through leaflets and other literature, named a press director to help gain support from major newspapers, and planned a series of lectures and speeches. They also urged women to turn out in large numbers for the 1893 school elections to show that, contrary to antisuffrage arguments, women did indeed wish to exercise the franchise. The National American Woman Suffrage Association (NAWSA), which had been formed in 1890 by the merging of the National and American Woman Suffrage associations, sent what funds it could; and Carrie Chapman Catt, an experienced organizer for the Association, came to Colorado to help. Fortunately for the suffragists, the liquor interests did not regard the movement as threatening; no other state issues were on the ballot and the opposition was not well organized. The amendment was approved by a comfortable margin, 35,798 to 29,451.[51]

Feminist historians have suggested several reasons for the change in voter behavior in Colorado between 1877 and 1893. Most point out that the timing of the second campaign was strategic. There was a great deal of discontent with economic and political conditions in Colorado in the early 1890s which led to an attitude of disillusionment with the old parties and old politicians. One news reporter suggested that men voted for women's suffrage because "They can't do any worse than men have."[52] According to another contemporary observer, "Some voted for it out of gallantry, others from a sense of justice. A small minority believed in it as a principle, but very many more gave a dubious support on account of dissatisfaction with existing conditions."[53] Susan B. Anthony credited the chivalry of Western men, the lack of prejudice against suffrage in new Western communities, and the strength of the Populist Party. Certainly Populist support was important in the Colorado campaign. The Populist Party gained control of the state government in 1892, and Populists supported the women's suffrage idea. Undoubtedly this influenced many voters. In addition, the suffragists had the support of organized labor, there was little organized opposition, and no other major issue appeared on the ballot. Thus, Colorado became the second state to approve full suffrage for women.[54]

In Idaho, the next state to approve women's suffrage, events followed a course roughly parallel to that in Colorado. The idea was first formally presented in 1870 when Dr. Joseph William Morgan introduced a women's suffrage bill in the territorial legislature. The bill passed on first and second reading, but following extensive debate there was some vote switching, and on third reading the bill was defeated on a tie vote. Despite the narrow margin of defeat, Morgan's measure was clearly premature. There appeared to be little support for, or interest in, the issue. There were no local or territorial suffrage associations; in fact, no women had spoken out in favor of suffrage. This general apathy continued for some time. Temperance lecturer Carrie F. Young and Oregon's well-known suffrage advocate Abigail Scott Duniway occasionally spoke on the topic in Boise and other Idaho towns, but no suffrage groups organized and the legislature took no action.[55] In 1885 and 1887 the territorial legislators defeated proposed bills, although the 1885 legislature did approve school suffrage and made some modifications in the laws related to married women's property rights. When the state constitutional convention met in 1889, Duniway and WCTU President Henrietta Skelton both addressed the delegates without success. Although a number of men favored women's suffrage they, like the Colorado delegates in 1876, feared that controversial provisions such as suffrage and prohibition would endanger statehood either at the polls or in Congress. The convention did provide for suffrage by constitutional amendment, but unlike the Colorado convention, it did not make such action mandatory on the first legislature. Moreover, the delegates did not adopt Duniway's suggestion that they provide for suffrage by simple majority vote of the legislature.[56]

Despite the defeat in the constitutional convention, Duniway and other suffrage supporters were optimistic. Much of the apathy of the 1870s and 80s had dissipated, and there was increasing interest in the issue. Duniway, who thought that "premature organization hurt the cause more than it helped,"[57] now thought the time right to launch a major campaign. She began organizing suffrage clubs and planning for the future. In the meantime the Boise *City Republican*, the Boise *Daily Statesman*, and other newspapers had taken up the cause, and suffrage won new adherents throughout the state. In 1894 both the Republican and Populist conventions went on record as favoring women's suffrage. When the legislature met in January 1895, the members approved a proposed constitutional suffrage amendment by a substantial margin (sixteen to zero in the Senate and thirty-three to two in the House) and set the election for November 1896.

Despite some initial antagonism between Idaho suffrage workers and the National American Woman Suffrage Association, once the campaign got underway both Western and Eastern leaders worked hard to ensure success. NAWSA sent Emma Smith DeVoe of Illinois and Laura M. Johns of Kansas to help organize new suffrage groups and revitalize old ones. NAWSA leader Carrie Chapman Catt spent a month in Idaho giving speeches and helping secure the endorsement of the major political parties.[58] She also helped develop an effective campaign strategy. Despite some concerns that miners in the Coeur d'Alene district and anti-Mormon voters in the north and west would vote against the amendment,[59] there was no effectively organized opposition. When the votes were counted, voters had approved the amendment 12,126 to 6,282; however, one more hurdle had to be cleared. The state board of canvassers ruled that the amendment had been defeated because 29,516 men had participated in the election but less than two-thirds of them had voted on the suffrage amendment. Three of Idaho's leading attorneys agreed to represent the suffrage interests in an appeal of the board's ruling and succeeded in winning a favorable decision in the courts.[60]

Although Populist and labor support was not as critical in Idaho as it was in Colorado, there were some similarities in both victories. In both states the support of one or more major political parties was important. In both states "the absence of public battles between suffragists and the WCTU, between wets and drys, and between Eastern and Western suffragists" contributed to the success of the campaign, and in both states a relatively small number of dedicated spokespersons and a carefully planned campaign helped assure victory.[61] In both Idaho and Colorado suffrage proved to be a "decided success." Women participated in increasing numbers in local and state elections, and a few ran for public office.[62] "We wanted it; we went after it and we got it," newspaper editor and suffrage advocate William Balderston wrote in 1905. "After we got it we liked it, and we find ourselves liking it better after an experience with it reaching over four campaigns." According to a statement by Governor James H. Brady a few years later, women participated in most elections and "often vote quite independently." Moreover, he noted, "they get elected to the offices of town clerk, county superintendent of schools, county treasurer, and state superintendent of public instruction and, less often, to the legislature."[63]

As Idaho women gained experience in the political process, suffrage leaders in Washington laid plans for a new campaign to reinstitute women's suffrage in that state. In 1906 Emma Smith DeVoe, who had played an important role in the 1896 Idaho campaign and had participated in the campaigns in a number of other states, moved to Washington. She soon rebuilt the state's suffrage organization and helped plan a new legislative campaign. In 1909 the legislature passed a bill calling for a referendum the following year. Despite a bitter dispute between DeVoe and recently arrived Idaho suffrage worker May Arkwright Hutton which threatened to undermine the entire campaign, the referendum carried by a substantial margin—52,299 to 29,676. After the bitter defeats in 1889 and 1898, the 1910 victory was especially pleasing to suffrage workers. It was also something of a surprise.[64] Carrie Chapman Catt credited the seemingly easy victory to the fact that the prohibition issue had been kept out of the campaign, noting that "the brewers were undoubtedly misled by the quiet character of the campaign." Whether this was a major factor in the victory is difficult to ascertain. Certainly DeVoe was able to persuade the prohibitionists to support the amendment actively but quietly, something the more militant Duniway had never been able to do. In addition, the 1909–10 campaign was much better organized and more smoothly run than the earlier ones. Perhaps most significant, the Washington victory, like those in Idaho and Colorado, was linked to a spirit of reform. Change was in the air, and many viewed women's suffrage as an important part of a progressive reform program.[65]

The Washington vote presaged a series of successes for women's suffrage. In rapid succession six additional states and one territory passed suffrage legislation—California in 1911; Oregon, Arizona, and Kansas in 1912; Alaska in 1913; and Montana and Nevada in 1914.[66] Western suffrage workers, invigorated by their victories, prepared to assist their suffering sisters in the Eastern states.[67] In the meantime, however, national leaders had finally agreed that the state-by-state method was too slow and too costly. Moreover, they believed that the Western victories had "aroused an opposition to woman suffrage which was not likely to be caught napping again" and that this opposition would increase in direct proportion to a state's political importance.[68] They therefore agreed to return to the program which Anthony had recommended fifty years earlier and attempt to secure a federal suffrage amendment.

Over the years since the so-called Anthony amendment was first discussed, the membership of the National American Woman Suffrage Association had changed. Unlike the older pioneer suffragists, the new members were young and well-educated; many were business and professional women. They had become increasingly impatient with what they considered far too conservative a program. Women should not "ask" for their rights, these women believed, they should "demand" them. Disgusted with the long years of sedate, piecemeal campaigning in the individual states, they urged a more militant and aggressive program to focus national attention on the suffrage cause and garner support for a federal amendment. When the NAWSA leadership refused to be pushed into a more militant stance, the insurgents under the leadership of Alice Paul formed the Congressional Union (later to become the Woman's Party) and planned a series of marches, speeches, and other events designed to bring pressure on the President and Congress.[69] In 1915 Paul and some of the California women conceived a dramatic plan that would "symbolize the offer of the political power of the enfranchised women of the West to their voteless sisters in the East." They arranged a cross-country automobile trip to carry a suffrage petition from Western voters to President Woodrow Wilson and the Congress. Along the route they planned to stage parades and rallies, make speeches, and gain additional names for the petition.[70]

A young Western writer and libertarian, Sara Bard Field, agreed to undertake the grueling trip. With two Swedish socialist women as companions and drivers, Field left San Francisco in September 1915. The automobile was a new conveyance, the suffrage issue a new frontier, and the trail led eastward not westward; but Field and her companions faced many of the problems pioneer women had faced half a century earlier. When the trio reached Reno and the edge of the long desert route to Salt Lake City, Field wrote her fiance, Charles Erskine Wood, "We are just about to start off on what is the only perilous part of our whole trip. . . . I say perilous because all the printed directions say it is and suggest that 'women and children' should never attempt the journey."[71] Obviously male guidebook writers' opinions of woman's delicate nature and her proper place had not changed since the first days of overland travel! Despite the guidebook warnings and a wrong road, the three women made it safely not only to Salt Lake but eventually to Washington where Field and a delegation of Western suffragists presented the petition, with more than half a million signatures, to President Wilson. Field received an enthusiastic reception in most of the cities she visited and a cordial reception in Washington, but the Western women's plea did not accomplish its purpose.[72] The "disenfranchised sisters" of the East remained without the vote for another five years. When Eastern women finally received the ballot in 1920, Wyoming women had been voting for half a century!

Why did women's suffrage come so much earlier in the West than in the East? Historians have suggested a number of reasons. The more romantic nineteenth-century writers, as well as some Eastern leaders such as Susan B. Anthony, believed that Western men were more chivalrous than Eastern men. Another popular nineteenth-century argument was that the West voted for women's suffrage in order to advertise and attract additional population. This was closely tied to the idea that Western men voted for women's suffrage to strengthen the "good, decent home element" against transient bachelors and the less virtuous elements in society. Still others suggested that Western men voted for women's suffrage to reward their wives for working beside them through the difficult pioneering years. Such an idea was clearly implied in the statement by one California suffragist:

> the countrymen's vote saved the day. The countrymen see women— all of them—working hard. They see no idle women. The city men see great numbers of parasitic, idle absurdly decorated snobs. Way underneath the city man has not the same respect for the women he sees, that the countryman has for all he sees. This is a cause [for the 1911 California suffrage vote], not a superficial one.[73]

A number of twentieth-century historians have associated Western women's suffrage with the supposed equality and democracy of the frontier. Others have associated it with the Puritan ethic and with the Populist and Progressive movements.[74]

All of these factors may have played some part in the Western suffrage votes, yet none of these explanations seems completely adequate. Certainly there was no evidence that Western men were more chivalrous. Rather, the argument was used so often in the nineteenth century that one modern historian suggested that Western men "were called chivalrous so often . . . that they came to believe it."[75] In the same vein, the population attraction contention was more propaganda than fact. Had it been true, Wyoming and Idaho would be among the most populous states in the country. Similarly, there seemed to be little basis for the strengthen-the-home arguments. On the contrary, one researcher concluded that suffrage lines in the West were not drawn between bachelors and married men.[76] The reward-the-helpmate theory may have been a factor in some places, but. Western men did not often work beside their wives. Indeed, many Western men were gone for long periods of time leaving their wives to carry on alone. If this factor did influence some men, it may have been more from guilt than from a sense of gratitude. Reform politics clearly influenced some suffrage elections. The rise of the Populist party was important in the Colorado suffrage vote and possibly had some influence on Idaho as well. Progressive reform appeared to have had some influence on the 1910 Washington vote and was probably a factor in California and Oregon. But if reform politics were a major factor in suffrage victories, what happened in Texas and Oklahoma (strong Populist states that refused suffrage), and in the Progressive Eastern States? Moreover, analysis of the legislative votes for the suffrage referenda in two states, Idaho and Washington, showed no significant relationship between party affiliation and the suffrage vote.[77]

The frontier democracy theory and the idea of a revival of the Puritan ethic coming out of the West are the most attractive arguments for Western leadership in women's suffrage.[78] It would be pleasant to believe Walter Prescott Webb's stirring phrase that "There is hidden somewhere in the cause [why Western men were first to grant the franchise to women] the spirit of the Great Plains which made men democratic in deed and in truth."[79] But as the analysis of the votes in the various states earlier in this chapter demonstrates, political expediency was more often the reason for granting suffrage than frontier egalitarianism. If Western men had a greater sense of justice and equality than Eastern men, one wonders what happened to that nebulous spirit in Kansas in 1867, in Colorado in 1877, in Oregon in 1884, 1896, 1906, and 1910 or, in fact, in the many Western states where women's suffrage victories came only after many unsuccessful referenda. Clearly, the question of the relationship between women's suffrage and the frontier experience is a very complex one. One is sometimes tempted to settle for the argument that on the frontier political actions were "the result largely of pure chance, coincidence, or a fortuitous combination of circumstances."[80] Before accepting such an unsatisfactory conclusion, however, it might be useful to consider two other factors which, although tied to the frontier experience, differ from the idea of Western egalitarianism. One is the point that because the trans-Mississippi states were relatively new, were formed at a time when questions of women's legal and political rights were being raised nationally, and had no deeply entrenched tradition of restriction, it was easier to convince Western legislators to pass women's rights legislation. Susan B. Anthony certainly recognized this. In a letter to the Utah *Woman's Exponent* in August 1894, she pointed out:

Now in the formative period of your constitution is the time to establish justice and equality to all the people. That adjective 'male' once admitted into your organic law, will remain there. . . . Once ignored in your constitution—you'll be powerless to secure recognition as are we in the older states.[81]

Although not all Western states granted full women's suffrage before 1920, it is significant that not only were all of the full-suffrage states in the West but that they were also the newest states. As another historian noted, "By 1914, eleven of the last eighteen states admitted into the Union had statewide woman suffrage; none of the first thirty states had accomplished this."[82] The idea of a lack of restrictive tradition also suggests a concept of innovation. Innovation was both common and necessary to the frontier. Frontier dwellers had to be innovators if they were to survive and prosper under new and difficult circumstances, and such innovative behavior may help explain political as well as social and economic changes. If one accepts the theories of several social scientists that the diffusion of innovations in society approximates an S-shaped curve, Western women's suffrage appears to conform to such theories.[83] Thus the diffusion of innovation—in this case women's suffrage—among legislators and decision makers may have had some effect in the Western territories and states.

Part of the problem in trying to analyze the Western suffrage movement

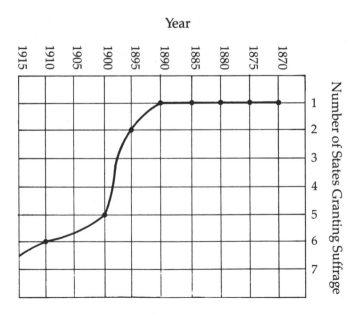

is that there has been so little work done in the field. With the exception of the pioneering efforts of T. A. Larson and some recent work by one or two young historians, most women's suffrage and feminist historians have almost entirely ignored the West.[84] Writers have concentrated on the national suffrage leaders and on the history of the movement in the Eastern states. Western suffrage votes are treated as some sort of aberrant political behavior rather than as part of the mainstream of the suffrage movement. Furthermore, no attempt has been made to analyze the seeming apathy on the part of most Western women in regard to suffrage. Clearly men, not women, took the lead in Wyoming and Utah and played a significant role in the other successful Western campaigns. In fact, little evidence exists that women were active in large numbers in any of the Western states.

This seeming apathy may be misleading, however. A number of women's diaries, journals, and reminiscences contained clear indications that they were aware of political events and supported women's rights even when they did not participate in suffrage campaigns. Several pointed out that since Western women had assisted their husbands in establishing new homes and had helped earn the family living without losing their femininity, there was no reason that they could not participate in politics without becoming less feminine or less attentive to domestic duties. Admitting she had taken only a small part in suffrage work, an Arizona woman nonetheless included an impassioned defense of votes for women in her reminiscences. If women were competent to care for their children, "train them morally and bear a fare [sic] share of their school education," she argued, "then why cannot she grasp the governmental questions as well and bring to bear her experience and intuition . . . without interfering with her home duties?" A Washington woman recalled with pride that during the years from 1883 to 1887 when Washington first opened the franchise to women, she "took my turn on petit and grand jury, served on election boards, walked in perfect harmony to the polls by the side of my staunch Democratic husband, and voted the Republican ticket— not feeling any more out of my sphere than when assisting my husband to develop the resources of our country."[85]

Even before suffrage was granted, some women used their influence indirectly. "In Pioneer times," one woman recalled, "women were a silent element in politics; but then, as now, individual women were strong partisans and ready, on occasion, to give a reason for the faith that was within them—especially when striving to influence the 'menfolks' of their own families who did the voting. . . ." Some did not confine their influence to the family circle. Writing from Kansas in 1855, Julia Lovejoy exhorted her friends back in New Hampshire to do all they could to secure the election of John C. Fremont. "There are ways without number, in which ladies in their own proper sphere, can assist in the coming election," she counseled. By the use of ornamental work, the making of Fremont cheese, and by similar devices, Lovejoy continued, women could keep Fremont's name "before the people till our object is gained. . . ." Even young girls indicated in their school diaries and journals that they were aware of political issues and took decided stands. "Boys and girls took a lively interest in politics," one recorded. "When General Houston and Mr. Runnels were opponents for the office of governor, many exciting speeches were made by the girls mounted on a school desk."[86]

Some women, of course, opposed suffrage. "Pray deliver me from women politicians," one cautioned. "When men write that the time will come when wives will walk beside their husbands to the polls and vote, depend upon it, there is some wily scheming behind the scenes." Others were not sure whether they approved of the new ways or not. "This is a deuced fast place," wrote one woman from Portland. "Most independent women here I ever seen. There are a number who will vote the coming election."[87] Other women were more interested in educational, legal, and economic reforms than in directly exercising the vote. One Texas woman, writing from the perspective of the 1870s, saw the issue in terms of a double moral and social standards rather than as purely political:

> I hate the doctrine that women ought by nature to be better than men! If there is any difference it ought to be that men should be better than women. . . . There is a great deal said about Women's Rights, but if I ever go on the platform, it will be as an advocate of Man's Rights and first of all I'll claim for them the right to as high a moral standard as women have and to be punished as severely as women are when they fail to reach that standard.

For California businesswoman Harriet Strong, the suffrage issue was directly related to property rights. "When wives and daughters are deprived of the privilege to act or to speak for their property, the voice of that property is silent," she wrote, "and there is a wrong permitted and practiced against that property."[88]

Some women who supported women's suffrage preferred to work outside formal suffrage organizations. Some were simply too busy. As one woman mine operator told a Colorado newspaper reporter, "A businesswoman has no time to spare for the turmoil of club or caucus." Others wished to avoid the bitter in-fighting and name-calling which characterized so much of the suffrage movement or became disgusted with the lack of clear programs and an often disorganized approach to suffrage campaigns. As one summed it up:

I have been in business long enough to have a certain sense of efficiency, and for the amount of money and energy expended, we developed only a low percentage of efficiency. . . . The campaign there
was run by club women, and I personally have not much respect for
the business ability of club women. . . . With, I think, a majority of
them it simply happened that they took up suffrage this year, in the
same manner and spirit that they took up French china or German
pottery or Japanese art. . . . A great deal of work was done . . . but
one woman of ability making a business of the work . . . could have
covered all that was done by seven or eight women . . . each in charge
of the same branch of work, but no one understanding the necessity
of allowing some one person to manage affairs. . . .[89]

For many business and professional women, such inefficiency discouraged
their participation in the suffrage movement. Moreover, many of them
believed that women's suffrage campaigns which tied enfranchisement
to temperance and other moral issues, rather than to economic and legal
reform, diluted women's power and left them with an empty victory. For
businesswomen, and other women as well, local suffrage was of more
immediate importance than voting in national, or even state, elections.
By 1910, twenty-three states had opened municipal, school, and/or tax
elections to women,[90] and many women believed these votes had more
direct bearing on their lives.

Western women were not indifferent to women's rights, but many were
disappointed or disgusted with the Eastern and national suffrage organizations and resented their interference in Western campaigns. Moreover,
many Western women who did participate in the suffrage movement developed their own unique political style and were far more sensitive to
local and regional issues than most of the Eastern and national leadership. Western suffrage leaders like Abigail Scott Duniway, Luna Kellie,
and May Arkwright Hutton were not popular with the more conservative
Eastern women because they emphasized political, economic, and social
reform as well as the suffrage issue. Many of these women had grown up
on the frontier, and, like Duniway, they "represented a particular segment
of . . . first-pioneers among whom women were welcome co-civilizers—
the independent farmers and small businessmen" whose economic and
social orientation "matched their own" and who clearly reflected the
"agrarian proto-populist political and social climate of nineteenth century
American frontier men and women."[91] Such an orientation was also evident among women who did not participate actively in suffrage campaigns but who chose instead to exercise their independence and to
emphasize their talents and skills through various economic enterprises
and who became successful entrepreneurs.

9

If All We Did
Was To Weep at Home[1]

Women as Frontier Entrepreneurs

The West offered challenges to women's skills and provided opportunities for them to develop and test new talents and to broaden the scope of their home and community activities. It also offered, for whatever reason, a significant degree of political participation. But did the West offer economic opportunity as well? Frederick Jackson Turner maintained that the West was a liberating influence in American life and that the frontier setting offered westering Americans, at least westering males, both economic and political opportunity. "So long as free land exists," he wrote in his famous essay on the significance of the frontier, "the opportunity for a competency exists and economic power secures political power."[2] In recent years, a number of historians have attacked portions of Turner's frontier hypothesis and especially its relevance to westering women. Indeed, several radical feminist authors have maintained that the West exerted a regressive rather than a progressive influence on women's lives. These authors contended that women on the frontiers were forced into unfamiliar, demeaning roles, and that although women in the Western settlements continued to try to reinstate a culture of domesticity, their work as virtual hired hands prevented them either from returning to older, more familiar roles in the social structure or from creating positive new roles. Unable to "appropriate their new work to their own ends and advantage," the authors of one article concluded, frontier women "remained estranged from their function as able bodies."[3] A similar point of view was offered by another author who also noted the conflict between women's sense of their proper sphere and the new roles and conditions imposed by the frontier. Women, she believed, "understood the westward migration as a masculine enterprise," and although she conceded that the frontier "seems in later stages to have yielded to newer social and legal forms for women," it failed to offer as many new opportunities for them as it did for men.[4] In a less strident interpretation another historian maintained that although the West may have offered opportunities for women to advance themselves economically and politically, few took advantage of these opportunities. "I had hoped to find that pioneer women used the frontier as a means of liberating themselves from stereotypes and behaviors which I found constricting and sexist," she wrote. "I discovered that they did not."[5]

Writing from a somewhat different perspective, several historians questioned the application of Turner's thesis to women's frontier experiences and concluded that women did not share in the freedom and opportunities the West offered to men. The stereotype of American women as the "virtuous, religious, progenitor of democracy—the cornerstone of the family and society," one maintained, was a product of an agrarian mythology (and by implication a frontier mythology as well). He argued that it was not on the farm, or on the frontier, that women won political and legal rights, but rather in the city. "It was the city," he wrote, "which became the catalyst for all the aspirations of freedom and equality held by American women." The frontier influenced women as well as men, another historian agreed, but "If we accept Turner's own assumption that economic opportunity is what matters, and that the frontier was significant as the context within which economic opportunity occurred, then we must observe that for American women . . . opportunity began pretty much where the frontier left off."[6] In a similar vein, another historian wrote that although there were independent Western women who may have been different from women in the urban East, industrialism and the city, not the Western farm, opened new avenues for women. The frontier, according to his interpretation, "strongly reinforced the traditional role of the sexes," and, he concluded, mill girls were likely to be "potentially far more 'revolutionary' than their rural, Western counterparts."[7]

Yet despite arguments to the contrary, there is clear evidence that Western women did not confine themselves to purely traditional domestic and community concerns. It is true that most Western women were not revolutionary. Like Western men, they did not completely break with tradition nor, with very few exceptions, attempt radically to change women's lives and role in society. They did enlarge the scope of woman's place, however, and countered prevailing Eastern arguments about woman's sphere and the cult of true womanhood. Indeed, the ideals of true womanhood never really applied to a large number of women. As one historian has pointed out, at the very time that domesticity and true womanhood were being expounded as an American ideal, an increasing number of women were leaving their homes to become factory workers and wage earners.[8] Factory work was obviously not available in frontier areas, but like many of their Eastern sisters, Western women were employed in a number of economic activities, and some of them engaged in new fields of endeavor outside what was considered their competency, skills, or proper sphere.

On the Western frontiers, as in other rural areas, much of women's work was tied to domestic manufacture. Historians have estimated that in the colonial period, when the United States was still predominantly rural, 60 to 75 percent of domestic manufacture, particularly in textiles, was carried out by women. Both Alexander Hamilton and Albert Gallatin acknowledged the important role of home textile production to the national economy. Hamilton noted that "in a number of districts" as much as four-fifths of the clothing was made "by the inhabitants themselves," while Gallatin estimated that "two-thirds of the clothing including hosiery and table linen" was the "product of family manufactures," products worth about "ten times by value what was produced outside the home."[9] Most of this domestic manufacture was done by women who also produced butter, cheese, preserved foodstuffs, soap, candles, and other domestic goods and were often in charge of the home dairy and chicken production. Most ordinary women, an eighteenth-century traveler reported, "take care of Cows, Hogs, and other small Cattle, make Butter and Cheese, spin cotton and flax, help sow and reap corn, wind silk from the worms, gather Fruit and look after the House."[10]

Such domestic manufacture continued on the Western frontiers for many years after it had ceased in the East. Although by the nineteenth century, factories were beginning to produce foodstuffs, clothing, and other goods previously provided by home production, frontier women continued to manufacture such items themselves because "neither the goods, nor the cash to obtain them were readily available."[11] Long, and often primitive, transportation made factory goods scarce and therefore expensive, and few frontier families, at least during the first years of settlement, had extra money to purchase what the women could, and did, produce at home. It was the women, as one Iowa man recalled, who saw that "the garden [was] tended, the turkeys dressed, the deer flesh cured and the fat prepared for candles or culinary use, the wild fruits were garnered and preserved or dried, that the spinning and knitting was done and the clothing made."[12] Such production was not considered gainful employment, of course, and female home manufacturers were rarely, if ever, listed by census takers as employed or working women. Yet such employment was essential to the family economy. Women, as one historian wrote, were "to their families what the factory was to an industrialized society;" they were "the key link in turning unusable raw materials into consumable finished goods."[13]

Not only did women provide needed goods and services for their families, which otherwise would have had to be purchased, but they often exchanged the produce of such work for needed goods or for cash. Margaret Murray recalled that her mother "sold Butter Eggs & Beeswax & anything we could spare off the farm, [and] in the summer and fall we gathered Black Berries wild grapes & anything we raised on the farm that would bring money or exchange for groceries." An Oklahoma woman invested a small gift from her mother in cotton goods which she made into sunbonnets for sale at the local stores, while an Iowa woman turned $230 of inheritance money into a profitable dairy business. A number of single women helped support themselves with such goods and services, and married women contributed substantially to the family income by plying their domestic skills. Indeed, according to one woman, "while the men were learning to farm, the women and children actually supported the families" through the manufacture and sale of various farm and home products.[14]

Most frontierswomen were justifiably proud of their skills and their contributions to the family economy, and such work won women a good deal of respect and admiration from their families and from frontier society. Although it is true that some women were exploited by their husbands who took their butter and egg money, sold jointly accumulated property without a "by your leave" or even sold laboriously acquired household and personal furnishings,[15] most families respected and acknowledged women's contributions to the comfort and often to the actual survival of the family's life. Women's domestic production was essential to the economic development of Mormon communities and it was actively encouraged by Church authorities. Church leaders openly endorsed and supported female home manufacturing societies and sometimes furnished the initial supplies for beginning home industries. Brigham Young delivered a series of sermons designed to stimulate home industry and "encouraged the exclusive purchase of homemade products [and] the expansion of home manufacturing. . . ."[16]

Through these contributions some women came to exert a good deal of influence on the family decision-making process. "The women were not unaware" of their contributions, one reported, and were "quite capable of scoring a point on occasion when masculine attitudes became too bumptious." Some women were openly aggressive or even contradictory in opposing male decisions, while others worked more subtly and were "careful to maintain the idea of male superiority." For example, one woman bought some milk cows and began a small dairy business while her husband was away doing carpenter work, but when he returned, he sold the cows since such work "did not appeal to him." The woman, however, without raising a fuss, simply took some inheritance money and reinvested in cows and "eventually the family acquired hogs to help consume the milk . . . [and] stock raising ended as the family's main economic activity."[17]

Often women's domestic skills became the basis for a profitable business. Cooks, seamstresses, and washerwomen were in demand, especially in the mining camps and in other areas where the population included a number of single men. Although such work was laborious, it was usually well paid, particularly during the early frontier period. "I know girls that is ritch," one woman reported, "just working out bie the month," while another wrote that wages for women's work were high, "$50 to $75 a month."[18] As late as 1880 in South Dakota, Cora Babcock reported that she and her friend "averaged for the winter $14.00 per week" taking in washing and ironing. "Our average expenses for groceries and fuel . . . was about $2.00 per week," she continued. "We carried well water, filled barrells and cleansed it with lye for washing. Had all the work we could possibly do and sometimes more."[19] Mary Jane Staples reported that when her husband became ill and they ran short of funds, she baked pies and "my venture was a success. I sold fruit pies for one dollar and twenty-five cents a piece and mince pies for a dollar and fifty cents. I sometimes made and sold a hundred a day." Ella Bird-Dumont noted that her income from making vests, gloves, and other items for cowboys and ranchers "made us a very comfortable living until the increase or revenue from my cattle began coming in," while an Oklahoma woman remembered that it was the sale of her garden produce that helped her family overcome hard times. "After our garden started producing," she wrote:

> I would load up the big wagon with vegetables and start at midnight, would drive all alone to Okla. City. I would get to the outskirts of town about one hour before dawn. I spread a quilt under the wagon and slept until daylight, then drove from door to door selling my vegetables. . . .[20]

Most of this type of work could be done at home, and women thus provided a small income for their families while they continued to carry out their household chores and care for their children within a familiar setting.

Some women preferred to hire out rather than run their own businesses or combined employment and home life. Some worked as housekeepers or cooks for single men or in the homes of more prosperous families. Others took jobs in hotels and boardinghouses. Ann Beisel reported that she "cooked in every hotel in Bartlesville [Oklahoma]" and "learned to take care of ourselves." Melissa Stroud and her sisters worked in a hotel in

Salem, Oregon, to "help make ends meet," and Carrie Nesbitt's mother worked as a chambermaid and waitress to help provide extra funds for her family. Many of these domestic jobs were undertaken by unmarried girls and widows. For widows, such work was often their only source of support. "I support our family by serving," one wrote to her brother in the East. "I must earn 10 dollars a week and then cannot live and eat enough hardly. . . ."[21] For single women, domestic service helped to pay for their education or provided a living until they found a suitable husband. In the Midwest, hired girls were in great demand as "essential domestic assistants on farms, especially during the spring and summer." According to one source, hired girls were in such demand that some pioneer families "wisely brought hired girls with them from the East."[22] Wages for domestic work were higher in the Western areas than in the East, and some women were able to accumulate a "tidy little nest egg."

In frontier areas, women also served an important function as hotel and boardinghouse keepers. Women frequently boarded hired hands or seasonal workers. One California woman wrote that during the harvesting she had ten men in the family. "Washing and cooking for this crew," she reported, "takes me all the time. . . ." A Texas woman recorded that her husband owned a cotton gin for twenty-two years, and "I had my part to play in this business as we boarded the hands and I did the cooking."[23] Other women opened their homes to boarders or operated small hotels to provide an income for themselves or their families. Shortly after her husband died, Amelia Barr wrote, "I have opened my house last week for boarders and intend to take about eight steady boarders," and a Texas woman recalled that her grandmother "kept a boarding house" to support her family when her Unionist husband left for Mexico."[24]

Boardinghouses varied in size and type of services provided. Some boarding establishments furnished only meals while others supplied both meals and lodging. Others offered a combination of services. A Kansas woman recorded that she had two lodgers for whom she provided breakfast and supper and two others who "cook their own food and lodge in our little hut." Most boarding establishments were relatively small operations. With limited space and cooking facilities, most women could not accommodate more than eight to ten boarders at a time, but a few attempted to run fairly substantial operations. "I took 77 boarders from Wisconsin and Canada," one Colorado woman recalled. Other women reported providing meals for large numbers of boarders, although usually they did not provide lodging. Some women, with little business experience, found it difficult to make these enterprises profitable. One woman reported that she fed her boarders "too good and ran behind on bills $70 and had to give up the job." But many of these operations were successful and provided their proprietress with a good living or a much needed supplementary income.[25]

A number of women worked with their husbands in operating hotels and boardinghouses. Usually the men kept the books, entertained the guests, and looked after building and maintenance while the women cooked and served the meals, cleaned the rooms, washed and mended the linens, and supervised the maids and other domestic workers. According to one report:

> At least four of the five prominent Yosemite hotels in the 1870s boasted culinary artists who bent over hot wood ranges, and brought forth memorable meals. All four were the hotelkeepers' wives whose cooking and housekeeping efforts, in a large measure, made their husbands' enterprises successful.

Other women took complete responsibility for the operation of such businesses. It is clear from the autobiography of Michigan pioneer Lettie Pennoyer that she was the better businessperson and was "saddled with much of the work of managing the hotel of which he was the proprietor."[26]

Such work, although often profitable, was difficult and time-consuming. Most frontier hotels were crude structures with few conveniences. "I should like to have you see my cook room," one woman wrote to her daughter; "in one corner I have a chest set up on end with shelves . . . then comes a champagne box sitting on a half-barrell for a rolling board." Her other provisions and utensils were stored in every available space and corner, and "my chamber beggars all description." According to another woman:

> All the kitchen that I have is four posts stuck down into the ground and covered over the top with a factory cloth no floor but the ground. this is a Boarding House kitchen. . . . I am scareing the Hogs out of my kitchen and Driving the mules out of my Dining room. You can see by the description of that I have given you of my kitchen that anything can walk into the kitchen that choeses [sic] to walk in. . . . there I hear the Hogs in my kitchen turning the Pots and kettles upside down, so I must drop the pen and run and drive them out.

Even when the facilities were adequate, women found running a hotel or boardinghouse hard work. One woman reported that her day began at seven when she began preparing the morning meal and supervising the women who were "sweeping and setting the table." After breakfast she did the baking, planned and prepared the other meals, made the beds, did the washing, and made or mended the sheets, pillowcases, and other linens. "I do not sit down until after eight o'clock at night," she reported, "and three nights out of a week I have to iron." Often women had to combine these arduous tasks with their own housework and the care of their children. "Oh, I am weary," one harassed mother-wife-hotelkeeper complained; "the work has been very difficult and the children have been fussy and no help at all. I do not know that I can go another step."[27]

Although domestic work was often difficult and required "the constitution of six horses," it did bring women a degree of community status and recognition. As an Oklahoma woman reported of her hotel, "It was a help to the town and trade was good. . . ." In many mining communities and lumber camps the few women, such as the legendary Nellie Cashman, who provided clean beds and the best meals in town became local institutions.[28] Moreover, domestic occupations also brought women a good deal of indirect economic power. One recent study indicated, for example, that women in Helena, Montana, controlled, either through property ownership or through work as boardinghouse and hotel keepers, as much as 80 percent of the available housing.[29] Women's work as cooks, seamstresses, and housekeepers gave them a good deal of buying power; women proprietors and boardinghouse and hotel managers were frequently purchasing agents as well. Thus women were a factor to be reckoned with in determining the types of goods and services supplied by storekeepers and merchants. On the frontier, women were actively sought not only as wives but as contributors to the local economy. Many community builders believed that a few good women would not only help in civilizing and taming the frontier but would add to its economic development as well. The Western agents for R. G. Dun and Company (the forerunner of Dun and Bradstreet) certainly were aware of women's potential economic contributions and recommended "equality of economic opportunity when it came to finding credit endorsements." Indeed, according to one analysis of Denver credit ratings for the period 1859 to 1877, "women without collateral could usually get recommendations for credit where men could not, even when everything was equal except their sex."[30]

However remunerative, domestic work was often boring as well as laborious, and it kept women confined within their domestic spaces. "There is something dull in sitting here day by day, planning this garment and making that, but that seems to be my destiny just now," mourned a young Nebraska girl who made a good living as a seamstress. "There does not seem to be much that a girl *can* do here." Other women, equally bored by dull work, tried to find an outlet for their energies and creative urges in quiltmaking, fancy sewing, or by adding artistic touches to their home manufactures. Texas pioneer Ella Bird-Dumont longed to be a sculptress but, denied the opportunity to study in her Panhandle home, she settled instead for creating beauty in the gloves and vests she made and sold to neighboring ranch hands and cowmen. Idaho settler Agnes Just Reid also longed to be an artist, and she was very excited when she met the Western landscape painter Thomas Moran. She reported to her father that Moran asked her how she "varnished" her rolls of butter to give them "such a glossy appearance." "This is one of the happiest experiences of my life," she continued, "for that man who knows everything to be ignorant in the lines that I know so well. . . . And do you know, since that day, the art of butter making has taken on a new dignity."[31]

Some frontier women refused to subvert their artistic talents to the tasks of sewing, butter making, and other home chores. A number of women were able to combine pioneering and domestic tasks and at the same time open new avenues into the "life of the mind." By the nineteenth century, writing was considered a fairly respectable occupation for women, and a number of them combined the pen with homemaking and child care. According to a recent study, between 1784 and 1860 at least one hundred magazines, most of which were devoted to women's interests, were founded in the United States and provided a market for articles by and for women. Many of these articles were about what women knew best—homemaking and the domestic arts—but the journals also published poetry, essays, and short stories by women. Women also became increasingly active in writing books as well as articles. Of the 1150 novels by American authors published in the United States between 1830 and 1850, a large proportion (perhaps as many as one-third) were written by women. So successful were some of these works that Nathaniel Hawthorne felt compelled to complain to his publisher that "America is wholly given over to a damned mob of scribbling women. . . ." Although many of the "damned mob" admittedly produced third and fourth-rate works, their books were nonetheless popular and brought their authoresses a good deal of attention as well as a source of income.[32]

The Western frontiers supported a number of successful women writers who drew on their pioneer experiences and the rich natural resources of their frontier homes for source material eagerly read by a fascinated Eastern public. During the early nineteenth century, Caroline Kirkland, Eliza Farnham, and Mary Austin Holley all gained moderately successful reputations with their books and articles about frontier life. A century later Laura Ingalls Wilder and Bess Streeter Aldridge wrote a series of successful and popular books based on their childhood experiences and the experiences of their pioneer ancestors. Mary Hallock Foote, Willa Cather, Mary Austin, Helen Hunt Jackson, and Gertrude Atherton achieved literary recognition for their works, most of which utilized their frontier experiences. Elizabeth Custer, as well as several other army wives, wrote of their Western experiences as did Jessie Benton Frémont and Susan Wallace, the wife of the New Mexico Territorial Governor and novelist Ben Wallace. Frances Fuller Victor, Sharlot Hall, and later Mari Sandoz combined history with literature and earned a national reputation for their work. Several Western women, such as California's Ina Coolbrith and Utah's Sarah Carmichael, were successful poetesses. A number of lesser-known Western women regularly contributed articles to various literary and women's magazines, and a few such as Amelia Bloomer, Mary Nolan, Abigail Scott Duniway, and Mormon leaders Emmeline Wells and Eliza Snow, edited magazines and newspapers of their own.[33]

Writing, like various domestic jobs and services, could be combined with homemaking and child rearing and thus it had a special attraction for women with families to care for. Writing permitted flexible hours and could be done at home. Moreover, it was a profession which a woman could enter without special training, provided she had some talent. Thus it was especially attractive to Western women who had few opportunities for advanced schooling or study and who had many home responsibilities and little or no domestic help. A combined career as wife, mother, homemaker, and writer was not easy, however, as one Texas poetess recorded in verse:

> Still I must sweep, and churn and brew,
> And make my dresses nice to view;
> And nurse the baby, read the news,
> Darn socks, keep buttons on the shoes,
> Play the piano, beat the steak,
> Then last, not least, this undertake.
> Not Euclid's problem intricate,
> Have half so puzzled my poor pate.
> If men to such a task were set,
> They's lock their doors, and swear and fret,
> And send for all their counselors.
> And say an age were time too short
> To learn this trade, perfect this art.
> But we must learn a hundred trades
> Without apprenticeship or aids,
> And practice all with equal skill,
> 'Tis their good pleasure, our good will.[34]

Other artistic careers, such as acting and other forms of public performance which took women outside the home and domestic sphere, were less well favored, but a number of Western women were also successful sculptresses, artists, musicians, and photographers. A few, like Texas sculptress Elisabet Ney, California artist Grace Carpenter Hudson, and Montana photographer Evelyn Cameron, achieved national recognition for their work.[35] Some women with musical ability chose to teach rather than to follow a stage or concert career. Some taught in schools or colleges, but many gave private lessons in their homes and thus combined a modest career with homemaking.[36]

Aside from the arts, teaching was about the only profession open to respectable women in the nineteenth century. As noted earlier (in chapter six), education was considered an extension of women's traditional roles as child rearers and moral and cultural guardians, and American education became increasingly feminized during the nineteenth century. As Catherine Beecher pointed out, teaching young children not only provided an essential service to the community, but it helped women prepare themselves for "the great purpose of a woman's life—the happy superintendence of a family." Beecher's advice did not go unheeded: a number of women taught school at one time or another.[37]

Although most women teachers were single, some women continued at least part-time teaching after their marriage. Especially in Western communities where men were engaged in the "multitudes of other employments that will . . . lead to wealth" (as Beecher so bluntly wrote), educated women, whatever their marital status, were frequently urged to help begin schools and teach for a term or two. The scarcity of teachers and the desire of frontier dwellers to provide an education for their children led to many attempts to recruit young women from the East. "We want good female teachers, who could obtain constant employment and the best of wages," a Kansas settler wrote home to a New England newspaper; "we want them immediately, and they would do much good."[38] Various Eastern groups attempted to respond to the demand. Catherine Beecher began a campaign to send women teachers to the West, warning that "Western children were growing up without the benefit of either a practical or a moral education." Beecher, and the Board of National Popular Education, formed in 1847, did recruit some teachers. The Board served as an agency for single teachers and provided job training as well as placement services, but the number of Eastern teachers provided by the group never approached the 90,000 young women Beecher believed were needed "if the tides of barbarism were to be pushed back." Far more helpful in recruiting teachers in the West than the actions of Eastern groups and agencies were the more practical solutions found by frontier residents who relied on the resources available and found local women with at least a modicum of education to fulfill the communities' educational needs.[39]

Teaching, like many other jobs, was complicated by frontier conditions.

Frontier schools were often poorly equipped, and teachers had to "make do" with improvised seating and teaching aids and a wide variety of books and supplies. One young woman reported that when she came from Kansas to teach an Oklahoma school she did not even have a building but "taught under a brush arbor until the weather got too cold. . . ." Teachers were often responsible for cleaning and heating the schoolrooms, carrying water, and trying to gather up enough pens, paper, slates, and books for their erstwhile scholars. Ellen Pennock reported that her first Colorado school was "undisciplined, the school house dirty, window lights broken, blackboards nearly paintless, and almost every pupil has a different kind of book." Another teacher reported that she had "a somewhat strange gathering of school books for they came from Maine, Missouri and many other states" and that "some difficulty was encountered in improvising seats and desks for the pupils."[40]

Teachers not only had to contend with cold buildings and lack of supplies, but they often had to cope with other hazards peculiar to the frontier. One Oklahoma woman described her problems when the creek overflowed and flooded her schoolroom; another recalled that her horse had been attacked by a wild stallion as she rode the seven miles to her district school. Yet another frontier teacher wrote of her fear of a herd of wild Texas steers near her school and her attempts to reach her schoolhouse "without coming in contact with those ferocious beasts." Frontier teachers battled rattlesnakes, tarantulas, scorpions, and other insects. Sometimes they even had to protect themselves and their pupils from marauding Indians, outlaws, or drunken cowboys and miners. One teacher, whose school was threatened by a man who "suddenly appeared, drew a pistol, and began shooting," fled with her students to the woods, then armed herself with a pistol. "I'm not going to be run off from this school," she declared. "I'm going to protect myself and those children. I'm going to be a second Belle Starr."[41]

Most frontier teachers taught all grades and ages and a variety of subjects. One Oklahoma teacher reported she taught everything "from the 'chart' class to the eighth grade." The records of an Idaho teacher noted than in 1878 her school enrolled thirteen boys ranging in age from eight to sixteen and seven girls from eight to twelve. Some of the children had been taught at home or had attended schools in the East before moving West, but others came with no previous educational experience, and it was often difficult to find suitable material and assignments for the many levels of student progress. One teacher reported that "we had three pupils . . . who were twenty-five years old and who were enrolled in the third grade." A typical curriculum included reading, writing, arithmetic, spelling, geography, history, and grammar, but some public schools and many private academies expected teachers to include instruction in botany, chemistry, "mental philosophy," and other advanced subjects.[42]

Discipline was often a problem for young Western teachers. Many times the older boys were rowdy and unattentive and imposed an implied physical threat to a small, sixteen or seventeen-year-old girl contending with her first school. Nineteen-year-old Clara Conron's diary was filled with references to the problems she had with these older boys. At one point she exclaimed in disgust, "Bert shot Osie in the eye with a popgun, and then skipped out . . . He is the most trying boy I ever knew." And the diaries and reminiscences of other frontier teachers contain many similar references to discipline problems.[43]

Teachers were at the mercy of male-dominated boards and the whims of "uneducated parents who expected instant learning." Contracts were usually granted on a one-term or one-year basis and were subject to frequent review. Teachers often lost their posts because one or two parents expressed dissatisfaction with their performance or for any number of personal slights or jealousies. Moreover, teaching did not provide much financial reward. Mattie Anderson wrote that she was attracted to her first school "by the certain salary of $75 a month . . . ," but more common was the thirty-five dollars a month Clara Conron earned when her school was in session or the fifty cents a day per pupil awarded to the teacher at Fort Laramie in 1871 or the dollar a day and board paid by a Colorado school.[44] To help compensate for low salaries many school boards made arrangements for teachers to live with local families who provided them with rooms and meals. Some, like Ellen Pennock, thought that "boarding around" was not too unpleasant. "Considering the times and circumstances, I enjoyed it," she wrote. "I found so many friends that I felt well paid for all the unpleasantness encountered." But Mollie Sanford wrote in her journal that she "stood the 'boarding around' just two weeks" before she secured "permanent quarters" of her own.[45]

Although many women reported that they enjoyed teaching, they also wrote that it was very difficult and tiring work. "I like teaching sometimes," one recorded, "and then again I don't. I think it is rather trying to ones nerves and mine are rather 'touchy' I am afraid."[46] Women who attempted to combine teaching with family responsibilities had an even more difficult time. One weary housewife-teacher noted in her diary, "Got Breakfast done up the work then got ready for school. . . . not very easy though to teach and keep house too." Another woman wrote to her father that although she enjoyed teaching, it placed too many demands on her family. "I am glad they wished me to take another [term] but my duty to my children forbids."[47]

As frontier conditions gave way to more settled communities and education became more professionalized, school boards began to demand that teachers secure additional education and pass certification examinations. Most state and territorial laws provided for three levels of certification and specified different age levels and educational requirements for each.[48] For those teachers who could not attend a regular school or college, some districts required attendance at summer normal schools held in the county seats or at a local town. Such requirements caused additional problems for married women attempting to improve their professional qualifications and still provide for their families, but they also undoubtedly improved the quality of education in rural schools.[49]

Despite poor working conditions, rowdy pupils, low salaries, and increasing educational requirements, some women chose full-time, lifetime careers in teaching and were able to advance themselves professionally. Many young women took advantage of the more liberal educational opportunities available to them in Western colleges and universities to improve their academic skills and qualify them for better-paying and more professionally fulfilling jobs in the educational system. When the franchise was opened to Western women, elective school offices were opened to them as well, and in most Western states, women held posts as principals, superintendents, and served on state boards of education.[50]

However, professional advancement presented a number of problems and challenges. Phoebe Sudlow of Iowa, reputedly the first woman principal and first woman city superintendent of schools in the United States, urged young women to enter the teaching field, but she also warned:

> Woman, in professional work, must learn to separate herself more from other seeming duties; to invest more as capital; to expect less in the present, and to provide more wisely for future usefulness and preferment.[51]

For some women, the exacting demands outlined by Sudlow were more than they wished to take on. Many, like Oklahoma pioneer teacher and county superintendent of schools Mrs. M. O. Bezanson, confessed they would prefer marriage and a family. Describing her election as county superintendent, Bezanson wrote of her male opponent, "I have always said that if he was smart at the time, he would have married me and won the race for the office. As I surely would not have refused him, if he had asked to marry me."[52] For other women like Sudlow, teaching provided a fulfilling career, and they enjoyed both the opportunities for advancement and the recognition which it brought them. Several, like Arizona's Sharlot

Hall (a popular and well-known teacher and historian), California's Mary Atkins (the founder of Benecia Academy, the forerunner to Mills College), Iowa's Kate Harrington Pollard (the author of a well-known series of textbooks and teachers' manuals), and Texas' Anna Pennybacker (the author of the most popular and widely used Texas history text) achieved national reputations as educational leaders.[53]

A number of women combined a desire to teach with religious zeal and entered the mission field. Indeed, for some women the principal motivation for going West was not family desires or economic betterment but an answer to a religious calling to minister to the Indians. Perhaps the best known of the Western missionary women were the martyred Narcissa Whitman (killed by the Indians at Waiilatpu mission, Oregon, in 1847) and her female missionary companions.[54] But long before Narcissa Whitman and Eliza Spalding gained fame as the "first white women over the Rockies," a number of women had already entered the Western mission field.

The first European missions to the Indians (Spanish and French as well as English) were formed during the colonial period and enjoyed modest success among the native peoples of New Mexico, Canada, New England, and the Appalachian region. Mission work was given additional impetus by the Great Awakening and the religious revivals of the eighteenth century, and during the decades following the American Revolution, a number of churches began to sponsor Indian schools and missions.[55] During the 1790s, the Second Awakening "spawned a whole family of state, regional, and national societies." Thus, by the beginning of the nineteenth century most denominations sponsored both foreign and home missions, and several interdenominational societies had been formed to carry the gospel to both the Indians and the white inhabitants of new Western settlements.[56]

The boards which organized and controlled Western missions were made up entirely of men, and decisions about the establishment and conduct of the missions were made in the East, not in the West.[57] Nonetheless, it was the missionaries in the field who were crucial to the success of the missionary effort, and women, living and working in the West, made important and significant contributions to mission work. At first a number of mission boards refused to allow women to enter the field, fearing the frontier and Indian villages too dangerous and unseemly a place for delicate females. Women filled with missionary ardor had to content themselves with fund-raising activities and quiet support of the mission effort.[58] Eventually, however, mission boards actively recruited both married and single women to wash, cook, and clean at the mission stations and to assist the male missionaries in teaching in the mission schools, in evangelizing among the Indian women, and in other aspects of mission work. Between 1820 and 1850, a growing number of women joined missions in the trans-Appalachian West and in Indian Territory. As the frontier moved further West, new mission fields opened, and women became increasingly prominent in missionary work. They broadened the scope of their activities, preached as well as taught, and occasionally had full responsibility for the establishment and operation of mission schools and churches. A few were ordained to the regular ministry, in order, as one put it, "to add in some ways to her power to serve. . . ."[59]

The missionary field was not the exclusive province of middle-class women of predominantly English background, however. Betsey Stockton, a former slave, was one of the first missionaries to the Hawaiian Islands in 1822 and later worked among the Indians of Canada. Spanish women had long found professions within the Church as an alternative to marriage and family. Although Spanish and Mexican women were not a part of the colonial mission effort on Mexico's northern frontiers, after 1800 they played an increasingly important role as teachers, nurses, and housekeepers at the missions. French women, too, often found professions within the Church, and the Ursuline sisters played an important role in the establishment of Indian schools in Canada and later in the establishment of schools and convents in French Louisiana. Moreover, a surprising number of Indian women entered the mission field to minister to their own people. Although most of them came from the Five Civilized Tribes (Cherokees, Choctaws, Chickasaws, Creeks, and Seminoles) and were educated in Eastern boarding schools before returning to their own people, a few women from the far Western peoples also felt called to a religious profession and entered Catholic sisterhoods or assisted the staff at various Protestant missions. Indeed, in 1891, the Catholic Church established the Congregation of American Sisters, an order for Native American women to help prepare Indians for eventual citizenship and to act as directors of Indian societies. Although not missionaries in the strictest sense of the word, Omaha Susan La Flesche and Paiute Sarah Winnemucca were effective spokeswomen for Indian rights and publicized the needs of their people through their books and public lectures.[60]

The missionaries' life was not an easy one. Often their Indian charges were less than enthusiastic about the new religion and learning the white man's ways, and sometimes they were openly rebellious. "They [the Indians] often have them [drunken scrapes] vary [sic] near our house," Mary Rice wrote to her sister Hannah, from Fort Gibson in 1835; "they will dance and hollow and scream all night." Mary Sagatoo, who married a young Boston-educated Chippewa and went to minister to his people in northern Michigan, worked hard to raise funds for a new church only to meet a lack of cooperation from the Indians in erecting the building. "Could the Indians know the very hard things I had to bear on their account," she wrote indignantly, "they would feel more gratitude than they have manifested toward me." Sometimes the white society of the West posed more difficult problems than the Indians. When the Presentation Sisters attempted to open a mission and school in Deadwood, South Dakota, in 1881, they soon "discovered the rowdy camp was not conductive to an enclosed community," and they retreated to the more civilized community of Fargo. Yet as these women struggled to learn the Indian languages, to help raise funds to support the mission work, and to teach their often reluctant, and sometimes recalcitrant, pupils, they were sustained by a deep commitment to their calling and by a certain knowledge that they were bringing civilization and Christian virtue to the frontier. They had their successes as well as their failures. As Mary Collins wrote of her years among the Sioux:

> They moved out on the land that I earnestly taught them to cultivate as homes. They have done this and I have visited them in almost every home in my district. . . . The women are good housekeepers now. . . . They work earnestly in their women's societies, giving over a dollar apiece to the native missionary society. . . . We have so far never gone backward but are constantly growing and pressing forward.[61]

Conservative and traditional in most of their views towards social progress and the role of women, the missionaries nonetheless helped broaden women's place within Western society and in the nation as a whole. Certainly they proved the ability of women to undertake successfully this strenuous and difficult calling. A number of them became strong advocates for improved education for women so that they could more effectively serve in the mission field, and their books about their mission life, their letters to newspapers and magazines, and their public speaking tours to raise funds provided a greater visibility for women as public rather than private participants in American life.[62]

At the opposite end of the social scale from the missionaries were the practitioners of a very different, publically visible, but traditional and exclusively female occupation, the so-called soiled doves or ladies of the night. A great deal has been written about Western prostitutes; much of it, of a popular, and often sensational, nature, concentrated on such colorful characters as Poker Alice, Tit Bit, Big Nose Kate, and Rose of the Cimarron.[63] These women were often portrayed as nice girls gone wrong, women of some character and experience who drank, gambled, and sold their favors but who still were of a basically honest nature and had "hearts of pure gold." Or they were pictured as women of "evil name and fame," depraved, vicious, and cruel "Cyprian sisters." Several recent and more scholarly studies have suggested that some girls entered the profession in order to advance themselves economically or to escape dull and dreary lives on isolated farms and ranches. Many were attracted by the bright lights and excitement of the mining camps and cattle towns and hoped to earn a little nest egg, meet a cowboy, farmer, or rancher, and eventually settle down to a respectable life.[64] Others hoped to become economically independent and viewed prostitution as one of the few professions where women had some chance of financial success. As one Denver woman succinctly noted, "I went into the sporting life for business reasons and no other. It was a way for a woman in those days to make money and I made it."[65]

A good deal of glamour has been attached to the lives of Western prostitutes, but their lot was a hard one, and many must have wished they had stayed at home. Lydia Taylor, a confessed former prostitute, in her little book *From Under the Lid*, told a story of a long, difficult, and often desperate life as she plied her trade in a number of Western towns. She hoped that her book would warn girls of the dangers and evils of prostitution; she wrote, "I could tell you stories of girls' lives that are so horrifying you would scarcely believe me."[66] An even more candid view of the life of a prostitute was conveyed by a Texas and Oklahoma oil town madame in an interview in the 1930s. "I've laid it in all of 'em, Borger, Kilgore. . . . I threw my fannie 21 times a night, 5 bucks a throw and time old red eye come up I was eatin' breakfast drunker'n an Indian." Nonetheless, she continued, she had no trouble in recruiting new girls:

> Some girl gets mad at her pa 'cause he won't let her stay out nights . . . so she pulls out. She hits for the lights and tries to save money by staying in the flops. I can pick one out just by lookin' at 'em . . . they're so hungry, and wishing to hell they was back home and afraid to go. Some "lady" ease up to her . . . and feed her a square . . . and give her a bed. . . . Get her in bed once and she's with you from then on. Can't go back then and wouldn't if she could.[67]

Often at the mercy of corrupt law enforcement officials, unscrupulous pimps and madames, and frequent law and order and purity campaigns, few of the girls found much glamour or financial success. Some madames, and women who worked in parlor houses with a prosperous local clientele, did fairly well. A few acquired some real estate or other property and eventually retired from business. Others, like the famous La Tules

(Doña Gertrudis Barceló) of New Mexico, operated prosperous gambling and saloon businesses, while a few were in business with their husbands in joint ventures in which the women ran the brothel while the men operated an adjoining saloon and gambling hall. Still others, like Cattle Kate Watson and Calamity Jane (Martha Canary), joined outlaw gangs or broke with convention and acquired reputations as scandalous Western characters.[68]

Brothel owners and operators and girls who worked in the better establishments generally scorned the dance hall and saloon girls who rented upstairs rooms over the taverns and the "crib" girls who sold their wares from small two-room establishments with a bedroom with a window on the street and a kitchen in the rear. At the bottom of the scale were the women who walked the streets and who were often ill and frequently subjected to cruel and violent treatment at the hands of both customers and law enforcement officials. But whatever their social or economic level—madame, parlor girl, saloon or crib girl, or streetwalker, their life was a hard one. Many committed suicide, died of disease and alcoholism, drifted away into other occupations or, among the more fortunate, found a husband or protector. One survey of prostitutes in the Kansas cattle towns found that the average age of these women was 23.1 years, and very few were over the age of thirty.[69] Despite the legendary success of a few women, prostitution was neither an attractive nor a rewarding occupation.

Prostitution was a town or city occupation as were other more respectable occupations such as domestic service, hotel and boardinghouse management, and teaching. The economic opportunities for rural women, especially in frontier areas, were more limited. Yet a surprising number of farm and ranch women were able to turn their knowledge of domestic production and farm and ranch management into prosperous business enterprises. In addition to their domestic occupations such as cloth production, and chicken, egg, dairy, and butter businesses, many rural women actually ran the family farm. As noted in chapter six, women often had to take over farm management when the men were ill or incapacitated or were gone from home prospecting, fighting Indians, working in town for cash, or just wandering. This was particularly true in Mormon settlements where the men were often required to be gone for one or two years on missions for the church or were involved in other church activities. Meanwhile, the women stayed at home to "milk the cows, plant the crops, and care for the children."[70] In many instances, women (non-Mormon as well as Mormon) provided most of the support for themselves and their families.[71] Even when their menfolk remained at home, most rural women worked with their husbands during especially busy times of the year, and they thus came to have a good understanding of the various farm operations. Wrote one young Iowa farm girl, "I can't describe a thrashing floor so you understand but some day I can show you just how it was done. . . ."[72] Such experience stood women in good stead when they were widowed or left alone and had to take over. In the East, single or widowed women probably would have relied on a father, brothers, or uncles to aid them, but in the West they had fewer of these support networks to draw on, hired help was scarce and expensive, and most simply took over and continued to operate the family farm until they remarried or retired and left the property to their children.

It was not easy for either men or women to make a good living on a frontier farm. Such work was particularly difficult for women who lacked the physical strength for some of the heavier field work and who had difficulty in finding and hiring labor for these tasks. One Oregon woman wrote her cousins that she had been obliged to sell part of her land and "put [the money] out at intrest [sic]" since her son refused to stay home and work and labor was "dear."[73] Some women were simply unable to "make a go of it" and sold out and moved to town or returned East. Others were more successful. One Oklahoma widow recalled that "I continued the farming with cotton the main crop. One year I picked 8000 lbs. . . . By so doing I supported my four children. . . ." Other women, fortunate enough to have sons to take over most of the physical labor of farming, continued to manage the family economy. One Montana ranch wife, widowed in her sixties, turned the daily operation of the ranch over to her sons, but "she took over the books . . . and continued to help manage them until her death at the age of ninety."[74]

A surprising number of Western women, both single and married, took up land in their own name. In the former Mexican states and territories, where Spanish rather than English law prevailed, married women could hold separate property in their own name, and many took advantage of the opportunity to purchase and administer their own land. Indeed, Jane McManus Storms Cazneau applied for, and received, an empresario grant from the Mexican government. During the Texas Revolution she offered to borrow money against her landholdings. "As a female, I cannot bear arms for my adopted country," she wrote in 1835, "but if the interest I possess in her soil, will be a guarantee for any money, I will with joy contribute my mite to purchase arms for her brave defenders."[75] In other former Mexican states other women, both of Mexican and English ancestry, owned farm and ranch property which they administered themselves.[76]

Between 1800 and 1850, many changes occurred in the social, economic, and legal position of women, and a number of states and territories outside the former Mexican provinces passed more liberal laws governing women's property rights. As one legal historian pointed out, the number of women with a stake in society increased rapidly during this period, and the English common law, primarily geared to the needs of the landed gentry, no longer was satisfactory for American needs. In fact, he wrote, "the tangle of rules and practices was potentially an impediment to the speed and efficiency of the land market. The statutes spoke of rights of husband and wife, as if the real issue was the intimate relations between the sexes. But the real point of the statutes was to rationalize more cold-blooded matters, such as the rights of a creditor to collect debts out of land owned by husbands and wives, or both."[77] In 1839, Mississippi made the first tentative reforms in the laws relating to married women's property, and other states and territories soon followed suit. By 1850, seventeen states, many of them in the West, had granted married women legal control over their property,[78] while in Oregon, the Donation Land Law of 1850 allowed wives of settlers to claim a half-section (320 acres) in their own right.[79] Most Western states' legal codes made some provision for women to purchase or homestead land and own and operate businesses in their own name. Husbands sometimes took advantage of these laws to escape debts or bankruptcy by transferring property to the wife's name, but this device often backfired, for women, once in legal possession of the property, frequently refused to return it, assisted in its administration, and used their legal ownership as a weapon to force their husbands to comply with their wishes.[80]

Following the Civil War, a number of both married and single women took advantage of the new Homestead Act to acquire property. Although some took up homestead claims simply to add to their husbands', fathers', or brothers' holdings, others, especially single women, intended to work their claims themselves. By the turn of the century, homesteading by young women had become so popular that one observer estimated that in 1886 one-third of the land in the Dakotas was held by women.[81] Often sisters or girl friends took up joint claims or a brother and sister established adjoining claims, assisting each other with the various tasks necessary to prove up their claims and acquire title. According to one report, most of these women did not intend to settle permanently but rather hoped to establish their claims and then "sell out to neighboring farmers, and to return to their small towns or to the city with a nest egg. In fact they used virgin land as their dowry . . . [and] few women worked the land themselves."[82]

Contemporary letters and diaries by homesteading women corroborate the suggestion that some young women intended to exploit their claims to earn money for other ventures. Abbie Bright, a Kansas homesteader, admitted that she looked on the opportunity as an adventure and as an investment rather than as a permanent home. North Dakota homesteaders Anna and Ethel Erickson intended to use their land to raise money for college.[83] Other women looked on their homesteads as permanent homes, however, and some remained on their land for a number of years.

Like any frontier farming venture, homesteading was difficult work, and many women were not successful in proving up their claims. Others found farming a much harder task than they had anticipated and gave it up after a few years. Cora Babcock, for example, made one successful crop of flax but then decided to "give up the claim idea and get married."[84] Others were more persevering. Some of them lived and worked on their claims during the spring and summer and then moved to town during the long winters, driving to their claims on weekends in order to meet the homestead requirements. Often they taught school or did sewing, cooking, laundry, or other domestic work to earn money to help make improvements on their land. Despite the hard work, many of them prospered. An enterprising group of Oklahoma women formed an all female "sooner company," raised $2500 to use in developing their claims, and successfully entered the Cheyenne and Arapaho Reservation ahead of the scheduled land run. Another legal company of twenty-two women established claim to 480 acres of land in the Cherokee Strip when it was opened in 1893, and by 1894 "they were the proud owners of three teams, two cows, chickens, and other stock."[85] Another successful, and enthusiastic, woman homesteader wrote that she believed homesteading offered city women an opportunity to become independent. "To me, homesteading is the solution of all poverty's problems," she insisted;

> . . . any woman who can stand her own company, can see the beauty of the sunset, loves growing things, and is willing to put in as much time at careful labor as she does over the washtub, will certainly succeed; will have independence, plenty to eat all the time, and a home of her own in the end.[86]

Like farm women, a number of ranchwomen worked alongside their husbands and learned a good deal about cattle, horses, and ranch management. Most ranchwomen visited roundup camps, helped with various chores, and occasionally lent a hand, when necessary, in the home corral, but they generally attempted to maintain a woman's proper place. Such a role was clearly preferred by ranchwomen such as Sophie Poe, the wife of the famous New Mexican lawman and rancher John William Poe, and Nannie Alderson, whose reminiscences of her ranch life have become one of the most popular books on women's lives in the West. Poe, Alderson, and a number of other ranchwomen spent most of their time at the home headquarters cooking, cleaning, caring for their children, tending a small garden, and attempting to introduce a little civilization into the wild West.[87] Other ranch wives chose the outdoor life and helped with the roundups, branding, mending fences, riding line, and searching out strays. "Pickey" Saunders recalled that her sister Alice Brown worked closely with her husband on their Big Bend ranch and was reputed to be an excellent shot and a daring and skilled rider. Another such woman noted that she found "real pleasure" in ranch work. "I love to work with cattle," she told an interviewer, "and have spent a good deal of my time on the range in Southern Arizona." When their husbands were absent on trail drives or business, these women could, and did, take over the day-to-day running of the ranch and seem to have done so quite skillfully.[88]

Widowed ranchwomen, like widowed farm women, often took over management of the ranch and herds after their husbands' death. Some of them, like Agnes Cleaveland's mother and Nannie Alderson, were barely able to hang on and make ends meet, but others were more successful. A Texas widow wrote with pride that she was able to provide a "safe and secure" living for herself and her two children in the ranching business and had begun "to feel more confidence in myself now and reconciled to living alone." Helen J. Stewart of Nevada took over extensive ranching and mining properties after her husband's death and earned a reputation as a good manager and businesswoman.[89] Some married women were better ranch managers than their husbands and took over the entire operation or ran separate businesses of their own. For example, Grace Fairchild, a Dakota rancher, was married to "a man not fitted to be a pioneer," and eventually had to manage their property herself to prevent bankruptcy. Similarly, a Texas woman married to a preacher "with little business sense" insisted on keeping her property and cattle in her own name and managing her own affairs. From time to time, she lent her husband money, although she always demanded repayment.[90] Some of these "cattle queens" actively participated in all aspects of ranch work. According to all reports, Colorado and Arizona cattlewoman Ann Bassett "could fit right in the toughest cow camp . . . take her place in the saddle with the rest and live the life they lived, doing with equal skill her share of the work on the range." Similarly, Texas rancher Sally Skull spent most of her time on the range supervising her men and protecting her herds from Indians and rustlers.[91] According to one reporter, the women ranchers she met took better care of their cattle than did men. She noted that a trio of New Mexico ranchwomen had made companions of their little herd of wild cattle, called them by name, nursed them when they were ill or injured, and fed better, particularly in the winter months, than did their male neighbors.[92] There was little to justify such an opinion in ranchwomen's statements, however. Those who worked their own cattle customarily used traditional male methods, while most women owners hired trusted foremen to supervise the actual handling of the cattle while they managed the business affairs.

Whether ranchwomen confined themselves to more traditional roles or actively participated in ranch operations, they tended to become increasingly self-reliant and independent. According to Nannie Alderson, "the new country offered greater personal liberty than an old and settled one," and although she admitted that her years of ranch life never taught her any business sense, she nonetheless believed that Western ranch life instilled a good deal of self-reliance in women and children. This opinion was shared by a number of outside observers. The English visitor Anthony Trollope wrote in 1862 that ranchwomen were "sharp as nails and just as hard." They were rarely obedient to their menfolk, he reported, and "they know much more than they ought to. If Eve had been a ranchwoman, she would never have tempted Adam with an apple. She would have ordered him to make his [own] meal."[93] This was particularly true of girls who grew up on Western farms and ranches. They were even more likely than their mothers to learn riding and roping skills, participate in ranch work, and understand business operations. According to one such young woman, "it is as beneficial for a woman as for a man to be independent," and, she continued, she knew of no reasons "why the judgement of women should not be as good as that of men if they gave the subject attention." In later life, many of these ranch girls assisted their husbands in the ranching business, operated ranches of their own, or turned their talents into careers in rodeo and wild west shows.[94]

Although ranch and farm management were certainly outside the strict domestic sphere prescribed by the cult of true womanhood, they were still closely enough linked to home and family to be considered respectable and proper. Some women enlarged upon their experiences in these accepted female occupations and ventured into previously male-dominated fields. We have been told, for example, that trail driving was an exclusively male enterprise and that women did not travel the cattle trails north or west from Texas to markets in Kansas or California. There were not many women on the cattle trails, but neither was this an entirely male domain. True, the women who accompanied the herds were not trail bosses, cowboys, or even cooks. They were usually the wives or daughters of owners or owners in their own right, and they stayed within accepted limits of behavior. When necessary they helped out with various chores, kept watch for Indians and rustlers, and occasionally helped load weapons or took up weapons themselves in defense of their own or their family's interests. Some viewed the journey as primarily a sight-seeing or pleasure trip, but most women who undertook the journey did so because they had an economic stake in the enterprise. Texas ranchwomen Margaret Borland and Lizzie Johnson Williams accompanied their own herds to Kansas and negotiated their own sales while another woman, Minta Holmsby, acted for her husband in this capacity.[95]

Some women turned their farm and ranch experience to the development of large-scale commercial agricultural enterprises, and others became very successful real estate investors. As early as 1742, a young frontierswoman, Eliza Lucas, assumed management of her father's extensive Carolina estates and developed a profitable indigo market. Mention has already been made of Margaret Brent who managed not only her own lands but was executrix for Leonard Calvert's estate as well.[96] These women established an early pattern for other women. By the late nineteenth century, a Western traveler commented on the number of "bright-minded women from other parts of the country" who were "engaged in real estate transactions in this country. . . . [I]t is not a rare thing," she continued, "for numbers of feminine speculators to attend the auction sales of land," and she estimated that of the sixty-five women teachers in the Los Angeles schools, "almost all own some land. . . ."[97] A number of California women engaged in commercial agriculture raising everything from raisins, oranges, and olives to commercial bulbs and seeds. Kate Sessions, a San Diego widow, developed a worldwide reputation as a horticulturist while another California woman, Mrs. Emily Robeson, operated a nationwide olive business. Several other California women, including Mrs. Theodosia Shepherd, Mrs. E. P. Buckingham, and Mrs. Georgia McBride, were all singled out in an article in the New York *World* as women who managed large and successful agricultural businesses.[98] Certainly the most successful of these female cultivators was Harriet Strong of Whittier whose extensive orange and walnut groves and very profitable pampas grass business earned her a place as the first woman on the Los Angeles Chamber of Commerce and "high rank in the business circles of the coast, despite her sex."[99]

California women were not the only ones who undertook such ventures, however. Texas schoolteacher and cattleowner Lizzie Williams also speculated in real estate, and at the time of her death had investments valued at $164,339. Sara Horton Cockrell of Dallas, whose husband was killed by the sheriff in 1858, took over his various business enterprises including several hotels, a lumber mill, and a toll bridge across the Trinity River. By the 1870s, R. G. Dun and Company agents reported that she was probably the largest property holder in Dallas County and "a good manager for a woman."[100] When Doña María Gertrudis de la Garza died in 1789, she left personal property which included fifty-nine leagues of land; monte dealer Doña Gertrudis Barceló owned a large amount of real estate and contributed lavishly to charity and even loaned the United States Army money to pay its troops after the Mexican invasion. Biddie Mason of Los Angeles and Clara Brown of Colorado, both former slaves, became well-known property owners and philanthropists to the black community. In Oregon, Portland teacher Helen Spalding had to resign her teaching position in order to attend to her growing real estate and business interests. Coloradoan Millie Ohmertz was so successful in real estate investment that she handled not only her own land but served as agent for Governor Hunt "as well as agent for others in Denver." A Spokane woman, Alice Houghton, speculated in real estate and served as emigration manager for the Great Northern and Northern Pacific railroads.[101] Although these women were undoubtedly exceptions, they were nonetheless indicative of the ways in which Western women were able to take advantage of more liberal property rights and economic opportunities and their own experience to improve their economic position.

In addition to real estate and commercial agriculture, Western women engaged in many other business and professional enterprises. A survey of the R. G. Dun and Company reports revealed a number of women in the Western states and territories owned and operated millinery shops, dressmaking establishments, grocery and dry goods stores, hotels and restaurants, and other similar establishments.[102] For some, these enterprises served as a basis for other businesses or professions. For example, an Oregon woman, Bethenia Owens-Adair, opened a millinery shop in order to earn money for medical school, and other women reported that the income from their shops helped to underwrite real estate and mining investments. Two enterprising westering women purchased a supply of cloth and other dry goods which they sold from the back of their spring wagon to help pay their expenses to California.[103]

Other women engaged in less-traditional businesses including manufacturing, mining, printing, and editing. Frontier women who had learned to "make-do" and who had devised various means to overcome shortages or unavailable goods applied for patents on various inventions, many of them developed out of their frontier experience. Most of these inventions were closely related to domestic and farm work—improvements for milk coolers, separators and churns, new types of wash tubs, quilting frames, beekeeping equipment, and new strains of farm and garden plants; but others, like Harriet Strong's patent for a "method and means for impounding debris and storing water," provided the basis for other businesses.[104] Strong used her patents and her knowledge of engineering to develop an irrigation and water company in the San Gabriel Valley and became an expert on underground water storage and flood control. Oregonian

Mathilde Cord developed and operated a pine needle industry for the production of various products. Another enterprising Oregon woman carefully studied the methods for raising flax and manufacturing linen and organized the Oregon Women's Flax Association which marketed various grades of linen in both the United States and abroad. Responding to the needs of their communities, Elizabeth Stone of Fort Collins and Sara Cockrell of Dallas operated a number of diverse business enterprises including hotels, flour mills, and brick kilns.[105]

Mining was generally considered a male enterprise, much too difficult, both mentally and physically, for women to undertake. However, a "few clever women" discovered that the "knowledge and skill" necessary for successful mining enterprises was "by no means beyond the grasp of the feminine brain."[106] Several women wrote of assisting their husbands and fathers during the gold rush days in California, Colorado, and Idaho, and a few bold souls participated in the Klondike and Alaska rushes. Other women who worked in the mining camps listened carefully to the miners talk and made shrewd investments which netted them large profits, and a few managed and supervised their own mines. Mrs. E. C. Atwood of Colorado declared in a paper read at the International Mining Congress in 1900 that mining could "be made to pay by any energetic woman who will pursue it in an intelligent way." Atwood, furious when she was cheated of $10,000 in mining investments, studied geology and minerology and became vice-president and general manager of the Bonacord Gold Mining and Milling Company and owned other mining interests in Cripple Creek and elsewhere in Colorado. Another Colorado woman, Delia McCarthy, was president and general manager of the Cooperative Mining and Milling Company of Cripple Creek and secretary in Atwood's Bonacord Company; two women operated the Silver Mountain Mining Company and the Clear Creek Mining Company near Denver; another managed the Highland Mining Company, owned seventeen mines, and supervised construction of a tunnel from the Las Animas River to her mine near Mary, Colorado. Utah also had several women mining entrepreneurs.[107]

Other Western women discovered smaller, but still lucrative, bonanzas in the printing trades and journalism. Indeed, a surprising number of Western women were engaged in these occupations. The well-known women's rights advocate Amelia Bloomer claimed she was one of the first women to edit and publish a paper when she established *The Lily*, a feminist journal in 1849, but women had been active in printing and publishing since the colonial period.[108] Bloomer and Ella Wentworth, editor of a literary journal in Cincinnati, both employed women in presswork as well as in writing and editing, and throughout the Western states and territories women secured employment in the printing trades. In 1868, a Woman's Cooperative Printing Union was established in San Francisco, "To give employment to women as typesetters and thereby enable them to earn an independent and honest living and to conduct and carry on a general printing business."[109]

Women were also employed as reporters and contributors for many Western journals and newspapers. After 1850, Ladies' Department columns began to appear in newspapers, often run by the editor's wife or one of the paper's more notable female contributors. Talented women journalists, however, also wrote regular columns or contributed articles on topics of general interest. Elizabeth Barstow Stoddard served as Our Lady Correspondent for the San Francisco *Daily Alta California* from 1854 to 1857. Californian Helen Burrell d'Apery was commissioned by a newspaper syndicate to write a series of articles on life in various European capitals. Flora Ellice Stevens was a reporter for the *Rocky Mountain News* in the 1870s, and Leonel Ross O'Bryan, writing under the pseudonym Polly Pry was one of the *Denver Post's* most popular reporters during the 1890s, often "scooping" her male contemporaries.[110]

Both Stevens and O'Bryan later published their own newspapers as did Caroline N. Churchill, a strong-minded and independent woman who launched several Western papers including the Denver based *Queen Bee*. In Utah, Louisa L. Greene founded the *Woman's Exponent* and Susa Young Gates published the *Young Woman's Journal*. Greene's successor at the *Exponent*, Emmeline B. Wells, served as editor of the popular Mormon journal for over forty years.[111] Many women helped their husbands operate papers and often took over the entire operation. One Oklahoma woman recalled that her mother-in-law "looked after the details of the office" while her politician husband "preserved the sacred principles of Republicanism. She gathered the locals while he wrote flaming editorials." After her husband's death, this intrepid newswoman published the paper herself:

> She read proof, corrected legals, kept the books, managed the foreign and domestic advertising, wrote want ads, addressed single wrappers . . . prepared stories about weddings and commencements, and penned fitting obituaries. . . . She . . . entered into the clamor of campaigns . . . and endured the clamor and din of state political battles.[112]

By the end of the nineteenth century, according to a recent survey, 1,238 women were engaged in printing and publication and another 1,127 were employed as compositors, linotype operators, and typesetters in eleven far-Western states. A separate study identified twenty-five women newspaper owners and editors in Missouri in the same period.[113]

Western women were also active in other professions including medicine and law. Although these women faced many of the same obstacles and discriminations as Eastern professional women,[114] they had less difficulty in establishing themselves and gaining recognition of their professional status. As noted in chapter six, frontier women often had to render medical assistance and treatment, and many were recognized as professional or near-professional practitioners of the healing arts. In Mexican-American communities and in many Indian societies, women were believed to have special gifts as healers, and *curanderas* and medicine women were valued for their skills in treating illness and reducing pain. A number of women assisted their physician-husbands and sometimes substituted for them in emergencies. Midwifery and nursing were common occupations for frontier women, although these services rarely earned them monetary remuneration, and they were not acknowledged as gainfully employed in the census or other official documents.[115] After Elizabeth Blackwell's successful assault on male domination of medicine in 1847, an increasing number of women attended medical school and became licensed physicians. In Utah, the Mormon community actively supported women's work in all aspects of medicine and dentistry and produced one of "the most remarkable groups of women doctors in American history". In 1873 Church leader Brigham Young suggested that women's classes be formed in Salt Lake City to study physiology and obstetrics and that "the Bishops see that such women be supported." Shortly thereafter, Romania B. Pratt went East to attend the Women's Medical College in Philadelphia, and she was followed by a number of other Mormon women including Ellis R. Shipp, Martha Hughes Cannon, Margaret Shipp Roberts, Mary McLean Green, Emma Atkins, Mary Emma Van Schoonhoven, Jane M. Skolfield, and Elvira Stevens Barney. In 1882, the Women's Relief Society founded the Deseret Hospital under the direction of resident physician and surgeon Dr. Ellen B. Ferguson. The hospital also served as a pioneer medical school which provided training in nursing and obstetrics.[116] Although Utah undoubtedly had the highest percentage of women doctors, other Western states and territories also had a fairly high percentage of professional women. By 1893, a number of coeducational medical schools had been established in the West and enrolled a number of women—19 percent at the University of Michigan, 20 percent at the University of Oregon, and 31 percent at Kansas Medical School.[117]

Women had more difficulty in obtaining legal training because of statutory prohibitions based on English common law which prohibited women from being called to the bar. Nonetheless, after 1870, a few women succeeded in winning admission to legal practice, and those who did frequently vied with each other for the honor of being named the first woman admitted to practice before their state bar or the first woman to try a case before a state supreme court. Among the most prominent female Western attorneys were Laura De Force Gordon and Clara Foltz who were among the first women to be admitted to practice before the United States Supreme Court.[118] Acceptance of professional women in the West was indicated by a recent survey which estimated that by 1890, 13 percent of the 936,534 women living west of Mississippi were engaged in the various professions, "giving the West the largest percentage of women lawyers, doctors, writers, and academicians in the nation. . . ."[119]

Other Western women pursued scientific careers. Martha Maxwell of Colorado gained an international reputation as a naturalist, taxidermist, and artist, and her display at the Centennial Exhibition at Philadelphia was one of the most popular at the exposition. Texan Maud Fuller Young studied biology and botany and wrote *Mrs. Young's Familiar Lessons in Botany with Flora of Texas*, the first science text written for use in Texas schools. Although born and educated in Boston, pioneer anthropologist Alice Cunningham Fletcher spent much of her adult life in the West preparing scientific studies of the American Indians, supervising the surveying and allotment of the Nez Perce lands, and lobbying for reforms in Indian policy. Alice Eastwood gained an international reputation as a botanist and served as Curator of Botany at the California Academy of Science in San Francisco.[120]

Indeed, Western women, conditioned by frontier conditions to try new ways of doing things, pioneered in many new fields of economic endeavor. A number of young Western women learned telegraphy, and some served as station agents as well as telegraphers for the railroads. A young Southwestern woman was one of the first of her sex to open a successful surveying and abstract office. Thérèse Schlinder was one of the most successful fur traders in the Great Lakes region during the 1820s as were Madeline La Framboise and Elizabeth Mitchell. All conducted their own businesses and became wealthy in the trade. After 1870, a number of government jobs were opened to women. Many served as postmistresses and others found employment as enrolling and engrossing clerks or other legislative positions, and a few successfully ran for public office. Mention has already been made of Esther Morris who served briefly as Justice of the Peace in South Pass City, Wyoming, in 1870, but other women were more active in political life. Luna Kellie of Nebraska was elected secretary of the State Farmer's Alliance, campaigned for the Alliance, the People's (Populist) Party, and the Union Reform Party and printed and edited a newspaper, *The Alliance*, which advocated various farm reform programs. Another farm reform politician, Mary E. Lease of Kansas, made a number of public speeches on behalf of the Alliance and the People's Party and gained a good deal of attention with her famous remark, "What you farmers need is to raise less corn and more hell!" May Arkwright Hutton of Idaho was also interested in political reform. She was an enthusiastic supporter of the labor union movement and women's suffrage, was active in Democratic state politics in Idaho and Oregon, and devoted a good deal of her time and her fortune (earned through a series of shrewd mining investments) to political and philanthropic activities.[121] So diverse were Western women's interests that one analysis of the 1900 census revealed that in addition to the expected milliners, dressmakers, laundresses, and teachers, Western women were employed as bank officials, wholesale merchants, butchers, blacksmiths, lighthouse keepers, and "boatmen."[122]

Everywhere in the West, by the end of the nineteenth century, women were entering new professions and businesses and were finding new roles outside the recognized scope of woman's place. Many of these Western female entrepreneurs first learned business skills by assisting their husbands,[123] but others learned because of necessity and gained economic and technical expertise through hard work and often bitter experience. According to one, her husband was "a rich man's son . . . fitted for no occupation." He knew nothing of business, she maintained, and "if he made $5000 a year he would be $10,000 in debt. . . ."[124] Other women were forced to become independent because of the absence or death of their husbands. Certainly some were reluctant capitalists and businesswomen, but others, often to their own amazement, found that they enjoyed earning their own livelihood and controlling their own lives, and they became enthusiastic entrepreneurs. "I am a great believer in the independence of women," one wrote. "I think married women should be allowed to go on with their career if they wish. . . ." Another, the very successful California businesswoman Harriet Strong, advocated business and economic education for all women so that they would be prepared to assume management of their property if necessary. She hoped to organize a Ladies Business League of America and establish a series of business colleges and training schools to teach women the basic principles of economics and business management. It was not easy for women to succeed in business, she cautioned. "Whatever vocation a woman would enter, she must give it the same scientific study and hard work that a man would in order to make a success." Moreover, she warned:

> A woman needs to have five times as much ability as a man in order to do the same thing. She may be permitted to conduct her own ranch and be a success in a small business enterprise—yes, but let her go into the business of incorporating a large enterprise and bonding it,

as a man would . . . and then see if the word does not go forth, "This woman is going too far; she must be put down."[125]

Despite these difficulties, Strong and other women did not choose to "weep at home." Whether through necessity or from choice, they entered the previously male-dominated business world, and they did so success-fully.

Whether the frontier provided a liberating experience and economic as well as social and political opportunities for women is still a question of much debate. Certainly there is some evidence that it did not. As noted at the beginning of this chapter, some historians have concluded, based on women's reminiscences, diaries, and letters, that the frontier did not offer as many opportunities for women as it did for men and that women often failed to take advantage of the frontier experience as a means of liberating themselves from constricting and sexist patterns of behavior. Yet these same reminiscences, diaries, and letters also contain evidence to support the contention that women on the frontiers modified existing norms and adopted flexible attitudes and experimental behavior patterns. For some these changes were easily made and enthusiastically accepted; for others they were reluctantly made and strongly resisted.[126] What has perhaps confused the various interpretations of woman's place and the westering experience is that the *reality* of women's lives changed dramat-ically as a result of adaptation to frontier conditions while the public *image* remained relatively static. Image, myth, and stereotype were contrary to what women were actually experiencing and doing. The ideal for women in the late nineteenth century moved more and more toward a romanti-cized view of the wife, mother, and lady, if not of leisure, at least of with-drawn and demure refinement. If frontier necessity, practice, and even law recognized female economic and political independence, social cus-tom and tradition ignored it. Despite a growing emphasis on women's rights, nineteenth-century writers overlooked—or at least chose not to draw attention to—Western life models on which other women might pat-tern their own lives. Temperance and suffrage rather than economic edu-cation and independence for women dominated the feminist literature, often to the detriment of effective women's rights. Women who did not marry or who effectively ran businesses or professional enterprises were often viewed as being not quite respectable or at least unfeminine no mat-ter how efficiently they also ran their homes or carried on family respon-sibilities in addition to challenging male domination of the marketplace.[127]

Yet women who survived the first or even the second wave of adjust-ment to frontier conditions and changed roles for women tended to ig-nore, or at least not slavishly strive toward, Eastern-dictated models of femininity or the ideal of true womanhood. These hardy and self-sufficient women stepped out of woman's place with few regrets. If they did not glory in their new freedom, they did express pride in their newfound talents and accomplishments. It was the later generations of Western women, those who no longer lived on a frontier, who began to emulate Eastern models of propriety and sought to perpetuate the myths of woman's proper sphere. Yet even these later generations betrayed their frontier heritage in their personal values and attitudes. This heritage was reflected in a survey in 1943 which showed that Western women, as compared to those in the North and the South, were far better educated, held a wider variety of jobs, and were more likely to continue working, were less prone to adhere to traditional religious and denominational beliefs, were more excited and more optimistic about their lives, were more open to change, and were more likely to approve equal standards for men and women.[128] Thus, the westering experience continued to influence Western women's values and attitudes long after the passing of the frontier.

Acknowledgment of Sources

The author is grateful to the following libraries and individuals for permission to quote from the works listed below. In many, indeed in most, instances, the libraries and depositories do not own literary rights to this material and often have no information on provenance. Where information on the original owners was available, an effort was made to locate them and secure their permission to quote. This was not always possible, but every effort was made to adhere to fair use doctrine.

Arizona Historical Society, Tucson

Sara Bennett, Letters, 1864, in Clarence E. Bennett Papers
Sarah M. Black, Reminiscences
Mrs. James Kilroy Brown, Biographical Sketch
Alice J. Curnow, The Journey With Tom
Rose Hattich, Examination Papers, in William and Rose Hattich
  Collection
John W. Kennedy, Reminiscence of Mary Elizabeth Corne Jennings
Aggie Loring, Letters, 1876, in George E. Loring Collection
Sarah E. Martin, My Desert Memories
Mrs. D. C. Martin, The A. B. Peach Family and Memories of Strawberry
  School
Rena Mathews, The Claim of Mrs. Rena (J. D.) Mathews of Being a
  Western Pioneer
Mabel W. Moffitt, Reminiscences of an Arizona Pioneer
Sister Monica, Sisters of Saint Joseph, Diary, 1870
Dora Osgood, To Arizona in 1901
Doña Jesus Moreno de Soza, Reminiscences, in Soza Family Papers
May H. Stacey, Letter to her mother, August 16, 1879
Cora Slaughter, Interview, in Charles M. Wood Collection

Sue H. Summers, Reminiscence of My Early Life in Arizona
Cedenia Bagley Willis, Journal of Nancy Cedenia Bagley Willis
Effie May Butler Wiltbank, Reminiscences
Mary E. Wood, Correspondence, 1890–1906
Charles McPhee Wright, Annals of Harriet S. Wright

Bancroft Library, Berkeley, California

Ellen Tompkins Adams, Diary, 1863
Catherine Jane Bell, Letter to her sister, October 31, 1859
Clara Burt, Journal, 1875–86
Mrs. Charles W. Dalton, Autobiography
Helen Burrell d'Apery, The Stormy Petrel
Sophia Eastman, Letters, 1851–54
Mary C. Fish, A Daily Journal, 1860
Mrs. Warren R. Fowler, A Woman's Experience in Colorado
William L. Fulkerth and Wife, Diary of the Overland Journey, 1863
Maggie Hall, The Story of Maggie Hall
Mrs. M. S. Hockensmith, Diary of a Trip Overland, 1866
Olivia Holmes, Diary, 1873
Mary Jatta, A Journey Across the Plains
Mrs. Mary A. Jones, Recollections
Doña Apolinaria Lorenzana, Memorias (Interview)
Emma Jane McIntyre, Observations of Her Life in the Pribilof Islands
Mrs. M. A. Minto, Female Pioneering in Oregon
Miss Millie Ohmertz, Female Pioneering
Doña Eulalia Pérez, Una Vieja (Interview)
Mrs. J. W. Prowers, Dictation, 1886
Louisa M. Rahm, Diary, 1862
Caroline Richardson, Diary, 1856
Sarepta A. Ross, Recollections of a Pioneer
Doña Atanacia Santa Cruz de Hughes, Interview
Mrs. Theodore Schultz, Early Anecdotes
Mary Pratt Staples, Reminiscences
Louisiana Strentzel, Letters, 1849
Susanna R. Townsend, Letters, 1852–53
Ruth S. Thompson, The Tragedy of Legion Valley
Dorotea Valdez, Reminiscences (Interview)
Mary Eliza Warner, Diary, 1864
Kittie Wilkins, The Idaho Horse Queen and Biographical Sketch
Mrs. Katie Wilson, Statement, 1887
Also consulted but not quoted in the text:

Doña Catarine Avíla de Rios, Recuerdos (Interview)
Mrs. M. G. Bancroft, New Mexico Miscellany
Refugio Redondo Biggs, Statement
Arcadia Bandini Brennan, Arcadian Memories of California
Mrs. Susan Cranston, Daily Journal, 1851
Mary E. Buffett Durant, Letter, 1853
Mrs. Henry D. Fitch, Dictation (Interview)
Carlota Koch, La Guipuzcoana, A Story of Early California
Doña Juana Machado de Ridington, Los Tiempos Pasados (Interview)
Malvinia Virginia Manning, Journal, 1860
Minnie L. Miller, The Road to Yesterday
Doña María Inocenta Pico, Cosas de California (Interview)
Matilda C. Stevenson, Letters, 1914

Barker Texas History Center, University of Texas, Austin

Mattie Belle Anderson, Reminiscences
Emily Andrews, Diary, 1874
Willie A. Andrews School Association Papers
Abigail Baldwin, Diary, 1853–54
Amelia Barr, Papers
Kate Brooks Bates, Biography of Mrs. Kate Brooks
Louisa R. Bell, Letters, 1864–65
Ella Bird-Dumont, Autobiography
Margaret Borland, Papers
Margaret Armstrong Bowie, Diary, 1872–77
Clara Brown, Journal, 1865
Mrs. W. L. Calohan, Some Reminiscences of Texas Life
Laura Clarke Carpenter, Papers,
Jane McManus Storms Cazneau, Papers
R. J. and Alice Crow, Papers
Fannie C. Crockett, Parson's Female Seminary
Lucy Jane Dabney, Walter Scales Dabney and Family
C. D. and William Donaldson, Papers
Mrs. Edward Dyer, Diary, 1860
Henrietta Embree, Diaries, 1856–61
Mary J. Eubank, A Journal of Our Trip to Texas, 1853
Abigail McLennan Fokes, Experiences . . . as Told by Her Daughter
Johnaphene S. Faulkner, Prairie Home
Doña María Gertrudis de la Garza, Last Will and Testament, 1789
Martha Nettie McFarlin Gray, Autobiography, in John G. McFarlin
  Papers

Milly R. Gray, Diary, 1851, in Vandale Collection
Mary Bounhanan Gordon, The Story of the Life of Mary Gordon
Mary Austin Holley, Literary Productions and Historical Notes
Helen Beall Houston, Memoirs
Margaret Lea Houston, Letters, 1840–67
Annie Hunt, Diary, 1850–51, in Louis W. Kemp Collection
Henrietta Chiles Knight, Trip Across the North Plains, 1850, in
    John A. E. Knight Papers.
Anne Legrand, Letters, 1846–84
Mrs. Charles Lavender, Biography of Eugenie Etinette Aubanel
    Lavender
Amanda Lindley, Autobiography
Mary Maverick, Diaries, 1849–52 and Reminiscences in Maverick Family
    Papers
Mary N. McDowell, Little Journey Through Memory's Halls
Patricia Mercer, Diary, 1840–41
Mary Minor, Civil War Letters
Margaret H. Mollenhauer, Letter, n.d.
Lizzie S. Neblett, Correspondence and Diaries, 1852–60
Susan E. Newcomb, Diaries, 1865–69, 1871–73
Elisabet Ney, Papers
Elizabeth Montgomery Neeley, History of the Montgomery Family
Cornelia Noble, Diary, 1861–63
Elizabeth Owens, Story of Her Life as Told by Elizabeth McAnulty
    Owens
Paine Female Institute, Goliad, Minutes of the Board of Trustees
Letitia Pendleton, Journal, 1854–59
Jane Lowe Quillen, A Saga of the Plains
Mary Rabb, Reminiscences of Mrs. John Rabb
Mrs. L. C. Saunders, Life Experiences of Pickey
Harriett Scott, Letter to her cousin, 1846
Lizzie Hatcher Simons, Diary, 1862
Julia Lee Sinks, Early Days in Texas
Mrs. Fracena Martin Sutton, Narrative
May Callan Tansill Collection
Texas Slave Narratives
Mollie Vannemon, Letters, 1857(?)
Mrs. John W. Wade, Recollections of an Octogenarian
Annie J. Wagner, Papers
Maud Jennie Fuller Young, Biographical Data
Also consulted but not cited in the text:
    Mrs. J. D. Bell, A True Story of My Capture By and Life with the
    Comanche Indians

Dorah Clegg, Diary of a Trip from Van Buren, Arkansas, 1870
Rebecca Ann Lamar, Journal and Letters
Mrs. Annie Page Slaughter, Day Book from Virginia to Texas, 1851–53
Adina de Zavala Collection

California State Library, Sacramento

Emeline L. S. Benson, From Beloit Wisconsin to San Pablo Valley,
  1853–54
Mary Jane Caples, Overland Journey to the Coast, 1849 (Reminiscence
  Written in 1911)
Roxanna C. Foster, The Foster Family California Pioneers of 1849
Mary Jane Guill, The Overland Diary . . . , 1860
Edith Highton, Journal of a Trip Through the Mountains . . . , 1881
Mary E. Hopping, Incidents of Pioneer Life
Mrs. Nicholas Harrison Karchner, Diary, 1862
Marie Nash, Diary, 1861
Harriet A. L. Smith, My Trip Across the Plains in 1849
Rebecca Woodson, Sketch of the Life of Rebecca Hiddreth Nutting
  (Woodson)

Colorado Historical Society, Denver

Benjamin F. and Harriett Carr, Letters, 1857–86
Rose Bell, Diary, 1862
Ella Bailey, Diary, 1869
Anna McKee, Letters, 1884

Dallas (Texas) Historical Society

Sarah Horton Cockrell Collection

Denver (Colorado) Public Library

Fannie Adriance, Reminiscence, in Jacob Adriance Papers
Cara G. Bell, Journal, 1872–76
Elmer F. Bennett, Pioneer Women of Colorado, Courage and Sacrifice
Kathleen Bruyn, Notes on Aunt Clara Brown
Julia Canby, Letter to Mrs. Carter, May 9, 1858 in William A. Carter
  Papers
Julia Dodge, Letters, 1856–80 in Dodge Family Papers
Harvey Doe, Letter to his parents, May 29, 1880
Daniel and Martha Graves, Diary of the Memoirs and Travels of Daniel
  and Martha Graves

Ellen R. Hinsdale, Letters, 1871–72
Mrs. Andrew Hively, Journal, 1863–64
Cora Bell Mitchell, Letter to "Dear Friends," n.d.
Mollie, Letter to Ann, September 26, 1871
Mrs. Isaac Moore, How I Went to Denver
Flora Ellice Stevens, Reminiscences
Sister Mary Joanna Walsh, Sketch, Pioneering to Denver, 1864
Mrs. Thomas Withers, Extracts from the Colorado Correspondence,
    1878–80
Esther Campbell, "Queen Ann" Bassett Willis
Also used at the DPL:
    Nellie Slater, Journal, Travels on the Plains in Eighteen Sixty-Two
        Restricted collection. Permission requested from R. F. Stanton,
        Salmon, Idaho
Also consulted but not quoted or cited in the text:
    Mrs. George McGrew, Diary Overland, 1864
    Robert C. Morris, Letter to "My Dear Cousin Lottie," March 30, 1870

Dun and Bradstreet

R. G. Dun and Company Papers, Baker Library, Harvard University

Dr. Carmen Finley, Palo Alto, California

Family History by Mrs. Clara Keithly Tarwater
Mrs. Clara Tarwater, Dairy Methods in the 1890s

Henry E. Huntington Library, San Marino California

Austin (Mary) Collection
    Rheta Childe Dorr to Mary Austin, February 15, 1922
    Inez Haynes Irwin to Mary Austin, May 3, 1923
    Anne Martin to Mary Austin, December, 1932
Robert Beeching, Journal of a Trip from New York . . . , 1849
Sarah M. Cool, Frontier Life; Incidents and Work in California
Mary Agnes Crank, Ranch Life Fifty Years Ago in James F. Crank
    Collection
Clara Colby, Letters
    Clara Folz Shortright to Clara Bewick Colby, June 26, 1908
    Ida Husted Harper to Clara Bewick Colby, June 30, 1900
Barsina French, Journal of a Wagon Trip, 1867
Esther Belle Hanna, Diary of Overland Journey, 1852

Catherine Margaret Haun, A Woman's Trip Across the Plains in 1849
Alice Locke Park Papers
  Omar E. Garwood to Alice Park, October 10, 1910
  Helen V. Bary to Idella Parker, November 23, 1911
  Memorandum, 1912 (?)
Severence (Caroline) Collection
  Caroline Severence to "Dear Friends," June 6, 1910
  Helen Cecilia Lewis to Caroline Severence, May 1896
  The Mother of Clubs, 1906 (printed)
Lura Case Smith Letters
  Lura Smith to Helen Case Hutting, March 22, 1854
  Lura Smith to Helen Case Hutting, August 12, 1854
  Lura Smith to Helen Case Hutting, September 21, 1854
Strong (Harriet W. R.) Collection
  Patent No. 528,823
  Rights of Property and Rights of Persons
Ada Adelaide Vogdes, Journal, 1866–72
Wood (Charles Erskine Scott) Collection
  Sara Bard (Field) Wood to Charles Erskine Scott Wood, September 29,
    1915
  Sara Bard (Field) Wood to Charles Erskine Scott Wood, October 10,
    1915
Also consulted but not quoted in the text:
  Anthony Family Papers
  Mrs. Angeline Jackson Ashley, Crossing the Plains in 1852
  Juliette G. Fish, Crossing the Plains in 1862
  Elizabeth B. Harbert Papers
  Ida H. Halsted Papers
  Esther and Joseph Lyman, Letters
  Dorthea Lummis Moore to Charles F. Lummis, 1884

Jack London Papers, Huntington Library

Restricted collection. Permission to quote from Dayelle Kittredge
Diary, courtesy of Mr. Milo Shepard, Jack London Ranch, Glen Ellen,
  California

Idaho Historical Society, Boise

Irene Corder, Mr. and Mrs. Obidah Corder's History of Their Pioneer
  Life
Hester A. Davis, Story of Hester Cory Davis, 1864

Federal Writers' Project
  Luna House (no author entry)
  Mrs. Catherine Marcus (no author entry)
Lida M. Johnson Isham, Pioneer Days, 1863–80
Mrs. William Justice, Pioneering in Hagerman from 1877 to 1900
McBeth-Crawford Collection
Wilford Ricks, A Sketch of the Life of Tabitha H. Ricks
Anna Moore Simpson, Annals of My Parsonage Life
Lizzie M. Sisk, Reminiscences
Mr. and Mrs. Jacob Stroup, Reminiscences
Emma Tate, Papers
Mary L. Wilson, John McClellan Family
Consulted but not quoted in the text:
  Mrs. James Hart, Westward Journey of Mrs. James H. Hart
  Eliza Hart Spalding to "Ever dear Parents," February 16, 1857

Kansas State Historical Society, Topeka

Chestina Allen, Diary, n.d. and Biography of Asabel G. Allen (1859?)
Minerva Austin, Letters, 1869–89
Emily Butcher, Diary Account, 1896–99
James, Jane, and Lucy Carruth, Life Pictures in Kansas, 1856
Clara Conron, Diary, 1884
Susan B. Diamond, Diaries, 1863–1916
Julia Hand, Diary, 1872–75
Julia Lovejoy, Diary, 1859 and Letters, 1855–59
Lucy Nettleton, Letters, 1863–64
Carrie Strong Robbins, Journal . . . Payson, Adams County, Illinois, 1887
Eliza B. Wyckoff, Reminiscences of Early Days in Kansas

Missouri Historical Society, St. Louis

Ella R. Gale, School Compositions and Diary in Daniel Gale Papers
William Carr Lane Papers
  Anne Lane to William Carr Lane, July 6, 1851
  William Carr Lane to Anne Lane, January 2, 1852
  Anne E. Lane to Sarah L. Glasgow, November 13, (1870?)
  William Glasgow, Jr. to Sarah L. Glasgow, October 14, 1842
  Sarah L. Glasgow to Susie (Glasgow), October 16, 1881
  Abby Eliot to Sarah L. Glasgow, March 22 (1847?)

Kate C. Bowen to William Carr Lane, January 5, 1853
William Glasgow, Jr. to William Carr Lane, January 18, 1853
Eliza G. Post, Memorandum Books, 1812–76
Mary A. Wilkinson, Diary, 1851–52, 1852–56 in Harlan Papers
Also consulted at the Missouri Historical, Permissions requested:
   Missouri Bishop Moore, Journals of the Trip to California, 1859
     Mrs. Francis B. Sweany, Denver, Colorado
   Mrs. William Poston Scott, Diary, 1852–55
     Mrs. Ellanore S. Arnold, Pasadena California
   Mary E. Smith, Diary, 1836
     Copyright, Lucious H. Cannon, St. Louis
Letter to Mrs. Fannie E. Steele, June 26, 1852
   C. Corwith Wagner, St. Louis

Montana Historical Society

Elizabeth Fisk, Papers
Lucia Darling, Crossing the Plains in a Covered Wagon, 1863

Nebraska Historical society

Nan Aspinwall (Mrs. Frank Gable), Scrapbooks
May Bennett Avery, Papers and Memories of Pioneer Days
Susan Bordeaux Bettelyoun, Interviews
Anna Cameron, Interview
Margaret J. Carns, Reminiscence and Biographical Sketch
Susan Ophelia Carter, Diary, 1887
Lillian A. Elliott, Reminiscences
Luna E. Kellie, Memoirs
Nebraska Farmer, Sod House Letters
Sarah Jane Price, Diaries, 1878–95
Hazel Perin Reeder, Amelia
Shaw Family Papers
Stella (no other identification), Correspondence, 1866

Newberry Library, Chicago

Edward E. Ayer Collection
   T. J. Ables, Letter, October 12, 1857
   Mrs. Francis H. Sawyer, Overland to California . . . , 1852
   Sara Wisner, A Trip Across the Plains in 1866

Everett D. Graff Collection
    Fannie Kelly, To the Senators and members of the House of
        Representatives . . . , 1871

Oregon Historical Society, Portland

Cecilia E. Adams, Diary, 1852
Ruth Jewett Bailey, Papers
Pamela Benson, Diary, 1878
Margaret Rice Brockway, Correspondence, 1869–75
Mrs. Isaac L. Bryson, Grandma's Story
Minerva Burbank, Correspondence, 1852–59
Emily L. Burrows, Correspondence, 1873–75
Maria C. Cable, After Thoughts
Laura R. Castor, Diary, 1887–99
Letitia A. Chambers, Correspondence, 1856
Harriet T. Clarke, Diary, 1851
Arvazena Angeline Cooper, Our Journey Across the Plains
Malinda S. Crouch, Recollections of the Rogue River Indian Wars
Mrs. Matthew Deady, Crossing the Plains in 1846
Mary Dunn, Biography
Margaret E. Irvin, Covered Wagon Days
Margaretta McClintock, My Trip Across the Plains, 1866
Mrs. Mary Gray McLench, Notes Relating to Trip to Oregon Early in
    1851
Laura Hawn Patterson, Recollections of 1843
Lucy Preston Peters, Diaries, 1867–1922
Frances D. Reed, Biography
Maria Jane Renshaw, Diary, 1858
Caroline Sexton, Biography
Smith Family, Account of Overland Journey in 1846
Melissa Stroud, Hardships of Pioneer Life
Sarah Sutton, Diary of Overland Journey from Illinois, 1854
Mary Elizabeth Warren, Life Story
Harriet W. Williams to Mary R. Shumway, March 14, 1865
Consulted but not quoted in the text:
    Sybel A. Collier, Correspondence, 1866
    Amanda Crandall, Compositions, 1850
    Louise Freeze, Memories of Tygh Valley
    Jane Silcott, Biography

Panhandle Plains Historical Museum, Canyon, Texas

C. May Cohea, Pioneer Women
Cora Milla Kirkpatrick, Interview
Luella MacIntire, Interview
Flossie L. Morris, Diaries, 1906, 1913–17
Mary F. M. Pierce, My First Days in Texas

Rio Grande Historical Collections, New Mexico State University, Las Cruces

Ada Chase, Daybooks, Chase Family Papers
Weatherby Family Papers (The Collection does not have literary rights)

Sharlot Hall Historical Society, Prescott, Arizona

Diary of Angeline M. Brown, 1880 (copy in Huntington Library)

South Dakota Historical Society, Pierre

Cora D. Babcock, Reminiscences and Diary, 1880–85
Mary C. Collins, Papers
Mother Gertrude, Biographical Sketch
Orpha LeGro Haxby, Manuscripts
Myrtle C. Hooper, Diaries, 1887, 1891
Lucie Emma D. Lott, Her Story
Jeanne Willemin, Letter, 1906 (?)
Irene Cushman Wilson, Diary, 1890–91
Consulted but not quoted in the text:
  Fanny McGillycuddy, Diary, 1877–78

University of Arizona, Special Collections, Tucson

Gertrude Gates, Papers
Ruth Gordon, Portrait of a Teacher, Mary Elizabeth Post ....

University of California at Santa Cruz, Library

Carrie Lodge, Interview, The Martin Castro Lodge Family (copy in
  Bancroft Library)

University of Washington, Archives, Seattle

Elizabeth Austin, Crossing the Plains, 1854
Martha Crumbaker, Letter, November 20, 1878
Anna Maria Goodell, Crossing the Plains in 1854

Mrs. Ben Harsuck, Reminiscing
Amelia Knight, Journal Kept on the Road from Iowa . . . , 1853
Lottie Roeder Roth, Reminiscences
Mrs. Elizabeth C. Rudene, Reminiscences
Louise Butler Swift, Hattie Swift and Fannie Butler, Letters, 1863–69
Chloe Ann Terry (Doyle), Diary Kept while Crossing the Plains in 1852

Western Americana Collection, Beinecke Library, Yale University

Wealthy Brown to her sister, June 12, 1855
Diary of Mary Burrell, Crossing the Plains, 1854
Eliza Dilworth to William Wallterton, July 13, 1856 in Bringhurst Family
    Papers
Sarah McAllister Hartman, New Market, Washington, 1845 (copy also
    in University of Washington Archives)
Mary Jane Hayden to her grandson, May 8, 1887
Mary Benjamin Kirkpatrick, Letters, 1864–65
Falvia Pease, Letter and Power of Attorney, 1855
Mary Rice to Hannah Rice, November 15, 1835(?)
William and Lucy Shively to her father, July 9, 1865
Abby to George Underwood, Letter, November 17, 1850

Western History Collections, University of Oklahoma, Norman

Indian-Pioneer Papers
Edna Hatfield Collection
Oil in Oklahoma, WPA Interviews
Oklahoma Women Collection
    Courtesy, Women's Studies Program
Barbara McQuitty, Oklahoma Textures: A Personal Research
Teresa Terrell, The Life of Emma A. Coleman

List of
Abbreviations

AHS— Arizona Historical Society, Tucson
BAH— Baker Library, Harvard University
BL— Bancroft Library, University of California, Berkeley
BTHC— Barker Texas History Center, University of Texas, Austin
CHS— Colorado Historical Society, Denver
CSL— California State Library, Sacramento
DPL— Western History Collection, Denver Public Library
HEH— Henry E. Huntington Library, San Marino California
IHS— Idaho Historical Society, Boise
ISHS— Iowa State Historical Society, Des Moines
KHS— Kansas Historical Society, Topeka
MHS— Missouri Historical Society, St. Louis
MoHS— Montana Historical Society, Helena
NARS— National Archives and Records Service, Washington, D.C.
NHS— Nebraska Historical Society, Lincoln
NL— Newberry Library, Chicago
NMSU—New Mexico State University Archives, Las Cruces
OHS— Oregon Historical Society, Portland
PPHA— Panhandle-Plains Historical Society, West Texas State University, Canyon
SDHS— South Dakota Historical Society, Pierre
UWA— University of Washington Archives, Seattle
WAC— Western Americana Collection, Beinecke Library, Yale University
WHC— Western History Collection, University of Oklahoma, Norman

Notes

Note on Sources

1. For a discussion of reminiscences and their analysis see: Sherrell Daniels, "The Archetypal Reminiscence," paper delivered at the Western History Association Conference, Kansas City, 1980 and John Browning White, "Published Sources on Territorial Nebraska, An Essay and Bibliography," Nebraska State Historical Society *Publications*, 23 (1956), pp. 11–23.

2. Robert A. Fothergill, *Private Chronicles: A Study of English Diaries* (London, 1974), p. 43.

3. Professor Julie R. Jeffrey, Goucher College, is undertaking a detailed study of women's travel and settlement diaries. Some of her preliminary findings were presented at the Western History Association Conference, Kansas City, 1980.

4. See, especially: pp. 199–203 for a discussion of this methodology.

5. Leon Howard, "Literature and the Frontier: The Case of Sally Hastings," *ELH: A Journal of English Literary History,* 7 (March 1940), p. 72.

Chapter 1

1. Portions of this chapter were presented at the World Conference on Records at Salt Lake City in August, 1980, and published as Sandra L. Myres, "Women and the North American Wilderness, Myth and Reality," *World Conference on Records, Proceedings*, III, *North American Family and Local History,* Paper #319 (Salt Lake City, 1980).

2. Hamlin Garland, *A Pioneer Mother* (Chicago, 1922), p. 18.

3. See, especially, O. E. Rölvaag, *Giants in the Earth: A Saga of the Prairie* (New York, 1927); Dorothy Scarborough, *The Wind,* reprint ed. (Austin, 1979); Michael Lesy, *Wisconsin Death Trip* (New York, 1973).

4. Willie Newbury Lewis, *Between Sun and Sod,* reprint ed. (College Station, 1976), p. 41.

5. William F. Sprague, *Women and the West: A Short Social History* (Boston, 1940), p. 30.

6. Dee Brown, *The Gentle Tamers: Women of the Old Wild West* (Lincoln, 1958), p. 297.

7. Everett Dick, *The Sod-House Frontier, 1854–1890* (New York, 1937), p. 234.

8. John M. Faragher, *Women and Men on the Overland Trail* (New Haven, 1979), p. 181.

9. Lillian Schlissel, "Women's Diaries on the Western Frontier," *American Studies*, 18 (Spring 1977), p. 92.

10. Glenda Riley, "Images of the Frontierswoman: Iowa as a Case Study," *Western Historical Quarterly,* 8 (April 1977), p. 191.

11. Elizabeth Ellet, *Pioneer Women of the West* (New York, 1852), p. 35.

12. Richard A. Bartlett, *The New Country: A Social History of the American Frontier, 1776–1890* (New York, 1974), p. 350.

13. Dawn Gherman, "From Parlour to Tepee: The White Squaw on the American Frontier," Ph.D. dissertation, University of Massachusetts, 1975, p. 20.

14. Ibid., pp. 30–31. Gherman points out that both Richard Slotkin, *Regeneration Through Violence: The Mythology of the American Frontier 1600–1860* (Middletown Ct., 1973) and Leslie A. Fiedler, *The Return of the Vanishing American* (New York, 1968) advance this general thesis.

15. Brown, *The Gentle Tamers*, p. 297.

16. Erick H. Erikson, *Childhood and Society*, 2nd ed. (New York, 1963), pp. 290–95.

17. Beverly J. Stoeltje, " 'A Helpmate for Man Indeed,' The Image of the Frontier Woman," *Journal of American Folklore*, 88 (January–March 1975), p. 32.

18. Randolph B. Marcy, *Thirty Years of Army Life on the Border* (New York, 1866), p. 372.

19. See, for example, Caroline Kirkland's description of Mrs. Danforth in *A New Home or Life in the Clearings*, reprint ed. (New York, 1953), pp. 32–43.

20. Helen Hunt Jackson, *Ramona, A Story* (Boston, 1885); Fray Angelico Chavez, *The Lady from Toledo* (Fresno, Ca., 1960).

21. Susanna Bryant Dakin, *Rose or Thorn? Three Women of Spanish California* (Berkeley, 1963) and Herbert E. Bolton, *An Outpost of Empire* (New York, 1931) both contain the story of the merry widow, Feliciana Arballo. Señora Penalosa's feat is described in Gaspar Pérez de Villagrá, *History of New Mexico*, Gilberto Espinosa, trans. (Los Angeles, 1933) and Nancy Benson, "Pioneering Women of New Mexico," *El Palacio*, 85 (Summer 1979), pp. 10–11. Benson also discusses the legend of La Conquistadora, Ibid., pp. 11–12.

22. Cecil Robinson, *With the Ears of Strangers: The Mexican in American Literature* (Tucson, 1963), pp. 239–63; Beverly Trulio, "Anglo-American Attitudes Toward New Mexican Women," *Journal of the West*, 12 (April 1973), pp. 229–39; Benson, "Pioneering Women," p. 13.

23. These images are portrayed in Mary Sifton Pepper, *Maid and Matrons of New France* (Boston, 1901) and Grace L. Nute, *The Voyageur* (New York, 1931).

24. George R. Lamplugh, "The Image of the Negro in Popular Magazine Fiction, 1875–1900," *Journal of Negro History*, 57 (April 1972), p. 179. Also see Lawrence B. de Graaf, "Race, Sex, and Region: Black Women in the American West, 1850–1920," *Pacific Historical Review*, 49 (May 1980), pp. 285–313 and Sue Armitage, Theresa Banfield, and Sarah Jacobus, "Black Women and Their Communities in Colorado," *Frontiers*, 2 (Summer 1977), pp. 45–51.

25. In Indian tradition the images were quite different. Women were viewed as an essential part of the domestic life of camp or village, and they were often portrayed as supernatural beings, cocreators with a male god of earth and its inhabitants. See: John Upton Terrell and Donna Terrell, *Indian Women of the Western Morning* (Garden City, 1976), pp. 1–13.

26. This term was widely used in the mid-nineteenth century, and writers "simply assumed—with some justification—that readers would intuitively understand exactly what they meant." Barbara Welter, "The Cult of True Womanhood: 1820–1860," *American Quarterly*, 18 (Summer 1966), p. 151. Welter's article is one of the best discussions of the cult of true womanhood and its effects on nineteenth-century women, but also see: Glenda Riley, "The Subtle Subversion: Changes in the Traditionalist Image of American Women," *Historian*, 32 (February 1970), pp. 210–227 and Ronald W. Hogeland, " 'The Female Appendage': Feminine Life-Styles in America, 1820–1860," *Civil War History*, 17 (June 1971), pp. 101–114.

27. See the discussion in Ruth Elson, *Guardians of Tradition: American Schoolbooks of the Nineteenth Century* (Lincoln, 1964), pp. 301–10.

28. Welter, "The Cult of True Womanhood," p. 152.

29. "A Lady's Gift," *Western Literary Journal and Monthly Review*, 1 (July 1836), p. 132.

30. *The Young Ladies' Progressive Reader* (New York, 1876), p. 177; G. S. Hillard, *A First Class Reader* (Boston, 1856), p. 485 quoted in Elson, *Guardians of Tradition*, pp. 306–07.

31. See, for example: Catherine Beecher, *The American Woman's Home: The Principles of Domestic Science* (New York, 1869) and *A Treatise on Domestic Economy* (New York, 1849) and Lydia Maria Child, *The American Frugal Housewife* (Boston, 1836).

32. See Julie Roy Jeffrey, *Frontier Women: The Trans-Mississippi West, 1840–1880* (New York, 1979), pp. 12–14.

33. Quoted in ibid., p. 23.

34. Ibid., p. 19.

35. Such characterizations were common in nineteenth-century accounts of Western travel written by both men and women. See, for example: Caroline Kirkland's *A New Home* and *Forest Life* (New York, 1844) and Eliza Farnham, *Life in Prairie Land* (New York, 1846). Similar men's accounts include John L. McConnel, *Western Characters; or, Types of Border Life in the Western States* (New York, 1853) and William Oliver, *Eight Months in Illinois*, reprint ed. (Chicago, 1924).

36. Even Turner's best-known successors and interpreters failed to deal adequately with women and provided only very general conclusions about women's life in the West. In *The Great Plains* (New York, 1931), Walter Prescott Webb included women in the "Mysteries of the Great Plains" and concluded that the Great Plains were "strictly a man's country," that women dreaded and feared the plains, and that women often refused to go West because frontier life, at least on the plains, "precluded the little luxuries that women love and that are so necessary to them." (pp. 505–6) Ray Allen Billington believed that the frontier experience altered the relationship between men and women but only insofar as women were more valued on the frontier. According to Billington, women were the "harbingers of civilization" and "desirable helpmates," and because they were few in number "they were to be sought after, venerated, and pampered to a degree unrecognizable in areas with a more equitable ratio of the sexes." Ray Allen Billington, *America's Frontier Heritage* (Hinsdale, Ill., p. 216.

37. T. A. Larson, "Women's Role in the American West," *Montana, The Magazine of Western History*, 24 (Summer 1974), p. 4. Richard Jensen also pointed out the failure of Turner and his successors to include women, in "On Modernizing Frederick Jackson Turner: The Historiography of Regionalism," *Western Historical Quarterly*, 11 (July 1980), pp. 316–17, as did Joan Jensen and Darlis Miller in "The Gentle Tamers Revisited: New Approaches to the History of Women in the American West," *Pacific Historical Review*, 49 (May 1980), pp. 176–77.

38. Frank Starr, *Hurricane Nell, Queen of the Saddle and Lasso* (New York, 1877); Percy B. St. John, *The Trapper's Bride: A Tale of the Rocky Mountains with The Rose of Wisconsin, Indian Tales* (London, 1845); Zilla Fitz-James, *Zilla Fitz-James, the Female Bandit of the Southwest; or, The Horrible, Mysterious, and Awful Disclosures in the Life of the Creole Murderess (!) . . . An Autobiographical Narrative*, edited by Rev. A. Richards (Little Rock, 1852).

39. See, for example: Ellett, *Pioneer Women*; William W. Fowler, *Women on the American Frontier* (Hartford, 1879); John Frost, *Heroic Women of the West* (Philadelphia, 1854); and H. Addington Bruce, *Woman in the Making of America* (Boston, 1912), pp. 115–55. There are also some recent additions to this genre including Elinor Bluemel, *One Hundred Years of Colorado Women* (n. p., 1973); Anne D. Pickrell, *Pioneer Women in Texas* (Austin, 1970); and Elinor Richey, *Eminent Women of the West* (Berkeley, 1975).

40. Larson, "Women's Role," p. 4. Also see: Jeffrey, *Frontier Women*, p. 206, and Jensen and Miller, "The Gentle Tamers Revisited," pp. 176–77.

41. John Unruh, *The Plains Across: The Overland Emigrants and the Trans-Mississippi West, 1840–60* (Urbana, 1979). Unruh's bibliography includes a number of women's accounts, but

the index has only five brief citations to women's role on the trail and the text presents women as passive rather than active participants.

42. Georgia Willis Read, "Women and Children on the Oregon-California Trail in the Gold Rush Years," *Missouri Historical Review,* 39 (October 1944), pp. 1–23. Read used only very brief selections from four women's accounts.

43. Nancy Ross, *Westward the Women* (New York, 1944) was based on the published accounts of fourteen pioneer women plus a number of secondary sources; Helena Huntington Smith, "Pioneers in Petticoats," *American Heritage,* 10 (February 1959), pp. 36–39, 101–3, was based on the lives of four women. Brown utilized only published accounts and relied heavily on men's diaries and journals and secondary sources. Christiane Fischer's *Let Them Speak for Themselves: Women in the American West, 1849–1900* (Hamden, Ct., 1977) contained excerpts from a wide selection of frontier women's writings, but the editor provided almost no interpretation. "It has not been my intention to make judgments nor to set down any definite pronouncements," she wrote, "but simply to share the enthusiasm and the delight I have experienced in reading these highly diversified narratives." (p. 21)

44. Sprague, *Women and the West,* p. 63. For a similar assessment of Sprague's work, see: Paula Treckel, "An Historiographical Essay: Women on the American Frontier," *The Old Northwest,* 1 (December 1975), pp. 393–95. Treckel also discusses the Frost and Fowler volumes and Page Smith's *Daughters of the Promised Land: Women in American History* (Boston, 1970).

45. See note 7 above.

46. See, for example: Sandra L. Myres, ed., *Ho for California! Women's Overland Diaries from the Huntington Library* (San Marino, 1980); Lillian Schlissel, *Women's Diaries of the Westward Journey* (New York, 1981); Robert L. Munkres, "Wives, Mothers, Daughters: Women's Life on the Road West," *Annals of Wyoming,* 42 (October 1970), pp. 191–224; Ruth B. Moynihan, "Children and Young People on the Overland Trail," *Western Historical Quarterly,* 6 (July 1975), pp. 279–92; B. J. Zenor, "By Covered Wagon to the Promised Land," *American West,* 11 (July 1974), pp. 30–41; June Sochen, "Frontier Women: A Model for All Women?" *South Dakota History,* 7 (Winter 1976), pp. 36–56; and Glenda Riley, "Women in the West," *Journal of American Culture,* 3 (Summer 1980), pp. 311–29 as well as the other articles cited in this chapter and in Jensen and Miller, "The Gentle Tamers Revisited."

47. *Journal of the West,* 12 (April 1973); *Montana, The Magazine of Western History,* 24 (Summer 1974); *Heritage of Kansas,* 10 (Spring 1977); *Utah Historical Quarterly,* 46 (Spring 1978); *Pacific Historical Review,* 49 (May 1980); and forthcoming issues of the *Journal of the West* and *New Mexico Historical Review.*

48. See, Sandra L. Myres, "The Westering Woman," *Huntington Spectator,* 1 (Winter 1980), p. 1.

49. Johnny Faragher and Christine Stansell, "Women and Their Families on the Overland Trail to California and Oregon, 1842–1867," *Feminist Studies,* 2 (1975), p. 161.

50. Schlissel, "Women's Diaries," pp. 94–97; David M. Potter, "American Women and the American Character," in *American History and the Social Sciences,* Edward N. Saveth, ed. (Glencoe, Ill., 1964), pp. 431–32.

51. Faragher, *Women and Men* and Jeffrey, *Frontier Women.*

52. Faragher, *Women and Men,* p. 187.

53. Jeffrey, *Frontier Women,* p. 202.

54. Particularly helpful are several articles by Glenda Riley, "Images of the Frontierswoman," cited in note 10 above; *Women on the American Frontier* (St. Louis, 1977); " 'Not Gainfully Employed': Women on the Iowa Frontiers, 1833–1870," *Pacific Historical Review,* 49 (May 1980), pp. 237–64; Mary W. M. Hargreaves, "Women in the Agricultural Settlement of

the Northern Plains," *Agricultural History*, 50 (January 1976), pp. 179–89; and the Stoeltje article cited in note 17 above.

55. Riley, *Women on the American Frontier*, p. 15.

Chapter 2

1. Ruth Elson, *Guardians of Tradition: American Schoolbooks of the Nineteenth Century* (Lincoln, 1964).

2. I am using the word frontier here in its modern sense as defined by Ray A. Billington in *America's Frontier Heritage* (New York, 1966), p. 25. Used in this way, frontier is both place (". . . a geographic region adjacent to the unsettled portions of the continent in which a low man-land ratio and unusually abundant, unexploited, natural resources provide an exceptional opportunity for social and economic betterment to the small-propertied individual") and a process ("through which the socioeconomic–political experiences and standards of individuals were altered by an environment where a low man-land ratio and the presence of untapped natural resources provided an unusual opportunity for individual self-advancement").

3. For a fuller discussion of the Spanish borderlands frontier see the many books by Herbert Eugene Bolton, but especially his four broad studies in *Wider Horizons in American History* (New York, 1939). Also see: John Francis Bannon, *The Spanish Borderlands Frontier, 1513–1821* (New York, 1970) and Donald J. Lehmer, "The Second Frontier: The Spanish," in *The American West: An Appraisal*, Robert G. Ferris, ed. (Santa Fe, 1963), pp. 141–50.

4. The French frontier in Canada is detailed in W. J. Eccles, *The Canadian Frontier, 1534–1760* (New York, 1969). French activities in the interior are well documented in two books edited by John F. McDermott, *The French in the Mississippi Valley* (Urbana, 1965) and *Frenchmen and French Ways in the Mississippi Valley* (Urbana, 1969).

5. Of course, the interior of the continent was not unsettled. It was inhabited by a number of Indian peoples, many of whom had long-established villages and towns, abundant agricultural production, and a vigorous and well-ordered society. Europeans were aware of these Indian peoples, but they tended to think of them as uncivilized and their lands as unsettled. This was particularly true of Anglo-Americans.

6. Frederick Jackson Turner, *The Frontier in American History* (New York, 1920), p. 3.

7. Michael Wigglesworth, 1662, quoted in Henry Nash Smith, *Virgin Land, The American West as Symbol and Myth* (Cambridge, 1950), p. 4.

8. Turner, *The Frontier*, p. 4.

9. Walter Rundell, Jr., "Concepts of the 'Frontier' and the 'West'," *Arizona and the West*, 1 (Spring 1959), p. 22.

10. Jedidiah Morse, *Geography Made Easy* (New Haven, 1784), p. 74.

11. The development and persistence of the Garden concept is discussed in Smith, *Virgin Land*, pp. 123–32. Also see Roderick Nash, *Wilderness and the American Mind* (New Haven, 1967), pp. 1–17, in which Nash relates the Garden myth to the Garden of Eden and places the American ambivalence towards wilderness in a Biblical context.

12. Cotton Mather, *The Wonders of the Invisible World* (London, 1862) quoted in Nash, *Wilderness*, p. 26.

13. Herman Mann, *The Material Creation: Being a Compendious System of Universal Geography and Popular Astronomy* (Dedham, Ma., 1818); W. H. Venable, *A School History of the United States* (Cincinnati, 1872) both quoted in Elson, *Guardians of Tradition*, p. 184.

14. Quoted in Peter N. Carroll, *Puritanism and the Wilderness, The Intellectual Significance of the New England Frontier, 1629–1700* (New York, 1969), p. 143.

15. Eliza W. Farnham, *Life in Prairie Land* (New York, 1846), p. iii.

16. Quoted in David Donald and Frederick A. Palmer, "Toward a Western Literature, 1820–1860," *Mississippi Valley Historical Review,* 35 (December 1948), p. 413.

17. Ibid., p. 414.

18. For these and similar comments by French explorers, priests, and settlers, see Dorothy A. Dondore, *The Prairie and the Making of Middle America: Four Centuries of Description,* reprint ed., (New York, 1961), pp. 3–90.

19. Herbert E. Bolton, ed., *Anza's California Expeditions,* 5 vols. (Berkeley, 1930), III, pp. 119–20.

20. Gaspar Pérez de Villagrá, *History of New Mexico,* Gilberto Espinosa, trans. (Los Angeles, 1933), pp. 42, 125–27.

21. Francis Parkman, *The Oregon Trail* and Josiah Gregg, *Commerce of the Prairies* as quoted in Ralph C. Morris, "The Notion of a Great American Desert East of the Rockies," *Mississippi Valley Historical Review,* 13 (September 1926), p. 194.

22. For an assessment of American reading habits in at least one part of the country, see Howard Peckman, "Books and Reading on the Ohio Valley Frontier," *Mississippi Valley Historical Review,* 44 (March 1958), pp. 649–63.

23. Zadok Cramer, *The Navigator or the Traders' Useful Guide in Navigating the Monongahela, Allegheny, Ohio and Mississippi Rivers* (Pittsburgh, 1806); Samuel Cummings, *The Western Pilot* (Cincinnati, 1836).

24. John Filson, *The Discovery, Settlement and Present State of Kentucke* (Wilmington, 1784), pp. 21, 26–27, 100.

25. Gilbert Imlay, *A Topographical Description of the Western Territory of North America,* 3rd ed. (London, 1797), p. 517.

26. Captain Bernard Romans, *A Concise History of East and West Florida* (New York, 1795), p. 117.

27. William Darby, *The Emigrant's Guide to the Western and Southwestern States and Territories* (New York, 1818), p. 187.

28. Jedidiah Morse, *The American Geography With a Particular Description of Kentucky, The Western Territory, The Territory South of Ohio and Vermont* (London, 1794), p. 458.

29. John Melish, *Travels in the United States of America,* 2 vols. (Philadelphia, 1812), II, p. 279 and *The Traveler's Directory Through the United States* (Philadelphia, 1816), p. 34.

30. Cummings, *Western Pilot,* p. 7.

31. Romans, *A Concise History,* p. 190.

32. Henry B. Fearon, *Sketches of America: A Narrative of a Journey Through the Eastern and Western States of America* (London, 1818), p. 441.

33. John Bradbury, *Travels in the Interior of America in the Years 1809, 1810, and 1811* (London, 1817); Henry M. Brackenridge, *Journal up the Missouri, 1811,* vol. 6 of Reuben Gold Twaites, *Early Western Travels,* 32 vols. (Glendale, Ca., 1904).

34. Matthew Bunn, *Narrative of the Life and Adventures of Matthew Bunn in an Expedition Against the Northwestern Indians. . . . ,* 7th ed. (New York, 1828). For other negative, or at least cautionary, views, see: F. W. Thomas, *The Emigrant, or Reflections While Descending the Ohio* (Cincinnati, 1833); Jervis Cutler, *Topographical Description of the State of Ohio, Indiana Territory, & Louisiana* (Boston, 1812); J. F. Schermerhorn & S. J. Mills, *A Correct View of that Part of the United States which Lies West of the Alleghany Mts. . . .* (Hartford, 1814); and other sources discussed in Dondore, *The Prairie,* pp. 91–152.

35. J. Olney, *A Practical System of Modern Geography,* 33rd ed. (New York, 1840) quoted in Elson, *Guardians of Tradition,* p. 184.

36. Charlotte Ludlow [Chambers] to her father in Lewis H. Garrard, *Memoirs of Charlotte Chambers* (Philadelphia, 1856).

37. Caroline Kirkland, *Forest Life,* 2 vols. (New York, 1842), II, pp. 19–20.

38. Ibid., II, p. 29. Also see her *A New Home—Who'll Follow* (New York, 1839).

39. Catherine Stewart, *New Homes in the West* (Nashville, 1843), p. 55.

40. Kirkland, *A New Home*, p. 235.

41. Eliza R. Steele, *A Summer Journey in the West* (New York, 1841), pp. 130–31. Also see her comments on p. 134.

42. Elizabeth A. Row, *Aunt Leanna or Early Scenes in Kentucky* (Chicago, 1855), p. 18.

43. Elson, *Guardians of Tradition*, p. 184. Also see Laurence M. Hauptman, "Mythologizing Westward Expansion: Schoolbooks and the Image of the American Frontier Before Turner," *Western Historical Quarterly*, 8 (July 1977), pp. 269–82.

44. Nash, *Wilderness and the American Mind*, pp. 47, 45.

45. Cramer, *The Navigator*, p. 25.

46. Timothy Flint, *The History and Geography of the Mississippi Valley*, 2 vols. (Cincinnati, 1832), I, pp. 339–40.

47. Mrs. John Kinzie, *Wau-Bun: The "Early Day" in the Northwest* (New York, 1856), p. 14.

48. Steele, *A Summer Journey*, p. 125.

49. Stewart, *New Homes*, p. 66.

50. Mary Coburn Dewees, *Journal of a Trip from Philadelphia to Lexington in Kentucky . . . in 1787* (Crawfordsville, In., 1936), p. 5.

51. Steele, *A Summer Journey*, p. 123.

52. Kirkland, *A New Home*, p. 21; Dewees, *Journal*, p. 4.

53. Joseph Schafer, "The Yankee and the Teuton in Wisconsin," *Wisconsin Magazine of History*, 6 (December 1922), p. 131. On the aversion of settlers to the prairies also see: Bohumil Shimek, "The Pioneer and the Forest," *Proceedings of the Mississippi Valley Historical Association*, 3 (1909–10), pp. 96–105; Richard Bartlett, *The New Country* (New York, 1974), pp. 190–91 and the sources cited in Dondore, *The Prairie*, p. 163, note 26.

54. For a discussion of this problem, see William F. Sprague, *Women and the West, a Short Social History* (Boston, 1940), pp. 51–53. Sprague contends that women suffered more from such diseases than did men, but there is no evidence for this in women's diaries.

55. Kirkland, *A New Home*, p. 55. In addition to the women's sources already cited, conditions in this part of the West are also discussed by several women who lived in the trans-Appalachian region. See: Christiana Holmes Tillson, *A Woman's Story of Pioneer Illinois*, Milo M. Quaife, ed. (Chicago, 1919); "The Letters and Diary of Sarah Fletcher," in *The Diary of Calvin Fletcher*, 7 vols., Gayle Thornbrough, ed. (Indianapolis, 1972), I, pp. 39–79; Jerusha Loomis Farnham, *Log City Days: Two Narratives on the Settlement of Galesburg, Illinois* (Galesburg, 1937); Margaret Van Horn Dwight, *A Journey to Ohio in 1810* (New Haven, 1914); Anna Howard Shaw, *The Story of a Pioneer* (New York, 1915), pp. 19–53; Ruth Hoppin, "Personal Recollections of Pioneer Days," *Michigan Pioneer and Historical Collections*, 38 (1912), pp. 410–17; Margaret Lafever, "Story of Early Day Life in Michigan," Ibid., pp. 672–77; Peggy Dow, *Vicissitudes in the Wilderness* (Norwich, Ct., 1833); Rebecca and Edward Burlend, *A True Picture of Emigration* (London, 1848); "Mrs. Caroline Phelps' Diary," *Illinois State Historical Society Journal*, 23 (July 1930), pp. 209–39; "Mrs. Lydia B. Bacon's Journal, 1811–1812," Cary M. Crawford, ed., *Indiana Magazine of History*, 40 (December 1944), pp. 367–86 and 41 (March 1945), pp. 59–79.

56. Mary Austin Holley to her brother-in-law, December 5, 1820, BTHC.

57. Stewart, *New Homes*, p. 14.

58. For typical men's comments on this topic, see: John Stillman Wright, *Letters from the West; or a Caution to Emigrants* (Ann Arbor, University Microfilms, 1966), pp. 61–62; Morris Birkbeck, "The Illinois Prairies and Settlers," James Hall, "Shawneetown and the Salines," and William Cullen Bryant, "The Illinois River: Morgan, Sangamon, and Tazwell Counties" in Paul M. Angle, ed., *Prairie State: Impressions of Illinois, 1673–1967 by Travelers and Other Observers* (Chicago, 1968), pp. 64–65, 91–92, 106–7.

59. Burlend, *A True Picture*, pp. 121, 153; Dewees, *Journal*, p. 16.

60. Joanna H. Haines, "Seventy Years in Iowa," *Annals of Iowa*, 27 (October 1945), p. 100; Anne Newport Royall, *The Tennessean* (New Haven, 1827), p. 34; Katharine Horack, "In Quest of a Prairie Home," *The Palimpsest*, 5 (July 1924), p. 249.

61. New York *Aurora*, July 20, 1843, quoted in John Unruh, *The Plains Across: The Overland Emigrants and the Trans-Mississippi West, 1840–60* (Urbana, 1979), p. 38.

62. Harriet W. Williams to Mary R. Shumway, Portland, March 14, 1865, OHS.

63. Merrill Mattes, *The Great Platte River Road: The Covered Wagon Mainline Via Fort Kearny to Fort Laramie*, Nebraska State Historical Society Publications, vol. 25 (Lincoln, 1969).

64. Mrs. Lodisa Frizzell, *Across the Plains to California in 1852* (New York, 1915), p. 8; Helen Carpenter, "A Trip Across the Plains in an Ox Wagon, 1857," in Sandra L. Myres, ed., *Ho for California! Women's Overland Diaries from the Huntington Library* (San Marino, 1980), p. 93.

65. William C. Woodbridge, *Rudiments of Geography*, 17th ed. (Hartford, 1833), p. 83; Thomas J. Farnham, *Travels in the Great Western Prairies, the Anahuac and Rocky Mountains, and in Oregon Territory, 1843*, in Ruben Gold Twaites, *Early Western Travels*, XXIII, pp. 108–9; S. Augustus Mitchell, *An Accompaniment to Mitchell's Reference and Distance Map of the United States* (Philadelphia, 1845), pp. 297, 300; *Niles' Weekly Register*, 35 (September 27, 1828), p. 70 quoted in Francis Paul Prucha, "Indian Removal and the Great American Desert," *Indiana Magazine of History*, 59 (December 1963), p. 309.

66. For these, and other newspaper quotations, I am indebted to John Unruh's fine survey in *The Plains Across*, pp. 28–29. For other assessments by newspapers and textbooks of the Western area see: Martyn J. Bowden, "The Great American Desert and the American Frontier, 1800–1882: Popular Images of the Plains" in Tamara K. Hareven, ed., *Anonymous Americans: Explorations in Nineteenth-Century Social History* (Englewood Cliffs, 1971), pp. 48–79.

67. New York *Daily Tribune*, July 19, 1843; St. Louis *Daily Missouri Republican*, June 11, 1844 and September 22, 1847 as quoted in Unruh, *The Plains Across*, pp. 36–49.

68. St. Joseph *Gazette*, August 18, 1852; St. Louis *Daily Missouri Republican*, February 27, 1849 in ibid., pp. 65–68.

69. J. N. Shively, *Route and Distance to Oregon and California* (Washington, D. C., 1846), reprinted in Dale Morgan, *Overland in 1846: Diaries and Letters on the California-Oregon Trail*, 2 vols. (Georgetown, Ca., 1963), II, pp. 734–42. There were a large number of guidebooks published for overland emigrants. Among the most popular and widely read were: Andrew Child, *New Guide for the Overland Route to California, 1852*, reprint ed. (Los Angeles, 1946); P. L. Edwards, *Sketch of the Oregon Territory or Emigrant's Guide* (Liberty, Mo., 1842); W. Clayton, *The Latter-Day Saints' Emigrants' Guide* (St. Louis, 1848); P. L. Platt and N. Slater, *Traveler's Guide Across the Plains Upon the Overland Route to California*, reprint ed., Dale Morgan, ed. (San Francisco, 1963); Hosea B. Horn, *Horn's Overland Guide* (New York, 1852); Landsford W. Hastings, *The Emigrants' Guide to Oregon and California*, reprint ed. (Princeton, 1932); Joseph E. Ware, *The Emigrants' Guide to California, 1849*, reprint ed. (Princeton, 1932); Overton Johnson and William H. Winter, *Route Across the Rocky Mountains, 1846*, reprint ed. (Princeton, 1932). The influence of these and later guides such as Randolph Marcy, *The Prairie Traveler, A Hand-book for Overland Expeditions* (New York, 1859); Capt. John Mullan, *Miners and Travelers' Guide* (New York, 1865); and J. L. Campbell, *Idaho: Six Months In the New Gold Diggings* (Chicago, 1864) and *The Great Agricultural & Mineral West* (Chicago, 1866) are perceptively evaluated by Ray Allen Billington in "Books That Won the West: The Guidebooks of the Forty-Niners & Fifty-Niners," *American West*, 4 (August 1967), pp. 25–32, 72–75.

70. Johnson and Winter, *Route*, p. 2; Horn, *Overland Guide*, p. 15; Ware, *Emigrants' Guide*, p. 23; Child, *Overland Guide*, p. 36.

71. Maria A. Belshaw, "Diary," in *New Spain and the Anglo-American West*, 2 vols. (Lancaster, Pa., 1932), II, p. 221.

72. Caroline Richardson, Diary, BL; Maria Shrode, "Journal," in Myres, *Ho For California!* p. 261; Nellie Slater, Travels on the Plains in Eighteen Sixty-Two, DPL.

73. Tamsen Donner to Allen Francis, June 16, 1846 in Eliza P. Donner Houghton, *The Expedition of the Donner Party and its Tragic Fate* (Los Angeles, 1920), p. 24; Kate Dunlap, *The Montana Gold Rush Diary of Kate Dunlap*, S. Lyman Tyler, ed. (Denver, 1969), p. B-10. Other comments on the potential of the Western country as viewed by women are found in: Benjamin F. and Harriet Carr, Letters, CHS (see especially Harriet to her parents, July 4, 1858); Anna Maria Goodell, Crossing the Plains in 1854, UWA; Charlotte Pegra, Diary . . . Kept by Her on a Trip Across the Plains, 1853 (Eugene, Oregon, 1966) copy in OHS; Missouri Bishop Moore, Journal of the Trip to California, MHS.

74. Martha M. Allen, "Women in the West: A Study of Book Length Travel Accounts by Women Who Traveled in the Plains and Rockies. . . . ," Ph. D. dissertation, University of Texas at Austin, 1972, p. 100.

75. Jennie Atcheson Wriston, *A Pioneer's Odyssey* (Menasha, Wi., 1943), p. 12.

76. See, for example: Frances Carrington, *My Army Life, and the Fort Phil Kearney Massacre* . . . (Philadelphia, 1910), p. 33; Emma Shepard Hill, *A Dangerous Crossing and What Happened on the Other Side*, 2nd ed. (Denver, 1924), pp. 4–5; Goodell, Crossing the Plains, and Ada Vogdes, Journal Describing the Life of an Army Officer's Wife . . . , HEH.

77. Agnes Stewart, "Journey to Oregon . . . ," C. W. Churchill, ed., *Oregon Historical Quarterly*, 29 (March 1928), p. 86; Lavinia H. Porter, *By Ox Team to California: A Narrative of Crossing the Plains in 1860* (Oakland, Ca., 1910), p. 63.

78. Julia L. Lovejoy, "Letters from Kansas," *Kansas Historical Quarterly*, 11 (February 1942), p. 37; Frizzell, *Across the Plains*, p. 13; Dayelle Kittredge, Diary 1865, HEH; Allen, "Women in the West," p. 103.

79. Mary Mathews, *Ten Years in Nevada, or Life on the Pacific Coast* (Buffalo, 1880), p. 30; Mrs. Lula L. Downen, *Covered Wagon Days in the Palouse Country* (Pullman, Wa., 1937), p. 6. Other negative reactions to the mountains are discussed in Allen, "Women in the West," pp. 129–31.

80. Susan Wallace, *Land of the Pueblos* (New York, 1890), p. 11; Eveline Alexander, *Cavalry Wife: The Diary of Eveline M. Alexander*, Sandra L. Myres, ed. (College Station, Tex., 1977), p. 82; Anna S. Gordon, *Camping in Colorado*, quoted in Allen, "Women in the West," p. 139; Mary Bailey, "Journal of Mary Stuart Bailey," in Myres, *Ho For California!* p. 75; "A Lady's View of Utah and the Mormons, 1858: A Letter from the Governor's Wife," Ray Canning, ed., *Western Humanities Review*, 10 (Winter 1955-56), p. 33.

81. Pauline Wonderly, *Reminiscences of a Pioneer*, John Barton Hassler, ed. (Placerville, Ca., 1965), p. 3; Henrietta Chiles Knight, Trip Across the North Plains, BTHC; Moore, Journal; Lucy Nettleton to her mother, July 14, 1863, KHS; Marie Nash, Diary of Marie Nash, Michigan to California, CSL. Most women's diaries and reminiscences contain similar descriptions of the natural wonders along the trails.

82. Ellen Biddle, *Reminiscences of a Soldier's Wife* (Philadelphia, 1907), p. 85; Catherine Haun, A Woman's Trip Across the Plains in 1849, HEH; Harriet Bunyard, "Journal," in Myres, *Ho For California!*, p. 217.

83. Harriet S. Ward, *Prairie Schooner Lady: The Journal of Harriet Sherrill Ward, 1853*, Ward G. DeWitt, ed. (Los Angeles, 1959), p. 91. For descriptions by both men and women of the curiosities such as Chimney Rock, Independence Rock, and Devil's Gate, see Mattes, *Platte River Road*.

84. Frizzell, *Across the Plains*, p. 24; Mary Blake, *On the Wing*, quoted in Allen, "Women in the West," p. 139; Biddle, *Reminiscences*, p. 199; Annie D. Tallent, *The Black Hills or the Last Hunting Ground of the Dakotahs* (St. Louis, 1899), p. 59. For other typical comments, see: Bailey, "Journal," 68; Carpenter, "Trip Across the Plains," p. 127; Alexander, *Cavalry Wife*,

p. 83; and Alice Baldwin, *An Army Wife on the Frontier: The Memoirs of Alice Blackwood Baldwin, 1867–1877*, Robert & Eleanor Carriker, eds. (Salt Lake City, 1975), p. 20.

85. Carpenter, "Trip Across the Plains," p. 130; Sarah Sutton, Diary of Overland Journey from Illinois, 1854, OHS; Teresa Vielé, *"Following the Drum:" A Glimpse of Frontier Life*, James Day, ed. (Austin, 1968), p. 100; Vogdes, Journal.

86. John G. Bourke, *On the Border with Crook*, reprint ed. (Chicago, 1962), p. 1; David M. Potter, ed., *Trail to California, The Overland Journal of Vincent Geiger and Wakeman Bryarly* (New Haven, 1945), p. 104.

87. Franklin Starr quoted in Mattes, *Great Platte River Road*, p. 388; Bailey, "Journal," p. 64.

88. Randolph B. Marcy, *Thirty Years of Army Life on the Border*, reprint ed. (Philadelphia, 1963), pp. 128–29.

89. Margaret Carrington, *Ab-sa-ra-ka: Home of the Crow* (Philadelphia, 1868), p. 2. Also see: Esther Belle Hanna, Diary of Overland Journey from Pillsburg . . . 1852, HEH; Mary Burrel, Crossing the Plains, WAC; Mrs. Isaac Moore, How I Went to Denver, DPL; Dunlap, *Montana Gold Rush*, p. B-10; Mollie Sanford, *Mollie: The Journal of Mollie Dorsey Sanford in Nebraska and Colorado Territories, 1857–1866*, reprint ed. (Lincoln, 1959), p. 21; Bunyard, "Journal," p. 221; and Shrode, "Journal," p. 274, for other descriptions by women of the plant life.

90. For various descriptions of animals, see Haun, A Woman's Trip; Moore, How I Went to Denver; Mary E. Ackley, *Crossing the Plains and Early Days in California's Golden Age* (San Francisco, 1928), p. 24; Francis D. Haines, *A Bride on the Bozeman Trail: The Letters and Diary of Ellen Gordon Fletcher, 1866* (Medford, Or., 1970), pp. 23, 50–51; Shrode, "Journal," p. 266; Carpenter, "Trip Across the Plains," p. 107.

91. Haun, A Woman's Trip and Diary of Sister Monica, 1870, AHS. Also see: Ward, *Prairie Schooner Lady*, p. 57; Frizzell, *Across the Plains*, p. 18; Shrode, "Journal," p. 283; Lucy Cooke, *Crossing the Plains in 1852* (Modesto, Ca., 1923), p. 66; and Sarah Royce, *A Frontier Lady: Recollections of the Gold Rush and Early California*, reprint ed. (Lincoln, 1977), pp. 44–45 for similar comments.

92. Hattie Swift to "Dear Auntie," Fort Gamble, Oregon, January 8, 1865 in Louise Butler Swift Papers, UWA; Phoebe Goodell Judson, *A Pioneer's Search for an Ideal Home* (Bellingham, Wa., 1925), p. 278; Hanna, Diary.

93. Interview with Mrs. John Bonham, July 22, 1937, Pioneer and Indian Papers, IX, pp. 286–87, WHC; Jeanne L. Wuillemin, Letter, 1906(?), SDHS.

94. Luella Day, *The Tragedy of the Klondike* (New York, 1906), pp. 24, 33; May Kellogg Sullivan, *A Woman Who Went to Alaska* (Boston, 1902), pp. 71, 24; Mary E. Hitchcock, *Two Women in the Klondike* (New York, 1899), p. 24. Other women's accounts of Alaska and the Yukon country include: Ella Higginson, *Alaska, The Great Country* (New York, 1910); Matilda Barns Luken, *The Inland Passage, A Journal of a Trip to Alaska* (n.p., 1889); Lula Alice Craig, *Glimpses of Sunshine and Shade in the Far North* (Cincinnati, 1900); Emily Craig Romig, *A Pioneer Woman in Alaska* (Caldwell, Id., 1948); and Mrs. Eva McClintock, ed., *Life in Alaska: Letters of Mrs. Eugene S. Williard* (Philadelphia, 1884).

95. Marie de l'Incarnation to her brother, April 15, 1639, quoted in Cornelius J. Jaenen, *Friend and Foe: Aspects of French-Amerindian Cultural Contact in the Sixteenth and Seventeenth Centuries* (New York, 1976), p. 27.

96. Arballo's experiences are discussed in Susanna B. Dakin, *Rose or Rose Thorn? Three Women of Spanish California* (Berkeley, 1963). Guadalupe Vallejo, "Ranch and Mission Days in Alta California," *Century Magazine*, 41 (December 1890), p. 184; "The Story of Mariana Díaz," Tucson *Citizen*, June 21, 1875, AHS. Also see: Raymond S. Brandes, ed., "Times Gone by in Alta California, Recollections of Señora Doña Juana Machado Alipaz de Riding-

ton," Historical Society of Southern California *Quarterly,* 41 (September 1959), pp. 195–240; Angustias de la Guerra Ord, *Occurrences in Hispanic California,* Francis Price and William Ellison, trans. and eds. (Washington, D. C., 1956); and Amalia Sibrian, "A Spanish Girl's Journey from Monterey to Los Angeles," *Century Magazine,* 41 (December 1890), pp. 469–70.

97. "Waheenee: An Indian Girl's Story Told by Herself to Gilbert L. Wilson," *North Dakota History,* 38 (Winter & Spring 1971), p. 7; Lucy Young, "Out of the Past, a True Indian Story," *California Historical Quarterly,* 20 (December 1941), p. 351; "An Indian Girl's Story of a Trading Expedition to the Southwest about 1841," Winona Adams, ed., *Montana Historical Collections,* no. 11 (Missoula, 1930), p. 10.

98. In an analysis of men's and women's overland diaries, feminist historian John Faragher found many differences in men's and women's trail experiences, but his study also revealed that aesthetically men and women viewed the westering experience in similar ways. See John M. Faragher, *Women and Men on the Overland Trail* (New Haven, 1979), pp. 14–15.

Chapter 3

1. This phrase, borrowed from the title of Ray Allen Billington's *Land of Savagery/Land of Promise: The European Image of the American Frontier in the Nineteenth Century* (New York, 1980) characterizes the contradictory view which westering women held of both the physical and the racial frontiers.

2. Leslie Fiedler, *The Return of the Vanishing American* (New York, 1969), p. 90.

3. Dee Brown, *The Gentle Tamers: Women of the Old Wild West* (Lincoln, 1958), p. 1.

4. Dawn Gherman, "From Parlour to Tepee: The White Squaw on the American Frontier," Ph.D. dissertation, University of Massachusetts, 1975, p. 236.

5. Ibid., pp. 214–215; Glenda Riley, "Through Women's Eyes: Indians in the Trans-Mississippi West," paper presented at the Twentieth Annual Western History Association Conference, Kansas City, Missouri, 1980.

6. Billington, *Land of Savagery,* p. 1.

7. Cornelius J. Jaenen, *Friend and Foe: Aspects of French–Amerindian Cultural Contact in the Sixteenth and Seventeenth Centuries* (New York, 1976), p. 24.

8. Billington, *Land of Savagery,* p. 8.

9. Ibid., p. 17.

10. Jaenen, *Friend and Foe,* p. 26. The matter of changing European images of American Indians is extremely complex and the discussion above very simplified. For a more detailed discussion, see: Billington, *Land of Savagery,* pp. 1–28; Gary B. Nash, "The Image of the Indian in the Southern Colonial Mind," in *The Wild Man Within: An Image in Western Thought from the Renaissance to Romanticism,* Edward Duley and M. E. Novak, eds. (Pittsburg, 1972); Nancy Black and Bette Weidman, eds., *White on Red: Images of the American Indian* (Port Washington, N.Y., 1976); Roy Harvey Pearce, *The Savages of America: A Study of the Indian and the Idea of Civilization* (Baltimore, 1953); Robert F. Berkhofer, Jr., *The White Man's Indian: Images of the American Indian from Columbus to the Present* (New York, 1979); and James Axtell, "Through a Glass Darkly: Colonial Attitudes Toward the Native Americans," *Essays from Sarah Lawrence Faculty,* 2 (October 1973).

11. On Spanish-Indian policy and relations see: Edward Spicer, *Cycles of Conquest: The Impact of Spain, Mexico and the United States on the Indians of the Southwest, 1533–1960* (Tucson, 1962), pp. 279–333.

12. Ibid., pp. 310–11.

13. Guadalupe Vallejo, "Ranch and Mission Days in Alta California," *Century Magazine,* 41 (December 1890), p. 185; Angustias de la Guerra Ord, *Occurrences in Hispanic California,* Francis Price and William H. Ellison, trans. (Washington, D.C., 1956), p. 6; "Times Gone

By in Alta California, Recollections of Señora Doña Juana Machedo Alipaz de Ridington,"
Raymond S. Brandes, trans., *Southern California Historical Society Quarterly*, 41 (September
1959), pp. 195–240. For similar views, see Memorias de Doña Apolinaria Lorenzana, 'La
Beata' . . . and Doña Eulalia Perez, Una Vieja y Sus Recuerdos, BL.

14. "The Story of Mariana Díaz," typescript of *Arizona Citizen*, June 21, 1875, AHS; "The
Colorado Massacre of 1781: María Montielo's Reports," Kieran McCarty, trans., *Journal of
Arizona History*, 16 (Autumn 1975), p. 223.

15. The terms are from Elliott Coues, ed., *On the Trail of a Spanish Pioneer: The Diary and
Itinerary of Francisco Gárces*, 2 vols. (New York, 1900), II, p. 449.

16. On the French attitude toward miscegenation see: Jaenen, *Friend and Foe*, pp. 161–64.

17. Marie de l'Incarnation to her brother, April 15, 1639, quoted in Jaenen, *Friend and
Foe*, p. 27.

18. Ibid., p. 172.

19. Ibid., p. 18.

20. For one version of this story, see Mary Sifton Pepper, *Maids and Matrons of New France*
(Boston, 1901), pp. 220–38.

21. Marie de l'Incarnation quoted in Jaenen, *Friend and Foe*, pp. 70–71. (l'Incarnation entered the Ursaline order after her husband's death.)

22. Nash, "The Image of the Indian," p. 61.

23. Ibid.

24. Robert Gray quoted in David B. Quinn, ed., *The Roanoke Voyages, 1584–1590*, 2 vols.
(London, 1955), I, pp. 368–72, 376.

25. Black and Weidman, *White on Red*, p. 8 and Pearce, *The Savages of America*, pp. 19–35
give a more detailed examination of the Puritan viewpoint.

26. Black and Weidman, *White on Red*, p. 8 and Pearce, *The Savages of America*, pp. 35–41
discuss the Quaker Role.

27. Mary Rowlandson quoted in Black and Weidman, *White on Red*, pp. 41–48.

28. William Penn, "A Letter from William Penn, Proprietary and Govenour of Pennsylvania in America, to the Committee of the Free Society of Traders," London, 1683, extracted
in Black and Weidman, *White on Red*, pp. 50–55.

29. Robert Montgomery Bird, *Nick of the Woods or the Jibbenainosay*, 3 vols. (London, 1837),
II, pp. 18–19.

30. Virginia R. Murphy, "Across the Plains in the Donner Party," *Century Magazine*, 42
(July 1891), p. 409.

31. Salem Town, *The Grammer School Reader* (Portland, 1852) quoted in Ruth Elson, *Guard-
ians of Tradition: American Schoolbooks of the Nineteenth Century* (Lincoln, 1964), p. 71.
For other textbooks views of the Indians see: Laurence M. Hauptman, "Mythologizing
Westward Expansion: Schoolbooks and the Image of the American Frontier Before Turner,"
Western Historical Quarterly, 8 (July 1977), pp. 269–82.

32. Quoted in Black and Weidman, *White on Red*, p. 132.

33. Ibid.

34. Ibid.

35. Gherman, "From Parlour to Tepee," p. 94. Gherman discusses the Jemison narrative
in some detail, pp. 91–110.

36. Mary Smith, *An Affecting Narrative of the Captivity and Sufferings of Mrs. Mary Smith. . . .*
(Providence, R.I., 1815), p. 13.

37. Margaret Helm, quoted in Julia Kinzie, *Waubun, the "Early Day" of the Northwest*, reprint ed. (Chicago, 1901), p. 176. Kinzie's book was first published in 1856. Kinzie maintained that she presented the Helm narrative without charge. However, like other editors of
captivity narratives, she may have made additions, deletions, or comments of her own.

38. Elizabeth Hanson, *God's Mercy Surmounting Man's Cruelty Exemplified in the Captivity . . . of Elizabeth Hanson* (Philadelphia, 1728). For a discussion of the Hanson narrative, see: Gherman, "From Parlour to Tepee," pp. 64–70.

39. Mary E. Crawford, ed., "Mrs. Lydia B. Bacon's Journal, 1811–1812," *Indiana Magazine of History*, 40 (December 1944), pp. 370, 385–86; Mary Eastman, *Dahcotah or Life and Legends of the Sioux* (New York, 1849), p. v; Kinzie, *Waubun*, pp. 88–90; "Mrs. Caroline Phelps' Diary," *Illinois State Historical Society Journal*, 23 (July 1930), p. 232.

40. Harriet E. Bishop, *Floral Home: or First Years of Minnesota* (New York, 1857), pp. 63, 71; Mary A. Sagatoo, *Wah-Sash-Kah-Moqua or Thirty-Three Years Among the Indians* (Boston, 1897), pp. 69, 78.

41. Sagatoo, *Wah-Sash-Kah-Moqua*, p. 61. For a similar analysis, see: Gherman, "Parlour to Tepee," p. 95.

42. See, for example: Rufus Anderson, *Memoir of Catherine Brown, A Christian Indian of the Cherokee Nation* (Boston, 1825); Kunigunde Duncan, *Blue Star, as Told from the Life of Corabelle Fellows* (Caldwell, Id., 1938); Mrs. Harriet S. Caswell, *Our Life Among the Iroquois Indians* (Boston and Chicago, 1892); Mary C. Collins, *Thirty Years with the Indians* (New York, n.d.) and Recollections of a Missionary, SDHS; and Mary Rice, Fort Gibson, Western Creek Nation to Hannah Rice, Keene New Hampshire, November 15, 1835, WAC.

43. Anna Howard Shaw, *The Story of a Pioneer* (New York, 1915), pp. 34–36; Mattie Lykins-Bingham, "Recollections of Old Times," *Westport Historical Quarterly*, 7 (Fall 1971), pp. 16–17; Madge E. Pickard and R. Carlyle Buley, *The Midwest Pioneer, His Ills, Cures & Doctors* (Crawfordsville, In., 1945), p. 1. Also see: Rowena Nye to Mrs. Stone, November 18, 1788 in Mildred Covey Fry, "Women on the Ohio Frontier: The Marietta Area," *Ohio History*, 90 (Winter 1981), p. 65.

44. Sarah Royce, *A Frontier Lady: Recollections of the Gold Rush and Early California*, Ralph H. Gabriel, ed., reprint ed. (Lincoln, 1977), p. 10. Also see: Lodisa Frizzell, *Across the Plains to California in 1852* (New York, 1915), p. 9 and Diary of Ellen Tompkins Adams, BL, for similar statements.

45. Mary Jane Caples (Mrs. James), Overland Journey to the Coast, CSL; E. Allene Taylor Dunham, *Across the Plains in a Covered Wagon* (n.p., n.d.), p. 4; Margaret Elizabeth Irvin, Covered Wagon Days, OHS; Amelia Knight, Journal Kept on the Road from Iowa to Oregon, 1853, UWA.

46. Arvazena Angeline Cooper, Our Journey Across the Plains, OHS; Harriet T. [Buckingham] Clarke, Journal, 1851, OHS; Charlotte Pegra, "Diary . . . Kept by Her on a trip Across the Plains, 1853" (Eugene, Oregon, 1966) copy in OHS; Virginia Wilcox Ivins, *Pen Pictures of Early Western Days* (n.p., 1908), p. 44.

47. Overton Johnson and William H. Winter, *Route Across the Rocky Mountains*, Carl L. Cannon, ed., reprint ed. (Princeton, 1932), p. 151.

48. Frizzell, *Across the Plains*, p. 18; Margaret M. Hecox, *California Caravan: The 1846 Overland Memoir of Margaret M. Hecox*, Richard Dillon, ed. (San Jose, 1966), pp. 32–34. Also see: Lucy Rutledge Cooke, *Covered Wagon Days: Crossing the Plains in 1852* (Modesto, Ca., 1923), p. 30 and Francis Haines, *A Bride on the Bozeman Trail, The Letters and Diary of Ellen Gordon Fletcher, 1866* (Medford, Or., 1970), pp. 28–29.

49. Sallie Hester Maddox, "The Diary of a Pioneer Girl," *Argonaut*, 97 (September 12, 1925); Mrs. Frances M. A. Roe, *Army Letters From An Officer's Wife, 1871–1888* (New York, 1909), p. 10; Marie Nash, Diary of Marie Nash, CSL.

50. John Unruh, *The Plains Across: The Overland Emigrants and the Trans-Mississippi West, 1840–60* (Urbana, 1979), pp. 156–71.

51. Ibid., p. 185. A number of fictional massacres were reported in the Eastern press.

Sometimes such reports were based on false information from the West, but in some instances they were created by newspaper writers simply to sell papers. See: Ibid., pp. 175–77.

52. Harriett Sherill Ward, *Prairie Schooner Lady, The Journal of Harriett Sherrill Ward, 1853,* Ward G. DeWitt and Florence DeWitt, eds. (Los Angeles, 1959), p. 77; Lavinia Honeyman Porter, *By Ox Team to California: A Narrative of Crossing the Plains in 1860* (Oakland, 1910), pp. 70, 82; Sarah Sutton, Diary of Overland Journey from Illinois, 1854, OHS. Also see: Helen Carpenter, "A Trip Across the Plains in an Ox Wagon, 1857" in Sandra L. Myres, ed., *Ho For California! Women's Overland Diaries from the Huntington Library* (San Marino, 1980), p. 116; Elisha Brooks, *A Pioneer Mother of California* (San Francisco, 1922), p. 23.

53. Hecox, *California Caravan,* p. 40; Mrs. Francis H. Sawyer, Overland to California, Notes from a Journal . . . 1852, NL. Also see: Lydia Waters, "Account of a Trip Across the Plains in 1855," *Quarterly of the Society of California Pioneers,* 6 (March 1929), pp. 59–79; Porter, *By Ox Team,* p. 125; Royce, *Frontier Lady,* p. 36; Diary of Overland Journey of William L. Fulkerth and Wife, BL; Rebecca Woodson, A Sketch of the Life of Rebecca Hiddreth Nutting Woodson, CSL; Nellie Slater, Travels on The Plains in Eighteen Sixty-Two, DPL.

54. Carpenter, "Trip Across the Plains," pp. 152–72; Emeline L. Fuller, *Left by the Indians: The Story of My Life* (Mt. Vernon, Ia., 1892), pp. 19–27. Other incidents are reported in: Royce, *Frontier Lady,* pp. 36–37; Mary Ackley, *Crossing the Plains and Early Days in California: Memories of Girlhood Days in California's Golden Age* (San Francisco, 1928), p. 32; Mrs. Isaac L. Bryson, Grandma's Story, OHS; Missouri Bishop Moore, Journal of the Trip to California, MHS; Catherine Haun, A Woman's Trip Across the Plains in 1849, HEH. For several similar men's accounts of the Indians of this region see: T. J. Ables, Letter from Petaluma California, 1857, NL; William A. Maxwell, *Crossing the Plains, Days of '57* (San Francisco, 1915), pp. 63–72, 124–26; and especially David Potter, ed., *Trail to California: The Overland Journal of Vincent Geiger and Wakeman Bryarly* (New Haven, 1945), pp. 45 and 175.

55. Maggie Hall, The Story of Maggie, BL; Barsina French, Journal of a Wagon Trip . . . 1867, HEH; Virginia V. Root, *Following the Pot of Gold at the Rainbow's End in the Days of 1850,* Lenore Rowland, ed. (Downey, Ca., 1960), pp. 9–10.

56. Maria Shrode, "Journal," in Myres, *Ho For California!,* p. 288; French, Journal; and Harriet Bunyard, "Diary of a Young Girl," in Myres, *Ho For California!,* p. 238.

57. "The Pioneer Mothers," *The Western Literary Journal and Monthly Review,* 1 (July 1836), p. 102.

58. Sarah McAllister Hartman, New Market Washington, WAC; Caroline Sexton, Biography, OHS.

59. Susan E. Newcomb, Diary, BTHC. Also see Tom Ladwig, "Hannah Cole and Her Fortress of Courage," *Missouri Life* (October 1981), pp. 40–41.

60. Ruth S. Thompson, The Tragedy of Legion Valley: A Narrative of the Experiences of the Grandmother, Matilda Jane Friend in an Indian Raid in Legion Valley, Llano Co., 1868, BL; Minnie Bruce Carrigan, *Captured by the Indians: Reminiscences of Pioneer Life in Minnesota* (Forest City, S.D., 1907); Helen Mar Tarble, *The Story of My Capture and Escape During the Minnesota Indian Massacre of 1862* (St. Paul, 1904); Josephine Meeker, *The Ute Massacre! Brave Miss Meeker's Captivity! Her Own Account of It Also The Narratives of Her Mother and Mrs. Price* (Philadelphia, 1879).

61. Hartman, Diary; Matilda Delaney, *A Survivor's Recollections of the Whitman Massacre* (Spokane, 1920), p. 6; Meeker, *The Ute Massacre,* p. 12. Also see: Mrs. J. D. Bell, A True Story of My Capture By and Life with the Comanche Indians, BTHC; Fannie Kelly, To the Senators and Members of the H of R of Congress, NL; Mrs. Sarah L. Larimer, *The Capture and Escape or Life Among the Sioux* (Philadelphia, 1870).

62. Elizabeth C. Rudene, Reminiscences, UWA; Olivia Holmes, Diary Written in 1872 by

Olivia Holmes, BL. Also see: Maria Cutting Cable, After Thoughts, OHS; Mary Rabb, Reminiscences of Mrs. John Rabb, BTHC; Mrs. Warren R. Fowler, A Woman's Experiences in Colorado, BL; Mrs. W. L. Calohan, Some Reminiscences of Texas Life, BTHC; and Mabel W. Moffitt, Reminiscences of an Arizona Pioneer, AHS, for similar experiences and statements.

63. Elizabeth Montgomery Neeley, History of the Montgomery Family, BTHC. Also see: Mrs. William Justice, Pioneering in Hagerman from 1877 to 1900, IHS; Johnaphene S. Faulkener, The Prairie Home, BTHC; Annie D. Tallent, *The Black Hills or the Last Hunting Ground of the Dakotahs* (St. Louis, 1899), pp. 57–58; Georgia McRoberts, "Pioneer Ranch Life Near Sterling," *Colorado Magazine,* 2 (March 1934), p. 66.

64. See, for example: Alice J. Curnow, The Journey with Tom, AHS; Mary Maverick, *Memoirs of Mary A. Maverick, San Antonio's First American Woman,* Rena M. Green, ed. (San Antonio, 1921), pp. 18–19; Eliza J. Wyckoff, Reminiscences of Early Days in Kansas, KHS; Hartman, Diary.

65. Ella Bird-Dumont, Autobiography, BTHC; Ellen Throop, *Reminiscences of Pioneer Days* (n.p., n.d.), copy in NHS.

66. See, for example: Frances Cooke Lipscomb Van Zandt, *Reminiscences of Frances Cooke Lipscomb Van Zandt, Wife of Isaac Van Zandt* (Fort Worth, 1905); Esther Belle Hanna, Diary of Overland Journey from Pittsburg to Oregon, 1852, HEH; Anne Cameron, Transcripts of Interviews, Burwell, Nebraska, NHS; Sarah Ellen Martin, My Desert Memories, AHS; Minerva Austin Letters, 1869–89, KHS; Barbara J. McQuitty, Oklahoma Texatures, a Personal Research, WHC.

67. Hartman, Diary.

68. See, for example: Mary Pratt Staples, Reminiscences, BL; Hartman, Diary; Ackley, *Crossing the Plains,* pp. 66–68; Martin, Desert Memories; Leola Lehman, "Life in the Territories," *Chronicles of Oklahoma,* 41 (Fall 1963), p. 375.

69. Mrs. Fracena Martin Sutton, Narrative, BTHC; Mary Ann Davidson, "An Autobiography and a Reminiscence," *Annals of Iowa,* 37 (Spring 1964), p. 257; Eva E. Dye, "Woman's Part in the Drama of the Northwest," *Oregon Pioneers Association Transactions of the 22nd Annual Reunion 1894,* p. 37.

70. See, for example: Hartman, Diary; Thomas W. Prosch, *David S. Maynard and Catherine T. Maynard, Biographies of Two of the Oregon Immigrants of 1850* (Seattle, 1906), p. 74; Porter, *By Ox Team,* p. 70.

71. Sandra L. Myres, ed., *Cavalry Wife: The Diary of Eveline Alexander* (College Station, 1977), pp. 106, 117; Martha Summerhayes, *Vanished Arizona: Recollections of the Army Life of a New England Woman* (Glorieta, N.M., 1970), pp. 162–64. Also see: "A Lady's View of Utah and the Mormons, 1858: A Letter from the Governor's Wife," Ray R. Canning, ed., *Western Humanities Review,* 10 (Winter 1955–56), p. 31.

72. Mary E. Hopping, Incidents of a Pioneer Life, as I Remember and As I Have Been Told, CSL; Haines, *Bride on the Bozeman Trail,* p. 132; Phoebe Judson, *A Pioneer's Search for an Ideal Home* (Bellingham, Wa., 1925), pp. 244–46, 225; Delaney, *A Survivor's Recollections,* p. 6.

73. "Mrs. Caroline Phelps' Diary," p. 237; Maria Brace Kimball, *My Eighty Years* (Boston, 1934), p. 97.

74. Reminiscences of Mr. and Mrs. Jacob Stroup and Mrs. G. W. Brinnon, Pioneers of Washoe, Payette County, in the Early Seventies, IHS; Mrs. Andrew Hively, Journal 1863–64, DPL. For similar views, see: Tallent, *The Black Hills,* pp. 697–99; Caroline Gale Budlong, *Memories of Pioneer Days in Oregon and Washington Territory* (Eugene, 1949), p. 38; Lida M. Johnson Isham, Pioneer Days, 1863–80, IHS; Mary Rabb, Reminiscences; and Thomas R.

Buecker, ed., "Letters of Caroline Frey Winne from Sidney Barracks and Fort McPherson Nebraska, 1874–1878," *Nebraska History,* 62 (Spring 1981), pp. 1–46.

75. Frances Carrington, *My Army Life and the Fort Phil Kearney Massacre* (Philadelphia, 1910), p. 44.

76. Contrasting views of this analysis are found in Gherman, "Parlour to Tepee" and Ronald J. Quinn, "The Modest Seduction: The Experience of Pioneer Women on the Trans-Mississippi Frontier." Ph.D. dissertation, University of California, Riverside, 1977. An interpretation similar to my own is suggested in Riley, "Through Women's Eyes."

77. Effie May Wiltbank, Reminiscences, AHS; Brooks, *A Pioneer Mother,* p. 13.

78. Potter, *Trail to California,* p. 82; Charles Gray, *Off at Sunrise: The Overland Journal of Charles Glass Gray,* Thomas D. Clark, ed. (San Marino, 1976), p. 27.

79. Potter, *Trail to California,* p. 120; Byron N. McKinstry, Diary, 1850–52, BL quoted in Unruh, *The Plains Across,* p. 178.

80. Cora Agatz, "A Journey Across the Plains in 1866," *Pacific Northwest Quarterly,* 27 (April 1936), p. 172.

81. A recent analysis of Western men's and women's perceptions and attitudes in the pre-World War II period suggested that men and women were very similar except in relation to aggression. Women were consistently much more passive than men. My own work suggests that this may be true for nineteenth-century attitudes as well. D'Ann Campbell, personal communications to the author.

82. See, for example: "The Narrative of a Southern Cheyenne Woman," Truman Michaelson, ed., *Smithsonian Miscellaneous Collections,* vol. 87, no. 5 (Washington, D.C., 1932); "Narrative of an Arapaho Woman," Truman Michelson, ed., *American Indian Anthropologist,* No. 35 (Menasha, Wi., 1933), pp. 595–610; "The Autobiography of a Fox Indian Woman," Truman Michaelson, ed., in Bureau of American Ethnology, *Fortieth Annual Report, 1918–19* (Washington, D.C., 1925), pp. 291–349.

83. Jaenen, *Friend and Foe,* p. 23.

84. Sarah Winnemucca (Hopkins), *Life Among the Piutes: Their Wrongs and Claims,* Mrs. Horace Mann, ed. (Boston, 1883), p. 20; Lalla Scott, *Karnee: A Paiute Narrative* (Reno, 1966), pp. 2, 66; Ruth Underhill, "Maria Chona, The Autobiography of a Papago Woman," *Memoirs of the American Anthropological Association,* 46 (1936), p. 8. Also see: Louise Lone Dog, *Strange Journey: The Vision Life of a Psychic Indian Woman* (Healdsburg, Ca., 1964), pp. 7–8.

85. Florence C. Shipek, ed., *The Autobiography of Delfina Cuero, a Diegueno Indian* (Los Angeles, 1968), pp. 14, 46; Frank B. Linderman, *Pretty Shield, Medicine Woman of the Crows* (Lincoln, 1972), p. 250; Kate Luckie (Wintu), quoted in Calvin Martin, *Keepers of the Game: Indian-Animal Relations and the Fur Trade* (Berkeley, 1978), p. 183.

86. Mary Cobb Agnew, Interview #5978, *Indian Pioneer Papers,* I, pp. 221–27, WHC; Winnemucca, *Life Among the Piutes,* p. 14; Lucy Young, "Out of the Past, a True Indian Story Told by Lucy Young," *California Historical Society Quarterly,* 20 (December 1941), p. 358; Scott, *Karnee,* p. 84 Also see: Agnew, Interview, and "Waheenee: An Indian Girl's Story Told by Herself to Gilbert L. Wilson," *North Dakota History,* 38 (Winter & Spring 1971), p. 175.

87. Spicer, *Cycles of Conquest,* pp. 161, 170; Ralph A. Smith, " 'Long' Webster and the Vile Industry of Selling Scalps," *West Texas Historical Association Yearbook,* 37 (October 1961), pp. 99–120; Young, "Out of the Past," p. 105. For a discussion of enslavement and indenturing of Indian women and children, see: Robert F. Heizer and Alan J. Almquist, *The Other Californians: Prejudice and Discrimination Under Spain, Mexico, and the United States to 1920* (Berkeley, 1971), pp. 44–58.

88. Winnemucca, *Life Among the Piutes,* p. 3; Young, "Out of the Past," p. 364. Also see:

the account of Amy Prowers, whose parents were killed in the Salt Creek Massacre, Mrs. J. W. Prowers, Dictation, BL.

89. Quoted in Jaenen, *Friend or Foe*, p. 63; Winnemucca, *Life Among the Piutes*, p. 30; Susan Bordeaux Bettelyoun, Memoirs, NHS.

90. Lizzie Bdly Bohanon, Interview #7204, Indian-Pioneer Papers, IX, pp. 175–77, WHC; Lehman, "Life in the Territories," p. 374; Winnemucca, *Life Among the Piutes*, p. 14. Also see: Linderman, *Pretty Shield*, p. 47 and Lola M. J. Anderson, Interview #10407, Indian-Pioneer Papers, II, p. 246, WHC.

91. Scott, *Karnee*, pp. 15–16; Alice Baldwin, *An Army Wife on the Frontier*, Robert C. and Eleanor Carriker, eds. (Salt Lake City, 1975), p. 79; Underhill, "Maria Chona," p. 38. Also see: Kate Shaw Ahrens, Interview #7474, Indian-Pioneer Papers, I, p. 322, WHC.

92. "Waheenee," p. 175; Linderman, *Pretty Shield*, p. 249; Belle H. L. Airington, Interview #6734, Indian-Pioneer Papers, II, pp. 349–50, WHC. A number of Indian women interviewed in the Oklahoma project made similar statements.

93. Susette LaFleasch [sic] Tibbs, "Inshta Theamba," Introduction to *Ploughed Under: The Story of an Indian Chief* (New York, 1881), p. 6.

94. *Mountain Wolf Woman, The Autobiography of a Winnebago Indian*, Nancy O. Lurie, ed. (Ann Arbor, 1961), p. 106.

Chapter 4

1. See, Peter Loewenberg, "The Psychology of Racism" in Gary B. Nash and Richard Weise, eds., *The Great Fear: Race in the Mind of America* (New York, 1970), pp. 186–201.

In this chapter, the terms *Mexican* or *Hispanic* are used to refer to Spanish-speaking peoples or people of Spanish-Mexican background living within the borders of what is now the United States. The term *American* is used to refer to the English-speaking peoples who began moving into the old Spanish Southwest in the 1830s and 40s. This is not meant to imply that Mexicans were not Americans; rather these terms, which were in common useage by both Hispanics and Americans in the nineteenth century, are used to avoid the awkwardness of hyphenated forms such as Mexican-American or Anglo-American.

2. James D. Hart, *American Images of Spanish California* (Berkeley, 1960), p. 1. Also see: W. Eugene Hollon, *The Southwest Old and New* (New York, 1961), pp. 86–87.

3. William Robertson, *The History of America*, 2 vols. (Albany, 1822), II, pp. 50, 205 quoted in David Weber, *Foreigners in Their Native Land: Historical Roots of the Mexican Americans* (Albuquerque, 1973), pp. 69–71. Also see: Harry Bernstein, *Making an Inter-American Mind* (Gainesville, 1961), pp. 1–32 and Philip W. Powell, *Tree of Hate: Propaganda and Prejudices Affecting United States Relations with the Hispanic World* (New York, 1971), pp. 3–38 for other discussions of anti-Spanish propaganda in the British colonies and the early years of the American Republic.

4. J. E. Worcester, *Elements of Geography, Ancient and Modern*, 2nd ed. (Boston, 1822) quoted in Ruth Elson, *Guardians of Tradition, American Schoolbooks of the Nineteenth Century* (Lincoln, 1964), p. 151.

5. Bernstein, *Making an Inter-American Mind*, p. 7. On the roots of anti-Catholic prejudice and the development of North American nativism, see Ray A. Billington, *The Protestant Crusade, 1800–1860: A Study of the Origins of American Nativism* (New York, 1938), pp. 1–31.

6. Alexander De Conde, *This Affair of Louisiana* (New York, 1976), p. 22; Jedidiah Morse, *The American Geography* (London, 1794), p. 569.

7. "Pike's Observations on New Spain," in *The Journals of Zebulon Montgomery Pike*, Donald Jackson, ed., 2 vols. (Norman, 1966), II, pp. 58, 60; William Shaler, *Journal of a Voyage*

Between China and the Northwestern Coast of America, Made in 1804, reprint ed. (Claremont, Ca., 1935), pp. 59, 60, 77.

8. Herman Mann, *The Material Creation: Being a Compendious System of Universal Geography and Popular Astronomy* (Dedham, Ma., 1818), quoted in Elson, *Guardians of Tradition*, p. 158.

9. Jedidiah Morse, *Geography Made Easy* (New Haven, 1784), pp. 102, 156; Laurence M. Hauptman, "Mythologizing Westward Expansion: Schoolbooks and the Image of the American Frontier Before Turner," *Western Historical Quarterly*, 8 (July 1977), pp. 279–80.

10. Rev. J. L. Blake, *A Geography for Children* (Boston, 1831) quoted in Elson, *Guardians of Tradition*, p. 159.

11. *Hunt's Merchant Magazine*, quoted in Hart, *American Images*, p. 13.

12. Richard Henry Dana, *Two Years Before the Mast*, quoted in ibid., p. 19. Other excellent sources of early American views of Mexicans include: John P. Bloom "New Mexico Viewed by Americans, 1846–1849," *New Mexico Historical Review*, 34 (July 1959), pp. 165–98; Cecil Robinson, *With the Ears of Strangers: The Mexican in American Literature* (Tucson, 1963), pp. 15–99; Weber, *Foreigners in Their Native Land*, pp. 51–86; David J. Langum, "Californios and the Image of Indolence," *Western Historical Quarterly*, 9 (April, 1978), pp. 181–96; Harry Clark, "Their Pride, Their Manners, and Their Voices: Sources of the Traditional Portrait of the Early Californians," *California Historical Quarterly*, 53 (Spring 1974), pp. 71–82; and Richard Peterson, "Anti-Mexican Nativism in California, 1848–1853: A Study of Cultural Conflict," *Southern California Quarterly*, 42 (Winter 1980), pp. 309–28.

13. See: Beverly Trulio, "Anglo-American Attitudes Toward New Mexican Women," *Journal of the West*, 12 (April 1973) pp. 229–39; James M. Lacy, "New Mexican Women in Early American Writings," *New Mexico Historical Review*, 34 (January 1959), pp. 41–51; and David J. Langum, "California Women and the Image of Virtue," *Southern California Quarterly*, 59 (Fall 1977), pp. 245–50.

14. Mary Austin Holley, *Texas* (Lexington, Ky., 1836), pp. 128, 151; Jane Cazneau, *Eagle Pass or Life on the Border* (New York, 1852), pp. 60, 81. Although Cazneau's book was not published until 1852, she had lived in Texas prior to the Revolution and wrote numerous letters to friends in the East including bankers, Congressmen, and newspaper editors asking for support for the Texas Revolution. She also appeared to have authored several newspaper articles. Thus, her opinions were widely circulated among influential people prior to the publication of *Life on the Border*.

15. Robinson, *Ears of Strangers*, p. 26; Lansford W. Hastings, *The Emigrants' Guide to Oregon and California*, reprint ed. (Princeton, 1932), pp. 106–116; Edwin Bryant, *What I Saw in California* (1849), reprint ed. (Palo Alto, 1967), pp. 417–27, 441–48 (this popular book was often used as a book of advice and sometimes as a guide by emigrants); Randolph B. Marcy, *The Prairie Traveler: A Hand-Book for Overland Expeditions* (New York, 1859), p. 100.

16. Mary Helm, *Scraps from Texas History* (Austin, 1884), pp. 8, 53. Other women's accounts of the Revolutionary period in Texas include: Mary Rabb, Reminiscences of Mrs. John Rabb; Elizabeth Owens, Story of Her Life . . . Set Down by Her Daughter; and the account of Angelina Eberly in Mary Austin Holley, Literary Productions and Historical Notes, all in BTHC. Like Helms these women were anti-Mexican.

17. Mary Maverick, *Memoirs of Mary A. Maverick*, Rena M. Green, ed. (San Antonio, 1921), pp. 16, 54.

18. Susan Magoffin, *Down the Santa Fe Trail and Into Mexico: The Diary of Susan Shelby Magoffin*, Stella M. Drumm, ed. (New Haven, 1926), pp. 130–31, 177, 192; Margaret Hecox, *California Caravan: The 1846 Overland Trail Memoirs of Margaret M. Hecox*, Richard Dillon, ed. (San Jose, 1966), pp. 44, 57, 63. Also see: Clara Brown, A Private Journel [sic], BTHC; Emeline Benson, From Beloit, Wisconsin to San Pablo Valley, January 1, 1853–December 31, 1854, CSL.

19. Hart, *American Images*, p. 22.

20. Ibid. Also see: Robinson, *Ears of Strangers*, pp. 135–161; Weber, *Foreigners in Their Native Land*, pp. 140–60.

21. Ellen McGowen Biddle, *Reminiscences of a Soldier's Wife* (Philadelphia, 1907), p. 199; Sandra L. Myres, ed. *Cavalry Wife: The Diary of Eveline M. Alexander* (College Station, Tex., 1977), pp. 73, 105; Lydia Lane, *I Married a Soldier*, reprint ed. (Albuquerque, 1964), pp. 34, 117–18; Robert C. and Eleanor R. Carriker, eds., *An Army Wife on the Frontier: The Memoirs of Alice Blackwood Baldwin* (Salt Lake City, 1975), p. 59; Martha Summerhayes, *Vanished Arizona: Recollections of My Army Life*, reprint ed. (Glorieta, N.M., 1970), pp. 271–77, 284–85; Mrs. Orsemus B. Boyd, *Cavalry Life in Tent and Field* (New York, 1894), pp. 300–301; and "The Diary of Eliza (Mrs. Albert Sidney) Johnston," *Southwestern Historical Quarterly*, 60 (April 1957), 497–99. Also see: Sandra L. Myres, "The Ladies of the Army—Views of Western Life," *The American Military on the Frontier*, Proceedings of the Seventh Military History Symposium (Washington, D.C., 1976), pp. 142–44.

22. Summerhays, *Vanished Arizona*, pp. 39, 157–58.

23. Teresa Vielé, *"Following the Drum": A Glimpse of Frontier Life* (New York, 1858), pp. 155–56.

24. Melinda Rankin, *Twenty Years Among the Mexicans: A Narrative of Missionary Labor* (St. Louis, 1875), p. 36; Anna McKee to her Mother, Christmas, 1884, CHS; Charles McPhee Wright, Annals of Harriet S. Wright, 1841–1932, AHS; Sophie A. Poe, *Buckboard Days* (Caldwell, Id., 1936), p. 207; Mary Ronan, *Frontier Woman, The Story of Mary Ronan*, H. G. Merriam, ed. (Missoula, 1973), p. 59. Also see: Marian Russell, *Land of Enchantment, Memoirs of Marian Russell Along the Santa Fe Trail* (Evanston, Il., 1954), pp. 29–30, and Diary of Sister Monica, Sisters of St. Joseph, 1870, AHS.

25. Vielé, *"Following the Drum,"* pp. 156, 113, 186; Lane, *I Married A Soldier*, p. 142; Sarah M. Cool, Frontier Life; Incidents and Work in California, HEH.

26. Maria Shrode, "Journal," in Sandra L. Myres, ed., *Ho for California!* (San Marino, 1980), p. 278; Virgina Root, *Following the Pot of Gold at the Rainbow's End in the Days of 1850*, Leonore Rowland, ed. (Downey, Ca., 1960), p. 8; Harriet Bunyard, "A Young Girl's Diary," in Myres, *Ho for California!* pp. 224–25; Shrode, "Journal," p. 278. Also see: Cecilia Bagley Willis, Journal, AHS.

27. Boyd, *Cavalry Life*, pp. 178–79; Lane, *I Married a Soldier*, p. 117; Bunyard, "Diary," p. 227; Susan Wallace, *The Land of the Pueblos* (New York, 1888), pp. 63, 65. Also see: Mrs. Sarah M. Black, Reminiscences, AHS.

28. Rachel Frazier, *Reminiscences of Travel from 1855 to 1867* (San Francisco, 1868), p. 29; Louise A. K. S. Clappe, *The Shirley Letters: Being Letters Written in 1851–1852 from the California Mines by "Dame Shirley"*, reprint ed. (Santa Barbara, 1970), pp. 109–10.

29. Emma Adams, *To and Fro in Southern California* (Cincinnati, 1887), pp. 132–33.

30. This summary is based on an excellent essay by Rodman Paul, "The Spanish Americans in the Southwest, 1848–1900," in John G. Clark, ed., *The Frontier Challenge: Responses to the Trans-Mississippi West* (Lawrence, 1971), pp. 31–56. In addition to the Paul essay and the sources he lists, see: Carey McWilliams, *North From Mexico: The Spanish-Speaking People of the United States* (Philadelphia, 1949); Leonard Pitt, *The Decline of the Californios: A Social History of the Spanish-Speaking Californians, 1846–1890* (Berkeley, 1966); Robert F. Heizer and Alan J. Almquist, *The Other Californians: Prejudice and Discrimination Under Spain, Mexico, and the United States to 1920* (Berkeley, 1971), pp. 138–53; and Alfredo Mirandé and Evangelina Enríquez, *La Chicana: The Mexican American Woman* (Chicago, 1979), pp. 53–95.

31. In the 1870s, H. H. Bancroft did arrange for a series of interviews with some of the older Mexican-American residents of California. The interviews were conducted and recorded in Spanish, and a number of women were included. Unfortunately, historians in

the 1870s were more interested in political history than in social history, and, of course, they were unaware of the kinds of questions that historians one hundred years later would like to have answered. The interviewers thus asked questions such as "Do you remember Governor Pio Pico?" "Were you in Los Angeles when Stockton landed?" "What do you recall of the Alvarado Revolt?" "What did your husband (father, brother) do at the presidio?" Thus the *Recuerdos* and *Memorias* dictated by these women centered on political and military events and not on their personal lives and feelings. The women who did mention their feelings about Americans were very circumspect in their remarks. Among the interviews conducted in the 1870s are those with Doña Juana Machado de Ridington, which is mostly concerned with her father's army service; Doña Catarina Avilá de Rios, an account of an 1849 murder at San Miguel Mission; Doña María Inocenta Pico, a history of her husband, Don Miguel Avila; and Doña Eulalia Pérez and Doña Apolinaria Lorenzana, both rather interesting accounts of mission life; and Doña Josepha Fitch, an account of her turbulent romance and elopement with a Yankee sea captain. Transcripts of these interviews and those of several other Mexican women are in the Bancroft Library which is preparing some of them for publication. In recent years, historians have become more interested in the experiences of Mexican-American women. Interviews with and reminiscences of several older women of Hispanic background are recorded in Rose de Tevis, Margaret Garcia and Edwin Rivera, eds., *El Oro y el Futuro del Pueblo* (Albuquerque, 1979).

32. Guadalupe Vallejo, "Ranch and Mission Days in Alta California," *Century Magazine,* 41 (December 1890), p. 190; Doña Atanacia Santa Cruz de Hughes, Mexican Troops Departure from Tucson as told to Donald W. Page, May 12, 1929, BL; Señora Doña Jesus Moreno de Soza, Soza Family Reminiscences, AHS; Fabiola Cabeza de Baca, *We Fed Them Cactus,* paperback ed. (Albuquerque, 1979), p. 63

33. Prudencia Higuera, "Trading With the Americans," *Century Magazine,* 41 (December 1890), p. 193; Vallejo, "Ranch and Mission Days," p. 190; Carrie Lodge, The Marina Castro Lodge Family, An Interview conducted by Elizabeth S. Calciano, Santa Cruz, 1965, transcript in BL; María Merced Williams de Rains to Benjamin Hayes, May 27, 1864 in Benjamin Hayes, Scraps, vol. 14, BL and reprinted in Esther B. Black, *Rancho Cucamonga and Dona Merced* (Redlands, Ca. 1975), p. 112. See also: Angustias de la Guerra Ord, *Occurrences in Hispanic California,* Francis Price and William Ellison, trans. and eds. (Washington, D.C., 1956), pp. 58, 62–63; and "Times Gone by in Alta California, Recollections of Señora Doña Juana Machado," Raymond S. Brandes, trans. and ed., *Historical Society of Southern California Quarterly,* 41 (September 1959), pp. 216–18. (Both the Ord book and the Machado article were prepared from the Bancroft interview transcripts.)

34. Iris Wilson Engstrand and Thomas L. Scharf, "Rancho Guajome: A California Legacy Preserved," *Journal of San Diego History,* 20 (Winter 1974), p. 7; Doña Victoria Reid, quoted in Susanna Dakin, *A Scotch Paisano: Hugo Reid's Life in California, 1832–1852* (Berkeley, 1939), p. 154; Vallejo, "Ranch and Mission Days," p. 190; Dorotea Valdez, Reminiscences, transcript of interview, BL.

35. See, for example, Maverick, *Memoirs,* 54; Baldwin, *An Army Wife,* pp. 59–60; Hecox, *California Caravan,* p. 63; and Ronan, *Frontier Woman,* pp. 55–57.

36. Ord, *Occurrences,* p. 59.

37. Although some older and a few recent studies have accepted the fact that there were few intercultural marriages, more detailed quantitative studies would seem to show just the opposite. See, particularly: Pitt, *The Decline of the Californios,* pp. 19, 124–25, 267; Jane Dysart, "Mexican Women in San Antonio, 1830–1860: The Assimilation Process," *Western Historical Quarterly,* 7 (October 1976), pp. 365–75; and Darlis Miller, "Cross-Cultural Marriages in the Southwest: The New Mexico Experience, 1846–1900," *New Mexico Historical Review,* 57 (October 1982), in press. Also, see: Paul, "The Spanish-Americans."

38. George M. Fredrickson, *The Black Image in the White Mind: The Debate on Afro-American Character and Destiny, 1817–1914* (New York, 1971), pp. 133–34.

39. "Emigration from Iowa to Oregon in 1843," *Oregon Historical Society Quarterly,* 15 (December 1914), p. 292.

40. Glenda Riley, *Frontierswomen: The Iowa Experience* (Ames, 1981), pp. 88–90; Lawrence B. de Graaf, "Race, Sex and Region: Black Women in the American West, 1850–1920," *Pacific Historical Review,* 49 (May 1980), pp. 286–87.

41. Sarah Kenyon to her family, 1856, quoted in Riley, *Iowa Frontierswomen,* p. 89. Also see: Mrs. R. A. Bass, Interview #4001, Indian-Pioneer Papers, VI, p. 13.

42. Myres, *Cavalry Wife,* p. 73; Bunyard, "Diary," p. 210; Elizabeth Custer, *"Boots and Saddles" or, Life in Dakota with General Custer,* reprint ed. (Norman, 1961), p. 5.

43. Interview, Georgia Ann Davis in Edna Hatfield Collection, WHC.

44. See de Graaf, "Race, Sex and Region," pp. 291–96. There was far less discrimination on the Hispanic and Indian frontiers where there were few legal or emotional prohibitions against miscegenation. On the Hispanic frontiers there were so many combinations of Spanish, Indian, and Negro alliances that government officials worked out an elaborate system of caste by which to identify the various racial combinations. In the Indian Territory (later Oklahoma), where Negroes first came as slaves of the Five Civilized Tribes (Cherokees, Chickasaws, Choctaws, Creeks, and Seminoles), Southern patterns of informal alliances between masters and slave women existed before the Civil War resulting in a number of children of mixed parentage. After the War there were a number of legal marriages between Indians and Negroes. Negroes generally supported the traditional Indians in their attempts to gain political control at the expense of Indian-white elements within the various tribes. However, mixed Indian-Negro marriages often brought increased discrimination from whites and sometimes resulted in the couples' isolation from both the black and the Indian community. See: Kenneth Wiggins Porter, *The Negro on the American Frontier: Select Preliminary Studies* (New York, 1971) and Irena Blocker, Interview #7462, Indian-Pioneer Papers, VIII, p. 510.

45. de Graaf, "Race, Sex and Region," pp. 290–91; John A. Andrew, "Betsey Stockton: Stranger in a Strange Land," *Journal of Presbyterian History,* 52 (Summer 1974), pp. 157–66; Dorothy Bass Spann, *Black Pioneers: A History of a Pioneer Family in Colorado Springs* (Colorado Springs, 1978); Sue Armitage, Theresa Banfield, and Sarah Jacobus, "Black Women and Their Communities in Colorado," *Frontiers,* 2 (1977), pp. 45–51; Robert Athearn, *In Search of Canaan: Black Migration to Kansas, 1879–80* (Lawrence, 1978), pp. 218, 238–39.

46. de Graaf, "Race, Sex and Region," p. 289; Robert L. Carlton, "Blacks in San Diego County, A Social Profile, 1850–1880," *Journal of San Diego History,* 21 (Fall 1975), p. 8. de Graaf suggests that because western blacks "were in many ways exceptional and represented a higher degree of initiative, aggressiveness, and tenacity than most Americans, black or white," black women in the West considered themselves to be part of an elite group. Also see: Rudolph M. Lapp, *Blacks in Gold Rush California* (New Haven, 1977), p. 269 and Douglas H. Daniels, *Pioneer Urbanites: A Social and Cultural History of Black San Francisco* (Philadelphia, 1980).

47. There is a voluminous literature on Mormons and Mormonism. Especially recommended as an impartial, objective account is Thomas O'Dea, *The Mormons* (Chicago, 1957). An excellent account of the early years of the Church is found in the biography of the founder, Fawn M. Brodie, *No Man Knows My History: The Life Story of Joseph Smith* (New York, 1945). On the Mormon move westward and the growth and development of the Mormon settlements in Utah see: Wallace Stegner, *The Gathering of Zion: The Story of the Mormon Trail* (New York, 1964); L. H. Creer, *The Founding of an Empire: The Exploration and Colonization of*

Utah, 1776–1856 (Salt Lake City, 1947); Nels Anderson, *Desert Saints: The Mormon Frontier in Utah* (Chicago, 1942); and LeRoy R. Hafen, *Handcarts to Zion: The Story of a Unique Western Migration* (Glendale, Ca., 1960). An excellent collection of primary sources is found in William Mulder and A. Russell Mortensen, *Among the Mormons: Historic Accounts by Contemporary Observers* (New York, 1958).

48. Gail F. Casterline, " 'In the Toils' or 'Onward for Zion': Images of the Mormon Woman, 1852–1890," M.A. thesis, Utah State University, 1976, pp. 31–58.

49. Leonard J. Arrington and Jon Haupt, "Intolerable Zion: The Image of Mormonism in Nineteenth Century American Literature," *Western Humanities Review*, 22 (Summer 1968), pp. 245–48. Other excellent articles dealing with various critiques and images of the Mormons include: Stanley S. Ivins, "Notes on Mormon Polygamy," *Western Humanities Review*, 10 (Summer 1956), pp. 229–39; Davis Britton and Gary L. Bunker, "Double Jeopardy: Visual Images of Mormon Women to 1914," *Utah Historical Quarterly*, 46 (Spring 1978), pp. 184–202; Leonard J. Arrington and Jon Haupt, "The Missouri and Illinois Mormons in Ante-Bellum Fiction," *Dialogue*, 5 (Spring 1970), pp. 37–50; Charles A. Cannon, "The Awesome Power of Sex: The Polemical Campaign Against Mormon Polygamy," *Pacific Historical Review*, 43 (February 1974), pp. 61–82; and David B. Davis, "Some Themes of Counter-Subversion: An Analysis of Anti-Masonic, Anti-Catholic, and Anti-Mormon Literature," *Mississippi Valley Historical Review*, 47 (September 1960), pp. 205–24.

50. Metta Victoria Fuller, *Mormon Wives: A Narrative of Facts Stranger Than Fiction* (New York, 1856), p. vi; Mrs. A. G. (Cornelia) Paddock, *In the Toils; or Martyrs of the Latter Days* (Chicago, 1879), p. 4. Also see: Mrs. Thomas Fitch, "The Mahomet of the West," *Overland Monthly*, 7 (September 1871), pp. 235–41.

51. J. H. Beadle, "Social Experiments in Utah," *Popular Science Monthly*, 9 (August 1876), pp. 479–80; Dr. Samuel Cartwright and Professor C. G. Forshey, *De Bow's Review*, 30 (February 1861), p. 206 quoted in Ivins, "Notes," p. 238; Testimonial of Angie Newman, U.S. Senate, *Report of the Education and Labor Committee on an Amendment intended to be proposed to the Sundry Civil Bill providing for an appropriation to aid in the establishment of a School in Utah . . . with a view to the suppression of polygamy therein*, Senate Report 1279, 49th Congress, 1st session, 1886 quoted in Casterline, " 'In the Toils,' " p. 51. See also: Fuller, *Mormon Wives*, p. xii.

52. See Ivins, "Notes," pp. 230–31 and Julie R. Jeffrey, *Frontier Women: The Trans-Mississippi West, 1840–1880* (New York, 1979), p. 164.

53. Amanda Dickinson, "Polygamy Degrades Womanhood," *Women's Journal* (Boston), March 29, 1870, p. 97 quoted in Casterline, " 'In the Toils,' " p. 56.

54. For a more complete discussion of these views, see Casterline, " 'In the Toils,' " pp. 7–58; Britton and Bunker, "Double Jeopardy," pp. 190–91 and 195–99; and Jeffrey, *Frontier Women*, pp. 148–49.

55. Britton and Bunker, "Double Jeopardy," pp. 188–90, 191–95.

56. Casterline, " 'In the Toils,' " pp. 7–58.

57. Arrington and Haupt, "Intolerable Zion," pp. 257–60.

58. Maria Ward [pseud.?], *Female Life Among the Mormons: A Narrative of Many Years Personal Experience by the Wife of a Mormon Elder Recently from Utah* (New York, 1856), p. 237.

59. Arrington and Haupt, "Intolerable Zion," p. 254. The authors point out that in Ward's *Female Life*, cited above, there are "no less than thirty-four references to and graphic descriptions of women being physically tortured with red-hot irons, with tomahawks, with whips, and with ice."

60. Mrs. T. B. H. [Fanny] Stenhouse, *Expose of Polygamy in Utah: A Lady's Life Among the Mormons* (New York, 1872), pp. 80, 82, 74; Ann Eliza Young, *Wife No. 19, or The Story of A Life in Bondage . . .* (Hartford, 1876), pp. 135, 161, 321.

61. Sarah Wood Kane, *Twelve Mormon Homes Visited in Succession on a Journey Through Utah and Arizona* (Philadelphia, 1876), p. 67. Casterline, " 'In the Toils,' " pp. 8–11. Also see: Richard F. Burton, *The City of the Saints, and Across the Rocky Mountains to California* (London, 1861); William Chandless, *A Visit to Salt Lake; being a Journey Across the Plains and a Residence in the Mormon Settlements at Utah* (London, 1857); J. W. Gunnison, *The Mormons, or, Latter-Day Saints in the Valley of the Great Salt Lake* (Philadelphia, 1852); and Jules Remy and Julius Brenchley, *A Journey to Great Salt Lake City with a Sketch of the History, Religion, and Customs of the Mormons, and an Introduction of the Religious Movement in the United States,* 2 vols. (London, 1861) for other objective reports on the lives of Mormon women. It might be observed that the majority of these objective reporters were Englishmen.

62. Lavinia Porter, *By Ox Team to California: A Narrative of Crossing the Plains in 1860* (Oakland, 1910), p. 105; Missouri Bishop Moore, Journal of the Trip to California, 1859, MHS; Porter, *By Ox Team,* p. 100; Roxanna C. Foster, The Foster Family, California Pioneers of 1849, CSL; Helen Carpenter, "A Trip Across the Plains in an Ox Cart in 1847," in Myres, *Ho for California!* p. 138. Also see: Ann Archbold, *A Book for the Married and Single, The Grave and the Gay: And Especially designed for Steamboat Passengers* (East Plainfield, Oh., 1850), pp. 38–39, 41–42.

63. Mary E. Ackley, *Crossing the Plains and Early Days in California: Memories of Girlhood in California's Golden Age* (San Francisco, 1928), p. 28; Harriett Sherrill Ward, *Prairie Schooner Lady: The Journal of Harriett Sherrill Ward,* Ward G. De Witt and Florence Stark DeWitt, eds. (Los Angeles, 1959), p. 199. Also see: Sarah Royce, *A Frontier Lady,* Recollections of the Gold Rush and Early California (Lincoln, Ne., 1977) p. 33; Harriet T. Clarke, Diary, OHS; Mary Jatta, A Journey Across the Plains, BL; Diary of Mary Elisa Warner, 1864, BL; and Mary Bailey, "Journal of Mary Stuart Bailey," in Myres, *Ho for California!* p. 75–76 for other descriptions of the city.

64. Diary of Mary Burrell Crossing the Plains, April–September, 1854, WAC; Bailey, "Journal," p. 76. Also see Diary of the Overland Journey of William L. Fulkerth and Wife, BL; and E. Allene Taylor Dunham, Across the Plains in a Covered Wagon, NL for other impressions of Young and the Mormon city.

65. Hecox, *California Caravan,* p. 23; Mary C. Fish, A Daily Journal Written During an Overland Journey to California, BL.

66. Diary of Sister Monica.

67. Sarah Hollister Harris, *An Unwritten Chapter of Salt Lake, 1851–1901* (New York, 1901), pp. 44–45, 40; Mrs. B. G. Ferris, *The Mormons at Home* (New York, 1856), pp. 103, 123, 117, 119. Also see: Fitch, "The Mahomet of the West."

68. Elizabeth Cumming to "dear Anne," September 24, 1858 in Mulder and Mortensen, *Among the Mormons,* p. 314. Also see: Ray R. Canning and Beverly Beeton, eds., *The Genteel Gentile: Letters of Elizabeth Cumming, 1857–58* (Salt Lake City, 1977); Frazier, *Reminiscences;* pp. 151–52; Kane, *Twelve Mormon Homes,* p. 46. Excerpts from Kane's book are printed in Mulder and Mortensen, *Among the Mormons,* pp. 339–403. Also see: Lucy Rutledge Cooke, *Covered Wagon Days: Crossing the Plains in 1852, Narrative of a Trip from Iowa to "The Land of Gold," as Told in Letters Written During the Journey* (Modesto, Ca., 1923), pp. 37–60; Mrs. C. V. Waite, *Adventures in the Far West and Life Among the Mormons* (Chicago, 1882); Sarah Raymond Herndon, *Days on the Road: Crossing the Plains in 1865* (New York, 1902), pp. 238–39; Mary Rockwood Powers, "A Woman's Overland Journal to California: The Overland Route Leaves from the Journal of a California Emigrant, April to October, 1856," *The Amateur Book Collector,* 1 (December 1950), p. 11; Margaretta F. McClintock, My Trip Across the Plains, OHS; Merrill Mattes, *Indians, Infants and Infantry: Andrew and Elizabeth Burt on the Frontier* (Denver, 1960), pp. 68–70; and Mary B. Kirkpatrick, Letters to her husband, 1864–65, WAC, for other women's comments.

69. Eliza Dilworth to William Wollerton, July 13, 1856, Bringhurst Family Papers, WAC. Also see: Casterline, " 'In the Toils,' " pp. 83–84, 90–93.

70. Lucy W. Kimball and Mercy Thompson quoted in Claudia L. Bushman, ed., *Mormon Sisters: Women in Early Utah* (Salt Lake City, 1976), p. 91; Mrs. Belinda M. Pratt to "Dear Sister," January 12, 1854, printed in Burton, *The City of the Saints*, pp. 526–34. Pratt's Biblical argument may be found on pp. 526–28.

71. Pratt letter, pp. 529, 530. Also see: Helen Mary Whitney, *Plural Marriage as Taught by the Prophet Joseph: A Reply to Joseph Smith, Editor of the Lamont (Iowa) "Herald"* (Salt Lake City, 1882) and *Why We Practice Plural Marriage* (Salt Lake City, 1884); and Casterline, " 'In the Toils,' " pp. 82–110.

72. "Statement of Policy," *Woman's Exponent*, January 1, 1873; "The 'Enslaved' Women of Utah," *Woman's Exponent*, July 1, 1872 both quoted in Casterline, " 'In the Toils,' " pp. 89, 90. Also see: Jeffreys, *Frontier Women*, pp. 149–51.

73. For an excellent summary of the views of this class in the Midwest, see: Richard Jensen, *Illinois: A Bicentennial History* (New York, 1978), pp. 4–31.

74. Caroline Kirkland, *A New Home or Life in the Clearings*, reprint ed. (New York, 1953), p. 89; Frances Trollope, *Domestic Manners of the Americans*, Donald Smalley, ed. (New York, 1949), pp. 116–26; Eliza W. Farnham, *Life in Prairie Land* (New York, 1846), pp. 41, 36, 65–66. Also see: Eliza R. Steele, *A Summer Journey in the West* (New York, 1841).

75. The influence of political convictions on the views of British writers is examined in some detail by Allan Nevins in *America Through British Eyes* (New York, 1948), pp. 79–102. Also see: Robert V. Hine, *The American West: An Interpretive History* (Boston, 1973), p. 257.

76. Powers, "A Woman's Overland Journal," p. 2; Elizabeth Custer, *Tenting on the Plains, or General Custer in Kansas and Texas*, 3 vols. (Norman, 1966), I, p. 120; Caroline Richardson, Diary, BL; Brown, A Private Journal. Such statements appear in many women's writings. See, for example: Porter, *By Ox Team*, p. 78; Carpenter, "A Trip Across the Plains," pp. 115, 140, 167; Harris, *An Unwritten Chapter*, pp. 8, 77; Christiana Holmes Tillison, *A Woman's Story of Pioneer Illinois* (Chicago, 1919), pp. 101–04; Pauline Wonderly, *Reminiscences of a Pioneer*, John B. Hassler, ed. (Placerville, Ca., 1965), p. 2; Fish, Daily Journal; Sarah Sutton, Diary of Overland Journey from Illinois, OHS; Mrs. Andrew Hively, Journal, DPL, and the books by army wives Teresa Vielé, *"Following the Drum,"* p. 81; Biddle, *Reminiscences*, p. 108; Lane, *I Married a Soldier*, p. 146; and Margaret Carrington, *Ab-sa-ra-ka: Home of the Crow* (Philadelphia, 1868), pp. 60–61.

77. Cooke, *Covered Wagon Days*, pp. 62–63. See also: Herndon, *Days on the Road*, p. 72 and Arvazena Cooper, Our Journey Across the Plains, OHS. Some poor women were aware of the resentment against them; even the Indians seemed aware of class differences. "Those Indians and especially this man's wife looked down on us very much," one woman wrote, "& in fact they always mistreated us when they had an opportunity. They seemed to think because we were so poor . . . they ought to take a particular pride in insulting us." Mrs. M. A. Minto, Female Pioneering in Oregon, BL.

78. The one possible exception to this statement is anti-Mormon prejudice. Perhaps because the Mormon practice of polygamy seemed a direct threat to women and women's place, female writers were often more derogatory and bitter in regard to Mormons than were men.

79. On the roots of nativist thought see: Billington, *The Protestant Crusade*, pp. 1–31; Davis, "Some Themes of Counter-Subversion," pp. 205–06; and John Higham, "Another Look at Nativism," *The Catholic Historical Review*, 44 (July 1958), pp. 147–58.

80. Andrew Rolle, *The Italian Americans: Troubled Roots* (New York, 1980), p. 61. Also see his *The Immigrant Upraised: Italian Adventurers and Colonists in an Expanding America* (Nor-

man, 1968), pp. 308–15. An opposite view point is John Hawgood, *The Tragedy of German-America* (New York, 1940), pp. 190–96.

Chapter 5

1. John M. Faragher, *Women and Men on the Overland Trail* (New Haven, 1979), pp. 14–15.
2. Richard Irving Dodge, Letters, WAC.
3. Margaret M. Hecox, *California Caravan: The 1846 Overland Memoir of Margaret M. Hecox*, Richard Dillon, ed. (San Jose, 1966), p. 17; Lodisa Frizzell, *Across the Plains to California in 1852* (New York, 1915), p. 8.
4. Margaret White Chambers, *Reminiscences* (n.p., 1903), p. 7.
5. Francis Parkman, *The Oregon Trail* (Boston, 1899), p. 40.
6. For example, Roxanna Foster recounted the story of the young bride who "looked around the dilapidated walls of the hotel, with the plaster cracked and falling off . . ." and was ready to return home immediately. Roxanna C. Foster, The Foster Family, California Pioneers of 1849, CSL.
7. Amelia Knight, Journal Kept on the Road from Iowa to Oregon, UWA; Lucy Rutledge Cooke, *Covered Wagon Days, Crossing the Plains in 1852* (Modesto, Ca., 1923), pp. 7–8.
8. Charles G. Gray, *Off at Sunrise*, Thomas D. Clark, ed. (San Marino, 1976), p. 5. Almost every Western diary, whether written by a man or a woman, expressed such sentiments at some point.
9. Diary of the Overland Journey of William L. Fulkerth and Wife, BL.
10. Glenda Riley, *Women on the American Frontier* (St. Louis, 1977), p. 3. The words and music to this song are included in the diary of Margaret Irvin, OHS.
11. Hiram Shutes quoted in Glenda Riley, "Women in the West," *Journal of American Culture*, 3 (Summer 1980), p. 315. Also see: Virginia Reed Murphy, "Across the Plains in the Donner Party (1846): A Personal Narrative of the Overland Trip to California," *Century Magazine*, 42 (July 1891), p. 411.
12. Margaret Irvin, Covered Wagon Days, OHS; John H. Clark, "Overland to the Gold Fields of California in 1852," Louise Berry, ed., *Kansas Historical Quarterly*, 11 (August 1942), p. 229.
13. Gray, *Off at Sunrise*, p. 23; Georgia W. Read and Ruth Gaines, eds., *Gold Rush: The Journals, Drawings, and Other Papers of J. Goldsborough Bruff* (New York, 1949), p. 14.
14. Katharine Horack, "In Quest of a Prairie Home," *The Palimpset*, 5 (July 1924), p. 250.
15. Helen Carpenter, "A Journey Across the Plains in an Ox Cart," in Sandra L. Myres, ed., *Ho for California! Women's Overland Diaries from the Huntington Library* (San Marino, 1980), p. 93; Sarah Sutton, Diary of Overland Journey 1854 from Illinois, OHS.
16. Glenda Riley, "Women on the Overland Trails: Iowa as a Case Study," paper presented at the Organization of American Historians, New Orleans, April 1979.
17. Faragher, *Women and Men*, pp. 18–20.
18. Virginia Ivins, *Pen Pictures of Early Western Days* (n.p., 1908), p. 72; Lavinia Porter, *By Ox Team to California: A Narrative of Crossing the Plains in 1860* (Oakland, 1910), p. 9; Arvazena Angeline Cooper, Our Journey Across the Plains, OHS. A number of other women mention similar problems with inexperience in housekeeping. See, for example: Mrs. Henrietta B. Embree, Diary 1856–61, BTHC; Susan E. Newcomb, Diary, August 1865–May 16, 1869, BTHC; Mrs. Ben Hartsuck, Reminiscences, UWA; Ada Vogdes, Journal, HEH.
19. Caroline C. Dunlap, "Ancotty (Long Ago): The Adventures of a Young Pioneer Girl on the Long Trek Westward," *The Oregonian*, June 28, 1959, p. 28, OHS; Catherine Haun, A Woman's Trip Across the Plains in 1849, HEH.

20. Porter, *By Ox Team*, p. 1; Agnes Steward, Journey to Oregon . . . ," C. W. Churchill, ed., *Oregon Historical Quarterly*, 29 (March 1928), p. 80; Celina Hines, "Diary," *Transactions of the Oregon Pioneers Association* (1918), p. 83; Mrs. Isaac Moore, How I Went to Denver, DPL.

21. Merrill Mattes, *The Great Platte River Road: The Covered Wagon Mainline via Fort Kearney to Fort Laramie*, Nebraska State Historical Society Publications, vol. 25 (Lincoln, 1969), pp. 90–91; Maria Shrode, "Journal," in Myres, *Ho for California!*, p. 271; Lydia Waters, "Account of a Trip Across the Plains in 1855," *Quarterly of the Society of California Pioneers*, 6 (March 1929), p. 61. For other accounts of men's lack of expertise with firearms see the accounts of Elisha Brooks, *A Pioneer Mother of California* (San Francisco, 1922), p. 13; Harriet T. Clarke, Journal, 1851, OHS; and Francis Haines, ed., *A Bride on the Bozeman Trail: The Letters and Diary of Ellen Gordon Fletcher, 1866* (Medford, Or., 1970) p. ix, which give hilarious accounts of men's attempts to hunt buffalo and bear.

22. J. M. Shively, "Route and Distances to Oregon and California," in Dale Morgan, ed., *Overland in 1846: Diaries and Letters of the California-Oregon Trail*, 2 vols. (Georgetown, Ca., 1963), II, p. 736; Lansford Hastings, *The Emigrants' Guide to Oregon and California*, reprint ed. (Princeton, 1932), p. 144. For an attempt at providing a guide for immigrant women see: Terry Brown, "An Emigrant's Guide for Women," *American West*, 7 (September 1970), pp. 12–17, 63.

23. "Diary of Mrs. Elizabeth Dixon Smith Geer," *Transactions of the Oregon Pioneers' Association* (1907), p. 157; Sarah Cummins, *Autobiography and Reminiscences of Sarah J. Cummins* (LaGrande, Or., 1914), p. 26; Cooper, Our Journey; Carpenter, "A Trip Across the Plains," p. 111. Also see Adrietta Applegate Hixon, *On to Oregon!* Waldo Taylor, ed. (Weiser, Id., 1947), p. 24.

24. Shrode, "Journal," pp. 274–75; John Fischer, *From the High Plains* (New York, 1978), p. 124.

25. Porter, *By Ox Team*, p. 9; Mrs. M. S. Hockensmith, Diary of a Trip Overland from the Mississippi to California, Nov. 16, 1865–Nov. 29, 1866, BL. Mary E. Ackley, *Crossing the Plains and Early Days in California: Memories of Girlhood Days in California's Golden Age* (San Francisco, 1928), p. 20; and Margaret Frink, *Journal of the Adventures of a Party of California Gold Seekers* (Oakland, 1897), p. 49 also describe the trench method of cooking. Although several of the guidebooks recommended the emigrant stoves, others, like J. L. Campbell's *Six Months in the Gold Diggings: The Emigrant's Guide Overland* (New York, 1864) advised emigrants that the stoves would not last through the trip or if they did they would be comparatively worthless at the end of the journey.

26. Catherine Jane Bell to her sister, Julia, October 31, 1859, BL; Moore, How I Went to Denver; Jane Augusta Gould, Diary, ISHS.

27. Herbert E. Bolton, *An Outpost of Empire*, reprint ed. (New York, 1965), pp. xi, 224; Martha Summerhayes, *Vanished Arizona: Recollections of the Army Life of a New England Woman*, reprint ed. (Glorieta, N.M., 1970), p. 26.

28. Mary E. Hopping, Incidents of Pioneer Life, As I Remember and As I Have Been Told, CSL, describes the method for making bean sandwiches. Cooke, *Covered Wagon Days*, p. 23; Emma Tate, Tales Our Grandmother Catherine Gekeler Told, IHS; Irene Corder, Mr. and Mrs. Obidiah Corder's History of Their Pioneer Life in the West from 1833 to 1929, IHS; and Olivia Holmes, Diary Written in 1872 by Olivia Holmes on Trip to Texas from Kansas by Wagon Train, BL, all mention making pies and other special treats, as do many other women's sources. Mary Burrell, Crossing the Plains, WAC and Haines, *A Bride on the Bozeman Trail*, both describe a number of luxury items as does Virginia Ivins in *Pen Pictures*, p. 63. Rebecca Woodson, A Sketch of the Life of Rebecca Hiddreth Nutting, CSL and Carpenter, "A Trip Across the Plains," pp. 128, 147 discuss the need for variety in the diet.

29. Nellie Slater, Journal of Travels on the Plains in Eighteen Sixty-Two, DPL; Mrs. Fran-

cis Sawyer, Overland to California, Notes from a Journal . . . 1852, NL; Carpenter, "A Trip Across the Plains," p. 171; Cooke, *Covered Wagon Days*, p. 60; Chambers, *Reminiscences*, p. 8.

30. Bolton, *An Outpost of Empire*, pp. 221–22; Carpenter, "A Trip Across the Plains," pp. 111–12; Lydia Lane, *I Married a Soldier*, reprint ed. (Albuquerque, 1964), pp. 131–32; Helen Clark, Diary, 1860, DPL.

31. Carpenter, "A Trip Across the Plains," p. 130; Porter, *By Ox Team*, p. 10; Cora Agatz, "A Journey Across the Plains in 1866," *Pacific Northwest Quarterly*, 27 (April 1936), p. 172. Mrs. Ashmun Butler reported that she wore men's clothing during a trip from California to Oregon. See: "Diary of the Rogue River Valley, 1852–1854," *Oregon Historical Quarterly*, 41 (December 1940), p. 338. For other comments on bloomers, see: Sawyer, Overland to California; Cooke, *Covered Wagon Days*, p. 24; Marie Nash, Diary of Marie Nash, Michigan to California . . . , CSL; Harriet T. Clarke, Diary, 1851, OHS; Emmeline Fuller, *Left By the Indians, The Story of My Life* (Mt. Vernon, Ia., 1892), p. 10; Julia A. Holmes, *A Bloomer Girl on Pike's Peak, 1858* (Denver, 1949), pp. 16–17; and Miriam Davis Colt, *Went to Kansas* (Watertown, Ia., 1862), p. 65.

32. Frizzell, *Across the Plains*, p. 16; Charlotte Pegra, "Diary . . . Kept by Her on a Trip Across the Plains, 1853," (Eugene, Oregon, 1966), copy in OHS; Dunlap, "Ancotty," p. 28.

33. Life Story of Mary Elizabeth Warren as told to Mildred Mitchell Sexton, OHS; Myra Eells, "Journal," *Transactions of the Oregon Pioneers Association* (1889), p. 67; Hockensmith, Diary of a Trip; Shrode, "Journal," p. 272; Mary Jane Guill, The Overland Diary of the Journey from Livingston County Missouri . . . 1869, CSL.

34. Missouri Bishop Moore, Journal of the Trip to California, MHS; Bell to her sister; Dunlap, "Ancotty," p. 29. Also see: Leo M. Kaiser and Priscilla Knuth, eds., "From Ithaca to Clatsop Plains: Miss Ketcham's Journal of Travel," *Oregon Historical Quarterly*, 62 (September 1961), p. 283.

35. Lizzie Moore Sisk, Reminiscences, IHS; Shrode, "Journal," p. 257; Cecilia Emily Adams, Diary 1852, OHS; Hockensmith, Diary; Haun, "A Woman's Trip." Also see: Louisa Rahm, Diary 1862, BL; Mary J. Eubank, A Journal of Our Trip to Texas, 1853, BTHC; Anna Maria Goodell, Crossing the Plains in 1854, UWA; Virginia V. Root, *Following the Pot of Gold at the Rainbow's End in the Days of 1850*, Lenore Rowland, ed. (Downey, Ca., 1960), p. 2; and S. Lyman Tyler, ed., *The Montana Gold Rush Diary of Kate Dunlap* (Denver, 1969), p. B–25 for other descriptions of layover days and associated duties.

36. Haun, A Woman's Trip; Haines, *A Bride on the Bozeman Trail*, p. 25. For other typical comments on Sundays, see: "Diary Kept by Mrs. Maria Belshaw," in *New Spain and the Anglo American West*, 2 vols. (Los Angeles, 1932), II, p. 228; Henrietta Chiles Knight, Trip Across the North Plains, BTHC; Missouri Moore, Journal; Cooke, *Covered Wagon Days*, p. 64; and Mary Bailey, "Journal of Mary Bailey," in Myres, *Ho for California!*, pp. 71, 74. Especially see the excellent discussion in John Reid, *Law for the Elephant: Property and Social Behavior on the Overland Trail* (San Marino, 1980), pp. 20–24.

37. "End of an Era: The Travel Journal of Mary Mahoney," *Nebraska History*, 47 (September 1966), p. 333; Moore, How I Went to Denver.

38. Shrode, "Journal," pp. 275–76; Cooper, Our Journey; Mrs. Matthew Deady, Crossing the Plains in 1846, OHS.

39. Brooks, *A Pioneer Mother*, p. 20; Knight, Journal. Two excellent articles dealing with children on the overland trails are Georgia Willis Read, "Women and Children on the Oregon-California Trail in the Gold Rush Years," *Missouri Historical Review*, 39 (October 1944), pp. 1–23 and Ruth Barnes Moynihan, "Children and Young People on the Overland Trail," *Western Historical Quarterly*, 6 (July 1975), pp. 279–94. Also see: Lillian Schlissel, "Mothers and Daughters on the Western Frontier," *Frontiers*, 3 (1978), pp. 29–33.

40. Irvin, Covered Wagon Days. Also see: Geer, "Diary," p. 155 and Brooks, *A Pioneer Mother*, p. 13, as well as the Read and Moynihan articles.

41. Waters, "Account of A Trip," p. 73; Chambers, *Reminiscences*, p. 16.

42. The problems faced by young mothers were discussed fairly candidly in some of the housekeeping and doctor's books of the period, and many of these manuals pointed out that the practice of simply drying rather than washing diapers was unsanitary. Enough of the writers mention the problem to make it clear that it was a fairly common practice. See, for example: William P. Dewees, *A Treatise on the Physical and Medical Treatment of Children*, 9th ed. (Philadelphia, 1847), p. 82 and John C. Gunn, *Gunn's Domestic Medicine . . .* (Springfield, Oh., 1835), p. 472.

43. Bolton, *An Outpost of Empire*, p. 247. For other specific accounts by mothers on their problems with childbirth, see: Pauline Wonderly, *Reminiscences of a Pioneer*, John B. Hessler, ed. (Placerville, Ca., 1965), pp. 6–7; Hester A. Davis, Story of Hester Cory Davis Crossing the Plains in 1864, IHS; Bell to her sister; Phoebe Judson, *A Pioneer's Search for an Ideal Home* (Bellingham, Wa., 1924), p. 40; Hixon, *On to Oregon*, p. 41.

44. Cummins, *Autobiography*, p. 26; Recollections of Mrs. Mary A. Smith Jones, Alamo, Contra Costa, Co., California, 1905, BL; Waters, "Account of a Trip," p. 77. For other accounts of women helping drive loose stock, see: Mrs. M. A. Minto, Female Pioneering in Oregon, BL; Simeon Ide, *The Conquest of California: A Biography of William B. Ide* (Oakland, 1944), p. 19; Carpenter, "A Trip Across the Plains," p. 94; and Moynihan, "Children and Young People," pp. 288, 290. Among other women who helped drive wagons, or did all of the driving, were Moore, How I Went to Denver; Sawyer, Journey to Oregon; Brooks, *A Pioneer Mother*; "The Diary of Luna E. Warner, A Kansas Teenager of the 1870's," *Kansas Historical Quarterly*, 35 (Autumn 1969), pp. 427–28; Jennie Atcheson Wriston, *A Pioneer's Odyssey* (Menasha, Wi., 1943), p. 16; Mrs. Isaac L. Bryson, Grandma's Story, OHS; Kaiser, "From Ithaca to Clatsop Plains," p. 355; and Agnes Sengstaken, *Destination West* (Portland, 1942), p. 43. Also see: Cooke, *Covered Wagon Days*; Porter, *By Ox Team*; and A. Knight, Journal, for other women's duties.

45. Moore, How I Went to Denver; Mary Powers, "A Woman's Overland Journal to California," *The Amateur Book Collector*, 1 (December 1950), p. 12; Cummins, *Autobiography*, p. 28; Geer, "Diary," p. 165; Tate, Tales.

46. Hopping, Incidents; "Mary Catharine Crossing the Plains," in Andy Rogers, *A Hundred Years of Rip and Roarin'; Rough and Ready, the Town that Won't Ghost* (Rough and Ready, Ca., 1952), p. 61. The story of the Southern huntresses is related in Theodore Potter, *The Autobiography of Theodore Edgar Potter* (Concord, N.H., 1913), pp. 27–28, 30–31, 66–67. Other women who mentioned standing guard duty included: Burrell, Crossing the Plains; Lucia Darling, Crossing the Prairies in a Covered Wagon, MoHS; and E. Allene Dunham, *Across the Plains in a Covered Wagon*, (n.p., n.d.), copy in Nl. Other fighting women are described in Hecox, *California Caravan*, pp. 52–54 and Louisiana Strentzel, Letter, in Strentzel Family Papers, BL.

47. Jeffrey, *Frontier Women: The Trans-Mississippi West, 1840-1880* (New York, 1979), p. 62; Hixon, *On to Oregon*, pp. 12, 21; Porter, *By Ox Team*, p. 82; Agatz, "A Journey," p. 173.

48. Hecox, *California Caravan*, p. 36. For the feminist viewpoint, see: Faragher, *Women and Men*; John Faragher and Christine Stansell, "Women and Their Families on the Overland Trail to California and Oregon," *Feminist Studies*, 2 (1975), pp. 150–166; and Lillian Schlissel, "Women's Diaries on the Western Frontier," *American Studies*, 28 (Spring 1977), pp. 87–100, and also Schlissel's edited book, *Women's Diaries of the Westward Journey* (New York, 1982), pp. 1–114.

49. A number of women's diaries, and several by men, mention this "easy" churning method. See for example: Ackley, *Crossing the Plains*, p. 20; Hopping, Incidents; Wonderly,

Reminiscences; Davis, Story of Hester Davis; Haun, A Woman's Trip; Sisk, Reminiscences; and Root, *Following the Pot of Gold.* I found only two women, Mrs. Isaac Moore (How I Went to Denver) and Chloe Ann Terry Doyle, (Diary Kept While Crossing the Plains, 1852, UWA), who mention the usual method of churning during the trips. Doyle also ironed her clothes, but most women did not.

50. Haun, A Woman's Trip; Maggie Hall, The Story of Maggie, BL; Mrs. Andrew Hively, Journal, 1863–64, DPL; Adams, Diary; and Reminiscences by Fannie A. Adriance for the Semicentennial at Golden, Colorado, DPL. Other women who discuss sewing, tatting, and similar pastimes include: Holmes, Diary; Carpenter, "A Trip Across the Plains," p. 100; Clark, Diary; Adams, Diary; Moore, How I Went to Denver; Cooke, *Covered Wagon Days;* and Nancy Hunt, "By Ox-Team to California: A Personal Narrative," *Overland Monthly,* 67 (April 1916), p. 12.

51. Although the term "Pikers" originally referred to people from Pike County, Missouri, the term, as well as "Missourians" was later extended to refer to all those of a particular social and economic class whose rough manners and uncouth ways earned them the enmity of their fellow travelers. See, especially, the comments by William A. Maxwell, *Crossing the Plains, Days of '57* (San Francisco, 1915), pp. 76–77.

52. Porter, *By Ox Team,* p. 78; Minto, Female Pioneering; Carpenter, "A Trip Across the Plains," pp. 114–15. Also see: Clara Brown, A Private Journal, BTHC; Cooper, Our Journey; and Brooks, *A Pioneer Mother,* p. 23, for other comments.

53. Haun, A Woman's Trip, described the variety of duties. Amelia Knight's description was also typical: "All hurry and bustle to get things in order, its children milk the cows, all hands help yoke these cattle, the d——ls in them . . . who tends these horses; Seneca don't stand there with your hands in your pockets, get your saddles and be ready to travel." Knight, Journal.

54. Priscilla Evans quoted in Leroy Hafen, *Handcarts to Zion* (Glendale, Ca., 1960), pp. 84–85; Hattie S. Benefield, *(Por el Bien del Pais) For the Good of the Country,* (Los Angeles, 1951), pp. 18–19; Hall, Story of Maggie; Mary Rabb, Reminiscences, BTHC.

55. Woodson, Sketch; Ivins, *Pen Pictures,* p. 63; Emily K. Andrews, Diary on a Trip from Austin to Fort Davis, BTHC.

56. Carpenter, "A Trip Across the Plains," p. 114; Irvin, Covered Wagon Days; "End of an Era," p. 333;, Warren, Life Story.

57. Harriet Ward, *Prairie Schooner Lady: The Journal of Harriet Sherrill Ward,* Ward G. De Witt and Florence S. De Witt, eds. (Los Angeles, 1959), p. 69; Bolton, *Outpost of Empire,* pp. 319, 312; Mary C. Fish, A Daily Journal Written During an Overland Journey to California, BL; Geer, "Diary," p. 156. Other dances and parties are described in Ackley, *Crossing the Plains,* p. 20; Clark, Diary; Mrs. Edward Dyer, Diary May 2–Sept. 19, 1860, BTHC; Diary of the Overland Journey of William L. Fulkerth and Wife, BL; Sarah R. Herndon, *Days on the Road: Crossing the Plains in 1864* (New York, 1902), p. 70; and Woodson, Sketch.

58. Evening pastimes and other entertainments are described in most journals. See especially: Goodell, Crossing the Plains; Shrode, "Journal," p. 264; Carpenter, "A Trip Across the Plains," p. 153; Frink, *Journal,* p. 58; Hunt, "By Ox-Team," p. 12; and Holmes, Diary.

59. Bailey, "Journal," p. 55; Porter, *By Ox Team,* p. 45; Mary Rockwood Powers, "A Woman's Overland Journal to California," *The Amateur Book Collector,* 1 (November 1950), p. 6, and 1 (October 1950), p. 2.

60. Bailey, "Journal," p. 84; Reid, *Law for the Elephant,* p. 11.

61. Shrode, "Journal," p. 269; Bunyard, "Diary," p. 236; Bailey, "Journal," pp. 80–81.

62. Judson, *A Pioneer's Search,* p. 23.

63. Haun, A Woman's Trip.

64. Frink, *Journal,* p. 128.

Chapter 6

1. Caroline Kirkland, *A New Home or Life in the Clearings*, reprint ed. (New York, 1953) originally published pseudonymously in 1839 under the title *A New Home—Who'll Follow?*

2. Anna Goodell, Crossing the Plains, UWA; Katherine Kirk, *Life in South Dakota, 1885–1895* (Birmingham, Al., [mimeograph] 1961). Also see: Mary Bailey, "Journal of Mary Stuart Bailey" in Sandra L. Myres, ed., *Ho for California: Women's Diaries from the Huntington Library* (San Marino, 1980), p. 99; Sarah Royce, *A Frontier Lady: Recollections of the Gold Rush and Early California* (Lincoln, 1977), p. 72. For a number of women's reminiscences of the trip and their role in home and community development, see: Fred Lockley, *Conversations with Pioneer Women*, Mike Helm, ed. (Eugene, Or., 1981).

3. Anna Shaw, *The Story of a Pioneer* (New York, 1915), p. 25; Lucy Jane Dabney, Walter Scales Dabney and Family, BTHC; Barbara Kilvert, "Pioneer Woman," *The Beaver* (Autumn 1957), p. 17; Mary Hopping, Incidents of Pioneer Life, As I Remember and as I have Been Told, CSL; Edith Eudora Kohl, *Land of the Burnt Thigh* (New York, 1938), pp. 2–3. For other, similar, reactions, see: Johnaphene Faulkner, The Prairie Home, 2 vols., I, p. 54, BTHC; Alice Curnow, The Journey with Tom, 2 vols., I, p. 10, AHS; Mrs. Catherine Marcus, IHS; Glenda Riley, "Pioneer Migration: The Diary of Mary Alice Shutes," *Annals of Iowa*, 44 (Spring 1977), p. 590.

4. Faulkner, Prairie Home, I, p. 4; Cedenia Bagley Willis, Journal of Nancy Cedenia Bagley Willis, AHS; Mary Rabb, Reminiscences of Mrs. John Rabb, BTHC.

5. Eugenie A. Leonard, Sophie H. Drinker, Mariam Y. Holden, *The American Woman in Colonial and Revolutionary Times, 1565–1800* (Philadelphia, 1962), p. 70; Miriam Davis Colt, *Went to Kansas* (Watertown, Ia., 1862), p. 46; Barbara J. McQuirty, Oklahoma Textures, University of Oklahoma Women's Study Project, 1978, WHC; Harris quoted in Robert G. Athearn, *In Search of Canaan: Black Migration to Kansas, 1879–80* (Lawrence, 1978), p. 239. For other descriptions of primitive homes, see: Wealthy Brown to her sister, June 12, 1855, WAC; Rose Bell, Diary, CHS; Emma Tate, Papers, IHS; Mrs. John Wade, Recollections of an Octogenarian, BTHC; Wilford Ricks, The History of Hans Christian Jensen and Helena Flamm Jensen, IHS; Jane Lowe Quillen, A Saga of the Plains, BTHC; Mary Cable, After Thoughts, OHS; Ellen R. Hinsdale, Letters, 1871–72, DPL; Susan Diamond, Diaries, KHS; Diary of Mary H. Parker Richards, 1846–48, HEH; Life Pictures in Kansas, Letters of James H., Jane G. and Lucy Carruth, KHS; Agnes R. Sengstacken, *Destination West!* (Portland, 1942), p. 100; "Diary of Mrs. Elizabeth Dixon Smith Geer," *Transactions of the Oregon Pioneer's Association* (1907), p. 174; Virginia V. Root, *Following the Pot of God at the Rainbow's End in the Days of 1850*, Leonore Rowland, ed. (Downey, Ca., 1960), p. 26.

6. Luna E. Kellie, Memoirs, NHS; May Bennett Avery, Memories of Pioneer Days, NHS; John W. Kennedy, Reminiscences of Mary Elizabeth Corne Jennings, AHS; May Callan Tansill Collections, BTHC; Riley, "Pioneer Migration," p. 590.

7. Faulkner, Prairie Home, I, pp. 35–46; Sarah Martin, Desert Memories, AHS; Mrs. Arthur Babcock in Nebraska Farmer Sod House Letters, NHS; Susan E. Newcomb, Diaries, BTHC; Faulkner, Prairie Home, I, p. 54.

8. Leonard, *American Woman*, p. 70; Mrs. L. C. Saunders, Life Experiences of Pickey, BTHC; Eva Denison in Sod House Letters; Paul Goeldner, "The Architecture of Equal Comforts, Polygamists in Utah," *Historic Preservation*, 24 (January-March 1972), pp. 14–17; Mary Maverick, *Memoirs of Mary A. Maverick*, Rena M. Green, ed. (San Antonio, 1921), p. 65; Rena Mathews, The Claim of Mrs. Rena Mathews of Being a Western Pioneer, AHS; Ella Bird-Dumont, Autobiography, BTHC; Sarah McAllister Hartman, Reminiscences of Life in Newmarket, WAC. Mexican homes are described in Susanna B. Dakin, *Rose or Rose Thorn? Three Women of Spanish California* (Berkeley, 1963), p. 32 and Helen S. Giffin, *Casas and Courtyards: Historic Adobe Houses of California* (Oakland, 1955), pp. 3–4; 7–8.

9. Margaret Murray, "Memoir of the William Archer Family," *Annals of Iowa*, 39 (Summer 1969), pp. 471–72.

10. The balloon houses are described in Julia Louisa Lovejoy, "Letters from Kansas," *Kansas Historical Quarterly*, 11 (February 1942), p. 41. Both Mary Jane Megquier, *Apron Full of Gold: The Letters of Mary Jane Megquier from San Francisco, 1849–1856*, Robert G. Cleland, ed. (San Marino, 1949), p. 7 and Mary Pratt Staples, Reminiscences, BL, mention shipping houses around the Horn.

11. Mrs. Andrew Paul Hively, Journal, 1863–64, DPL; Aggie Loring to her mother, December 21, 1876, George E. Loring Collection AHS. Other women who describe their experiences in boarding out include Benjamin and Harriet Carr, Letters, 1857–86, CHS; Mrs. Thomas Withers, Extracts from the Colorado Correspondence, 1878–80, DPL; Letter to Fanny Steele, MHS; Mrs. Henrietta B. Embree, Diary 1856–61, BTHC; Mary Luster, *The Autobiography of Mary R. Luster* (Springfield, Mo., 1935); Chestina Allen, Diary, KHS; Cornelia Noble, Diary, BTHC; Mrs. Mary McNair Mathews, *Ten Years in Nevada or Life on the Pacific Coast* (Buffalo, N.Y., 1880).

12. Murray, "Memoir," pp. 365–66; Joanna Haines, "Seventy Years in Iowa," *Annals of Iowa*, 27 (October 1945), p. 101; Fanny Adriance to her brother, Henry Rogers, May 15, 1861, DPL; Mrs. Nellie Bush, Interview, Indian-Pioneer Papers, XIV, p. 53, WHC; Lizzie Sisk, Reminiscences, IHS. Also see: Ellen Pennock, "Incidents in My Life as a Pioneer," *Colorado Magazine*, 30 (April 1953), p. 126.

13. Martha Summerhayes, *Vanished Arizona: Recollections of the Army Life of a New England Woman*, 2nd ed. (Salem, Ma., 1911).

14. Hartman, Reminiscences; Effie May Butler Wiltbank, Reminiscences, AHS; Rodman Paul, ed., *A Victorian Gentlewoman in the Far West: The Reminiscences of Mary Hallock Foote* (San Marino, 1972), p. 178; Mrs. Dan Bain, Interview #10531, Indian-Pioneer Papers, IV, pp. 101–2.

15. Mrs. Mary Minto, Female Pioneering in Oregon, BL; Phoebe Judson, *A Pioneer's Search for a New Home* (Bellingham, Wa., 1925), p. 88; Wiltbank, Reminiscences. Also see: Carruth, Life Pictures in Kansas.

16. Guadalupe Callan, untitled manuscript in May Callan Tansill Collection, BTHC; Colt, *Went to Kansas*, pp. 49–53; Pennock, "Incidents," p. 126. For other discussions of fireplace cooking, see: Anna McKee to Lizzie and Winnie McKee, October 19, 1884, CHS; Saunders, Life Experiences; Sisk, Reminiscences; Lida M. Johnson Isham, Pioneer Days, 1863–80, IHS; Aggie Loring to her mother; Carruth, Life Pictures in Kansas; Luster, *Autobiography*, pp. 74, 79; Kilvert, "Pioneer Woman," p. 20; Carrie Robbins, Journal, KHS; Mrs. Lee Whipple-Haslam, *Early Days in California: Scenes and Events of the 50s as I Remember Them* (Jamestown, Ca., 1925), p. 11; and Martha Atkinson, Interview, Indian-Pioneer Papers, III, p 254. For a discussion of Mexican and Spanish cooking arrangements, see: Ana Bégué de Packman, *Early California Hospitality* (Glendale, Ca., 1938), pp. 19–21 and Janet LeCompte, *Pueblo, Hard Scrabble, Greenhorn* (Norman, 1978), p. 71.

17. Packman, *California Hospitality*, p. 13; Mrs. Matthew Deady, Crossing the Plains in 1846, OHS; Emma Hill Shepard, *A Dangerous Crossing and What Happened on the Other Side* (Denver, 1924), p. 54; Cable, Afterthoughts; Laura A. Patterson, Recollections of 1843, OHS; Mary Dunn, Biography, OHS; Smith Family, Account of Overland Journey, 1846, OHS; Matilda Delaney, *A Survivor's Recollections of the Whitman Massacre* (Spokane, 1920), p. 29; Teresa Vielé, *"Following the Drum:" A Glimpse of Frontier Life*, James M. Day, ed. (Austin, 1968), p. xiii; Allen, Diary. Also see: "Experiences of Mrs. Sarah N. Worthington in Frontier Illinois" in William F. Sprague, *Women and the West: A Short Social History* (Boston, 1940), pp. 259–60; Lovejoy, "Letters from Kansas," pp. 39–40; Leola Lehman, "Life in the Territories," *Chronicles of Oklahoma*, 41 (Fall 1963), p. 379; Whipple-Haslam, *Early Days*, p. 11; Abbie Beggs,

Interview, Indian-Pioneer Papers, VI, p. 437; "Letters of Caroline Frey Winne from Sidney Barracks and Fort McPherson, Nebraska, 1874–1878," Thomas R. Buecker, ed., *Nebraska History,* 62 (Spring 1981), pp. 8, 11.

18. Francis Judge, "Carrie and the Grand Tetons," *Montana,* 18 (July 1968), p. 51; Wiltbank, Reminiscences. Also see the sources noted above in note 16. The "vinegar" pies were ones in which vinegar was substituted for lemon.

19. Catherine Beecher, *The American Woman's Home: The Principles of Domestic Science* (New York, 1869), p. 171. Also see: Beecher, *A Treatise on Domestic Economy* (New York, 1849); Lydia Maria Child, *The American Frugal Housewife* (Boston, 1836); and Sarah J. Hale, *The Ladies' New Book of Cookery . . . ,* 3rd ed. (New York, 1852).

20. Sandra L. Myres, ed., *Cavalry Wife: The Diary of Eveline M. Alexander, 1866–1867* (College Station, Tex., 1977), pp. 108–11; Ella Bailey, Diary 1869, CHS; Rebecca Woodson, A Sketch of the Life of Rebecca Hiddreth Nutting Woodson, CSL; Emeline L. S. Benson, From Beloit Wisconsin to San Pablo Valley, January 1, 1853–December 31, 1854, CSL. Also see: Mary Jane Caples, Overland Journey to the Coast, CSL; Margaret Armstrong Bowie, Diary, 1872–77, BTHC; Mary Ronan, *Frontier Woman: The Story of Mary Ronan,* H. G. Merriam, ed. (Missoula, 1973), p. 47; James E. Potter, ed., "The Ranch Letters of Emma Robertson, 1891–1892," *Nebraska History,* 56 (Fall 1975), p. 221; Mary B. Ballou, *"I Hear the Hogs in My Kitchen," A Woman's View of the Gold Rush* (New Haven, 1962); and Sengstacken, *Destination, West!,* pp. 103–4.

21. Kitturah Belknap, "Family Life on the Frontier: The Diary of Kitturah P. Belknap," Glenda Riley, ed., *Annals of Iowa,* 44 (Summer 1977), p. 35. Also see: Murray, "Memoirs," p. 361; Howard Johnson, *A Home in the Woods: Pioneer Life in Indiana* (Bloomington, In., 1978), pp. 34–37; Kennedy, Reminiscences; Tate, Papers; Newcomb, Diary; Olivia Holmes, Diary 1873, BL; Bowie, Diary; Rabb, Reminiscences; Pennock, "Incidents," p. 129; and Ellen Throop, *Reminiscences of Pioneer Days* (n.p., n.d.), copy in NHS, pp. 6–7, for other descriptions of cloth making and sewing.

22. Summerhayes, *Vanished Arizona,* p. 158.

23. Belknap, "Family Life," p. 47. There are a number of excellent, firsthand accounts of housekeeping and home life by Mormon women. See especially: Juanita Brooks, ed., *Not by Bread Alone: The Journal of Martha Spence Heywood, 1850–56* (Salt Lake City, 1978); Fae D. Dix, ed., "The Josephine Diaries, Glimpses of the Life of Josephine Streeper Chase, 1881–94," *Utah Historical Quarterly,* 46 (Spring 1978), pp. 167–83; Annie Clark Tanner, *A Mormon Mother* (Salt Lake City, 1976); Mary Ann Hafen, *Recollections of a Handcart Pioneer of 1860* (Denver, 1938); and S. George Ellsworth, ed., *Dear Ellen: Two Mormon Women and Their Letters* (Salt Lake City, 1974).

24. Brooks, *Not by Bread Alone,* p. 41; Bird-Dumont, Autobiography; Embree, Diary; "Imbentarios de los bienes que quedan por fin y muerte de Margarita Martin, Año 1744" and "El siete día del mes de mayo del año 1753, Juana Galvana Coyta," in Carmen Espinosa, *Shawls, Crinolines, Filigree: The Dress and Adornment of the Women of New Mexico* (El Paso, 1970), pp. 12, 16; Carr, Letters; Hopping, Incidents. Also see: Letter to Fannie Steele; Brigida Briones, "A Glimpse of Domestic Life in 1827," *Century Magazine,* 41 (January 1891), p. 470 and "Inspection Made by Don Juan de Gordejela," in George P. Hammond and Agapita Rey, trans., *Don Juan de Onate: Colonizer of New Mexico, 1595–1628,* 2 vols. (Albuquerque, 1953), II, pp. 539–40.

25. Quoted in Patricia Cooper and Norma Bradley Buferd, *The Quilters: Women and Domestic Art* (New York, 1978). For a similar description, see: John M. Faragher, *Women and Men on the Overland Trail* (New Haven, 1979), p. 56.

26. Wiltbank, Reminiscences. An excellent account by a woman who took in laundry to supplement her income is The Diary of Cora D. Babcock, SDHS.

27. For example, a Texas woman wrote, "now I have not washed any in 2 weeks on the account of the cold wether and out of Soap but I am going to make Soap next week. I cent some eggs to the stor [sic] yesterday and bought too [sic] boxs of lye . . ." Anne Legrand to her mother, January 23, 1878, BTHC.

28. Beecher suggested that for a barrel of soap one needed "5 to 6 bushels of ashes and 4 qts unslacked stone lime or 8 qts. slacked. Add lime to boiling water, add to the ashes and let it drain thro to the lye. 3lbs of grease to a pailful of lye. Strength of the lye is the secret in getting soap to 'come.' " Catherine Beecher, *Miss Beecher's Domestic Receipt-Book*, 5th ed. (New York, 1871). Also see her *Treatise on Domestic Economy for the Use of Young Ladies at Home* (Boston, 1841) and *Miss Beecher's Housekeeper and Healthkeeper* (New York, 1873), pp. 112–121, for other discussions of washing techniques.

29. Jerusha Loomis Farnham, *Log City Days* (Galesburg, Il., 1937), p. 47; Lehman, "Life in the Territories," p. 376; Julia Hand, Diary of Julia Hand, 1872–75, KHS; Guadalupe Vallejo, "Ranch and Mission Days in Alta California," *Century Magazine*, 41 (December 1890), pp. 191–92.

30. Kennedy, Reminiscences; Isham, Pioneer Days; Embree, Diary; Ella Bailey, Diary. For other comments on the problems of washdays see: Abigail Baldwin, Diary, BTHC; Curnow, Journey, I, p. 91; Carr, Letters; Benson, From Beloit; Mrs. Ashman Butler, "Diary of the Rogue River Valley, 1852–1854," *Oregon Historical Quarterly,* 41 (December 1940), pp. 345–56; Mollie Vannemon, Letters, BTHC; Avery, Memories; and Christiana H. Tillson, *A Woman's Story of Pioneer Illinois* (Chicago, 1919), pp. 147–48. The "shug stick" was a large dasherlike stick that was moved up and down to agitate the clothes.

31. Hand, Diary; Sarah Price, Diary 1878–95, NHS; Myrtle Carter Hooper, Diaries, 1887, 1891, SDHS; Sod House Letters. For other good descriptions of women's general day-to-day work see: Embree, Diary; Butler, "Diary of the Rogue River Valley"; Diamond, Diaries; Laura Rice Caster, Diary 1887–99, OHS; Benson, From Beloit; and Mary and Esther St. John, "Prairie Diary," Glenda Riley, ed., *Annals of Iowa,* 44 (Fall 1977), pp. 103–17. Maria Jane Renshaw, Diary 1858, OHS gives a particularly good overall description of indoor and oand outdoor activities. For three excellent secondary accounts of women's housekeeping activities on the frontier, see: Glenda Riley, *Frontierswomen: The Iowa Experience* (Ames, 1981), pp. 56–87; Jerena East Giffin, " 'Add a Pinch and a Lump,' Missouri Women in the 1820s," *Missouri Historical Review,* 65 (July 1971), pp. 478–504; and Dorothy Schwieder, "Labor and Economic Roles of Iowa Farm Wives, 1840–80," in Trudy Peterson, ed., *Farmers, Bureaucrats, and Middlemen: Historical Perspectives on American Agriculture* (Washington, D.C., 1981).

32. On nineteenth-century birth rates, see: Robert V. Wells, "Demographic Change and the Life Cycle of American Families," in Theodore K. Rabb and Robert I. Rotberg, eds., *The Family in History: Interdisciplinary Essays* (New York, 1971), pp. 85–94 and John Modell, "Family and Fertility on the Indiana Frontier, 1820," *American Quarterly,* 23 (December 1971), pp. 615–32.

33. A. M. Mauriceau, *The Married Woman's Private Medical Companion* (New York, 1847), p. 107; Eliza B. Duffey, *What Women Should Know: A Women's Book About Women* (Philadelphia, 1873), pp. 134–35. For excellent discussions of the medical and moral problems of birth control in the nineteenth century, see: James Reed, *From Private Vice to Public Virtue: The Birth Control Movement and American Society Since 1830* (New York, 1978), pp. 3–35 and Carl N. Degler, *At Odds: Women and the Family from the Revolution to the Present* (New York, 1980), pp. 210–26.

34. Careful study of a number of collections of women's papers has led me to conclude that references to marital intimacy, contraception, and other delicate matters related to sex were carefully expurgated from the materials before they were placed in libraries, archives, and other depositories. This was probably done not by the original writers but by children

or grandchildren horrified to think that their parents ever "talked about things like that." In one case I was allowed to look at a private collection of letters only if I promised not to reveal that the husband and wife discussed her pregnancies and that he referred to her legs rather than to her limbs! The existence of some rather explicit material on sexual matters and the tantalizing omissions from letter collections, missing pages, or inked or cut out paragraphs of diaries when the preceding or succeeding materials suggests that intimate topics might have been discussed leads one to suspect later-day censorship.

Several recent studies have suggested that nineteenth-century women were far more aware of their sexuality than historians once thought. An 1890 survey by a California female physician revealed that women she interviewed were familiar with such terms as coitus, intercourse, and orgasm, words a proper Victorian woman was not expected to have even heard. Although these studies make it clear that women were aware of sexual desires and the sex drive, how they viewed it is less clear. See: Charles Rosenberg, "Sexuality, Class and Role in Nineteenth Century America," *American Quarterly*, 25 (May 1973), pp. 131–53; Carroll Smith-Rosenberg and Charles Rosenberg, "The Female Animal: Medical and Biological Views of Woman and Her Role in Nineteenth-Century America," *Journal of American History*, 60 (September 1973), pp. 332–56; Carl N. Degler, "What Ought to Be and What Was: Women's Sexuality in the Nineteenth Century," *American Historical Review*, 79 (December 1974), pp. 1467–90, and *At Odds*, pp. 249–78; Sarah J. Stage, "Out of the Attic: Studies of Victorian Sexuality," *American Quarterly*, 27 (October 1975), pp. 480–85. Certainly it is clear from some women's diaries that they were very reticent to discuss physical relationships. One young woman confided to her journal that her new husband "got up quite early because we were ashamed to see each other dress" (Diamond, Diaries). Another young woman wrote that her mother "could never overcome her timidity and natural shyness regarding sex subjects. . . . what I learned regarding adolescence, I learned later from my sister and other girls." Mary Bennet Ritter, *More than Gold in California 1849–1933* (Berkeley, 1933), p. 107.

35. Lizzie Neblett to her husband, May 24, 1864, Neblett Collection, BTHC (Neblett later discussed the use of a vaginal sponge in correspondence with her cousin Fannie); Alice Clow to her sister, April 9, 1854, Clow Papers, BTHC.

36. For a discussion of the widespread use of abortion in the nineteenth century, see: James C. Mohn, *Abortion in America: The Origins and Evolution of National Policy, 1800–1900* (New York, 1978), pp. 3–118 and Degler, *At Odds*, pp. 227–48. The quote is from Lu Lee Cook, Navarro County, Texas, in Texas Slave Narratives, Works Progress Administration, BTHC. The attempt of a young neighbor girl to terminate her pregnancy by abortion is discussed by both Susan and Samuel Newcomb in their diaries, 1864, BTHC.

37. Summerhayes, *Vanished Arizona*, pp. 76, 78. For other discussions of women's problems in labor and delivery, see: Hand, Diary; Embree, Diary; Neblett, Diary and Letters; Holmes, Diary; Withers, Extracts; Bird-Dumont, Autobiography; Peggy Dow, *Viscissitudes, or Journey of Life and Supplementary Reflections* (Norwich, Ct., 1833), p. 434; Margaret White Chambers, *Reminiscences* (n.p., 1903), pp. 16, 27–28; Lillian A. Elliott, Reminiscences, NHS; "The Diary of Mary Richardson Walker, June 10–December 21, 1838," Rufus A. Coleman, ed., Historical Reprints, *Sources of Northwest History*, no. 15 (Missoula, 1931), pp. 18–19; Mary Maverick, Diary, BTHC; Susanna Robert Townsend to Dear Sister Mary, April 6, 1882, BL; and the summary discussion in Degler, *At Odds*, pp. 59–63.

One difficult delivery which had tragic consequences was described by a young Missouri girl: "[She] was in labor from 8 o'clock (Sunday) until Wednesday at 11 o'clock am. . . . It took three men to hold her in bed for two days & one night." The child was finally born dead and the mother died as well. "Had been married a little over a year. They could not put on her bridal dress as she was swollen too much." Diary of Sally Smith, MHS.

38. Mrs. William Poston Scott, Diary, MHS; Anne Legrand to her mother, October 5,

1876, BTHC. Also see: Embree, Diary; Bird-Dumont, Autobiography; Maverick, Diary; Susanna Townsend to Mary, April 6, 1852, BL; Minerva Burbank to "Dear Sister and Brother," May 6, 1856, OHS; Dow, *Viscissitudes,* p. 437; Diary of Alice Gray Sears, 1853–64, courtesy of Sears McGee, University of California, Santa Barbara; Mary Fannie Miles Pierce, My First Days in Texas, PPHA; Belknap, "Frontier Life," p. 42; Lovejoy, "Letters from Kansas," p. 37.

39. Among some of the more popular books of medical advice were Henry Wilkins, *The Family Adviser* (New York, 1818), a book prepared for Methodist missionaries; John C. Gunn, *Gunn's Domestic Medicine . . . Expressly Written for the Benefit of Families in the Western and Southern States* (Springfield, Oh., 1835); Daniel Whitney, *The Family Physician and Guide to Health . . . Together with the History, Causes, Symptoms, and Treatment of the Asiatic Cholera* (Penn-Yan, N.Y., 1833); and A. Weyer, *The Family Physician, or Poor Man's Friend* (St. Clairsville, Oh., 1831). Both Beecher and Child included extensive instructions on the care and feeding of sick children, but as noted above, neither included instructions for caring for broken limbs, burns, the bites of venemous reptiles or insects, or other common frontier problems. Moreover, both assumed the mother would have access to both skilled medical and nursing care. See: Lydia Maria Child, *The Mother's Book* (Boston, 1831); *The Family Nurse* (Boston, 1837); and Catherine Beecher, *Housekeeper and Healthkeeper.* Also see: Madge E. Pickard and R. Carlyle Buley, *The Midwest Pioneer: His Ills, Cures & Doctors* (Crawfordsville, In., 1945), especially pp. 35–97.

40. Wiltbank, Reminiscences; Maverick, Diary; Fabiola Cabeza de Baca, *We Fed Them Cactus* (Albuquerque, 1954), p. 59; Leonard Arrington, "Blessed Damozels: Women in Mormon History," *Dialogue,* 6 (Summer 1971), pp. 27–30. Also see: Hattie Stone Benefield, *For the Good of the Country (Por el Bien del Pais)* (Los Angeles, 1951), pp. 24–25; Eve Ball, "The Angel of the Pecos," in Western Writers of America, *The Women Who Made the West* (Garden City, 1980), pp. 1–14; and Claudia Bushman, ed., *Mormon Sisters: Women in Early Utah* (Salt Lake City, 1976).

41. Curnow, Journey, I, pp. 113–14. Despite the mothers' worries, the children generally enjoyed their rough-and-tumble life. See for example: Judge, "Carrie and the Grand Tetons;" Amelia Murdock Wing, "Early Days in Clayton County," *Annals of Iowa,* 27 (April 1946), pp. 257–96; "The Diary of Luna E. Warner, A Kansas Teenager of the Early 1870s," Venola L. Bivans, ed., *Kansas Historical Quarterly,* 35 (Autumn 1969), pp. 276–311 and 35 (Winter 1969), pp. 411–41; Dorothy M. Johnson, "A Short Moral Essay for Boys and Girls: Or How to Get Rich in a Frontier Town," *Montana,* 24 (Spring 1974), pp. 26–35; and Florence Sayer, "My Valley," *Idaho Yesterdays,* 8 (Fall 1964), pp. 18–25 for discussions of childhood memories of the frontier.

42. Harriett Carr to "Dear Father Carr," August 21, 1860, CHS; Ellen Hunt quoted in Elmer Bennett, "Pioneer Women of Colorado—Courage and Sacrifices," DPL; Lizzie Neblett to her husband, August 13, 1863. Another woman wrote a friend, "Our husbands ought to be precious good, and their gratitude to us for staying home and taking care of their children should be *unbounded!*" Abby Eliot to Sarah Glasgow, March 22, 1847, William Carr Lane Collection, MHS.

43. Holmes, Diary; Lizzie Clow to her sister, August 1851; Belknap, "Family Life," pp. 41–42; Pierce, My First Days; Martha Crumbaker to her sister, November 20, 1878, UWA; "End of an Era: The Travel Journal of Mary Mahoney," David Mahoney, ed., *Nebraska History,* 47 (September 1966), p. 336.

44. Hopping, Incidents; Benefield, *For the Good of the Country,* pp. 24–25. Also see: Bird-Dumont, Autobiography; Wiltbank, Reminiscences; Throop, *Reminiscences,* p. 4; Luster, *Autobiography,* p. 80; Tate, Papers; Kellie, Memoirs; Minerva Austin to her mother, December 4, 1870, KHS; Diary of Susan Ophelia Carter, NHS; Reminiscences of Mr. and Mrs.

Jacob Stroup, IHS; Minerva Burbank to her sister, September 25, 1856, OHS; Mary Leona Wilson, Short History of John McClellan Family, IHS; Carruth, Life Pictures in Kansas. Tillson, *A Woman's Story,* pp. 149–50 gives a particularly good description of candle making.

45. Bowie, Diary; St. John, "Prairie Diaries," p. 116; Belknap, "Family Life," p. 35. Also see: Tillson, *A Woman's Story,* p. 149.

46. Neblett, Diary; May McKeen Benton to her sister, undated letter, William J. Weatherby Family Papers, Laura Weatherby Correspondence, Box 1, NMSU.

47. Caples, Overland Journey to the Coast; Clara Tarwater, Dairy Methods in the 1890s, courtesy of Carmen Finley; Irene Corder, Mr. and Mrs. Obidiah Corder's History of Their Pioneer Life in the West from 1833 to 1929, IHS; Mrs. C. E. Baldwin, Interview, Indian-Pioneer Papers, IV, pp. 307–10; Delaney, *A Survivor's Recollections,* p. 29; Mary McKeen Benton to her sister, undated letter, Weatherby Family Papers. Mormon women were especially active in such money-making enterprises. Many had to support themselves and their children when their husbands were absent on missions or when there were two or more plural families to be fed and clothed. The church encouraged women to learn some skill or profession and contribute income to the family and church.

48. Frances Leon Swadesh, *Los Primeros Pobladores: Hispanic Americans of the Ute Frontier* (Notre Dame, 1974), pp. 178–79; Julia C. Spruill, "Women in the Founding of the Southern Colonies," *North Carolina Historical Review,* 13 (April 1912), pp. 212–13; Hon. Harvey Munsill, "Bristol," *The Vermont Historical Gazetteer,* 1 (1867), p. 20; Mrs. Bettie Bellah, Interview, Indian-Pioneer Papers, II, pp. 66–71.

49. Faulkner, Prairie Home, I, p. 75; Mrs. Mary Edmonson, Interview, Edna Hatfield Collection, WHC; Cable, After Thoughts; Eliza Farham, *California Indoors and Out: or How We Farm, Mine and Live Generally in the Golden State* (New York, 1856), pp. 107–8. Also see: Bellah, Interview; Ronan, *Frontier Woman,* p. 55; "Life and Journal of Eliza Maria Partridge Lyman," quoted in *Utah Historical Quarterly,* 46 (Spring 1978), p. 120; and Arrington, "Blessed Damozels," p. 23 for other accounts of women as home-builders.

50. Warner, "A Kansas Teenager," p. 295; Margaret M. Hecox, *California Caravan: The 1846 Overland Memoir of Margaret M. Hecox,* Richard Dillon, ed. (San Jose, 1966), p. 52; Rabb, Reminiscences. Also see: Judson, *A Pioneer's Search,* p. 109; Caroline Sexton, Biography, OHS; Elizabeth Austin, Crossing the Plains, UWA; Thomas Prosch, *David S. Maynard and Catherine Maynard: Biographies of Two of the Oregon Immigrants of 1850* (Seattle, 1906), p. 74; and Katherine Horack, "The Quest for a Prairie Home," *Palimpsest,* 5 (July 1924), p. 256 for other accounts of women joining in the defense of their homes.

51. Gaspar Peréz de Villagra, *History of New Mexico* (Los Angeles, 1933), p. 224; Mary Sifton Pepper, *Maids and Matrons of New France* (Boston, 1901), pp. 220–38; William W. Fowler, *Woman on the American Frontier* (Hartford, 1877), p. 93; Curnow, Journey with Tom, II, p. 83. Also see: Barbara B. Zimmerman and Vernon Carstensen, eds., "Pioneer Woman in Southwestern Washington Territory: The Recollections of Susanna Maria Slover McFarland Price Ede," *Pacific Northwest Quarterly,* 4 (October 1976), pp. 143, 147 and Mary Ann Davidson, "An Autobiography and a Reminiscence," *Annals of Iowa,* 37 (Spring 1964), p. 256.

52. Annie Pike Greenwood, *We Sagebrush Folks* (New York, 1934), p. 51; Barbara E. Gannon Baker, Interview, Indian-Pioneer Papers, IV, pp. 144–54; Joseph Bodenhammer, Interview, Indian-Pioneer Papers, IX, p. 83; Ruby Boggs, Interview, Indian-Pioneer Papers, IX, p. 112; Francis D. Reed, Biography, OHS; Ritter, *More Than Gold in California,* pp. 65–66.

53. Rebecca Burlend, *A True Picture of Emigration,* Milo Quaife, ed. (Secaucus, N.J., 1972), p. 92; Hafen, *Recollections,* pp. 74–76, 79–80; Tanner, *A Mormon Mother,* p. 129; Malinda S. Crouch, Recollections of Rogue River Indian Wars, OHS; Lizzie Hatcher Simons, Diary, August 31–December 31, 1862, BTHC; Mrs. W. O. Bishop in Sod House Letters. Also see: Elinore Pruitt Stewart, *Letters of a Woman Homesteader* (New York, 1914), pp. 17–18, 87; Kilvert,

"Pioneer Woman," p. 19; Elizabeth Shor, "Problems in the Land of Opportunity," *American West*, 8 (January–February 1976), p. 25; Murray, "Memoir," p. 368; Walker D. Wyman, *Frontier Woman: The Life of a Homesteader on the Dakota Frontier* (River Falls, Wi., 1972); Kellie, Memoirs; Kennedy, Reminiscence; Diary of Emily Butcher, KHS for other women's descriptions of taking on men's chores or assisting with farm work.

54. Rachel W. Bash, Interview, Indian-Pioneer Papers, VI, p. 8; Mrs. Theodore Schultz, Early Anecdotes, BL; Stewart, *Letters*, p. 282; Judge, "Carrie and the Grand Tetons," p. 52. Also see: Bird-Dumont, Autobiography; Bowie, Diary; Farnham, *California*, p. 108; Anna McKee to her sisters Lizzie and Winnie, October 19, 1884, CHS; and Charles McPhee Wright, Annals of Harriet S. Wright, AHS for other women's descriptions of their pride and pleasure in their ability to undertake successfully men's work.

55. Hazel P. Reeder, Amelia, NHS; Abigail Scott Duniway, "A Few Recollections of a Busy Life," in Mary O. Douthit, ed., *The Souvenir of Western Woman* (Portland, 1905), pp. 9–10; Ella R. Gale, Diary, MHS; Willie Newbury Lewis, *Between Sun and Sod: An Informal History of the Texas Panhandle*, 2nd ed. (College Station, Tex. 1976), p. 41; Inez Bennett, Interview, Indian-Pioneer Papers, VII, p. 209.

56. See, for example: Adriance, Reminiscence; Lura Case Smith, Papers, HEH; Butler, "Diary of the Rogue River Valley," pp. 345, 349; Withers, Extracts; Letter to Fannie Steele; Ronan, *Frontier Woman*, pp. 81–82; "Mary Catharine Crossing the Plains" in Andy Rogers, *A Hundred Years of Rip and Roarin': Rough and Ready the Town That Won't Ghost* (Rough and Ready, Ca., 1952), p. 60; and Aggie Loring to her mother, July 7, 1879, AHS.

57. Faragher, *Women and Men*, pp. 80–81; Lewis, *Between Sun and Sod*, p. 93; Harriet West, *The Life and Travels of Harriet C. West* (Kahoka, Mo., 1910), p. 80. Also see: Jeanne L. Wuillemin, undated letter, SDHS; Butler, "Diary of the Rogue River Valley," pp. 342, 345; Susan Carter, Diary; Dora Osgood, To Arizona in 1901, AHS; Allen, Diary; Castor, Diary; and Mildred C. Fry, "Women on the Ohio Frontier: The Marietta Area," *Ohio History,* 90 (Winter 1981), p. 65 for other women's descriptions of men's "domestic" occupations. One man admitted, "I have a strange hobby for a man; I crochet beautiful bedspreads and table pieces." Bodenhamer, Interview, p. 83.

58. Glenda Riley, "Women on the Overland Trails: Iowa as a Case Study," paper presented at Organization of American Historians, New Orleans, 1979. Also see: Johnny Faragher and Christine Stansell, "Women and Their Families on the Overland Trail to California and Oregon, 1842–1867," *Feminist Studies*, 2 (1975), pp. 150–66 and Lillian Schlissel, "Women's Diaries on the Western Frontier," *American Studies*, 18 (Spring 1977), pp. 87–100.

59. As May Lacey Crowder pointed out, "Frequently enough, while the men were learning to farm, the women and children actually supported the families. . . . The women were not unaware of this fact and were quite capable of scoring a point on occasion when masculine attitudes become too bumptious." Quoted in Riley, *Frontierswomen*, pp. 86–87. Among the many women whose diaries and letters reveal a thorough knowledge and understanding of family enterprises are: Mrs. James Kilroy Brown, Reminiscences, AHS; Julia Dodge, Letters, DPL; Withers, Extracts; Neblett, Diary and various letters to her husband; Legrand Letters; Bird-Dumont, Autobiography; Kellie, Memoirs; Ronan, *Frontier Woman;* Murray, "Memoirs," pp. 364, 368. Also see the discussions of the later careers of Harriet Strong and Sarah Cockrell in chapter nine. Recent studies have suggested a similar role for women among the Southern yeoman class. See especially: Keith L. Bryant, Jr., "Role and Status of the Female Yeomanry in the Antebellum South, The Literary View," *The Southern Quarterly,* 18 (Winter 1980), especially pp. 76–77.

60. Blues, melancholia, and depression were a prevalent nineteenth-century disease which afflicted men as well as women. Thus it is not surprising to find such feelings expressed in frank terms in diaries, reminiscences, and letters. For Henrietta Embree, problems of poor

health, her husband's frequent absences from home, and the cares of her growing family were simply too much to bear, and she turned first to laudanum and later to opium to relieve her worries and concerns (Embree, Diary). Sarah Sim became suicidal and attempted to kill herself and her children. (Shor, "Problems in the Land of Opportunity," pp. 24–29. For most women, however, the condition was not so severe and quickly passed away. For many middle-class women, even on the frontiers, blues were compounded by the lack of anything else to think about. They often found their lives a dreary round of shopping and calls and church with little to distract their attention. They had servants to do much of their work, their husbands were engaged in business, and they had little to stimulate their minds or thoughts and thus easily became despondent. The affliction was much less apparent in women who had heavy burdens and responsibilities or whose days were full of other than household activities. Men were also affected, but the problem appeared to have been more common among professional men—lawyers, doctors, teachers—than among their more active brothers who simply did not have time during the day and were too tired at night to care, or, at least, to write or comment about their depression.

61. These women would have been surprised, perhaps shocked to be called heroines, and most of them would have denied their right to the title, although most were proud to be called pioneers. As a recent study pointed out, "these women realized now how strong and successful they had been in meeting the challenges of frontier life." Julie Jeffrey, *Frontier Women: The Trans-Mississippi West, 1840-1880* (New York, 1979), p. 202.

62. Glenda Riley, " 'Not Gainfully Employed': Women on the Iowa Frontier, 1833–1870," *Pacific Historical Review*, 49 (May 1980), p. 257. Riley's findings and interpretations are similar to my own.

Chapter 7

1. Phoebe G. Judson, *A Pioneer's Search for an Ideal Home* (Bellingham, Wa., 1925). Judson's reminiscences of her pioneer days described many of the concerns and activities discussed in this chapter.

2. Everett Dick, "Sunbonnet and Calico, The Homesteader's Consort," *Nebraska History*, 47 (March 1966), p. 13.

3. May McKeen Benton to Laura Weatherby, March 26, 1905 in William J. Weatherby Family Papers, Box 1, NMSU; Julia Louisa Lovejoy, Diary, KHS.

4. For example, Emily Hawley, a twenty-two-year-old Iowa woman, entertained a steady stream of neighbors, boarders, and visitors yet she "rarely missed a day of recording in her diary that she was homesick, lonely, and sometimes despondent." See: Dorothy Schwieder, "Labor and Economic Roles of Iowa Farm Wives, 1840–1880," in Trudy H. Peterson, ed., *Farmers, Bureaucrats, and Middlemen: Agricultural Perspectives on American History* (Washington, D.C., 1981). I am indebted to Professor Schwieder for pointing out the differences in isolation and loneliness.

5. Lou Conway Roberts, *A Woman's Reminiscences of Six Years in Camp with the Texas Rangers* (Austin, 1928), p. 40.

6. Sarah E. Martin, My Desert Memories, AHS. For similar comments, see: Mrs. Chestina B. Allen, Diary, KHS; Susan E. Newcomb, Diary, BTHC; Lottie Roeder Roth, Historical Sketch of Mrs. Roeder's Eventful Life, and Mrs. Elizabeth Cornelis Rudene, Reminiscences, UWA; Reminiscences of Mr. and Mrs. Jacob Stroup, IHS; Emma Jane McIntyre, Observations of Her Life in the Pribilof Islands, BL; Rebecca Woodson, A Sketch of the Life of Rebecca H. Nutting (Woodson), CSL; Emily Jane Burrows to Cousin Mary, November 10, 1873, in Emily Jane Burrows, Correspondence, 1873–75, OHS; Matha Crumbaker to H. and C(ynthia) Law-

rence, November 20, 1878, UWA; Polly Jane Purcell, *Autobiography and Reminiscences of a Pioneer* (Freewater, Or., n.d.), p. 5; Matilda Delaney, *A Survivor's Recollections of the Whitman Massacre* (Spokane, 1920), p. 29; Mrs. Hester Pattison quoted in Dick, "Sunbonnet and Calico," p. 10; Sara Roberts, *Alberta Homestead: Chronicle of a Pioneer Family* (Austin, 1971), p. 79; and the perceptive discussion by Mary W. M. Hargreaves in "Women in the Agricultural Settlement of the Northern Plains," *Agricultural History*, 50 (January 1976), pp. 179–89.

7. See, for example: Marian Russell, *Land of Enchantment: Memoirs of Marian Russell Along the Santa Fe Trail*, Garnet M. Brayer, ed. (Evanston, 1954), pp. 101, 109; Teresa Vielé, *"Following the Drum:" A Glimpse of Frontier Life*, James Day, ed. (Austin, 1968), pp. 217–18; Martha Summerhayes, *Vanished Arizona: Recollections of the Army Life of a New England Woman*, reprint ed. (Glorieta, N.M., 1970), pp. 109, 112.

8. Elizabeth Minerva Byers quoted in Elmer Bennett, Pioneer Women of Colorado—Courage and Sacrifice, DPL; Mary Pratt Staples, Reminiscences, BL; Ella Bailey, Diary, 1869, CHS.

9. Ella Bailey, Diary; Emeline L. S. Benson, From Beloit Wisconsin to San Pablo Valley, CSL; Barbara Kilvert, "Pioneer Woman," *The Beaver*, (Autumn 1957), p. 19; O. E. Rölvaag, *Giants in the Earth* (New York, 1927), p. 156; Sarah Sim quoted in Elizabeth Shor, "Problems in the Land of Opportunity," *American West*, 13 (January–February 1976), pp. 27, 28.

10. Mary Ronan, *Frontier Woman, The Story of Mary Ronan*, H. G. Merriam, ed. (Missoula, 1973), p. 81.

11. Frances Dragoo Reed, Biography, OHS; James E. Potter, ed., "The Ranch Letters of Emma Robertson, 1891–1892," *Nebraska History*, 56 (Summer 1975), p. 222.

12. See, for example: Kitturah P. Belknap, "Family Life on the Frontier: The Diary of Kitturah P. Belknap," Glenda Riley, ed., *Annals of Iowa*, 44 (Summer 1944), pp. 40–41 and Emily Hawley Gillespie, Diary, ISHS, quoted in Schwieder, "Labor and Economic Roles." Schwieder's article contains an excellent discussion of alternate forms of neighboring as they developed on the Iowa frontier.

13. On Mexican-American settlement patterns, see: D. W. Meining, *Imperial Texas: Essays in Cultural Geography* (Austin, 1969), pp. 23–37; Angelico Chavez, *My Penitente Land: Reflections on Spanish New Mexico* (Albuquerque, 1974), pp. 55–59; Leonard Pitt, *The Decline of the Californios* (Berkeley, 1966), pp. 1–25; and Oakah Jones, *Los Paisanos: Settlers on the Northern Frontier of New Spain* (Norman, 1979), pp. 3–15, 237–48. Some idea of the life of Spanish-American women in these settlements will be found in Janet Lecompte, *Pueblo, Hardscrabble, Greenhorn: The Upper Arkansas, 1832–1856* (Norman, 1978), pp. 63–73; Jones, *Los Paisanos*, pp. 136–66; Frances Leon Swadesh, *Los Primeros Pobladores: Hispanic Americans of the Ute Frontier* (Notre Dame, 1974), pp. 178–82; and Alfredo Mirandé and Evangelina Enríquez, *La Chicana: The Mexican American Woman* (Chicago, 1979), pp. 53–95.

14. Mary Hallock Foote quoted in Rodman W. Paul, "When Culture Came to Boise, Mary Hallock Foote in Idaho," *Idaho Yesterdays*, 20 (Summer 1976), p. 4; Sara Stebbins to "Dear Mother," in "Frontier Life: Loneliness and Hope," Donald F. Carmony, ed., *Indiana Magazine of History*, 61 (March 1965), p. 54; Ann England LeGrand to her mother, October 5, 1867, BTHC. See also: Lura C. Smith to sister, August 12, 1854, HEH; Sarah R. Herndon, *Days on the Road, Crossing the Plains in 1865* (New York, 1902), p. 72.

15. On army customs, see: Sandra L. Myres, "The Ladies of the Army—Views of Western Life," in *The American Military on the Frontier Proceedings of the Seventh Military History Symposium, USAF Academy, 1976* (Washington, D.C., 1978), pp. 138–39 and Patricia Y. Stallard, *Glittering Misery, Dependents of the Indian Fighting Army* (Fort Collins, 1978), pp. 61–62. Hispanic class structure is discussed by Jane Dysart, "Mexican Women in San Antonio, 1850–1860: The Assimilation Process," *Western Historical Quarterly*, 7 (October 1976), pp. 365–75 and Lynn Perrigo, *Our Spanish Southwest* (New York, 1971), pp. 73–77.

16. E. R. Pratt to his brother, February 2, 1850 in Walker D. Wyman, ed., *California Emigrant Letters* (New York, 1952), p. 128; Bruce Siberts, *Nothing but Prairie and Sky: Life on the Dakota Range in the Early Days*, Walker D. Wyman, comp. (Norman, 1954), p. 34. Also see: Ella Bird-Dumont, Autobiography, BTHC, for a woman's comments on male loneliness.

17. Newcomb, Diary; Malinda Sutherlin Crouch, Recollections of Rogue River Indian Wars, OHS.

18. Mary Ann Hafen, *Recollections of a Handcart Pioneer of 1860* (Denver, 1938), pp. 75–76. For similar experiences of other Mormon women, see: Annie Clark Tanner, *A Mormon Mother: An Autobiography* (Salt Lake City, 1969), pp. 59–61, 71–73; Fae D. Dix, ed., "The Josephine Diaries: Glimpses of Life of Josephine Streeper Chase, 1881–94," *Utah Historical Quarterly*, 46 (Spring 1978), pp. 171–72.

19. Julia Hand, Diary 1872–75, KHS. See also: Diary of Alice Gray Sears, 1853–64, courtesy of Sears McGee, University of California at Santa Barbara; Newcomb, Diary, for similar comments.

20. For an excellent discussion of the different roles of men and women and the relationship between the sexes in the rural Midwest see: John M. Faragher, *Women and Men on the Overland Trail* (New Haven, 1979), pp. 110–43.

21. John Demos, "The American Family in Past Time," *American Scholar*, 43 (Summer 1974), p. 445. Also see: Rowland Berthoff, *An Unsettled People: Social Order and Disorder in American History* (New York, 1971), pp. 204–17 and Carl N. Degler, *At Odds: Women and the Family in America from the Revolution to the Present* (New York, 1980).

22. Margaret Lea Houston to Sam Houston, June 20, 1849, in Margaret Lea Houston Letters, 1840–67, BTHC; Ronan, *Frontier Woman*, p. 89; Carrie Strong Robbins, The Journal of Carrie Strong Robbins, Payson, Adams County, Illinois, KHS. See also: Bird-Dumont, Autobiography; Emma Shepard Hill, *A Dangerous Crossing and What Happened on the Other Side* (Denver, 1924), pp. 143–206; Mrs. Thomas Withers to her mother, December 2, 1878, extracts from the Colorado Correspondence of 1878–80, DPL; Luna Kellie, Memoirs, NHS; and Martin, Desert Memories, for other descriptions of happy, traditional marriages.

23. Kellie, Memoirs; Reminiscences of Mrs. James Kilroy (Olive S.) Brown, AHS; Annals of Harriet S. Wright, 1841–1932, in Charles McPhee Wright Papers, AHS; Sara Bennett to Clarence E. Bennett, April 1, 1864, in Clarence E. Bennett Papers, AHS; Newcomb, Diary.

24. Lizzie Scott Neblett, Diary, BTHC; Mary Maverick, Diary, in Maverick Family Papers, BTHC. Also see: Henrietta Embree, Diary 1856–61, BTHC; "The Diary of Mary Richardson Walker, June 10–December 21, 1838," Rufus A. Coleman, ed., *Historical Reprints, Sources of Northwest History*, no. 15 (Missoula, 1931), p. 16; Mrs. William P. Scott, Diary, MHS; Mary R. Powers, "A Woman's Journal," *Amateur Book Collector*, 1 (September 1950), p. 2; Harvey Doe to his parents, March 29, 1880, DPL.

25. Ella Bailey, Diary; Orpha LeGro Haxby Manuscripts, SDHS; The Claim of Mrs. Rena J. D. Mathews of Being a Western Pioneer, AHS.

26. Berthoff, *An Unsettled People*, pp. 213–14. Also see: Robert L. Griswold, "Apart But Not Adrift: Women, Divorce, and Independence in California, 1850–1890," *Pacific Historical Review*, 49 (May 1980), pp. 265–84, a perceptive recent study which discusses the rising divorce rate and the effect of divorce on women's lives. On Western divorce mills, see: Harry Hazel and S. L. Lewis, *The Divorce Mill: Realistic Sketches of the South Dakota Divorce Colony* (New York, 1895) and Jane Burr, *Letters of a Dakota Divorcee* (Boston, 1909). For other discussions of divorce by Western women see: Thomas Prosch, *David S. Maynard and Catherine T. Maynard: Biographies of Two of the Oregon Immigrants of 1850* (Seattle, 1906), p. 33; Sue H. Summers, Reminiscences of My Early Life in Arizona, AHS; Walker D. Wyman, *Frontier Woman: The Life of a Woman Homesteader on the Dakota Frontier* (River Falls, Wi., 1972); Annie Hunt Diary in Louis W. Kemp Collection, BTHC; Mary E. Wood, Correspondence, AHS;

Amanda Lindley, Autobiography, BTHC; Louie Boyd, Notes on Mrs. Murat, DPL; Robert Glass Cleland, ed., *Apron Full of Gold: The Letters of Mary Jane Megquier from San Francisco, 1849–1856* (San Marino, 1949), pp. vii, 87; Anne E. Lane to Sarah L. Glasgow, 1851, in William Carr Lane Collection, MHS; Ruth Jewett Bailey, Papers, OHS; Sarah Cool, Frontier Life, Incidents and Work in California, HEH; Pamela F. Benson, Diary, 1878, OHS; C. Richard King, ed., *Victorian Lady on the Texas Frontier: The Journal of Ann Raney Coleman* (Norman, 1971); Emeline L. Fuller, *Left By the Indians: The Story of My Life* (Mount Vernon, Ia., 1892), pp. 39–40; Francis D. Haines, Jr., ed., *A Bride on the Bozeman Trail: The Letters and Diary of Ellen Gordon Fletcher, 1866* (Medford, Or., 1970), p. 87; Agnes Just Reid, *Letters of Long Ago*, reprint ed. (Salt Lake City, 1973), pp. 17–19; R. Dean Galloway, "Rowena Granice," *Pacific Historian*, 24 (Spring 1980), pp. 105–24. The changing nature of the relationship between wives and husbands is discussed in Degler, *At Odds*, pp. 26–51. The high rate of Western divorce is discussed in Henry Pang, "Highest Divorce Rates in Western United States," *Sociology and Social Research*, 52 (1968), pp. 228–36.

27. See David J. Langum, "Expatriate Domestic Relations Law in Mexican California," *Pepperdine Law Review*, 7 (1979), pp. 41–66.

28. "Old Time Counsel to a Bride, 1847," Missouri Historical Society, *Glimpses of the Past*, 1 (February 1934), pp. 5–6.

29. See, for example: Embree, Diary.

30. Hill, *A Dangerous Crossing*, p. 73.

31. See, for example: Julia Lee Sinks, Early Days in Texas, BTHC; Harriet Virginia Scott to her cousin Bartholomew Slade, 1846, BTHC; Ellen Roselle Hinsdale, Letters, May 23, 1871–August 2, 1872, DPL; A Journal of Cara Georginia Whitmore Bell . . . 1872–76, DPL; Mary Agnes Crank, Ranch Life Fifty Years Ago, in James F. Crank Papers, HEH; and Ralph M. Wardle, "Territorial Bride," *Nebraska History*, 50 (Summer 1969), pp. 207–28, especially p. 215.

32. Two excellent descriptions of court week are C. May Cohea, Pioneer Women, PPHA and Summers, Reminiscences. Also see: Marion Blake, Interview #9602, Indian-Pioneer Papers, VIII, pp. 378–79, WHC.

33. Mary E. Hopping, Incidents of Pioneer Life, As I Remember and As I Have Been Told, CSL; Mrs. William Justice, Pioneering in Hagerman from 1877 to 1900, IHS; Ella Bailey, Diary; Angie Debo, *Prairie City* (New York, 1969), p. 23 quoted in *Women's World: A Patchwork of Time and Space* (Lawton, Oklahoma, 1978). Other descriptions of the rigors of all night dancing and parties can be found in: Haines, *A Bride on the Bozeman Trail*, pp. 90–91; Cleland, *Apron Full of Gold*, p. 47; and Mrs. Ashmun Butler, "Diary of the Rogue River Valley, 1852–1854," *Oregon Historical Quarterly*, 41 (December 1940), p. 343. There are numerous descriptions of frontier dances. See, for example: Lizzie Moore Sisk, Reminiscences, IHS; Irene Corder, Mr. and Mrs. Obidiah Corder's History of Their Pioneer Life in the West, IHS; Bird-Dumont, Autobiography; Reminiscences of Mr. and Mrs. Jacob Stroup; Diary Account of Emily Butcher, 1896–99, KHS; Hinsdale, Letters; Diary of Mrs. Milly R. Gray, BTHC; Myrtle Carter Hooper, Diaries, SDHS; Louise Palmer, "How We Live in Nevada," *Overland Monthly*, 2 (May 1869), p. 459; Dick, "Sunbonnet and Calico," p. 11; Mrs. Sallie Hester Maddox, "The Diary of a Pioneer Girl," *Argonaut*, September 12, 1925; Elizabeth Therese Baird, "Reminiscences of Life in Territorial Wisconsin," *Wisconsin Historical Collections*, 15 (Madison, 1900), pp. 212–16; Venola L. Bivans, ed., "The Diary of Luna E. Warner, A Kansas Teenager of the Early 1870s," *Kansas Historical Quarterly*, 35 (Autumn 1960), pp. 284, 286–87; Hafen, *Handcart Pioneer*, p. 49; Conway, *A Woman's Reminiscences*, p. 14; Reid, *Letters of Long Ago*, pp. 13–16; Sophie Poe, *Buckboard Days* (Caldwell, Id., 1936), pp. 152–55.

34. Pauline Graham, "Play-Party Games," *Palimpsest*, 10 (February 1919), p. 33; Sarepta Ross, "Recollections of a Pioneer," BL. There is an extensive literature on the play-party.

See, for example: Leah Jackson Wolford, *The Play Party in Indiana*, rev. ed (Indianapolis, 1959); William A. Owens, *Swing and Turn: Texas Play-Party Games* (Dallas, 1936); B. A. Botkin, "The Play Party in Oklahoma," *Publications of the Texas Folklore Society*, 7 (1928), pp. 7–24; and the following articles in the *Journal of American Folklore:* Emelyn E. Garnder, "Some Play-Party Games in Michigan," 33 (April–June 1920), pp. 91–133; Carl Van Doren, "Some Play-Party Songs from Eastern Illinois," 32 (October–December 1919), pp. 486–96; Mrs. L. D. Ames, "The Missouri Play-Party," 24 (July–September 1911), pp. 295–318; Harriet L. Wedgwood, "The Play-Party in Nebraska," 25 (July–September 1912), pp. 268–72; Edwin S. Piper, "Some Play-Party Games of the Middle West," 28 (July–September 1915), pp. 262–89; Goldy M. Hamilton, "The Play-Party in Northeast Missouri, 27 (July–September 1914), pp. 289–303. (My thanks to Professor Warren Beck for these references.)

35. Brigida Briones, "A Glimpse of Domestic Life in 1827," *Century Magazine*, 41 (January 1891), p. 470; Briones, "A Carnival Ball at Monterey in 1829," Ibid., p. 468; Doña Juana Machado, "Times Gone By in Alta California," Ray S. Brandes, ed. and trans., *The Historical Society of Southern California Quarterly*, 41 (September 1959), p. 214. In addition to these articles, other women's descriptions of Mexican-American frontier social life may be found in Angustias de la Guerra Ord, *Occurrences in Hispanic California* (Washington, D.C., 1956), p. 50; Guadalupe Vallejo, "Ranch and Mission Days in Alta California," *Century Magazine*, 41 (December 1890), pp. 190–91; Amalia Sibrian, "A Spanish Girl's Journey from Monterey to Los Angeles," *Century Magazine*, 41 (January 1891), pp. 469–70; May Banks Stacey to her mother, August 16, 1869, AHS; Ronan, *Frontier Woman*, pp. 55–56; Reminiscences of Señora Doña Jesus Moreno de Soza, AHS; Anna McKee to her Mother, Christmas, 1884, CHS. On the custom of throwing *cascarones*, see: Ralph E. Twitchell, *Leading Facts of New Mexico History*, reprint ed., 2 vols. (Albuquerque, 1963), II, p. 162. Spanish-American folk-dramas are discussed and described by Arthur L. Campa in "Spanish Religious Folktheatre in the Spanish Southwest, (First Cycle)" and "Spanish Religious Folktheatre in the Southwest (Second Cycle)," *University of New Mexico Bulletin*, 245 (February and June 1934), pp. 5–69 and 5–157 and "Los Comanches, A New Mexican Folk Drama," *University of New Mexico Bulletin*, 376 (April 1942), pp. 5–43. "Los Pastores" or "Bartolo" and other religious and secular dramas were "interspresed with moral and religious teachings, with music and songs, with farce and buffonery and thus served a religious as well as social function." Machado, "Times Gone By," p. 235.

36. Letter to Fannie E. Steele, June 26, 1852, MHS; Eloise Sargent Lehow, Reminiscences, DPL. Other typical descriptions of more formal frontier calling may be found in Embree, Diary; Gray, Diary; Mary A. Wilkenson, Diary, March 1851–January 1852 and January 1852–February 1856, MHS; Laura Rice Castor, Diary 1887–99, OHS; Lura C. Smith, Papers; Eliza G. Post, Memorandum Books, MHS; C. D. and William Donaldson Papers, BTHC; Wright, Annals; and Virginia Wilcox Ivins, *Pen Pictures of Early Western Days* (n.p., 1908).

37. Louise Butler Swift to her mother, August 3, 1863, UWA; Christiana Tillson, *A Woman's Story of Pioneer Illinois* (Chicago, 1919), 103–4; Mrs. Matthew Deady, Crossing the Plains in 1846, OHS; Allen, Diary. Also see: Mrs. Andrew Hively, Journal, DPL; Margaret A. Bowie, Diary, 1872–77, BTHC; Olivia Holmes, Diary Written in 1872, BL; Mary Fannie Pierce, My First Days in Texas, PPHA; Julia T. Dodge, Letters 1856–80, DPL; and Jane Carruth to Melinda Evans, 1891, KHS; Hooper, Diaries, 1887, 1891; Julia Hand, Diary, KHS; Lura C. Smith, Papers; Fanny Adriance, Reminiscences, DPL; Butler, "Diary of Rogue River."

38. See, for example: Briones, "A Glimpse of Domestic Life," p. 470; "Literate Woman in the Mines: The Diary of Rachel Haskell," *Mississippi Valley Historical Review*, 31 (June 1944), p. 85; Rodman Paul, ed., *A Victorian Gentlewoman in the Far West: The Reminiscences of Mary Hallock Foote* (San Marino, 1972), pp. 178, 180–81; Irene Cushman Wilson, Diary, 1890–91, SDHS.

39. Mrs. Isaac Moore, How I Went to Denver, DPL; Emily Andrews, Diary; and May Callan Tansill, Narrative, BTHC. See also: Summers, Reminiscences; Bivans, "The Diary of Luna E. Warner," p. 289; Agnes Sengstaken, *Destination West!* (Portland, 1942), p. 125; Louise Swift to her mother, August 31, 1864, UWA; Nannie T. Alderson, *A Bride Goes West* (New York, 1942), p. 269; Mrs. Clara Tarwater, "Family History," private collection. A typical selection of frontier musical instruments and musical groups is pictured in Heather S. Hatch, "Music in Arizona Territory," *Journal of Arizona History,* 12 (Winter 1971), pp. 263–80. The growth of musical organizations in the larger cities is discussed in Julia Cooley Altrocchi, "Paradox Town, San Francisco in 1851," *California Historical Quarterly,* 28 (March 1949), pp. 38–40.

40. Diary of Mary Elizabeth Smith, MHS; Irene S. Wilson, Diary; Caroline Cock Dunlap, "Ancotty (Long Ago)," *The Oregonian,* June 28, 1959, copy in OHS.

41. Mrs. Frances M. A. Roe, *Army Letters from an Officer's Wife, 1871–1888* (New York, 1909), p. 37; Katherine Gibson Fougera, *With Custer's Cavalry* (Caldwell, Id., 1942), p. 132. Eliza Johnson painted wildflowers as a hobby and some of her watercolors were recently published in *Texas Wild Flowers* (Austin, 1972). Eliza Burt assembled an herbarium of pressed flowers as did Ada Vogdes. Mrs. Orsemus Boyd amused herself with games like cribbage while Elizabeth Custer reported that the ladies of the Seventh Cavalry "painted, drew, or learned new guitar accompaniments." See: Merrill Mattes, *Indians, Infants and Infantry: Andrew and Eliza Burt on the Frontier, 1866–98* (Denver, 1960), p. 8; Ada Vogdes, Journal Describing Army Life of an Officer's Wife, HEH; Mrs. Orsemus Boyd, *Cavalry Life in Tent and Field* (New York, 1894), p. 66; Elizabeth Custer, *Following the Guidon,* reprint ed. (Norman, 1966), p. 256. Also see the descriptions of army amusements in Forrest R. Blackburn, "Families on the Frontier," *Military Review,* 49 (October 1969), pp. 24–26 and Stallard, *Glittering Misery,* pp. 42–52.

42. Effie May Butler Wiltbank, Reminiscences, AHS; Robbins, Journal. For descriptions of the various social activities described see: Delaney, *A Survivor's Recollections,* pp. 32–34; Adriance, Reminiscences; Margaret Lea Houston to Sam Houston, June 20, 1849, BTHC; Poe, *Buckboard Days,* pp. 148–49, 178–79; Hill, *A Dangerous Crossing,* pp. 53–63; Hattie Swift to "My Dear Ella," July 16, 1865, UWA; Mary Austin Holley, Papers, BTHC; Eliza Ferry Leary, Letters, WAC; Diary Account of Emily Butcher, KHS; Nebraska Farmer Sod House Letters, NHS; Johnaphene Faulkner, "Prairie Home," BTHC; Emily L. Burrows to Cousin Mary, April 10, 1874, Emily Burrows Correspondence, 1873–75, OHS; Kellie, Memoirs; Leola Lehman, "Life in the Territories," *Chronicles of Oklahoma,* 41 (Winter, 1963–64), p. 377; Mrs. John W. Wade, Recollections of an Octogenarian, BTHC; and Mildred C. Fry, "Women on the Ohio Frontier: The Marietta Area," *Ohio History,* 90 (Winter 1981), pp. 71–72.

43. Shirley Sargent, *Pioneers in Petticoats: Yosemite's Early Women, 1856–1900* (Los Angeles, 1966), pp. 15–18, 45–50; Sarah Haight, *The Ralston-Fry Wedding and the Wedding Journey to Yosemite May 20, 1858 from the Diary of Miss Sarah Haight,* Francis P. Farquhar, ed. (Berkeley, 1961). See also: Diary of Edith Highton—Journal of a Trip Through the Mountains from June 4th 1881 and Harriet Jane Kirtland Lee, Journal of a Trip Through the Southern Mines by Harriet J. Kirtland May 13–June 3, 1859, both in CSL.

44. See, for example: Julia Holmes, *A Bloomer Girl on Pike's Peak,* Agnes Wright Spring, ed. (Denver, 1940); Hill, *A Dangerous Crossing,* pp. 79, 93–111; Elmo Scott Watson, *The Professor Goes West* (Bloomington, Il., 1954), pp. 8–9; Mrs. Jacob Rideout, *Camping Out in California* (San Francisco, 1889); E. P. Stewart and Flora Smalley, "We Slept in the Wagon: An Arizona Camping Trip, 1902," *Journal of Arizona History,* 12 (Autumn 1971), pp. 183–212; May Stacey, to "My dear Ma," August 16, 18[79], AHS; Lucy Preston Peters, Diary, 1867–1922, OHS; Ellen Hinsdale to "My Dear Sarah," May 23, 1871, DPL; Dayelle Kittredge, Diary, 1876 in Jack London Papers, HEH. After the completion of the transcontinental railroad many Eastern and European tourists visited these areas as well, although they remained

favorite vacation spots for Westerners who often mourned the increased number of people who shared their wilderness beauty. See: Mrs. Mary B. Richards, *Camping Out in Yellowstone: A Letter Written in 1882 to The Salem Observer* (Salem, Ma., 1910); S. Anna Gordon, *Camping in Colorado with Suggestions to God-Seekers, Tourists and Invalids* (New York, 1879); Mrs. Mallie Stafford, *The March of Empire Through Three Decades Embracing Sketches of California History* (San Francisco, 1884); Sue A. Sanders, *A Journey To, On and From The "Golden Shore,"* (Delavan, Il., 1887); Annie B. Schenck, "Camping Vacation," *Colorado Magazine*, 42 (Summer 1965), pp. 185–215.

45. Katharine Horack, "The Quest for a Prairie Home," *Palimpsest*, 5 (July 1924), pp. 255–56; McIntyre, Observations. See also: Butler, "Diary of the Rogue River Valley," p. 349; Sara Bennett to her husband, AHS; Maddox, "The Diary of a Pioneer Girl;" Ronan, *Frontier Woman*; Paul, *A Victorian Gentlewoman*; and Myres, "Romance and Reality," pp. 138–39.

46. Hand, Diary; Mary Byram Wright, "Personal Recollections of the Early Settlement of Carlinville, Illinois," *Journal of the Illinois State Historical Society*, 18 (October 1925), p. 679; Ellen Pennock, "Incidents in My Life as a Pioneer," *Colorado Magazine*, 30 (April 1953), p. 126. Other typical descriptions of holiday celebrations include: Laura Hawn Patterson, Recollections of 1843, OHS; Haxby, Manuscripts; Letitia A. Chambers to her brother, July 18, 1856, OHS; Martin, Desert Memories; Tarwater, Family History; and Armand W. Reeder, "Memories of Christmas Customs in the West," St. Louis *Post Dispatch*, December 5, 1965, p. 5N.

47. For example, Wisconsin settler Elizabeth Baird recalled that their parties were all instigated by the men. "I never knew a lady to start any of these parties herself, although always ready to join in them." Baird, "Reminiscences," p. 216.

48. Sarah Sim quoted in Shor, "Problems in the Land of Opportunity," p. 25; Mary Pratt Staples, Reminiscences, BL.

49. Anne LeGrand to her mother, January 23, 1878, BTHC; Horack, "The Quest for a Prairie Home," p. 255.

50. Mabel Wakefield Moffitt, Reminiscences of an Arizona Pioneer, AHS. For similar comments, see: Cora Belle Mitchell to "Dear Friends," n.d., DPL; Clara Burt, Journal 1875–86, BL; and Sengstacken, *Destination, West!*, p. 218. The problems associated with sending children east to school are discussed in Ellen McGown Biddle, *Reminiscences of a Soldier's Wife* (Philadelphia, 1907), p. 139.

51. Staples, Reminiscences; Mrs. D. C. Martin, The A. B. Peach Family and Memories of Strawberry School, AHS; Lucia Darling, Diary, MoHS. For other comments concerning the founding of schools see: Horack, "Quest," pp. 255–56; Emma Tate, Papers, IHS; Eliza S. Warren, *Memoirs of the West* (Portland, 1916), p. 16; Wiltbank, Reminiscences; Ellen Throop, "Reminiscences of Pioneer Days" (n.p.), copy in NHS, p. 7; de Soza, Reminiscences; Recollections of Mrs. Mary A. Jones, BL; Mary Atkins, *The Diary of Mary Atkins* (Mills College, 1937); Joanna Harris Haines, "Seventy Years in Iowa," *Annals of Iowa*, 27 (October 1945), pp. 110–13; Sarah M. Black, Reminiscences, AHS; Brown, Biographical Sketch; Mrs. A. Avery, Interview #7974, Indian-Pioneer Papers, III, pp. 391–411; Martha Andrews, Interview #9700, Ibid., II, pp. 401–13; Mrs. Lee Whipple Haslam, *Early Days in California: Scenes and Events of the 50s as I Remember Them* (Jamestown, Ca., 1925), p. 25; Flower Valley School District, Edna Hatfield Collection, WHC; Isaac Holman to Col. Moore, April 17, 1835 in C.D. and William Donaldson Papers, BTHC; Biography of Mrs. Charles Lavender, BTHC; Willie Andrews, Pioneer School Association Papers, BTHC; "Early Settlements in Illinois: Some Recollections of Harriet Baker Winston," *Journal of the Illinois State Historical Society*, 18 (October 1925), p. 692; Willie Newbury Lewis, *Between Sun and Sod: An Informal History of the Texas Panhandle* (College Station, 1976), pp. 112–13; Martin, Desert Memories; Minerva Austin Smith to "Dear Folk," December 19, 1869, Minerva Austin Letters, 1869–89, KHS; Summers, Reminiscences and Mr. and Mrs. Jacob Stroup, Reminiscences.

A good summary of the development of schools and educational systems in the West is

Robert V. Hine, *The American West: An Interpretive History* (Boston, 1973), pp. 238–51. On the importance of the school as a civilizing agent see: Bernard Bailyn, *Education in the Forming of American Society: Needs and Opportunities for Study* (Chapel Hill), 1960, pp. 26–29; Lawrence A. Cremin, *Traditions of American Education* (New York, 1977), pp. 45–56; and Merle Curti, *The Making of An American Community: A Case Study of Democracy in a Frontier County* (Stanford, 1959), pp. 379–81.

52. Briones, "A Glimpse of Domestic Life," p. 470. On schools in the Spanish-Mexican Southwest, see: Perrigo, *Our Spanish Southwest*, pp. 81–87; Warren A. Beck, *New Mexico: A History of Four Centuries* (Norman, 1962), pp. 206–9; I. J. Cox, "Education Efforts in San Fernando de Bexar," *Southwestern Historical Quarterly*, 6 (July 1902), pp. 27–63; and Jones, *Los Paisanos*, p. 249. Beck included an excellent discussion of the difficulty in establishing public schools in these areas after the American occupation. This problem is also discussed in Simon F. Kropp, "Albert F. Fountain and the Fight for Public Education in New Mexico," *Arizona and the West*, 11 (Winter 1969), pp. 341–58. On the schools established by Roman Catholic sisters, see: Sister Mary Joanna Walsh, Sketch, Pioneering to Denver, Opening of the School—St. Mary's Academy, June 1864, DPL (copy of a ms. in the Archives of Loretto Motherhouse, Loretto, Kentucky); Diary of Sister Monica, 1870 and 100 Years in Arizona, The Sisters of St. Joseph Carondelet, AHS; Sister Lilliana Owens, "Our Lady of Light Academy, Santa Fe," *New Mexico Historical Review*, 13 (April 1938), pp. 129–45; and Sister Blandina Segale, *At the End of the Santa Fe Trail* (Columbus, Oh. 1932).

53. Of the 182 colleges founded before the Civil War that lasted into the twentieth century, 49 were Presbyterian, 34 Methodist, 25 Baptist, and 21 Congregationalist. Hine, *The American West*, p. 244. These figures, of course, do not include the numerous small academies and mission schools or the colleges which did not survive into the modern period. Also see: Beck, *New Mexico*, pp. 211–12. A typical Protestant mission school is described in Walter N. Vernon, "Early Echoes from Bloomfield Academy," *Chronicles of Oklahoma*, 52 (Summer 1974), pp. 237–43.

54. Ross, Recollections; Margaret E. Murray, "Memoirs of the William Archer Family," *Annals of Iowa*, 39 (Summer 1968), p. 366; Curti, *The Making of an American Community*, p. 384; Martha Nettie McFarlin Gray, Adventures of John Green McFarlin and Autobiography, BTHC.

55. Mrs. George Brauer, Interview, Indian-Pioneer Papers, X, p. 402; Mabel Sharpe Beavers, Interview, Ibid., VI, p. 307. According to another woman, "the people held a meeting . . . and decided to have a school. Everyone worked, some men plowed up the sod, women worked carrying it to the men who were erecting this sod house." Madge Alford, Interview, Indian-Pioneer Papers, II, p. 37.

56. See: Joan Hoff Wilson, "The Illusion of Change: Women and the American Revolution," in Alfred F. Young, ed., *The American Revolution: Explorations in the History of American Radicalism* (De Kalb, Ill., 1976), pp. 410–14 and Nancy F. Cott, *The Bond of Womanhood, "Women's Sphere" in New England, 1780–1835* (New Haven, 1977), pp. 101–25 for discussions of the reforms in women's education.

57. Horace Mann, *Common School Journal*, 8 (1846), p. 117 quoted in Willard S. Elsbree, *The American Teacher: Evolution of a Profession in a Democracy* (New York, 1939), p. 201. Elsbree included a discussion of the reasons for the influx of women into the teaching profession, pp. 144–208. Also see: Redding S. Sugg, *Mother Teachers: The Feminization of American Education* (Charlottesville, Va., 1979).

58. The difference in pay between male and female teachers was often substantial and the disparity became greater as time went on. For example in Kansas in 1880 "the average monthly salary for male teachers was $6.49 more than for female teachers, $6.84 more in 1900, and nearly $17.00 more in 1914." In Nebraska men made $4.20 more a month than women teachers in 1880, $9.80 in 1900, and $21.89 in 1914. Wayne E. Fuller, "Country School-

teaching on the Sod-House Frontier," *Arizona and the West*, 17 (Summer 1975), p. 124. When Esther Selover got her first teaching job, she recalled, "I won out against my competitors, probably because I was willing to accept a dollar and a half a week . . . while my illustrious opponents [all male] held out for two dollars." Sengstacken, *Destination, West!* p. 28. See also: Phoebe W. Sudlow quoted in Cornelia M. Banhart, "Phoebe W. Sudlow," *Palimpsest*, 51 (January 1970), pp. 169–76.

In 1870 in twelve states and territories (California, Colorado, Dakota, Idaho, Kansas, Montana, Nebraska, Nevada, New Mexico, Oregon, Washington, and Wyoming), 2,708 teachers were males and 3,054 were females. William Sprague, *Women and the West: A Short Social History* (Boston, 1940), p. 148.

59. Robert E. Belding, "Iowa's Brave Model for Women's Education," *Annals of Iowa*, 43 (Summer 1976), p. 347; Vernon Carstensen, "The State University of Iowa: The Collegiate Department from the Beginning to 1878," Ph.D. dissertation, State University of Iowa, 1936, 2 vols; I, p. 192. Women's education improved on all levels during the last half of the nineteenth century. In 1900 in eleven states of the Far West, 78,416 women between the ages of fifteen and twenty were enrolled in educational institutions, but only 68,580 young men in the same category. According to the compiler of these statistics, "These figures are even more impressive in view of the fact that the percentage of young people in this age group in schools or colleges was higher for this group of Western states than for any other section of the country, and the fact that men outnumbered the women in the West." Sprague, *Women and the West*, pp. 192–93. Also see: Hine, *The American West*, pp. 248–49.

60. Even Western school trustees, who were often hard-pressed to find teachers, sometimes were dubious about hiring young women whom they feared would not be able to control the rowdier boys. "Father seen some of the directors in both districts," a young Oregon woman wrote, "but they were not in favor of women teacher's [sic] he spoke to them a good while ago about the school for you but they wanted men teachers and they have got them." Emily L. Burrows, to "Dear Friend," April 10, 1874 in Burrows Correspondence.

61. On the crucial role of women as civilizers on the frontier, see: Erick Erickson, *Childhood and Society*, 2nd ed. (New York, 1963) pp. 291–92 and Julie Jeffrey, *Frontier Women: The Trans-Mississippi West* (New York, 1979), pp. 11–14.

There is a rich literature on women as teachers. See, for example: Clara S. Conron, Diary 1884, KHS; Diary of Angeline Brown, copy in HEH; Examination Papers of Rose Hattich, William and Rose Hattich Papers, AHS; Memories of Strawberry School; Andrews, Pioneer School Association Papers; Ruth Gordon, Portrait of a Teacher: Mary Elizabeth Post and Something of the Times in Which She Lived, University of Arizona Special Collections; Sarah Jane Price, Papers, 1878–95, NHS; Notes of Mrs. Mary Gray McLench, OHS; Darling, Diary; Eleanor Elizabeth Gordon, *A Little Bit of A Long Ago Story* (Humboldt, Ia., 1934); Lila Gravatt Scrimsher, ed., "The Diary of Anna Webber: Early Day Teacher of Mitchell County," *Kansas Historical Quarterly*, 38 (Autumn 1972), pp. 320–37; Pennock, "Incidents in My Life as a Pioneer," pp. 128–29; Jennie A. Wriston, *A Pioneer's Odyssey* (Menasha, Wi., 1943), pp. 89–90; Michael B. Husband, ed., "The Recollections of a Schoolteacher in the Disappointment Creek Valley," *Colorado Magazine*, 51 (Spring 1974), pp. 141–56; Anna Johnson, "Recollections of a Country School Teacher," *Annals of Iowa*, 42 (Winter 1975), pp. 485–505; Alice Applegate Peil, "Old Oregon School Days," *Oregon Historical Quarterly*, 59 (September 1958), pp. 197–207; Louis Fuller, ed., *An Ohio Schoolmistress: The Memoirs of Irene Hardy* (Kent, Oh., 1980); James Smallwood, *And Gladly Teach: Reminiscences of Teachers from Frontier Dugout to Modern Module* (Norman, 1976).

62. Sprague, *Women and the West*, p. 201. Kentucky granted limited school suffrage in 1838, and full school suffrage was voted in Kansas in 1861; Michigan and Minnesota, 1875; Colorado, 1876; New Hampshire and Oregon, 1878; Massachusetts, 1879; New York and

Vermont, 1880; Nebraska, 1883; North and South Dakota, Montana, Arizona, and New Jersey, 1887. Eugene A. Hecker, *A Short History of Women's Rights,* reprint ed. (Westport, Conn. 1971), p. 167.

63. Faragher, *Women and Men,* p. 181. Also see his discussion on pp. 112–21.

64. Ibid., p. 119.

65. Daniel Chaplin, *A Discourse Delivered before the Charitable Female Society in Groton, October 19, 1814* (Andover, Ma., 1814), p. 9 and Dr. John Gregory, *A Father's Legacy to his Daughters* (London, 1822), pp. 11–12 quoted in Cott, *Bonds of Womanhood,* pp. 128–29.

66. Barbara Welter, "The Feminization of American Religion, 1800–1860," in Welter, *Dimity Convictions: The American Woman in the Nineteenth Century* (Athens, Oh., 1976), pp. 83–102. Also see: Wilson, "The Illusion of Change," pp. 406–10.

67. Lovejoy, Diary; Embee, Diary; Francis Ingalls, Diary, State Historical Society of Wisconsin quoted in Curti, *The Making of An American Community,* p. 27. For the comments of several ministers in a similar vein, see: Walter R. Hauf, ed., "American Home Missionary Society Letters from Iowa," *Annals of Iowa,* 37 (Summer and Fall, 1963), pp. 45–76, 95–120. Also see: Benson, From Beloit Wisconsin.

68. Martin, Desert Memories; Mary and Esther St. John, "Prairie Diary," Glenda Riley, ed., *Annals of Iowa,* 44 (Fall 1977), p. 110. Also see: Robert M. Gatke, ed., "Kitturah Belknap's Chronicle of the Bellfountain Settlement," *Oregon Historical Quarterly,* 38 (September 1937), pp. 268–71. The classic description of the itinerant preacher is Edward Eggleston's 1874 novel *The Circuit Rider.* Also see: R. J. Eidem, "North Dakota Preaching Points: A Synopsis of Settlement," *North Dakota History,* 45 (Winter 1978), pp. 10–13 for a demographic study of the relationship between settlement and establishment of churches in one Western area.

69. Delaney, *A Survivor's Recollections;* Kitturah Belknap, "Family Life on the Frontier: The Diary of Kitturah Penton Belknap," Glenda Riley, ed., *Annals of Iowa,* 44 (Summer 1977), p. 43. Also see Belknap's descriptions of two Oregon camp meetings in Gatke, "Kitturah Belknap's Chronicle," pp. 263–99. For other women's comments on camp meetings and the social aspects of church affairs see: Memoirs of Mrs. Luella Harrah MacIntire to Grace Tyree Lewellen, Memoirs of Mrs. Cora Milla Kirkpatrick, and At Home in a Dugout, all in PPHA; John Hutto, "Mrs. Elizabeth (Aunt Hank) Smith," *West Texas Historical Association Yearbook,* 15 (October 1939), p. 43; Life Experiences of Pickey: Written by Mrs. L. C. Saunders, BTHC; Bivans, "The Diary of Luna E. Warner," p. 423; Wilson, Diary; Mrs. Isabel Eldridge, A Bit of Local History, UWA. An excellent discussion of the camp meeting is Charles A. Johnson, *The Frontier Camp Meeting: Religion's Harvest Time* (Dallas, 1955), especially pp. 122–44.

70. See Georgia Harkness, "Pioneer Women in the Ministry," *Religion in Life,* 39 (1970), pp. 261–71 for a discussion of these and other early female ministers.

71. Lucy Jane Dabney, Walter Scales Dabney and Family, BTHC; M.E.D. Trowbridge, *Pioneer Days: The Life Story of Gershom and Elizabeth Day* (Philadelphia, 1895). See also: Peggy Dow, *Vicissitudes, or The Journey of Life,* 3rd ed. (Philadelphia, 1816); Mary W. Gaylord, *Life and Labors of Rev. Reuben Gaylord* (Omaha, 1889); Ann James Marshall, *The Autobiography of Mrs. A. J. Marshall, Age 84 Years* (Pine Bluff, Ar., 1897); and Anna M. Simpson, Annals of My Parsonage Life, IHS.

72. Allen, Diary; Diary of Jerusha Loomis Farnham in *Log City Days: Two Narratives on the Settlement of Galesburg, Illinois* (Galesburg, Il., 1937), pp. 38–39. For other descriptions of women's activities, see: Cool, Frontier Life; Minerva Austin to "Dear Folks," April 17, 1870 in Minerva Austin Letters, KHS; Sisk, Reminiscences; Maria Jane Renshaw, Diary, 1858, OHS; Susan B. Diamond, Diary, 1866, KHS; Mrs. Warren R. Fowler, A Woman's Experiences in Colorado, BL; Moffitt, Reminiscences; Tillson, *A Woman's Story,* pp. 146–47; Pennock, "Incidents in My Life," pp. 126–27; Luella Shaw, *True History of Some of the Pioneers of Colorado* (Hotchkiss, Co., 1909), p. 238; Lois L. Murray, *Incidents of Frontier Life* (Goshen, In.,

1880), pp. 103–5, 163–64; Gatke, "Kitturah Belknap's Chronicle," pp. 263–99; and Fry, "Women on the Ohio Frontier," p. 70. On women's growing role in the church, see: Cott, *Bonds of Womanhood*, pp. 126–59 and Welter, "The Feminization of American Religion."

73. On Mormon women and their role in the church see: Leonard Arrington, "Blessed Damozels: Women in Mormon History," *Dialogue*, 6 (Summer 1971), pp. 24–25; Cheryll May, "Charitable Sisters," in Claudia L. Bushman, ed., *Mormon Sisters, Women in Early Utah* (Salt Lake City, 1976), pp. 225–39; Juanita Brooks, ed., *Not by Bread Alone: The Journal of Martha Spence Heywood* (Salt Lake City, 1978); S. George Ellsworth, *Dear Ellen: Two Mormon Women and Their Letters* (Salt Lake City, 1974), and Dix, "The Josephine Diaries," pp. 167–83; Cedenia Bagley Willis, Journal, AHS; A Sketch of the Life of Tabitha Hendricks Ricks by Herself, IHS; The History of Hans Christian Jensen and Helen Flamm Jensen, IHS.

74. Emma Tate Papers, IHS; Judson, *A Pioneer's Search*, p. 279.

75. Mattie Lykins-Bingham, "Recollections of Old Times," *Westport Historical Quarterly*, 7 (Fall 1971), pp. 18–19; Potter, "The Ranch Letters of Emma Robertson," p. 229. In Florence, Arizona, women were influential in organizing Protestant services and eventually in securing a Presbyterian minister and building a church. Summers, Reminiscences. The efforts of another group of women to secure a church for their community are discussed in Mildred Searcy, "The Little Brown Jug," *Historical Magazine of the Protestant Episcopal Church*, 43 (March 1974), pp. 57–64. For other women's descriptions of church organization and building see: Belknap, "Family Life," p. 43; Bird-Dumont, Autobiography; Mrs. Ben Hartsuck, Reminiscing, UWA; Conway, *Thirty Years in Camp with the Texas Rangers*, p. 29; de Soza, Reminiscences; Throop, *Reminiscences of Pioneer Days*, p. 7; Lewis, *Between Sun and Sod*, pp. 112–16; Sarah Royce, *A Frontier Lady: Recollections of the Gold Rush and Early California*, reprint ed. (Lincoln, 1977), p. 104. An interesting view of the same subject from the prospective of a missionary minister is Virginia McLoughlin, ed., "Establishing a Church on the Kansas Frontier: The Letters of the Rev. O. L. Woodford and His Sister Henrietta, 1857–1859," *Kansas Historical Quarterly*, 37 (Summer 1971), pp. 153–91. Good general descriptions of the problems of frontier congregations and ministers can be found in Curti, *The Making of an American Community*, pp. 127–31; Richard Bartlett, *The New Country: A Social History of the American Frontier, 1776–1890* (New York, 1974), pp. 368–80; and Hine, *The American West*, pp. 222–37.

76. Welter, "The Feminization of American Religion," p. 316.

77. Murray, "Memoirs," p. 366.

78. Almost every pioneer reminiscence or diary mentions such activities. See, for example: Mrs. Walter Ferguson, "The Trail to No-Man's Land," courtesy of Anne Morgan; Tarwater, Family History; Recollections of Mrs. Mary A. (Smith) Jones, BL; Anna Cameron, Transcripts of Interviews, NHS; May Bennett Avery, Memories of Pioneer Days, NHS; Brown, Biographical Sketch; Pennock, "Incidents in My Life," p. 126.

79. Tilitha Jane Blackburn, Interview #9183, Indian-Pioneer Papers, VIII, p. 283. See also: Myrel Kirkpatrick Gastil, Interview, Edna Hatfield Collections, WHC; Cameron, Transcripts of Interviews; Avery, Memories of Pioneer Days; Summers, Reminiscence; Elizabeth B. Harbert Papers, HEH; Elizabeth Greenfield, "Shakespearean 'Culture' in Montana, 1902," *Montana*, 22 (April 1972), pp. 48–55; and Altrocchi, "Paradox Town," pp. 35–37.

80. Alexis de Tocqueville, *Democracy in America*, II, p. 106 quoted in Keith Melder, "Ladies Bountiful, Organized Women's Benevolence in Early Nineteenth Century America," *New York History*, 48 (July 1967), p. 231.

81. Ibid., p. 232. Also see: Louise Moede Lex, "Mary Newbury Adams: Feminist Forerunner from Iowa," *Annals of Iowa*, 43 (Summer 1976), pp. 323–26; T. Scott Miyakawa, *Protestants and Pioneers* (Chicago, 1964), pp. 199–201, 213–16, 229–32; and Carroll Smith Rosenberg, "Beauty, The Beast and the Militant Woman: A Case Study in Sex Roles and Social Stress in Jacksonian America," *American Quarterly*, 23 (October 1971), pp. 562–84.

82. Farnham in *Log City Days*, p. 43; "Diary of Mary Walker," p. 15; Eveline Alexander

to her mother, February 22, 1867, private collection quoted in Sandra L. Myres, ed., *Cavalry Wife: The Diary of Eveline M. Alexander* (College Station, Tex., 1977), p. 160 n24. Also see Clifford M. Drury, "The Columbia Maternal Association," in Helen K. Smith, ed., *With Her Own Wings* (Portland, 1948), pp. 169–71; Melder, "Ladies Bountiful," pp. 231–54; Louisa J. Roberts, *Biographical Sketch of Louisa J. Roberts with Extracts From Her Journal and Selections from Her Writings* (Philadelphia, 1895).

83. Caroline M. Seymour Severence, *The Mother of Clubs: An Estimate and an Appreciation,* Ella G. Ruddy, ed. (Los Angeles, 1906), pp. 23, 24. On the women's club movement, in addition to Severence, see: Mrs. J. C. Croly, *The History of the Woman's Club Movement in America* (New York, 1898) and Mary I. Wood, *The History of the General Federation of Women's Clubs* (New York, 1912). The diverse activities of one of the largest and best-known Western women's clubs are described in Thelma Lee Hubbell and Gloria R. Lothrop, "The Friday Morning Club: A Los Angeles Legacy," *Southern California Historical Quarterly,* 50 (March 1968), pp. 59–90.

84. Adriance, Reminiscences; Dunlap, "Ancotty"; Aggie Loring to her mother, December 21, 1876, AHS. According to the Texas Women's Resource Center, Women's Club members organized 85 percent of all the public libraries in Texas. *Texas National Dispatch,* 1 (November 1981), p. 1.

85. Summers, Reminiscences; "The Women's Club Movement in Texas," unpublished essay in private collection; Wood, *History of the General Federation,* p. 3. Also see: Staples, Reminiscences; Shaw Family Papers, NHS; Claim of Mrs. Rena Mathews; Prosch, *David S. Maynard and Catherine T. Maynard,* p. 78; and Nelson A. Ault, "The Earnest Ladies: The Walla Walla Women's Club and the Equal Suffrage League of 1886–1889," *Pacific Northwest Quarterly,* 42 (April 1951), pp. 123–37; Katherine Clinton, "Pioneer Women in Chicago, 1830–1837," *Journal of the West,* 12 (April 1973), pp. 317–24; Lykins-Bingham, "Recollections of Old Times," pp. 15–24; Grace R. Pratt, "The Great-Hearted Huttons of the Coeur d'Alenes," *Montana,* 17 (Spring 1967), pp. 20–23; Barbara Lowney, "Lady Bountiful: Margaret Crocker of Sacramento," *California Historical Quarterly,* 47 (June 1968), pp. 99–112; and Helen Cannon, "First Ladies of Colorado: Jane Olivia Barnes Cooper," *Colorado Magazine,* 44 (Spring 1967), pp. 129–38 for other discussions of women's civic and philanthropic acitvities.

86. Dr. Ruth Flowers quoted in Sue Armitage, Theresa Banfield, and Sarah Jacobus, "Black Women and Their Communities in Colorado," *Frontiers,* 2 (1977), p. 46. This article contains an excellent discussion of the role of black women in community development. See also: Williard Gatewood, "Kate D. Chapman Reports on 'The Yankton Colored People,' 1889," *South Dakota History,* 7 (Winter 1976), pp. 28–35; Dorothy Bass Spann, *Black Pioneers: A History of a Pioneer Family in Colorado Springs* (Colorado Springs, 1978); and Mrs. Nellie Bush, Interview, Indian-Pioneer Papers, XIV, p. 53.

87. Elizabeth Fisk to her mother, Fisk Family Papers, MoHS, quoted in Petrik, "The Bonanza Town: Women and Family on the Frontier," unpublished essay, SUNY Binghamton, 1979; Susan Wallace, *The Land of the Pueblo* (New York, 1888), p. 69; Elizabeth Thorpe, "The Owls of Newcastle," *Montana,* 19 (April 1969), pp. 71–73.

88. Mary Bailey, "Journal of Mary Stuart Bailey," in Sandra L. Myres, ed., *Ho For California!* (San Marino, 1980), p. 66; Louise A. K. Clappe, *The Shirley Letters from the California Mines, 1851–1852* (New York, 1961), p. 49; Chicago doctor quoted in Clinton, "Pioneer Women in Chicago," p. 318; Julia Lovejoy, "Letters from Kansas," *Kansas Historical Quarterly,* 11 (February 1942), p. 34.

89. Haines, *A Bride on the Bozeman Trail,* p. 76; Whipple-Haslam, *Early Days in California,* p. 15.

90. For typical remarks by women on frontier violence, see: Julia T. Dodge, Letters, 1856–80, DPL; Adriance, Reminiscence; Hutto, "Mrs. Elizabeth (Aunt Hank) Smith," pp.

40–47; Martin, *My Desert Memories*; Brown, *Biographical Sketch*; Ferguson, "The Trail to No-Man's Land;" de Soza, *Reminiscences*; Haxby, *Manuscripts*; Julia Canby to Mrs. Carter, May 9, 1858, DPL; John McClellan Family, *Short History*, IHS; Hively, *Journal*; Susanna Roberts Townsend to "Dear Sister," April 16, 1852, BL; Stella to "My Dear Little Sister," January 28, 1866, NHS; and Caroline Richardson, *Diary*, BL.

91. Richard M. Brown, "Historical Patterns of Violence in America," in Hugh Graham and Ted Gurr, eds., *Violence in America: Historical and Comparative Perspectives* (New York, 1969), pp. 45–46.

92. There are several good studies of the vigilance committees. For an overview, see Hine, *The American West*, pp. 300–309 and the Brown article cited above. More detailed studies include: Wayne Gard, *Frontier Justice* (Norman, 1949); Philip D. Jordan, *Frontier Law and Order: Ten Essays* (Lincoln, 1970); and Alan C. Valentine, *Vigilante Justice* (New York, 1956). Also see: David J. Bodenhamer, "Law and Disorder on the Early Frontier: Marion County, Indiana, 1823–1850," *Western Historical Quarterly*, 10 (July 1979), pp. 323–36 for a discussion of the effects of violence in a frontier community.

93. Durango, Colorado *Record*, April 9, 1881 quoted in David Lavender, "The Petrified West and the Writer" in Gerald Haslam, ed., *Western Writing* (Albuquerque, 1974), p. 148; Clappe, *The Shirley Letters*, pp. 97–98. For other women's comments on vigilante activity, see: Maddox, "The Diary of a Pioneer Girl;" Stella to her sister, 1866, NHS; and Roger Lotchin, *San Francisco, 1846–1856* (New York, 1974), pp. 255–60.

Chapter 8

1. Most of the books on women's suffrage also deal with married women's property rights, or lack thereof. For typical treatments, see: Andrew Sinclair, *The Emancipation of American Woman* (New York, 1965), pp. 83–91; Page Smith, *Daughters of the Promised Land: Women in American History* (Boston, 1970), pp. 103–21; and Eleanor Flexner, *Century of Struggle: The Woman's Rights Movement in the United States* (Cambridge, 1959), pp. 1–22. Also see: James P. Louis, "The Roots of Feminism: A Review Essay," *Civil War History*, 17 (June 1971), pp. 162–70 and Ellen C. DuBois, *Feminism and Suffrage: The Emergence of an Independent Woman's Movement in America, 1848–1869* (Ithaca, 1978).

2. Mary S. Benson, *Women in Eighteenth-Century America: A Study of Opinion and Social Usage* (New York, 1935), p. 238. For full discussions of the legal status of women in colonial America see, in addition to Benson, pp. 223–58: Richard B. Morris, *Studies in the History of American Law* (New York, 1930), pp. 126–200 and Mary R. Beard, *Woman as Force in History: A Study in Traditions and Realities* (New York, 1946), pp. 77–169. All three point out that colonial women had more legal freedom than the leaders of the women's suffrage movement assumed they had and that the concept of "civil death" was strongly modified in American practice.

3. Morris, *Studies*, pp. 133, 134. Also see, Sinclair, *Emancipation*, pp. 21–32 and Flexner, *Century of Struggle*, pp. 9–13. Sinclair maintains that women like Brent and Hutchinson were not feminists but "rebels who happened to be women." Sinclair, *Emancipation*, p. 32.

4. Charles Francis Adams, *Familiar Letters of John Adams and His Wife Abigail Adams During the Revolution* (New York, 1876), pp. 149–50 quoted in Flexner, *Century of Struggle*, p. 15; Caroline Gilman, ed., *Letters of Eliza Wilkinson . . .* , reprint ed. (New York, 1969) quoted in Mary Beth Norton, " 'What an Alarming Crisis Is This': Southern Women and the American Revolution," in Jeffrey J. Crow and Larry E. Tise, eds., *The Southern Experience in the American Revolution* (Chapel Hill, 1978), pp. 221–22.

5. Joan Hoff Wilson, "The Illusion of Change: Women and the American Revolution," in Alfred F. Young, ed., *The American Revolution: Explorations in the History of American Radi-*

calism (DeKalb, Il., 1976), pp. 383–445. Norton offers a somewhat different interpretation in her essay.

6. Sinclair, *Emancipation,* p. 42.

7. "The Forgotten Feminist of Kansas: The Papers of Clarina I. H. Nichols, 1854–1885," Joseph G. Gambone, ed., *Kansas Historical Quarterly,* 39 (Spring 1973), p. 20. This idea is discussed in T. A. Larson, "Woman Suffrage in Wyoming," *Pacific Northwest Quarterly,* 56 (April 1965), p. 57.

8. Theodora W. Youmans, "How Women Won the Ballot," *Wisconsin Magazine of History,* 5 (September 1921), pp. 3–4, 6; Ann L. W. Wilhite, "Sixty-Five Years Till Victory: A History of Woman Suffrage in Nebraska," *Nebraska History,* 49 (Summer 1968), p. 150; "Forgotten Feminist," pp. 22–24.

9. Ruth A. Gallaher, *Legal and Political Status of Women in Iowa* (Iowa City, 1918), pp. 152–5 quoted in Glenda Riley, *Frontierswomen: The Iowa Experience* (Ames, 1981), p. 155.

10. Other early reforms came in Kentucky where women were granted a limited school franchise in 1838, in Mississippi where an 1839 bill gave married women control of their own property, and in Texas and California which also provided protection for married women's property in their first state constitutions. See William F. Sprague, *Women and the West: A Short Social History* (Boston, 1940), pp. 93–94 and Lawrence M. Friedman, *A History of American Law* (New York, 1973), pp. 185–86. Peggy A. Rabkin, *Fathers to Daughters: The Legal Foundations of Female Emancipation* (Westport, Conn., 1980).

11. Youmans, "How Women Won," p. 7. On women's work during the Civil War, see Flexner, *Century of Struggle,* pp. 105–14; Mary Elizabeth Massey, *Bonnet Brigades: American Women and the Civil War* (New York, 1966); and the contemporary work on the Sanitary Commission, Linus P. Brockett and Mary C. Vaughan, *Women's Work in the Civil War* (Boston, 1867).

12. On the split between the two organizations, see Flexner, *Century of Struggle,* pp. 145–66; Robert Riegel, "The Split in the Feminist Movement," *Journal of American History,* 49 (December 1962), pp. 485–96; James M. McPherson, "Abolitionists, Woman Suffrage, and the Negro, 1865–1869," *Mid-America,* 47 (January 1965), pp. 40–47; and William O'Neill, *Everyone was Brave: A History of Feminism in America* (Chicago, 1971), pp. 18–21.

13. Youmans, "How Women Won," p. 9.

14. Wilhite, "Sixty-Five Years Till Victory," p. 151. The school suffrage was partially revoked in 1875 when it was restricted to include only unmarried women.

15. On the Iowa vote, see Riley, *Frontierswomen,* pp. 158–60; Gallaher, *Legal and Political Status,* pp. 176–79; and Frank E. Horack, "Equal Suffrage in Iowa" in Benjamin F. Shambaugh, *Applied History,* 6 vols. (Iowa City, 1914), II, pp. 298–300. On the Kansas campaign, see: Sister Jeanne McKenna, " 'With the Help of God and Lucy Stone,' " *Kansas Historical Quarterly,* 36 (Spring 1970), pp. 13–26; Flexner, *Century of Struggle,* pp. 149–50; and the accounts of Henry Blackwell, Lucy Stone, and Susan Anthony in Elizabeth Cady Stanton, Susan B. Anthony, and Matilda Joslyn Gage, eds., *History of Woman's Suffrage,* 6 vols. (Rochester, N.Y., 1881–1922), II, pp. 229–43, and "Campaigning for Women Suffrage in Kansas as Told by Mrs. Elizabeth Cady Stanton," in Sprague, *Women and the West,* pp. 262–66.

16. Flexner, *Century of Struggle,* p. 178. For example, referendum campaigns were carried on in Michigan in 1874, Colorado in 1877, Nebraska in 1882, Oregon in 1884, Washington in 1889, and South Dakota in 1890. Washington approved women's suffrage in 1910 and became the fifth state to extend the franchise to women.

17. Moreover, argued Howard B. Furer in "The American City: A Catalyst for the Women's Rights Movement," *Wisconsin Magazine of History,* 52 (Summer 1969), pp. 285–305, only when people were well settled in urban communities did they feel "secure and settled enough to question the established ways" in regard to the status of women. Even in the

West, he concluded, "the greater social and political advances were occurring in the cities. Suffrage sentiment moved westward across the plains and mountains as towns and new cities were being formed," p. 296.

18. Quoted in Lynne Cheney, "It All Began in Wyoming," *American Heritage,* 24 (April 1973), p. 64.

19. As national organizer, Carrie Chapman Catt, noted, "The better the campaign, the more certain that suffrage would be defeated at the polls." Carrie C. Catt, *Woman Suffrage and Politics: The Inner Story of the Suffrage Movement* (New York, 1926), p. 130.

20. Edward M. Lee, *The Galaxy,* June 1872, quoted in T. A. Larson, "Woman Suffrage in Western America," *Utah Historical Quarterly,* 38 (Winter 1970), p. 13.

21. Historians in the late nineteenth and early twentieth century usually credited Mrs. Esther Morris with a much more crucial role in the suffrage movement in Wyoming than she seemed to have actually played. Larson contends, with a good deal of substantiating evidence, that Morris' role was more the invention of later suffragists looking for heroines than actual fact. See Larson, "Woman Suffrage in Wyoming," pp. 57–66. A view similar to Larson's is in Cheney, "It All Began in Wyoming." For the traditional suffragist viewpoint, see: Sprague, *Women and the West,* pp. 174–177; Mae Urbanek, "Justice of the Peace," in Western Writers of America, *The Women Who Made the West* (Garden City, 1980), pp. 198–203.

22. *The Woman's Journal,* March 9, 1872 quoted in Larson, "Woman Suffrage in Western America," p. 15.

23. The small number of legislators in Wyoming may be another key to the success of the suffrage proposal; there simply were not as many men to convince.

24. In addition to the articles cited above, see: T. A. Larson, "Dolls, Vassals, and Drudges: Pioneer Women in the West," *Western Historical Quarterly,* 3 (January 1972), pp. 5–9; "Petticoats at the Polls: Woman Suffrage in Territorial Wyoming," *Pacific Northwest Quarterly,* 44 (April 1953), pp. 74–79; and "Wyoming's Contribution to the Regional and National Women's Rights Movements," *Annals of Wyoming,* 52 (Spring 1980), pp. 2–14; G[race] R. Hebard, "The First Woman Jury," *Journal of American History,* 7 (November 4, 1913), pp. 1293–1341; and Alan P. Grimes, *The Puritan Ethic and Woman Suffrage* (New York, 1967), pp. 47–77.

25. *Deseret Evening News,* March 17, 1869, quoted in Larson, "Dolls, Vassals and Drudges," p. 10.

26. Ibid., p. 11. To reinforce the Mormon leaders' belief in women's support for polygamy, the women held a mass meeting in January 1870 to protest a pending Congressional antipolygamy bill.

27. In addition to Larson's "Dolls, Vassals, and Drudges," pp. 9–13 see: Thomas G. Alexander, "An Experiment in Progressive Legislation: The Granting of Woman Suffrage in Utah in 1870," *Utah Historical Quarterly,* 38 (Winter 1970), pp. 20–30; Beverly Beeton, "Woman Suffrage in Territorial Utah," *Utah Historical Quarterly,* 46 (Spring 1978), pp. 100–120; and Grimes, *The Puritan Ethic,* pp. 27–46.

28. Larson, "Dolls, Vassals, and Drudges," p. 12; Alexander, "An Experiment in Progressive Legislation," p. 27. Some of the women, however, were not so enthusiastic about exercising the vote. At one women's meeting in Salt Lake City some women "admitted they had always considered politics beneath women and were thus not interest in voting." Beeton, "Woman Suffrage," pp. 115–16.

29. Beeton, "Woman Suffrage," pp. 106–10.

30. Grimes, *The Puritan Ethic,* p. 41; Alexander, "An Experiment in Progressive Legislation," pp. 29–30; Beeton, "Woman Suffrage," pp. 116–18; Larson, "Dolls, Vassals, and Drudges," pp. 12–13.

31. Jean B. White, "Woman's Place Is In the Constitution: The Struggle for Equal Rights in Utah in 1895," *Utah Historical Quarterly,* 42 (Fall 1974), pp. 344–69.

32. A. H. De France quoted in Billie Barnes Jensen, "Colorado Woman Suffrage Campaigns of the 1870s," *Journal of the West*, 12 (April 1973), p. 257.

33. Wilbur F. Stone, *History of Colorado*, 5 vols. (Chicago, 1918), I, p. 689. Also see Larson, "Woman Suffrage in Western America," p. 16.

34. Jensen, "Colorado Woman Suffrage Campaigns," pp. 256–60.

35. Ibid., pp. 260–63; Colin B. Goodykoontz, "Some Controversial Questions Before the Colorado Constitutional Convention of 1876," *Colorado Magazine*, 17 (January 1940), pp. 1–17.

36. Jensen, "Colorado Woman Suffrage Campaigns," pp. 265–71 recounts the campaign in some detail. The charge by Anthony that the Mexican vote was responsible for the failure of suffrage is effectively refuted in William B. Faherty, "Regional Minorities and the Woman Suffrage Struggle," *Colorado Magazine*, 33 (July 1956), pp. 212–17.

37. Larson, "Woman Suffrage in Western America," p. 9.

38. G. Thomas Edwards, "Dr. Ada M. Weed: Northwest Reformer," *Oregon Historical Quarterly*, 78 (March 1977), pp. 10–23.

39. T. A. Larson, "The Woman Suffrage Movement in Washington," *Pacific Northwest Quarterly*, 67 (April 1976), pp. 49–50. See also: Stella E. Pearce, "Suffrage in the Pacific Northwest, Old Oregon and Washington," *Washington Historical Quarterly*, 3 (April 1912), pp. 106–10 and Sprague, *Women and the West*, pp. 171–72.

40. *New Northwest*, October 27, 1871, quoted in Larson, "The Woman Suffrage Movement," p. 50.

41. *Statutes of the Territory of Washington . . . 1871* quoted in Larson, "The Woman Suffrage Movement," p. 50.

42. Duniway reported in 1884 that "she had divided her time about equally between Oregon and Washington and had lectured in each about seventy times a year for twelve and one-half years." Larson, "The Woman Suffrage Movement," p. 53. Also see: Elizabeth F. Chittenden, " ' By No Means Excluding Women,' " *American West*, 12 (March 1975), pp. 24–27; Helen K. Smith, *The Presumptuous Dreamers: A Sociological History of the Life and Times of Abigail Scott Duniway, Volume 1, 1834–1871* (Lake Oswego, Or., 1974), pp. 151–53, 161–203; and Ruth B. Moynihan, "Abigail Scott Duniway of Oregon: Woman and Suffragist of the American Frontier," 2 vols., Ph.D. dissertation, Yale University, 1979, II, pp. 343–50.

43. Larson, "The Woman Suffrage Movement," pp. 50–52; Pearce, "Suffrage in the Pacific Northwest," pp. 110–11; Sprague, *Women and the West*, p. 172. For a contemporary account, see John Miller Murphy, "Woman Suffrage in Washington Territory," in Mary O. Douthit, ed., *The Souvenir of Western Women* (Portland, 1905), p. 104.

44. Larson, "The Woman Suffrage Movement," p. 54; Murphy, "Woman Suffrage," p. 106. On the connection between prohibition and suffrage see: Flexner, *Century of Struggle*, pp. 184–89; Sinclair, *Emancipation of the American Woman*, pp. 220–29; Janet Giele, "Social Change in the Feminist Role: A Comparison of Woman's Suffrage and Woman's Temperance, 1870–1920," Ph.D. dissertation, Radcliffe College, 1961; and Ruth Bordin, *Woman and Temperance: The Quest for Power and Liberty, 1873–1900* (Philadelphia, 1981).

45. The territorial code of 1881 made all electors and householders eligible for service on grand juries and all electors qualified to serve as petit jurors. Since the 1883 law made women electors and since married women were considered householders jointly with their husbands, married women obviously qualified for grand jury service. See Cladius O. Johnson, "George Turner of Supreme Court of Washington Territory," *Oregon Historical Quarterly*, 44 (December 1943), pp. 375–76.

46. Ibid., p. 378. In an earlier, very similar case, *Rosencrantz v. Territory of Washington*, the Court had held that both the jury provision and the suffrage portion of the 1883 act were valid. Turner dissented in that opinion; pp. 376–77.

47. Ibid., pp. 377–82. This decision was reaffirmed in 1888 by the court in *William M.*

White v. *Territory of Washington,* but in 1891 the ruling was reversed when the State Supreme Court unanimously held in *Marston* v. *Humes* that the code of 1881 was a valid and binding body of laws and could be amended by section number without any designation of the subject matter. Larson, "The Woman Suffrage Movement," p. 55. See also: Pearce, "Suffrage in the Pacific Northwest," pp. 111–12 and Nelson A. Ault, "The Earnest Ladies: The Walla Walla Women's Club and the Equal Suffrage League of 1886–1889," *Pacific Northwest Quarterly,* 42 (April 1951), pp. 128–31. Suffragists charged that Harland was simply a dupe for the liquor dealers and that he had been employed to help bring a case before the courts. Ault, "The Earnest Ladies," p. 130.

48. Larson, "The Woman Suffrage Movement," p. 55.

49. Ibid. Also see: Pearce, "Suffrage in the Pacific Northwest," pp. 112–13; Sprague, *Women and the West,* pp. 173–74; Murphy, "Woman Suffrage," pp. 106–7; and Ault, "The Earnest Ladies," pp. 132–37.

50. *House Journal of the General Assembly of the State of Colorado* (Denver, 1893), p. 195 as cited in Billie B. Jensen, "Let the Women Vote," *Colorado Magazine,* 41 (Winter 1964), p. 14.

51. Jensen, "Let the Women Vote," pp. 13–19; Sprague, *Women and the West,* pp. 178–80.

52. *Rocky Mountain News,* January 1, 1894 as quoted in Jensen, "Let the Women Vote," p. 23.

53. William McLeod Raine, "Truth About Woman Suffrage," *The Circle* (October 1907), p. 220 as quoted in Jensen, "Let the Women Vote," p. 22.

54. The importance of Populist support is clear from Jensen's analysis of the election. In the General Assembly she found that twenty-two Populists, eleven Republicans, and one Democrat supported the measure while four Populists, twenty-one Republicans, and three Democrats were opposed. In the Senate, twelve Populists, eight Republicans, and no Democrats supported the bill while one Populist, four Republicans, and five Democrats were opposed. In the election, thirty counties that had voted Populist in the previous election supported suffrage and only one Populist county did not. "The combined Republican and Democratic counties gave a total majority of 471 votes against," she concluded, ". . . while the combined Populist counties gave a majority of 6,818 for it." Jensen, "Let the Women Vote," p. 23. Although the source of some of Jensen's figures is questionable, they nonetheless point out the importance of the Populist Party in the women's victory. See also: Sprague, *Women and the West,* pp. 179–80 and T. A. Larson, "Woman Suffrage," in Howard Lamar, ed., *The Reader's Encyclopedia of the American West* (New York, 1977), pp. 1283–84.

55. According to T. A. Larson, "the story of the woman's rights movement in Idaho for more than twenty years after Dr. Morgan's abortive effort in 1871 is mainly the story of Mrs. Duniway's work . . ." T. A. Larson, "The Woman's Rights Movement in Idaho," *Idaho Yesterdays,* 16 (Spring 1972), p. 4.

56. Ibid., pp. 6–7. Larson suggested that some men opposed women's suffrage, others opposed prohibition, and still others opposed statehood. "Rather than invite a combination of such forces," he concluded, "the constitutional convention postponed woman suffrage and prohibition as well."

57. Ibid., p. 8.

58. Catt and other Eastern suffrage women effectively sidetracked Duniway whose participation they feared would upset the WCTU interests. Despite the seeming peace prevailing between the Idaho women and the NAWSA organizers and speakers, Catt noted that the Idaho women were "exceedingly touchy and we will have to be very cautious about helping them," for "there is always antagonism against the outsider as she is thought to be running things." Catt to Emma Smith Devoe, August 6, 1896 and Catt to Mrs. C. Holt Flint, December 29, 1894, both quoted in Larson, "Idaho's Role in America's Woman Suffrage Crusade," *Idaho Yesterdays,* 18 (Spring 1974), p. 3. The major parties at the time were the

Republicans, Democrats, Populists, and Silver Republicans. Suffrage won endorsement from all four. Larson, "The Woman's Rights Movement in Idaho," p. 11.

59. Resistance in the two areas was based on different reasons. The Populist miners feared that women, having used Populist support to obtain the vote, would then turn them out of office as they appeared to have done in Colorado. Anti-Mormon voters feared Mormon political strength in Idaho if Mormon women were allowed to vote. Ibid., p. 14.

60. On the final successful campaign, see ibid., pp. 14–15; Sprague, *Women and the West,* pp. 187–89; and William Balderston, "Women Suffrage in Idaho," in Douthit, *Souvenir,* pp. 117–18.

61. Larson, "The Woman's Rights Movement in Idaho," pp. 15, 18. Larson points out that although there were at least 15,000 women age twenty-one or over in Idaho in 1896, no more than a thousand were affiliated with the Idaho Equal Suffrage Association, and the key to victory rested in the hands of nineteen dedicated women and men, p. 14. Also see: Sprague, *Women and the West,* pp. 189–90 and statements by Carrie Chapman Catt and William Balderston quoted in Larson, "The Woman's Rights Movement in Idaho," p. 15 for other reasons advanced for the success of the Idaho campaign.

62. Larson, "The Woman's Rights Movement in Idaho," p. 19 and "Idaho's Role," p. 4. According to Larson, women occupied the state superintendent's office from 1898 until 1933 and several were elected to the legislature—three in 1898, two in 1908, one in 1914, one in 1916, and one in 1918. Larson, "Idaho's Role," p. 4.

63. Balderston, "Women Suffrage in Idaho," p. 117; James H. Brady in *The Woman's Journal,* September 25, 1909, quoted in Larson, "Idaho's Role," p. 4.

64. At the same time that suffrage carried in Washington by more than twenty-two thousand votes, it lost in Oregon by almost the same margin. Larson, "The Woman Suffrage Movement in Washington," p. 62.

65. Ibid., pp. 56–62. See also: C. H. Bailey, "How Washington Women Regained the Ballot," *Pacific Monthly,* 26 (1911), p. 9 and Benjamin H. Kizer, "May Arkwright Hutton," *Pacific Northwest Quarterly,* 57 (April 1966), pp. 53–55.

66. Despite the need for more extensive investigation and analysis of the successful campaigns in some areas, there is a fairly extensive literature on the Western suffrage movement. On the successful campaigns, see, in addition to the sources cited above: Jean Loewy, "Katherine Philips Edson and the California Suffragette Movement, 1919–1920," *California Historical Society Quarterly,* 47 (December 1968), pp. 343–50; Ronald Schaffer, "The Problem of Consciousness in the Woman Suffrage Movement: A California Perspective," *Pacific Historical Review,* 45 (November 1976), pp. 469–94; Ronald W. Taber, "Sacagawea and the Suffragettes," *Pacific Northwest Quarterly,* 58 (January 1967), pp. 7–13; Elinor Richey, "The Unsinkable Abigail," *American Heritage,* 26 (February 1975), pp. 72–75, 86–89; Meredith A. Snapp, "Defeat the Democrats: Union for Woman Suffrage in Arizona, 1914–1916," *Journal of the West,* 14 (October 1975), pp. 131–59; Mattie L. Williams, "History of Woman Suffrage in Arizona and the Nation," *Arizona Historical Review,* 1 (January 1929), pp. 69–72; Martha B. Caldwell, "The Woman Suffrage Campaign of 1912," *Kansas Historical Quarterly,* 12 (August 1943), pp. 300–18; Walter T. Nugent, "How the Populists Lost in 1894," *Kansas Historical Quarterly,* 31 (Autumn 1965), pp. 245–55; T. A. Larson, "Montana Women and the Battle for the Ballot," *Montana,* 23 (January 1973), pp. 24–41; Ronald Schaffer, "The Montana Woman Suffrage Campaign, 1911–14," *Pacific Northwest Quarterly,* 55 (January 1964), pp. 9–15; John C. Board, "The Lady from Montana," *Montana,* 17 (Summer 1967), pp. 2–17; Austin Hutcheson, ed., "The Story of the Nevada Equal Suffrage Campaigns, The Memoirs of Anne Martin," *University of Nevada Bulletin,* 42 (August 1948); and Reda Davis, *California Women: A Guide to Their Politics 1885–1911* (San Francisco, 1967). On other Western states where full women's suffrage did not come until after the amendment, see: Mary Semple

Scott, ed., "History of Woman Suffrage in Missouri," *Missouri Historical Review*, 14 (April–July 1920), pp. 281–384; Monica Cook Morris, "The History of Woman Suffrage in Missouri, 1867–1901," *Missouri Historical Review*, 25 (October 1930), pp. 67–82; Elizabeth A. Taylor, "The Woman Suffrage Movement in Arkansas," *Arkansas Historical Quarterly*, 15 (Spring 1956), pp. 17–52 and "The Women Suffrage Movement in Texas," *Journal of Southern History*, 17 (May 1951), pp. 194–215; Necah S. Furman, "Women's Campaign for Equality," *New Mexico Historical Review*, 53 (October 1978), pp. 365–74; Louise Moede Lex, "Mary Newbury Adams: Feminist Forerunner from Iowa," *Annals of Iowa*, 43 (Summer 1976), pp. 323–41; James R. Wright, "The Assiduous Wedge: Woman Suffrage and the Oklahoma Constitutional Convention," *Chronicles of Oklahoma*, 51 (Winter 1973–74), pp. 421–43; Gayle Barrett, "The Woman Suffrage Movement in Oklahoma," Women's Study Program, WHC; Winton Solberg, "Martha G. Ripley, Pioneer Doctor and Social Reformer," *Minnesota History*, 39 (Spring 1964), pp. 1–17; Marilyn Ziebarth, "MHS Collections: Woman's Rights Movement," *Minnesota History*, 42 (Summer 1971), pp. 225–30; Mary Kay Jennings, "Lake County Woman Suffrage Campaign in 1890," *South Dakota History*, 5 (Fall 1975), pp. 390–409; Dorinda Riessen Reed, *The Woman Suffrage Movement in South Dakota*, Governmental Research Bureau Report, no. 41 (Vermillion, 1958); T. A. Larson, "Emancipating the West's Dolls, Vassals, and Hopeless Drudges: The Origins of Woman Suffrage in the West," *University of Wyoming Publications*, 37 (1971), pp. 1–16. Stanton et. al., *History of Woman Suffrage*, emphasizes the Eastern suffrage movement but it does include material on and reports from all of the Western states. However, the information, including statistics, should not be considered completely reliable and care should be taken in using the material. In this regard, see: James H. Hutson, "Women in the Era of the American Revolution: The Historian as Suffragist," *The Quarterly Journal of the Library of Congress*, 32 (October 1975), pp. 290–303.

67. For example, the Colorado Equal Suffrage Aid Association was an organization of distinguished office holders and community leaders formed to advance the cause of suffrage in other states. According to the association's letterhead, they were "A nonpartisan organization of Colorado men who favor the cause of Equal Suffrage, believing that the women of Colorado have exercised the privileges of the elective franchise with credit to themselves and to the State." Omar E. Garwood to Alice Park, Oct. 10, 1910, Alice Park Papers, Box 2, Folder 35, HEII. Shortly after the successful Washington campaign, Emma DeVoe and Idaho Governor James H. Brady took the lead in forming the National Council of Women Voters "designed to mobilize the voting women in the five suffrage states" and carry on a program of voter education and assistance to suffragists in other parts of the country. Larson, "Idaho's Role," pp. 8–9.

68. Flexner, *Century of Struggle*, p. 269. Although suffrage leaders were pleased to have full suffrage states, this had little impact nationally because of the small number of electoral votes in the Western states. For example, in 1912 the nine Western states with full suffrage had a total of only forty-five electoral votes and thus were not "of decisive political importance." Ibid. This situation was altered somewhat by the approval of Presidential suffrage in Illinois in 1913. These electoral votes, along with those from Nevada and Montana, brought the 1914 total to ninety-one and helped the more militant, younger women in the NAWSA push for the more aggressive national campaign discussed below. See: Aileen S. Kraditor, *The Ideas of the Woman Suffrage Movement, 1890–1920* (New York, 1965), pp. 231–32.

69. On the organization and work of the Congressional Union and the Woman's Party, see: Inez Haynes Irwin, *Up Hill with Banners Streaming: The Story of the Woman's Party*, reprint ed. (Penobscot, Me., 1964); Flexner, *Century of Struggle*, pp. 271–85; and Sinclair, *Emancipation of the American Woman*, pp. 326–30. O'Neill, *Everyone Was Brave*, pp. 126–30 gives a brief biographical sketch of Alice Paul.

70. The trip was carefully scheduled to present the petition on the opening day of the

1915–16 Congressional session. Amelia Fry, "Along the Suffrage Trail: From West to East for Freedom Now!" *American West*, 6 (January 1969), pp. 16–17; Flexner, *Century of Struggle*, p. 278.

71. Sara Bard Field to Charles Erskine Scott Wood, September 29, 1915, Sara Bard Field Papers, HEH. Another interesting piece of *déjà vu* in the Field Collection is a card to Wood from Toll Gate Rock, October 1915. "We have passed the most curious rock formations all day long and yesterday. They remind me of ancient Egyptian architecture. . . . There are those resembling palaces and grotesque shapes like heads . . . and obelisks."

72. Fry, "Along the Suffrage Trail," pp. 16–25; Irwin, *Up Hill*, pp. 107–118.

73. Alice Park, Memorandum, 1912, Alice Park Papers, Box 2, Folder 156, HEH.

74. See: Larson, "Dolls, Vassals, and Drudges," pp. 13–16 and "Woman Suffrage in Western America," pp. 10–11; Grimes, *Puritan Ethic*, pp. 15–26; Kraditor, *Ideas of the Woman Suffrage Movement*, pp. 219–31; and Sprague, *Women and the West*, pp. 189–91 for summaries of the various arguments.

75. Larson, "Dolls, Vassals, and Drudges," p. 14.

76. Ibid., p. 13, and see note 77.

77. In Idaho, "The eleven men who voted Yes were younger, averaging 33 years, while those who voted No averaged 39.8. . . . Otherwise there was little to distinguish the two sets of men. . . . Two married men and five bachelors voted Yes; four married men and six bachelors voted No. . . . Nine Democrats and two Republicans voted Yes; ten Democrats and one Republican voted No." Larson, "The Woman's Rights Movement in Idaho," p. 4. In Washington, Larson found a similar situation in 1883. There were no significant differences between the votes of married men and bachelors nor were there significant differences based on age, years of residence in the territory, or religion. More farmers supported the suffrage bill than men in other occupations, but the division was not partisan. "Republicans approved 12 to 8, Democrats 9 to 4." Larson, "The Woman Suffrage Movement in Washington," pp. 52–53.

78. Grimes, *The Puritan Ethic*, p. 119. Grimes makes a partial case for his arguments in Utah and Wyoming but not in the other Western states.

79. Walter Prescott Webb, *The Great Plains* (Boston, 1931), p. 505.

80. Grimes, *The Puritan Ethic*, p. 53.

81. *Woman's Exponent*, August 1894 quoted in White, "Woman's Place Is In the Constitution," p. 345.

82. Grimes, *Puritan Ethic*, p. 14.

83. See Everett M. Rogers, *The Diffusion of Innovations* (New York, 1962); Jack L. Walker, "The Diffusion of Innovation Among the American States," *American Political Science Review*, 63 (September 1969), pp. 880–99; James S. Coleman, Eliha Katz, and Herbert Menzel, *Medical Innovation: A Diffusion Study* (Indianapolis, 1966). The chart given in the text is a very simplistic one and does not incorporate any of the elaborate mathematical formulae used in these studies. Nonetheless the theory seems to have some relevance here.

84. For example, Flexner devoted eight out of 345 pages to the West; Sinclair, fifteen out of 367; and O'Neill made only passing mention of the Western movement.

85. Rena Mathews, The Claim of Mrs. Rena Mathews for Being a Pioneer, AHS; Phoebe Judson, *A Pioneer's Search for an Ideal Home* (Bellingham, Wa., 1925), p. 277. Also see: Lou Conway Roberts, *A Woman's Reminiscences of Six Years in Camp with the Texas Rangers* (Austin, 1928), p. 31; Mrs. Ashmun Butler, "Diary of the Rogue River Valley, 1852–1854," *Oregon Historical Quarterly*, 41 (December 1940), p. 343; The Life Story of Mary Elizabeth Warren, OHS; Mrs. L. L. Dalton, Autobiography, WAC, for similar comments.

86. Catharine A. S. Coburn, "Women's Station in Pioneer Days," in Harvey W. Scott, *History of the Oregon Country*, 6 vols. (Cambridge, 1924), I, p. 316; Julia Lovejoy, "Letters

from Kansas," *Kansas Historical Quarterly,* 15 (May 1947), p. 138; Fannie C. Crockett, Parson's Female Seminary, BTHC. Also see: Letitia Pendleton, Journal Kept at Mary Sharpe College, Tennessee, 1854–59, BTHC; Chestina Allen, Diary, KHS; Sarah L. Glasgow to Susie [Glasgow], October 16, 1881 and Anne E. Lane to Sarah L. Glasgow, November 13, 1870 (?) in William Carr Lane Collection, MHS.

87. Rachel Frazier, *Reminiscences of Travel from 1855 to 1867* (San Francisco, 1868), p. 154; Mollie, Letter to Ann, 1871, DPL. Also see: Ann Archbold, *A Book for the Married and Single, The Grave and the Gay, And Especially Designed for Steamboat Passengers* (East Plainfield, Oh., 1850), pp. 140–50.

88. Guadalupe Callan in May Callan Tansill papers, BTHC; Harriet Strong, Rights of Property and Rights of Persons, Harriet Strong Papers, HEH.

89. Helen V. Barry to Idella Parker, November 23, 1911, Alice Park Correspondence, Box 3, HEH. For similar comments see: Rheta Childe Dorr to Mary Austin, February 15, 1922, Mary Austin Collection, Box 8, HEH; Mary Austin, *Earth Horizon* (New York and Boston, 1932), p. 327; Ida Husted Harper to Clara B. Colby, June 30, 1900, Colby Correspondence, HEH; Clara Shortridge Folz to Clara Colby, June 26, 1908, Colby Correspondence.

90. See Eugene A. Hecker, *A Short History of Women's Rights,* reprint ed. (Westport, Ct., 1971), p. 167, for a list of the states having limited suffrage.

91. Moynihan, "Abigail Scott Duniway," pp. 632–33. Moynihan is now revising her study for publication.

Chapter 9

1. Susan E. Kennedy, *If All We Did Was to Weep at Home: A History of White Working-Class Women in America* (Bloomington, In., 1979).

2. Frederick Jackson Turner, *The Significance of the Frontier in American History,* reprint ed. (El Paso, 1960), p. 24. There are many editions and reprints of Turner's essay, a paper read originally at the meeting of the American Historical Association in Chicago, July 12, 1893 and first printed in the Proceedings of the State Historical Society of Wisconsin, December 14, 1893.

3. Johnny M. Faragher and Christine Stansell, "Women and Their Families on the Overland Trail to California and Oregon, 1842–1867," *Feminist Studies,* 2 (1975), p. 161.

4. Lillian Schlissel, "Women's Diaries on the Western Frontier," *American Studies,* 18 (Spring 1977), pp. 94–97.

5. Julie Roy Jeffrey, *Frontier Women: The Trans-Mississippi West, 1840–1880* (New York, 1979), pp. xv–xvi.

6. Howard B. Furer, "The American City: A Catalyst for the Women's Rights Movement," *Wisconsin Magazine of History,* 52 (Summer 1969), p. 286. Furer does concede, however, that Western, as well as Eastern, cities helped to nourish the movement. Ibid., p. 296; David M. Potter, "American Women and the American Character," in Edward N. Saveth, ed. *American History and the Social Sciences* (Glencoe, Illinois, 1964), pp. 431–32.

7. Robert V. Hine, *The American West: An Interpretive History* (Boston, 1974), p. 174.

8. Gerda Lerner, "The Lady and the Mill Girl: Changes in the Status of Women in the Age of Jackson," *Midcontinent American Studies Journal,* 10 (Spring 1969), p. 12 and passim, as quoted in Carl Degler, *At Odds: Women and the Family in America from the Revolution to the Present* (New York, 1980), p. 375.

9. Quoted in Degler, *At Odds,* p. 367.

10. Quoted in Julia Cherry Spruill, *Women's Life and Work in the Southern Colonies* (Chapel Hill, 1938), p. 82.

11. Glenda Riley, " 'Not Gainfully Employed': Women on the Iowa Frontier, 1833–1870," *Pacific Historical Review,* 49 (May 1980), p. 240.

12. George C. Duffield, "An Iowa Settler's Homestead," *Annals of Iowa,* 6 (1903), p. 210, quoted in Ibid.

13. Riley, " 'Not Gainfully Employed'," pp. 241–42.

14. Margaret Murray, "Memoir of the William Archer Family," *Annals of Iowa,* 39 (Summer 1968), p. 362; Mary Austin, Interview, Indian-Pioneer Papers, III, p. 357; E. May Lacey Crowder, "Pioneer Life in Palo Alto County," *Iowa Journal of History and Politics,* 46 (April 1948), p. 178. Also see: Jeffrey, *Frontier Women,* pp. 59–61 and chapter six, above.

15. Abigail Scott Duniway wrote in 1905 that this type of male behavior was not uncommon. Duniway, "A Few Recollections of a Busy Life," in Mary O. Douthit, *A Souvenir of Western Women* (Portland, 1905), pp. 9–12. A concrete example is found in the life of Amelia Perrin, Amelia, NHS.

16. See Leonard J. Arrington, "The Economic Role of Pioneer Mormon Women," *Western Humanities Review,* 9 (Spring 1955), pp. 145–64.

17. Crowder, "Pioneer Life in Palo Alto County," p. 181; Jeffrey, *Frontier Women,* p. 64.

18. Mollie Vannemon Letters, December 24, 1857, BTHC. Also see: Nancy A. Hunt, "By Ox-Team to California, Personal Narrative of Nancy A. Hunt," *Overland Monthly,* 67 (April 1916), p. 325 and Jeffrey, *Frontier Women,* pp. 124–25.

19. Diary of Cora D. Babcock, SDHS. Also see: Notes on Mrs. Murat, DPL; Matilda Delaney, *A Survivor's Recollections of the Whitman Massacre* (Spokane, 1920), p. 41; Agnes Just Reid, *Letters of Long Ago* (Salt Lake City, 1973), p. 13; Fanny Steele, Letter, MHS; and Kathleen Bruyn, Notes on Aunt Clara Brown, DPL for other descriptions and discussions of washerwomen. The important role of laundresses on Western army posts is discussed in several sources including Miller J. Stewart, "Army Laundresses: Ladies of 'Soap Suds Row'," *Nebraska History,* 61 (Winter 1980), pp. 421–36. Sewing is discussed in John Hoffman, ed., "The Life of Lettie Teeple Pennoyer," *Michigan History,* 58 (Summer 1974), pp. 297–99; Ella Bird-Dumont, Autobiography, BTHC; Life Experiences of Pickey: Written by Mrs. L. C. Saunders, BTHC; Mary B. Ballou, *"I Hear the Hogs in My Kitchen": A Woman's View of the Gold Rush* (New Haven, 1962); Mollie Dorsey Sanford, *Mollie: The Journal of Mollie Dorsey Sanford in Nebraska and Colorado Territories 1857–1866* (Lincoln, 1959), p. 98; and Juanita Brooks, ed., *Not By Bread Alone: The Journal of Martha Spence Heywood, 1850–56* (Salt Lake City, 1978). The R. G. Dunn and Company papers, Baker Library, Harvard University, are an excellent source of information on women milliners, dressmakers, and seamstresses.

20. Mary Jane Caples, Overland Journey to the Coast, CSL; Bird-Dumont, Autobiography; Mary Bennett, Interview, Indian-Pioneer Papers, VII, pp. 230–34. Also see: the discussion in Jeffrey, *Frontier Women,* pp. 124–26, and other descriptions of women's domestic businesses in chapter six, above.

21. Ann Beisel, Interview, Indian-Pioneer Papers, VI, p. 455; Melissa Stroud, Hardships of Pioneer Life, OHS; Frances Judge, "Carrie and the Grand Tetons: Fanciful Memories of a Little Girl," *Montana, The Magazine of Western History,* 18 (July 1968), p. 45; From his sister Abby to George Underwood, November 17, 1850, WAC. Also see: Margaret W. Chambers, *Reminiscences* (n.p., 1903) pp. 36–37; May Avery, Papers and Memories of Pioneer Days, NHS; Notes on Mrs. Murat; Mrs. Isaac L. Bryson, Grandma's Story, OHS; Dicey S. Adams, Interview, Indian-Pioneer Papers, I, pp. 169–71; and Ellen P. Paullin, ed., "Etta's Journal, January 2, 1874–July 25, 1875," *Kansas History,* 3 (Autumn 1980), pp. 201–19 for other descriptions of "working out" as well as the discussion in Degler, *At Odds,* pp. 272–73. In Western communities, black women and Mexican women from the poorer classes often worked as domestics. See Dorothy Bass Spann, *Black Pioneers: A History of a Pioneer Family in Colordao Springs* (Colorado Springs, 1978); Sue Armitage, Theresa Banfield, and Sarah

Jacobus, "Black Women and Their Communities in Colorado," *Frontiers,* 2 *(1977),* pp. 45–51; Fabiola Cabeza de Baca, *We Fed Them Cactus* (Albuquerque, 1954); Hattie Stone Benefield, *For the Good of the Country (Por el Bien del Pais)* (Los Angeles, 1951); and Darlis A. Miller, "Cross-Cultural Marriages in the Southwest: The New Mexico Experience (1846–1900)" unpublished paper.

22. David E. Schob, *Hired Hands and Plowboys: Farm Labor in the Midwest 1815–60* (Urbana, 1975), p. 191.

23. Emeline Benson, From Beloit Wisconsin to San Pablo Valley, CSL; Autobiography of Martha Nettie McFarlin Gray, BTHC. Also see: Lillian Elliott, Reminiscences, NHS.

24. Amelia E. Barr, Letter, November 1867, BTHC; Helen Beall Houston, Memoirs 1873–1940, BTHC.

25. Chestina Allen, Diary, KHS; Cora Belle Mitchell, Letter to "Dear Friends," DPL. Also see: Ella Brown Spooner, *Tabitha Brown's Western Adventures* (New York, 1959), pp. 19–22; Lois Murray, *Incidents of Frontier Life* (Goshen, In., 1880), pp. 163–64; Mrs. Milly R. Gray, Diary, BTHC; and Mary C. Withington, *A Catalogue of Manuscripts in the Collection of Western Americana Founded by William R. Coe* (New Haven, 1952), p. 282, entry 474; Mary L. Herrod, Interview, Indian-Pioneer Papers, I, p. 312; and Lucy E. Boyce, Interview, Indian-Pioneer Papers, X, p. 69 for other accounts of women boardinghouse keepers.

26. Shirley Sargent, *Pioneers in Petticoats: Yosemite's Early Women, 1856–1900* (Los Angeles, 1966), p. 20; Hoffmann, "The Life of Lettie Teeple Pennoyer," pp. 297–99.

27. Robert G. Cleland, ed., *Apron Full of Gold: The Letters of Mary Jane Megquier* (San Marino, 1949), p. 33; Ballou, "*I Hear The Hogs in My Kitchen,*" pp. 8–9, 11; Cleland, *Apron Full of Gold,* p. 47; Sargent, *Pioneers in Petticoats,* p. 22. Also see: Virginia V. Root, *Following the Pot of Gold at the Rainbow's End in the Days of 1850* (Downey, Ca., 1960) p. 26; "Luna House," IHS; Caroline Sexton, Biography, OHS; and Life Experiences of Pickey for other experiences of women hotelkeepers.

28. Christine Bates, Interview, Indian-Pioneer Papers, VI, p. 37; Harriet Rochlin, "The Amazing Adventures of a Good Woman," *Journal of the West,* 12 (April 1973), pp. 285–86.

29. Paula E. Petrik, "The Bonanza Town: Women and Family on the Frontier, Helena, Montana, 1865–1920," Ph.D. dissertation, SUNY-Binghamton, in progress.

30. Lyle W. Dorsett, "Equality of Opportunity on the Urban Frontier: Access to Credit in Denver, Colorado Territory, 1858–1876," *Journal of the West,* 18 (July 1979), pp. 75–81.

31. Sanford, *Mollie,* p. 98; Bird-Dumont, Autobiography; Just, *Letters,* pp. 12–13.

32. Degler, *At Odds,* pp. 377–79.

33. There is a rich secondary literature on Western women writers. See, for example: Robert Price, "Mary Hartwell Catherwood and Cincinnati," *Cincinnati Historical Society Bulletin,* 22 (July 1964), pp. 162–69; Anthony Amaral, "Idah Meacham Strobridge: First Woman of Nevada Letters," *Nevada Historical Society Quarterly,* 10 (Fall 1967), pp. 3–28; Philip Graham, "Texas Memoirs of Amelia E. Barr," *Southwestern Historical Quarterly,* 69 (April 1966), pp. 473–98; Maureen Ursenbach, "Three Women and the Life of the Mind," *Utah Historical Quarterly,* 43 (Winter 1975), pp. 26–40; Rodman Paul, "In Search of 'Dame Shirley,' " *Pacific Historical Review,* 33 (May 1964), pp. 127–46; Paul, "When Culture Came to Boise: Mary Hallock Foote in Idaho" Idaho Historical Series, no. 19 (Boise, March 1977); Richard W. Etulain, "Mary Hallock Foote (1847–1938)"; *American Literary Realism,* 5 (Spring 1972), pp. 144–50; John B. Byers, "Helen Hunt Jackson," *American Literary Realism,* 6 (Summer 1973), pp. 197–241; Virginia McConnell, "H. H., Colorado, and the Indian Problem," *Journal of the West,* 12 (April 1973), pp. 272–80; Carolyn Forrey, "Gertrude Atherton and the New Woman," *California Historical Quarterly,* 55 (Summer 1976), pp. 194–209; Elinor Richey, "The Flappers Were Her Daughters: The Liberated, Literary World of Gertrude Atherton," *America West,* 11 (July 1974), pp. 4–10; J. Wilkes Berry, "Mary Hunter Austin (1868–1934)," *Ameri-*

can Literary Realism, 2 (Summer 1969), pp. 125–31; Lawrence C. Powell, "A Dedication to the Memory of Mary Hunter Austin, 1868–1934," *Arizona and the West*, 10 (Spring 1968), pp. 1–4; Edward K. Brown and Leon Edel, *Willa Cather: A Critical Biography* (New York, 1953); Rebecca L. Smith, *Mary Austin Holley: A Biography* (Austin, 1962); Pamela Herr, "Jessie Benton Fremont, The Story of a Remarkable Nineteenth-Century Woman," *American West*, 16 (March/April 1979), pp. 4–13, 59–63; Jane Apostol, "Jeanne Carr: One Woman and Sunshine," *American West*, 15 (July/August 1978), pp. 28–33, 62–63; Miriam B. Murphy, "Sarah Elizabeth Carmichael: Poetic Genius of Pioneer Utah," *Utah Historical Quarterly*, 43 (Winter 1975), pp. 52–66; Agnes Graham, "My Aunt, Ina Coolbrith," *Pacific Historian*, 17 (Fall 1973), pp. 12–19; Josephine DeWitt Rhodenhamel and Raymund Francis Wood, *Ina Coolbrith: Librarian and Laureate of California* (Provo, Ut., 1973); Hazel E. Mills, "The Emergence of Frances Fuller Victor, Historian," *Oregon Historical Quarterly*, 62 (December 1961), pp. 309–36; James J. Weston, "Sharlot Hall: Arizona's Pioneer Lady of Literature," *Journal of the West*, 4 (October 1965), pp. 539–52; Lawrence C. Powell, "Letter from the Southwest," *Westways*, 47 (January 1975), pp. 24–27, Mamie J. Meredith, "Mari Sandoz," in Virginia Faulkner, ed., *Roundup: A Nebraska Reader* (Lincoln, 1957), pp. 382–86.

34. Helena Gillespie, "A Dress to Make," in Sam H. Dixon, *The Poets and Poetry of Texas* (Austin, 1855) quoted in Betty Sue Flowers, " 'The Crosswise Bar': Women Poets of Texas, 1836–1936," unpub. ms., Austin, Tex.

35. I. K. Stephens, "Edmund Montgomery, Hermit Philosopher of Liendo Plantation," *Southwest Review*, 16 (January 1931), pp. 200–235; Bride Neill Taylor, *Elisabet Ney, Sculptor* (New York, 1916); Searles R. Boynton, *The Painter Lady: Grace Carpenter Hudson* (Eureka, 1978). Also see: Raye Price, "Utah's Leading Ladies of the Arts," *Utah Historical Quarterly*, 38 (Winter 1970), pp. 65–85; Elizabeth H. Smith, "The Story of Emma Wixom, The Great Operatic Diva from the Mother Lode," *California Historian*, 13 (March 1967), pp. 85–88; R. Dean Galloway, "Rowena Granice," *Pacific Historian*, 24 (Spring 1980), pp. 105–24; Peter Palmquist, *With Nature's Children: Emma B. Freeman (1880–1928): Camera and Brush* (Eureka, 1976); Teresa Terrell, "The Life of Emma A. Coleman: Early Day Norman Photographer," Women's Studies Program, University of Oklahoma, 1978, WHC; Elisabet Ney Papers and Biography of Mrs. Charles Lavender, Eugenie Etinette Aubanel Lavender, BTHC for other accounts of women artists. Douglas Daniels records the career of several prominent black women musicians in *Pioneer Urbanites: A Social and Cultural History of Black San Francisco* (Philadelphia, 1980), p. 16. Donna Lucey of Brooklyn, N.Y. is currently writing a biography of Evelyn Cameron.

36. See, for example: Kate Brookes Bates, Biography of Mrs. Kate Brookes Arnall Bates, A Daughter of Texas and Her Ancestors and Mary Nicholson McDowall, Little Journey Through Memory's Halls, BTHC.

37. Beecher quoted in Degler, *At Odds*, p. 380. Degler cites a study of teachers in Massachusetts before 1860 which showed that although only about 2 percent of all working women were teachers during any one time period, about 20 percent had "worked at one time or another in the course of their lives as teachers." Degler, *At Odds*, p. 381. Figures for the West would undoubtedly be as high or even higher.

38. Beecher quoted in Jeffrey, *Frontier Women*, p. 12; "Letters of Julia Louisa Lovejoy, 1856–1864," *Kansas Historical Quarterly*, 15 (August 1947), p. 318.

39. Jeffrey, *Frontier Women*, pp. 12, 34–35. Also see notes of Mrs. Mary Gray McLench, Relating to Her Trip to Oregon Early in 1851, OHS for a reminiscence by a young Vermont woman recruited "through a teacher's agency, by Samuel R. Thurston, Congressional delegate from Oregon, to go there to teach." Jeffrey also quotes several of these young women.

40. Mabel Sharpe Beavers, Interview, Indian-Pioneer Papers, VI, p. 303; Ellen C. Pennock, "Incidents in My Life as a Pioneer," *Colorado Magazine*, 30 (April 1953), p. 128; Lucia Darling, Crossing the Prairies in a Covered Wagon, MoHS.

41. Rachel W. Bash, Interview, Indian-Pioneer Papers, VI, p. 6; Jennie Atcheson Wriston, *A Pioneer's Odyssey* (Menasha, Wi., 1943), pp. 89–91; Lottie Ross quoted in James Smallwood, ed., *And Gladly Teach: Reminiscences of Teachers from Frontier Dugout to Modern Module* (Norman, 1976), pp. 42, 43–44. Also see: Reminiscences of Mrs. Mattie Belle Anderson, Fort Davis, BTHC; Diary of Angeline M. Brown, copy in HEH; Clara Conron, Diary 1884, KSH; and Mary Ley and Mike Bryan, *Journey From Ignorant Ridge: Stories and Pictures of Texas Schools in the 1800s* (Austin, 1976), pp. 133 and 150, for other discussions of problems faced by frontier teachers.

42. Bash, Interview; Teacher's Register in Emma Tate Papers, IHS; Agness [sic] Francis quoted in Smallwood, *And Gladly Teach*, p. 52; Patricia Mercer, Diary, 1840–41, Margaret Mollenhauer, Letter, 1894, and Paine Female Institute, Goliad, Minutes of the Board of Trustees, December 18, 1852, all in BTHC.

43. Conron, Diary. Also see: Sanford, *Mollie*, pp. 89–91; Pennock, ''Incidents of My Life,'' pp. 128–29.

44. Anderson, Reminiscences; Conron, Diary; Fort Laramie Papers, June 11, 1871 from the notes of David Lavender, Ojai, California; Pennock, ''Incidents of My Life,'' p. 128. The many personal requirements and regulations imposed on teachers are discussed by Jessie May Hines, Gertrude Gates Patton, Jane E. Davis, and others in Smallwood, *And Gladly Teach*, pp. 30–33.

45. Pennock, ''Incidents of My Life,'' p. 128; Sanford, *Mollie*, pp. 87–88.

46. Conron, Diary. Also see: Sanford, *Mollie*, pp. 91–93 and Pennock, ''Incidents of My Life,'' pp. 128–29 for similar comments.

47. Susan B. Diamond, Diaries 1872, KHS; Harriet Carr to her father, February 1864, Benjamin and Harriet Carr Letters, CHS.

48. The certification requirements for Oklahoma are described in some detail in Smallwood, *And Gladly Teach*, p. 6.

49. Several frontier teachers mention attendance at these institutes. See, for example: Conron, Diary; Sarah Jane Price, Diaries 1878–79, NHS; Mabel Baldwin Couch in *And Gladly Teach*, pp. 29–30; and Ley and Bryan, *Journey From Ignorant Ridge*, p. 131. The examination papers of Rose Hattich in the William and Rose Hattich Papers, AHS include both the questions and answers in arithmetic, grammar, history, geography, reading, mental arithmetic, methods of teaching, school law, physiology, and natural philosophy which she was required to pass for a first-grade certificate in 1892. Another typical teacher's examination is reproduced in Ley and Bryan, *Journey From Ignorant Ridge*, pp. 146–49.

50. See chapter seven, notes 59 and 61.

51. Cornelia M. Banhart, ''Phoebe W. Sudlow,'' *Palimpsest*, 51 (January 1970), p. 174.

52. Interview, Mrs. M. O. Bezanson, Indian-Pioneer Papers, VII, p. 503.

53. C. Gregory Crampton, ed., *Sharlot Hall on the Arizona Strip* (Flagstaff, 1975); Mary Atkins, *The Diary of Mary Atkins* (Mills College, 1937); Marie Haefner, ''Kate Harrington,'' *Palimpsest*, 51 (January 1970), pp. 163–64; Ley and Bryan, *Journey from Ignorant Ridge*, pp. 102–4. Also see: Willie Andrews Pioneer School Association Papers, BTHC; Lucy Jane Dabney, Walter Scales Dabney and Family, BTHC; Ruth Gordon, ''Portrait of a Teacher, Mary Elizabeth Post and Something of the Times in Which She Lived,'' typescript, University of Arizona; and Eleanor E. Gordon, *A Little Bit of A Long Story* (Humboldt, Ia., 1934) for other accounts of women who made teaching a career. Additional information on women as teachers is found in Anna McKee, Letters, 1884, CHS; Annie Josephine Wagner papers, BTHC; Louisa Rahm, Diary, 1862, BL; Myrtle Carter Hooper Diaries, 1887, 1891, SDHS; Mabel Wakefield Moffitt, Reminiscences of an Arizona Pioneer, AHS; The Story of the Life of Mary Bounhanan Gordon, BTHC; Ella Bailey, Diary 1869, CHS; Mrs. Charles W. Dalton, Autobiography, BL; Laura Clarke Carpenter Papers, BTHC; Louise Butler Swift, Letters, UWA; Anderson, Reminiscences; Sarah M. Black, Memoirs, AHS; Edna Helm Ahrens, Interview,

Indian-Pioneer Papers, I, pp. 313–15; Emma Shephard Hill, *A Dangerous Crossing and What Happened on the Other Side* (Denver, 1924), pp. 119–22; Lulu Alice Craig, *Glimpses of Sunshine and Shade in the Far North* (Cincinnati, 1900), p. vii and the citations in note 61, chapter seven for other accounts by Western women about their teaching experiences.

54. Whitman and Spalding accompanied their husbands to Oregon in 1836. They were joined two years later by four other missionary wives, Mary Walker, Myra Eells, Mary Gray, and Sarah Smith. Their diaries and letters and an account of their lives are found in Clifford M. Drury, *First White Women Over the Rockies: Diaries, Letters, and Biographical Sketches of the Six Women of the Oregon Mission Who Made the Overland Journey in 1836 and 1838*, 2 vols. (Glendale, Ca., 1963).

55. On the colonial mission effort, see William W. Sweet, *The Story of Religion in America* (New York, 1930) pp. 225–49 and Sydney E. Ahlstrom, *A Religious History of the American People* (New Haven, 1972), pp. 41–69, 156–57, 289. Ahlstrom points out that "the missionary spirit itself was a fruit of the Awakening . . ." p. 289.

56. Sweet, *The Story of Religion*, pp. 350–72; Ahlstrom, *A Religious History*, pp. 859–64.

57. Ahlstrom, *A Religious History*, p. 863. Ahlstrom also pointed out that the early missionary leaders anticipated "Frederick Jackson Turner's belief in the force of the West in determining the future cast of the emerging nation," p. 459.

58. For example, the Massachusetts Missionary Society was supported by the "Boston Female Society for Promoting the Diffusion of Christian Knowledge," and a number of missionary societies had female auxiliaries who helped raise funds to purchase Bibles, catechisms, and religious tracts for use in the mission field. Sweet, *The Story of Religion*, p. 352.

59. "Winona," *The Autobiography of Rev. Mary C. Collins* (New York, n.d.). Copy in the Mary C. Collins Papers, folder II, SDHS.

60. John A. Andrews, "Betsey Stockton: Stranger in a Strange Land," *Journal of Presbyterian History*, 52 (Summer 1974), pp. 157–66 (the article includes excerpts from Stockton's diary and letters published in the *Christian Advocate* for 1823); Guadalupe Vallejo, "Ranch and Mission Days in Alta California," *Century Magazine*, 41 (December 1890), pp. 183–92; Susanna Bryant Dakin, *Rose or Rose Thorn? Three Women of Spanish California* (Berkeley, 1963); Doña Eulalia Perez, *Una Vieja y Sus Recuerdos*, Dictated to A. D. Thomas Savage at San Gabriel Mission in 1877, BL; *Memorias de Doña Apolinaria Lorenzana, "La Beata" vieja de unos sentente y cinco anos Dictados por ella* in Sta. Barbara en Marzo de 1878 a Tomas Savage, BL; Heloise Hulse Cruzat, "The Ursulines of Louisiana," *Louisiana Historical Quarterly*, 2 (January 1919), pp. 6–23; Marie E. Chabor, "Les Ursulines de Quebec en 1850," *Sessions d'Etude: Soc. Canada d'Historie de l'Eglise Catholique*, 36 (1969), pp. 75–92; Guy Fregault, "La Nouvalle France a l'Epoque de Marie de l'Incarnation," *Review d'Historie de l'Amerique Francaise*, 18 (1964), pp. 167–75; Rufus Anderson, *Memoir of Catherine Brown, A Christian Indian of the Cherokee Nation* (Boston, 1825); Althea Bass, *A Cherokee Daughter of Mount Holyoke* (Muscatine, Ia., 1937); Paula Waldowski, "Alice Brown Davis: A Leader of Her People," *Chronicles of Oklahoma*, 58 (Winter 1980–81), pp. 455–63; Elizabeth Ross, "Woman Superintendent, Cherokee Female Seminary" in Indian-Pioneer Papers, CVIII: 265–68; Mary Lewis Herrod, Interview, Indian-Pioneer Papers, I, pp. 312–16; Kate Shaw Ahrens, Interview, Indian-Pioneer Papers, I, pp. 317–28; Isabell Kiowa Crawford, *The History of a Blanket Indian Mission* (New York, 1915); Valerie Mathes, "American Indian Women and the Catholic Church," *North Dakota History*, 47 (Fall 1980), pp. 20–25; Susan Bordeaux Bettelyoun, Papers, NHS; Elinor Richey, "Sagebrush Princess with a Cause: Sarah Winnemucca," *American West*, 12 (November 1975), pp. 30–33; Mrs. Sarah Winnemucca Hopkins, *Life Among the Piutes: Their Wrongs and Claims*, Mrs. Horace Mann, ed. (Boston, 1883); Valerie Mathes, "Portrait for a Western Album," *American West*, 16 (May–June 1979), p. 39 (an article on Susan La Flesche who was a doctor, effective spokeswoman for Indian rights and also was appointed missionary to her tribe by the Presbyterian Board of Home Missions).

61. Mary Rice, Fort Gibson, Western Creek Nation to Hannah Rice, Keene, N.H., Nov. 15, 1835, WAC; Mary Sagatoo, *Wah-Sash-Kah-Moqua or Thirty-Three Years Among the Indians* (Boston, 1897), p. 61; Sue Peterson, "From Paradise to Prairie: The Presentation Sisters in Dakota, 1880–1896," *South Dakota History,* 10 (Summer 1980), p. 217; Mary C. Collins, *Thirty Years With the Indians* (New York, n.d.), pp. 5–6.

62. There is a rich literature by missionary women. In addition to the sources cited above, see: Mrs. Harriet S. Caswell, *Our Life Among the Iroquois Indians* (Boston and Chicago, 1892); Sara Tuttle, *Letters on the Chickasaw and Osage Missions* (Boston, 1831); Peggy Dow, *Vicissitudes, of Journey of Life and Supplementary Reflections* (New York, 1856); Harriet Bishop, *Floral Home, or First Years of Minnesota* (New York, 1857); Mary M. Crawford, *The Nez Perces Since Spalding* (San Francisco, 1936); Mrs. Mary Eastman, *Dahcotah or Life and Legends of the Sioux* (New York, 1849); Elaine Goodale Eastman, *Sister to the Sioux: The Memoirs of Elaine Goodale Eastman, 1885–91,* Kay Graber, ed. (Lincoln, 1978); Kunigunde Duncan, *Blue Star, As Told from the Life of Corabelle Fellows* (Caldwell, Id., 1938); Deane G. Carter, "A Place in History for Ann James," *Arkansas Historical Quarterly,* 28 (Winter 1969), pp. 309–23; McBeth-Crawford Collection, IHS; Mary C. Collins Papers, SDHS; Mother Gertrude, Biographical Sketch, SDHS. On missionaries in the Southwest who ministered to the Mexican as well as to the Indian population, see: R. Douglas Brackenridge, Francisco D. Garcia-Treto, and John Stover, "Presbyterian Missions to Mexican Americans in Texas in the Nineteenth Century," *Journal of Presbyterian History,* 49 (Summer 1971), pp. 105–32; Melinda Rankin, *Twenty Years Among the Mexicans: A Narrative of Missionary Labor* (St. Louis, 1875) and *Texas in 1850* (Boston, 1850); Harriet S. Kellogg, *Life of Mrs. Emily Harwood* (Albuquerque, 1903); Sister Blandina Segale, *At the End of the Santa Fe Trail* (Milwaukee, 1948); Anna McKee Letters, 1884, CHS; Sister Mary Joanna Walsh, Sketch, Pioneering to Denver, Opening of the School, St. Mary's Academy, June 1864, DPL; Diary of Sister Monica, 1870, AHS; Lucille McDonald, "Mother Joseph" in Western Writers of America, *The Women Who Won the West* (Garden City, 1980), pp. 120–29; Thomas Richter, ed., "Sister Catherine Mallon's Journal," *New Mexico Historical Review,* 52 (April 1977), pp. 135–55, and 53 (June 1977), pp. 237–58; Sister Lilliana Owens, "Our Lady of Light Academy, Santa Fe," *New Mexico Historical Review,* 13 (April 1938), pp. 129–45.

63. See, for example: Ronald Miller, *Shady Ladies of the West* (Los Angeles, 1964); Caroline Bancroft, *Six Racy Madames of Colorado* (Boulder, 1965); Herbert Asbury, *The Barbary Coast* (New York, 1933); Cy Martin, *Whiskey and Wild Women* (New York, 1974); and Harry Sinclair Drago, *Notorious Ladies of the Frontier* (New York, 1969).

64. Among the better recent studies of Western prostitution are Joseph W. Snell, "Painted Ladies of the Cowtown Frontier," *Trail Guide,* 10 (December 1965), pp. 3–24; John S. McCormick, "Salt Lake City's Stockade: The Beginning of Prostitution on West Second South," *Utah Historical Quarterly,* forthcoming, and "Prostitution in Salt Lake City: The History of Three Brothels," *Utah Preservation,* 1 (May 1979); Marion Goldman, "Sexual Commerce on the Comstock Lode," *Nevada Historical Quarterly,* 21 (Summer, 1978), pp. 99–129; George M. Blackburn and Sherman L. Ricards, "The Prostitutes and Gamblers of Virginia City, Nevada, 1870," *Pacific Historical Review,* 48 (May 1979), pp. 239–58; Carol Leonard and Isidor Wallismann, "Prostitution and Changing Morality in the Frontier Cattle Towns of Kansas," *Kansas History,* 2 (Spring 1979), pp. 34–53; Paula Petrik, "Prostitution in Helena, Montana, 1865–1900," *Montana, The Magazine of Western History,* 31 (April 1981), pp. 28–40; Eliott West, "Scarlett West: The Oldest Profession in the Trans-Mississippi West," ibid., pp. 16–27; Gary L. Cunningham, "Moral Corruption and the American West: A Socio-Historical Investigation of the Origins and Nature of Prostitution and Gambling in the Primary Cattle Towns of Kansas, 1867–1886, As a Means of Ascertaining the Extent of Its Significance in American Western History," Ph.D. dissertation, University of California at Santa Barbara, 1980; Anne P. Diffendal, "Prostitution in Grand Island, Nebraska, 1870–1913," paper read at the Western History Association Conference, San Diego, California, October, 1978; and Marion

S. Goldman, *Gold Diggers and Silver Miners: Prostitution and Social Life on the Comstock Lode* (Ann Arbor, 1981).

65. Quoted in Jeffrey, *Frontier Women*, p. 121.

66. Mrs. Lydia Taylor, *From Under the Lid* (n.p., 1913). There is some question as to the authenticity of Mrs. Taylor's book. She may indeed have been a former prostitute or she may have been a reformer who hoped to prevent young women from entering prostitution by writing a sensational, but false, narrative.

67. "Tale of the Booms: Reminiscences of a Prostitute," WPA Writer's Project, "Oil in Oklahoma," WHC. The interviewer described the woman as "Annie, a beautiful Madam with two gold teeth, a battered puss, and the form of a lopsided watermelon."

68. Several accounts of prosperous madames are found in Jeffrey, *Frontier Women*, pp. 121–22 and Petrick, "Prostitution in Helena." However, Petrick's study clearly showed that in Helena, at least, opportunities for such entrepreneural activities by the demimonde decreased as the community became more settled and began to curtail prostitution. Also see: Burton S. Hill, "A Girl Called Nettie," *Annals of Wyoming*, 37 (Fall 1965), pp. 147–56; W. R. Hogan, "Pamela Mann: Texas Frontierswoman," *Southwest Review*, 20 (Summer 1935), pp. 360–70; and Mary'n Rosson, "A Good Old Gal," in Western Writers of America, *The Women Who Won the West* (New York, 1980), pp. 88–103. There several accounts of La Tules. See: Janet Lecompte, "La Tules and the Americans," *Arizona and the West*, 20 (Autumn 1978), pp. 215–30; Angelico Chávez, "Doña Tules, Her Fame and Her Funeral," *El Palacio*, 57 (August 1950), pp. 227–34 and Janet Lecompte, "The Independent Women of Hispanic New Mexico, 1821–1846," *Western Historical Quarterly*, 12 (January 1981), pp. 25–26. Two husband-and-wife teams are described in Diffendal, "Prostitution in Grand Island." There are numerous accounts, mostly popularized, of the famous bandit queens and Western characters, as well as reminiscences purportedly written by two of the best known: Mrs. E. J. Guerin, *Mountain Charley* (Norman, 1968) and Mrs. Martha Canary Burke (Calamity Jane), *Life and Adventures* (n.p., 1898).

69. Snell, "Painted Ladies," pp. 11–12. Also see: Jeffrey, *Frontier Women*, pp. 122–23; Robert Schick, "Prostitution," in Howard Lamar, ed., *The Reader's Encyclopedia of the American West* (New York, 1977), pp. 972–73; and Warren J. Brier, "Tilting Skirts and Hurdy-Gurdies: A Commentary on Gold Camp Women," *Montana, The Magazine of Western History*, 19 (October 1969), pp. 58–67.

70. Leonard Arrington, "Women as a Force in the History of Utah," *Utah Historical Quarterly*, 38 (Winter 1970), p. 4.

71. Ibid.; Riley, " 'Not Gainfully Employed,' " pp. 263–64.

72. Murray, "Memoir of the William Archer Family," p. 364. Also see: Joanna H. Haines, "Seventy Years in Iowa," *Annals of Iowa*, 27 (October 1945), p. 105; Mary W. M. Hargreaves, "Women in the Agricultural Settlement of the Northern Plains," *Agricultural History*, 50 (January 1976), pp. 179–89; R. J. and Alice Clow Papers, BTHC; Nebraska Sod House Letters, NHS; Sarah E. Martin, My Desert Memories, AHS; and the sources listed in note 52, chapter six. On women running farms and ranches during their husband's absence, see: note 53, chapter six and Louisa R. Bell, Letters, BTHC; M. E. D. Trowbridge, *Pioneer Days: The Life Story of Gershom and Elizabeth Day* (Philadelphia, 1895); Civil War Letters of Mary Minor, BTHC; Perrin, Amelia; Mary Rabb Diary, BTHC; Lizzie S. Neblett, Correspondence, BTHC; and Jack D. L. Holmes, "Ann White Hutchins: Anthony's Better Half?" *Journal of Mississippi History*, 37 (1975), pp. 203–8.

73. Margaret Rice Brockway Correspondence, OHS.

74. Ozena Young Anthony, Interview, Indian-Pioneer Papers, II, pp. 458–62; Monique Urza, "Catherine Etchart: A Montana Love Story," *Montana, The Magazine of Western History*, 31 (January 1981), p. 15. Also see: William and Lucy Shively to her father, July 9, 1865,

WAC; Falvia Pease to her brother-in-law, 1855, WAC; Mary Jane Hayden to her grandson, 1887, WAC; Rebecca Woodson, A Sketch of the Life of Rebecca Hiddreth Nutting (Woodson), CSL; "Diary of Mrs. Elizabeth Dixon Smith Geer," in *Oregon Pioneer's Association Transactions of the 35th Annual Reunion* (1907), p. 175; William J. Weatherby Family Papers, Laura Weatherby Correspondence, 1899–1911, NMSU; and Miriam Davis Colt, *Went to Kansas* (Watertown, Ia., 1862) for other accounts of widows as farmers or farm managers.

75. Jane Cazneau to Joseph D. Speers, October 29, 1835, in Jane McManus Storms Cazneau Papers, BTHC.

76. See, for example: Lecompte, "Independent Women of Hispanic New Mexico," p. 24–27; Memorias de Doña Apolinaria Lorenzaná; Carrie Lodge, The Martina Castro Lodge Family, Interview conducted by Elizabeth S. Calcianao, Santa Cruz, 1965, BL; Experiences of Abigail McLennan Fokes and Family, BTHC; Johnaphene Faulkner, Our Prairie Home, BTHC. On the Spanish and Mexican laws which enabled married women to hold separate property, see: Nina N. Pugh, "The Spanish Community of Gains in 1803: *Sociedad de Gananciales*," *Louisiana Law Review*, 30 (1969), pp. 1–43.

77. Lawrence M. Friedman, *A History of American Law* (New York, 1973), pp. 183–85. Also see: Kay Ellen Thurman, "The Married Woman's Property Acts," LL.D. thesis, University of Wisconsin, 1966.

78. Friedman, *History of American Law*, pp. 184–85.

79. Dorothy O. Johansen, *Empire of the Columbia*, 2nd ed. (New York, 1967), p. 231. For the experiences of two women, both widows, who took up donation claims, see: Smith Family, Account of Overland Journey in 1846, OHS; Mary Frost, "Experiences of a Pioneer," *Washington Historical Quarterly*, 7 (April 1916), pp. 123–25.

80. A number of such cases were reported by the agents of R. G. Dun and Company. For typical entries see: R. G. Dun and Company Papers, Western Territories, vol. 2, entry for Mrs. Demming, Fort Smith and vol. 3, August Bittner and Mrs. E. Bittner, Baker Library, Harvard University.

81. Emma Haddock, "Women as Land Owners in the West," Association for The Advancement of Women, *Proceedings, 14th Annual Convention*, (Louisville, 1886), quoted in Hargreaves, "Women in the Agricultural Settlement," p. 249.

82. Ibid., quoted in Andrew Sinclair, *The Better Half: The Emancipation of the American Woman* (New York, 1965), p. 207.

83. Joseph W. Snell, ed., "Roughing It on Her Kansas Claim: The Diary of Abbie Bright, 1870–1871," *Kansas Historical Quarterly*, 38 (Autumn 1971), pp. 233–68, (Winter 1971), pp. 394–428; Enid Bern, ed., "They Had a Wonderful Time: Homesteading Letters of Anna and Ethel Erickson," *North Dakota History*, 45 (Fall 1978), pp. 4–31.

84. Babcock, Reminiscences.

85. Lonnie E. Underhill and Daniel F. Littlefield, "Women Homeseekers in Oklahoma Territory, 1889–1901," *Pacific Historian*, 17 (Fall 1973), pp. 36–47.

86. Elinore Pruitt Stewart, *Letters of a Woman Homesteader*, reprint ed. (Lincoln, 1961), p. 215. There are a number of sources on women homesteaders. In addition to the articles cited above, see: Marie Snedecor, "The Homesteaders: Their Dreams Held No Shadows," *Montana, Magazine of Western History*, 19 (April 1969), pp. 10–27 which includes the letters of Lillie Klein Rasmussen; Gertrude S. Young, *Dakota Again* (Brookings, S.D., 1950), pp. 3–16; Mary W. M. Hargreaves, "Homesteading and Homemaking on the Plains: A Review," *Agricultural History*, 47 (April 1973), pp. 156–63; Roger Welsch, "North American Houses and Barns: Sod Houses," *Shelter II* (1978), p. 54; Deborah Frazier, "Woman Homesteader Recalls Strolls, Snakes and a Shotgun," Dallas *Morning News*, April 19, 1978, p. 1C; Edith Eudora Kohl, *Land of the Burnt Thigh* (New York, 1938); Frances J. Fulton, *To and Through Nebraska by a Pennsylvania Girl* (Lincoln, 1884); Jeanne L. Wuillemin, Letter, SDHS; The Diary of Susan

Ophelia Carter, NHS; and Edna Helm Ahrens, Interview, Indian-Pioneer Papers, I, pp. 306–8.

87. Sophie Poe, *Buckboard Days*, reprint ed. (Albuquerque, 1981); Nannie T. Alderson and Helena Huntington Smith, *A Bride Goes West*, reprint ed. (Lincoln, 1969). Also see: Agnes Morley Cleaveland, *No Life for a Lady*, reprint ed. (Lincoln, 1977); Una Brooks, "The Influence of the Pioneer Women Toward a Settled Social Life on the Llano Estacado," M. A. thesis, West Texas State University, 1942; Mrs. Fannie E. Borden, Interview, Indian-Pioneer Papers, IX, pp. 365–85, Flossie Lill Morris, Diaries, PPHA.

88. Life Experiences of Pickey; Bulah Rust Kirkland, interview, in J. Marvin Hunter, ed., *The Trail Drivers of Texas*, 2 vols. (San Antonio, 1920), I, p. 491. Also see: Mary Kidder Rak, *A Cowman's Wife* (New York, 1934) and *Mountain Cattle* (New York, 1936); James E. Potter, "The Ranch Letters of Emma Robertson, 1891–1892," *Nebraska History*, 17 (April–June 1936), pp. 91–102; William J. Weatherby Family Papers, Laura Weatherby Correspondence, 1899–1911, NMSU; Mrs. Alvis P. Belcher, interview, in Hunter, *Trail Drivers of Texas*, II, p. 219; and Charles M. Wood, "Arizona Argonauts" in Charles Morgan Wood Papers, Box 2, AHS (an interview with Cora Viola Slaughter).

89. Bird-Dumont, Autobiography; Carrie Miller Townley, "Helen J. Stewart: First Lady of Las Vegas," *Nevada Historical Society Quarterly*, 16 (Winter 1973), pp. 214–44 and 17 (Spring 1974), pp. 2–32. Also see: Joyce Roach, *The Cowgirls* (Houston, 1977), pp. 17–38 and Margaret Borland, Papers, BTHC.

90. Walker D. Wyman, *Frontier Woman: The Life of a Woman Homesteader on the Dakota Frontier* (River Falls, Wi., 1972); Emily Jones Shelton, "Lizzie E. Johnson: A Cattle Queen of Texas," *Southwestern Historical Quarterly*, 50 (January 1947), pp. 349–66.

91. Esther Campbell, "Queen Ann" Bassett Willis, DPL; Everett Dick, *Vanguards of the Frontier* (New York, 1941), p. 477. Also see: Roach, *The Cowgirls*, pp. 41–71; Mrs. Libby Smith Collins, *The Cattle Queen of Montana*, Alvin E. Dyer, ed. (Spokane, 1912?); Underhill and Littlefield, "Women Homeseekers," pp. 45–46; Joyce Roach, "Horse Trader," in Western Writers of America, *Women Who Made the West*, pp. 178–85; Armand Reeder, "Katie Lawder (Lady Moon)," unpublished ms., Denver, Colorado, copy in possession of author; Gertrude Gates, Papers, University of Arizona. For accounts of Spanish and Mexican women as ranch managers, see: Lecompte, "Independent Women of New Mexico," p. 25; J. N. Bowman, "Prominent Women of Provincial California," *Historical Society of Southern California Quarterly*, 39 (June 1957), pp. 149–66; and Edith O. Parker, "María Gertrudis Perez Cordero Cassiano (1790–1832)," in Evelyn M. Carrington, ed., *Women in Early Texas* (Austin, 1975), p. 54, describing the career of María del Carmen Calvillo Delgado.

There are a number of reminiscences and descriptions of women's ranch life written by English women who either lived briefly on Western ranches or visited them as tourists. See, especially: Edith M. Nicholl, *Observations of a Ranchwoman in New Mexico* (London, 1898); Isabelle Randall, *A Lady's Ranch Life in Montana* (London, 1887); Mary J. Jaques, *Texas Ranch Life with Three Months Through Mexico in a "Prairie Schooner"* (London, 1894); Rose Pender, *A Lady's Experience in the Wild West in 1883*, reprint ed. (Lincoln, 1978); and Cornelia Adair, *My Diary, August 30th to November 5th 1874* (Austin, 1965).

92. Mary Gay Humphreys, "The Ways of Women Ranchers," *Century Magazine*, 83 (February 1912), pp. 527–29, 533–34.

93. Alderson, *A Bride Goes West*, pp. 109, 223; Trollope quoted in Stan Steiner, *The Ranchers, A Book of Generations* (New York, 1980), p. 104.

94. Kittie Wilkins, The Idaho Horse Queen, Biographical Sketch, BL (includes transcript of an interview from the San Francisco *Examiner*, December 14, 1887). Also see: Roach, *The Cowgirls*, pp. 83–138; Fred Pass, "Women of the West," Dallas *Morning News*, January 24, 1979; Nan Aspinwall (Mrs. Frank Gable), Papers, boxes 3–5, NHS.

95. Borland Papers; Shelton, "Lizzie E. Johnson," pp. 356–58; Roach, *The Cowgirls*, pp. 5–15. Also see: Mary Taylor Bunton, *A Bride on the Old Chisolm Trail in 1886* (San Antonio, 1939); Fannie Borden Interview; Amanda Burks in Hunter, *The Trail Drivers*, I, pp. 368–77; and Mrs. Alvis P. Belcher in Hunter, *The Trail Drivers*, II, pp. 217–19 for other accounts of women who traveled on the cattle trails.

96. Sam S. Baskett, "Eliza Lucas Pinckney: Portrait of an Eighteenth Century American," *South Carolina Historical Magazine*, 72 (October 1971), pp. 207–19; chapter eight p. 214, above.

97. Emma H. Adams, *To and Fro in Southern California* (Cincinnati, 1887), p. 239. Also see: Mary C. F. Hall-Wood, *Santa Barbara As It Is: Topography, Climate, Resources and Objects of Interest* (Santa Barbara, 1884), pp. 86–87.

98. "Women as Farmers," unidentified newspaper clipping June 19, 1894, copied from the New York *World*, Harriet Strong Collection, Box 18, HEH. Also see: Elizabeth Macphail, *Kate Sessions, Pioneer Horticulturist* (San Diego, 1976); San Francisco *Chronicle*, January 20, 1895; San Francisco *Bulletin*, Sunday Magazine, December 25, 1904; and *Colliers*, September 3, 1910. Copies of the newspaper and magazine articles are in the Strong Collection, Box 18.

99. San Francisco *Evening Post*, November 26, 1892, p. 2. Copy in Strong Collection, Box 18.

100. Shelton, "Lizzie E. Johnson," pp. 359–60, Sara Horton Cockrell Papers and Frank M. Cockrell, ms., Early Dallas, Dallas Historical Society; Dun and Bradstreet Papers, Texas, volume 8, p. 66.

101. Will of Doña María Gertrudis de la Garza, August 1789, BTHC; Lecompte, "Independent Women of Hispanic New Mexico," p. 25; Alfredo Mirandé and Evangelina Enríquez, *La Chicana: The Mexican-American Woman* (Chicago, 1979), pp. 66–68; Sherman W. Savage, *Blacks in the West* (Westport, Ct., 1976), pp. 14, 84; Bruyn, Notes on Aunt Clara Brown and *"Aunt" Clara Brown: Story of a Black Pioneer* (Boulder, 1970); Douthit, *The Souvenir of Western Women*, p. 103; Miss Millie Ohmertz, Female Pioneering, BL; Mary E. Stickney, "Colorado Women Successful in Managing Mining Business," Denver *Times*, January 19, 1902, p. 19, copy in "Women in Colorado" File, DPL (includes interview with Houghton). Also see: Kate Nye-Starr, *A Self-Sustaining Woman* (Chicago, 1888), pp. 10–58, 112; Mary Mathews, *Ten Years in Nevada* (Buffalo, 1880), p. 342; and Margaret Lea Houston Letters, BTHC for accounts of other women who successfully managed their own property.

102. See Lyman S. Tyler, *The Montana Gold Rush Diary of Kate Dunlap* (Denver, 1969), pp. A9–A10; Mrs. J. L. Vaughn, "First Business Woman" in Mary L. Cox, *History of Hale County Texas* (Plainview, 1937), p. 211; C. Raymond Woodward, Jr., "A Frontier Leader of Men and Women," *Nebraska History*, 18 (July–September, 1937), pp. 200–202; Alderson, *A Bride Goes West*, pp. 266–69; Arrington, "The Economic Role of Mormon Women," pp. 150–52; Mrs. Katie Wilson, Statement, Monrovia California, November 1, 1887, BL; and Mrs. Catherine Marcus, IHS, for typical accounts of women in these businesses.

103. Bethenia Owens-Adair, *Dr. Bethenia Owens-Adair: Some of Her Life Experiences* (Portland, 1906); Mathews, *Ten Years in Nevada*; Nye-Starr, *A Self-Sustaining Woman*. The two enterprising ladies are described in R. Beeching, Diary, 1849, HEH.

104. Patent #528,823 in Strong Papers, Box 14. Other accounts of women inventors can be found in Jennie McCowen, "Women in Iowa," *Annals of Iowa*, 1 (October 1884), pp. 105–6, and Caroline Romney, "Women As Inventors and the Value of Their Inventions in Household Economics," *Journal of Industrial Education*, 9 (September 1894), pp. 1–11, 22–26, copy in Elizabeth Harbert Papers, HEH. A more detailed study of women inventors is being prepared by Autumn Stanley of Wilbur Springs, California, as part of a larger study on women and agriculture. I am indebted to Ms. Stanley for sharing the results of her research with me.

105. Strong Papers, Boxes 11, 12, 14; Douthit, *Souvenir of Western Women*, pp. 128–31, Nolie Mumey, *The Saga of "Auntie" Stone and Her Cabin* (Boulder, 1964), pp. 34, 64–70; Cockrell Papers.

106. Stickney, "Colorado Women Successful in Managing Mining Business."
107. For accounts of women who assisted their husbands and fathers, see: Mrs. Theodore Schultz, Early Anecdotes, BL; August Tabor, Interview, BL; an account in Elmer F. Bennett, "Pioneer Women of Colorado—Courage and Sacrifice," DPL; and Harriet A. L. Smith, My Trip Across the Plains, CSL. A Mrs. Bulingame recounted her adventures in prospecting for gold in Mrs. C. B. Waite, *Adventures in the Far West* (Chicago, 1882), pp. 132–36. On two of the Northern adventuresses, see: Luella Day, *The Tragedy of the Klondike* (New York, 1906); Carolyn Niethammer, "The Lure of Gold" in Western Writers, *Women Who Won the West*, pp. 69–87; and Rochlin, "The Amazing Adventures of a Good Woman," pp. 82, 93–95. Among the most successful investors were washwoman Clara Brown of Colorado and boardinghouse operator May Arkwright Hutton of Idaho. See: Savage, *Blacks in the West*, 84; Bruyn, *Aunt Clara Brown*; Benjamin H. Kizer, "May Arkwright Hutton," *Pacific Northwest Quarterly*, 57 (April 1966), pp. 49–56; and Hutton's own book, *The Coeur d'Alenes or a Tale of the Modern Inquisition in Idaho* (Wallace, Id., 1900). For Utah, see: Laurence P. James and Sandra C. Taylor, " 'Strong Minded Women': Desdemona Stott Beeson and Other Hard Rock Mining Entrepreneurs," *Utah Historical Quarterly*, 46 (Spring 1978), pp. 136–50.
108. Lorle Porter, "Amelia Bloomer: An Early Iowa Feminist's Sojourn on the Way West," *Annals of Iowa*, 41 (Spring 1973), p. 1244; Margorie D. Barlow, *Notes on Women Printers in Colonial America and the United States, 1639–1975* (Charlottesville, Va., 1976). Also see: Edna Parratt, "Women Printers," *Bulletin of the New York Public Library*, 56 (1952), pp. 42–43 and Lois Rather, *Women as Printers* (Oakland, 1970).
109. Porter, "Amelia Bloomer," pp. 1248, 1256; Incorporation Papers, Women's Cooperative Printing Union, California State Archives, quoted in Rather, *Women as Printers*, p. 24. The expereinces of a woman typesetter are found in Caroline Gale Budlong, *Memories of Pioneer Days in Oregon and Washington Territory* (Eugene, Or., 1949), p. 40.
110. Frances W. Kaye, "The Ladies Department of the *Ohio Cultivator*, 1845–1855, A Feminist Forum," *Agricultural History*, 50 (January 1976), pp. 414–23; James H. Matlack, "The *Alta California*'s Lady Correspondent," *New York Historical Society Quarterly*, 58 (October 1974), pp. 280–303; Helen Burrell d'Apery, The Stormy Petrel, unpublished manuscript, 2 vols., BL; Flora Ellice Stevens, Reminiscences, DPL; Mary Lou Pence, "Polly Pry," in Western Writers, *Women Who Won The West*, pp. 104–19; and "Women in Colorado" File, DPL. The *Cultivator* employed a number of popular Midwestern women journalists including Louisa Bateman, Hannah Maria Tracy-Cutler, and Frances Dana Gage who were all active Western boosters as well as advocates of a broadened sphere for women's activities.
111. Caroline N. Churchill, *Active Footsteps* (Colorado Springs, 1909), excerpted in Christiana Fischer, *Let Them Speak for Themselves: Women in the American West, 1849–1900* (Hamden, 1977), pp. 166–76; Leonard J. Arrington, "Blessed Damozels: Women in Mormon History," *Dialogue*, 6 (Summer 1971), p. 26.
112. Mrs. Walter Ferguson, The Trail to No-Man's Land, unpublished manuscript, copy courtesy of Ann Morgan, University of Oklahoma, Norman. Also see: Galloway, "Rowena Granice," pp. 105–24; David Lavender, "The Petrified West and the Writer," in Gerald Haslam, ed., *Western Writing* (Albuquerque, 1974), pp. 146–49; Abigail Scott Duniway, "A Few Recollections of a Busy Life," in Douthit, *Souvenir of Western Women*, pp. 9–12 and *Pathbreaking, An Autobiographical History of the Equal Suffrage Movement in Pacific Coast States* (Portland, 1914); Helen F. Spalding, "Mrs. Catherin A. Coburn," in Douthit, *A Souvenir of Western Women*, p. 173; Robert F. Karolevitz, *Newspapering in the Old West* (Seattle, 1965) which contains accounts of several women editors and publishers including Abigail Scott Duniway of Oregon, Nettie Watson and Faye Fuller of Washington, and Gertrude and Laura Huntington of Wyoming; Alma F. Vaughan, "Pioneer Women of the Missouri Press," *Missouri Historical Review*, 64 (July 1970), pp. 289–305; and file of *The Central Magazine*, MHS.

113. Nancy Yamane, "The Working Role of Women in the American West, 1880–1910," *Passports, San Jose State University Studies in History*, 3 (1979), p. 42; Vaughan, "Pioneer Women of the Missouri Press." The eleven states included in the Yamane survey were California, Washington, Colorado, Oregon, Utah, New Mexico, Montana, Idaho, Arizona, Wyoming, and Nevada.

114. The problems encountered by women who attempted to enter the professions are discussed in Barbara J. Harris, *Beyond Her Sphere: Women and the Professions in American History* (Westport, Ct., 1978). See especially, pp. 73–126.

115. On *curanderas* and medicine women, see: Mirandé and Enríquez, *La Chicana*, pp. 59–60, 79–86; Cabeza de Baca, *We Fed Them Cactus*, pp. 59–60; Valerie Mathes, "Native American Women in Medicine and the Military," *Journal of the West*, forthcoming. On midwives, nurses, and doctors' assistants, see: Helen Olson Halvorsen, "Nineteenth Century Midwife: Some Recollections," *Oregon Historical Quarterly*, 70 (March 1969), pp. 39–49; Tyler, *The Montana Gold Rush Diary of Kate Dunlap*, p. A-9; Thomas Prosch, *David S. Maynard and Catherine T. Maynard: Biographies of Two of the Oregon Immigrants of 1850* (Seattle, 1906), pp. 71–72, 78; Eve Ball, "Angel of the Pecos," in Western Writers of America, *Women Who Won the West*, pp. 1–14; Mrs. C. E. Baldwin, Interview, Indian-Pioneer Papers, IV, pp. 307–10; Mrs. Walter Banks, Interview, Indian-Pioneer Papers, V, pp. 132–34; The Diary of the Memoirs and Travels of Daniel and Martha Graves, DPL; Sophia Eastman, Letters, BL.

116. Arrington, "The Economic Role of Mormon Women," pp. 161–63; "Blessed Damozels," pp. 27–30; Miriam B. Murphy, "The Working Women of Salt Lake City: A Review of the *Utah Gazeteer*, 1892–93," *Utah Historical Quarterly*, 46 (Spring 1978), pp. 123–25; Robert T. Divett, "Utah's First Medical College," *Utah Historical Quarterly*, 31 (Winter 1963), pp. 51–59; Kate B. Carter, *Our Pioneer Heritage*, 11 vols. (Salt Lake City, 1958–1963), VI, pp. 361–424; and also see: Ellis Shipp Musser, ed., *The Early Autobiography and Diary of Ellis Reynolds Shipp, M.D.* (Salt Lake City, 1962).

117. Harris, *Beyond Her Sphere*, p. 107. For some of the problems and triumphs of Western women in the medical profession, see: Esther C. Lovejoy, "My Medical School (1890–1894)," *Oregon Historical Quarterly*, 75 (March 1974), pp. 7–36; Winton Solberg, "Martha G. Ripley, Pioneer Doctor and Social Reformer," *Minnesota History*, 39 (Spring 1964), pp. 1–17; Mathes, "Portrait," pp. 38–39; McCowan, "Women in Iowa," pp. 106–8; Mary Bennett Ritter, *More than Gold in California* (Berkeley, 1933); Helen Doyle, *A Child Went Forth: The Autobiography of Dr. Helen MacKnight* (New York, 1934); Owens-Adair, *Dr. Bethenia Owens-Adair*; and Dorothea Moore Papers, HEH.

118. Harris, *Beyond Her Sphere*, pp. 110–12; Catherine M. Rottier, "Ellen Spencer Mussey and the Washington College of Law," *Maryland Historical Magazine*, 69 (Winter 1974), pp. 361–82; "Women Are Too Easily Made Tools of Men," undated clipping from *Bancroft Magazine* in the author's files; Corinne L. Gilb, "Laura de Force Gordon," in Edward T. James, Janet W. James, and Paul S. Boyer, eds., *Notable American Women, 1607–1950*, 3 vols. (Cambridge, 1971), II, pp. 68–69; and "Clara Foltz," Ibid., I, pp. 641–43; McCowen, "Women in Iowa," p. 108; Margaret J. Carns Papers, NHS; Clara (Bewick) Colby Papers, HEH; and Joanna L. Stratton, *Pioneer Women: Voices from the Kansas Frontier* (New York, 1981), p. 19.

119. Gloria R. Lothrop, review of Ray A. Billington's *Westward Expansion* in *Southern California Historical Society Quarterly*, 59 (Spring 1977), p. 125. A similar study based on the 1890 census reported that although only about "4 percent of the nation's women lived west of the Mississippi, they comprised 14 percent of the nation's women lawyers, 10 percent of the women doctors, 15 percent of the women writers and scientists, 11 percent of the women artists, [and] 10 percent of the women journalists. . . . In all there were nearly 20,000 women professionals on the frontier." Steiner, *The Ranchers*, pp. 103–4.

120. Floyd and Marion Rinhart, "Marsha Maxwell's Peaceable Kingdom," *American West*, 8

(September–October 1976), pp. 34–35, 62–63; "Pioneer Boulder Woman, Martha Maxwell, Brought Fame to Colorado," Boulder *Camera*, August 21, 1958, copy in "Women in Colorado File," DPL; Mary Dartt, *On The Plains and Among the Peaks; or How Mrs. Maxwell Made Her Natural History Collection* (Philadelphia, 1879); Maud Jeannie Fuller Young, Biographical Data, BTHC; Nancy O. Lurie, "The Lady From Boston and the Omaha Indians," *American West*, 3 (Fall 1966), pp. 31–33, 80–84; Ruth Carson, "Indians Called Her 'The Measuring Woman': Alice Fletcher and the Apportionment of Reservation Lands," *American West*, 2 (July 1975), pp. 12–15; E. Jane Gay, *With the Nez Perces: Alice Fletcher in the Field, 1889–92*, Frederick Hoxie and Joan Mark, eds. (Lincoln, 1981); Maurine S. Fletcher, "Portrait for a Western Album," (a brief account of Alice Eastwood), *American West*, 17 (January–February 1980), p. 30

121. Accounts of women telegraphers are in Nye-Starr, *A Self-Sustaining Woman*, p. 154 and Lucie Emma Dickinson Lott, Her Story, SDHS. On women abstractors, see: Michael Miller, "The Avery–Bowman Company: The First Women Abstractors in Santa Fe," *Llano Estacado Southwest Heritage*, 11 (Spring 1981), pp. 10–16. The women fur traders are discussed in John E. McDowell, "Thérèse Schindler of Mackinac: Upward Mobility in the Great Lakes Fur Trade," *Wisconsin Magazine of History*, 61 (Winter 1977–78), pp. 125–43. Accounts of women in government service include Charles W. Cowley, "Catherton Post Office," *Nebraska History*, 54 (Winter 1973), pp. 625–32; Anderson, Reminiscences; John Hutto, "Mrs. Elizabeth (Aunt Hank) Smith," *West Texas State Historical Association Yearbook*, 15 (October 1939), p. 45; Diary Account of Emily Butcher, 1896–99, KHS; and Brown, Diary. On women as political reformers, see: Douglas A. Bakken, "Luna E. Kellie and the Farmer's Alliance," *Nebraska History*, 50 (Summer 1969), pp. 185–206; Luna E. Kellie, Memoirs, NHS; Gene O. Clanton, "Intolerant Populist? The Disaffection of Mary Elizabeth Lease," *Kansas Historical Quarterly*, 34 (Summer 1968), pp. 189–200; Kizer, "May Arkwright Hutton," pp. 53–55.

122. Owens-Adair, *Dr. Bethenia Owens-Adair*, pp. 536–37. For more specific studies, see McCowen, "Women in Iowa," pp. 97–113; Murphy, "The Working Women of Salt Lake City," pp. 121–35; Joyce D. Goodfriend and Dona K. Flory, "Women in Colorado Before the First World War," *Colorado Magazine*, 53 (Summer 1976), pp. 201–28, especially pp. 219–22; Lillian Schlissel, "Mothers and Daughters on the Western Frontier," *Frontiers*, 3 (1978), p. 32; Yamane, "The Working Role of Women in the American West," pp. 29–48; *Buffalo Chips to Senate Seats: Women at Work in Oklahoma* (Norman, 1978); T. A. Larson, "Women's Role in the American West," *Montana, The Magazine of Western History*, 24 (Summer 1974), pp. 4–9.

123. Ada Chase, Daybook entry, Saturday, February 4th, 1886, Chase Family Papers, NMSU; Carrie Adell Strahorn, *Fifteen Thousand Miles by Stage* (New York, 1911); Christiana Holmes Tillson, *A Woman's Story of Pioneer Illinois* (Chicago, 1919); and Mrs. Thomas Withers, Extracts from Colorado Correspondence, 1878–80, DPL all wrote of assisting their husbands with bookkeeping and other financial management tasks. It is clear from the Cockrell papers that Sara Cockrell handled many of the business arrangements for her husband; Harriet Strong gained much of her knowledge of business and engineering through correspondence and conversations with her mining engineer-husband.

124. Nye-Starr, *A Self-Sustaining Woman*, pp. 10, 52.

125. The Life Story of Mary Elizabeth Warren as told to Mildred Mitchell Sexton, OHS; Strong Papers, Box 14 contains papers related to her plans for the "Queen Isabella" schools of business for women. The quotes are from an interview with the Whittier *News*, January 1913 and an article in *California Outlook*, March 22, 1913, copies in Strong Papers, Box 18. Also see her paper entitled "Rights of Property and Rights of Persons," prepared "at the request of Susan B. Anthony," Strong Papers, Box 14.

126. See: Schlissel, "Mothers and Daughters," p. 32 and notes 1–8 above.

127. A similar viewpoint is expressed in Goodfriend and Flory, "Women in Colorado," pp. 205–10.

128. D'Ann Campbell, "Was the West Different? Values and Attitudes of Young Women in 1943," *Pacific Historical Review,* 47 (August 1978), pp. 453–63. The interpretation and analysis in this chapter is based partly on the Campbell article and partly on the model suggested by Patricia Branca, "A New Perspective on Women's Work: A Comparative Typology," *Journal of Social History,* 9 (Winter 1975), pp. 129–53.

Index